SECOND EDITION

Literacy Development in the Early Years

Helping Children Read and Write

LESLEY MANDEL MORROW
Rutgers, The State University

ALLYN AND BACON
Boston   London   Toronto   Sydney   Tokyo   Singapore

Copyright © 1993 by Allyn & Bacon
A Division of Simon & Schuster, Inc.
160 Gould Street
Needham Heights, MA 02194

Editor in Chief: Nancy Forsyth
Series Editor: Sean W. Wakely
Series Editorial Assistant: Carol L. Chernaik
Production Administrator: Deborah Brown
Editorial-Production Service: P. M. Gordon Associates
Composition Buyer: Linda Cox
Cover Administrator: Suzanne Harbison
Cover Designer: Seed Design
Manufacturing Buyer: Louise Richardson

Library of Congress Cataloging-in-Publication Data

Morrow, Lesley Mandel.
   Literacy development in the early years : helping children read and write / Lesley Mandel Morrow. —2nd ed.
     p. cm.
   Includes bibliographical references (p.) and index.
   ISBN 0–205–14043–2
   1. Language arts (Preschool)—United States. 2. Reading (Preschool)—United States. 3. Children—United States—Books and reading. I. Title.
LB1140.5.L3M66 1993
372.6—dc20   92—4822
                                                        CIP

Printed in the United States of America
10 9 8 7 6 5   96 95

Four line drawings, Morrow Literacy Center, floor plan of a classroom, a contract, and bookmaking directions: Pamela Cromey
Photographs: Lenore Arone, Susan Arone, Joyce Caponigro, Lori Harrje, Milton E. Mandel, Franklin A. Morrow, Lesley Mandel Morrow, Andrea Shane

To Frank and Stephanie
my very special husband
and my very special daughter

Contents

Foreword

Dramatic changes occurred during the last decade in our understanding of early literacy development. Whereas we once thought that children learned to speak and listen during their early years and later learned to read and write at school age of five or six years, we now know that they develop language-related abilities "all of a piece" (simultaneously) from the days of infancy onward.

During the last decade, we also discovered that the conditions that promote first language learning are the very same conditions that promote total literacy development. These conditions, created in the social context surrounding a child, involve immersion, approximation, opportunity to practice, feedback, and modeling (Cambourne, 1984).

Lesley Morrow demonstrates the value of immersing children in the language we want them to learn—that includes the language of literature as well as the language of daily living. She provides numerous examples of children's approximations of writing and reading as she establishes the necessity of giving them unlimited opportunities to practice. Further, she illustrates the ways adults provide feedback and models for young language learners as they make attempts to read and write.

Children's literature, the area I know best, is central to Morrow's literacy environment. Literature serves as a model for language learning and provides strong motivation for learning to read and write. It is a springboard for all sorts of literacy-related activities. Most important, literature is a way of knowing. It is shaped around story—a primary act of human minds.

Dr. Lesley Morrow knows about children's literature, too. She recognizes the impact of fathers, mothers, siblings, baby-sitters, grandparents and other caregivers reading to children and enjoying the wealth of books. She shows how reading to babies influences their grasp of language and story patterns that serve them well as they learn to read and write. She illustrates how children learn concepts about print, book handling, and conventions of stories as they interact with books. Morrow establishes that adults teach by example as they enjoy shared reading and shared writing with children. She shows the impact of having a literacy center in a classroom and the effects of storybook reading aloud by a teacher. She shows that when children know authors and illustrators as real people, they want to read their works and write in a manner similar to their idols. She states that storytelling is similar to reading aloud in its impact on children. Speaking from her own experiences as a teacher, researcher, and parent, she charts a path that leads to successful literacy learning.

Lesley Morrow has taken a long view of literacy development in the early years, showing the historical roots of ideas that are valid today. She also knows and draws upon the trend-setting research of today's leaders because she is a member of that research community. She succinctly summarizes language theories and relates current research to shape sound practices. She has conducted much of the original research herself, testimony to the fact that she can bridge the gap between theory, research, and practice. Her examples are anchored in real classroom experiences—her own and those of other teachers with whom she works collaboratively. The examples have the ring of authenticity and add credibility to her argument.

Morrow's treatment of literacy development is on the cutting edge of current knowledge. She is well informed about her subject and makes connections among all aspects of literacy learning. She is a sensitive observer and writer as she lets children and teachers speak for themselves through their work.

Morrow states that few children learn to love books by themselves. Someone must lure them into the joys of the printed work and the wonderful world of stories. She shows us how to do that and enriches our lives and the lives of children through her work. Her contribution to the literary development of young children is a lasting one.

Bernice E. Cullinan
Professor of Early Childhood Education
and Elementary Education
New York University

Preface

Literacy Development in the Early Years is for teachers, readings specialists, administrators, students in teacher education programs, and parents. It is appropriate for both graduate and undergraduate courses in early literacy, and it complements texts on the teaching of reading in the elementary school, child development, the early childhood curriculum, teaching language arts in the elementary school, and children's literature.

I wrote the book because of my special interest in literacy development in early childhood. I taught in preschools, kindergartens, and the primary grades, and then went on to teach early childhood curriculum and early literacy courses at the university level. My research has focused on instructional strategies in early literacy. A wealth of research information has been created in this area over the past several years. That research has generated new theory and given new strength to certain older theories of learning. It has implications for new instructional strategies and reinforces certain older practices that had little or no research to establish their validity. It describes a program that nurtures literacy development from birth through second grade.

Although the book is about early literacy, its content has strong ramifications for reading instruction in the elementary grades. The fundamental ideas presented in this volume should eventually be incorporated in texts on reading in the elementary school. As we all recognize, there is little in education that is really new; what we know about it simply gets refined, reorganized, or verified. In many respects, some parts of this book may sound like some of the earliest volumes on early literacy.

This book does not offer a prescription. Formula programs stop teachers from thinking for themselves and therefore do not reflect the traditional ideals of American education. The ideas offered in this book have been tried and they have worked, but not all of them are appropriate for all teachers or all children. The good teacher functions most effectively with teaching strategies he or she feels most comfortable with. The teacher needs to be a decision-maker who thinks critically about the design of his or her literacy program and the selection of materials. Children, too, are individuals who come to school with diverse cultural backgrounds, experiences, exposures to literacy, and abilities. Instructional programs can differ in different parts of the country, in different localities, and for different children in the same classroom.

Underlying this book is the merging of the art and the science of teaching. The science has developed theories based on research that have generated instructional strategies. The book contains descriptions of strategies and steps for carrying them out. But, the scientific research does not necessarily take into account individual differences among teachers and children. The art of teaching concentrates on those human variables.

Chapter 1 provides a framework of theory and research, past and current, that has influenced strategies for developing emergent literacy. Chapter 2 discusses the strong influence of the home on the development of literacy, especially in a child's earliest years.

Chapters 3 through 8 deal with areas of literacy development, oral language, reading, and writing. These chapters discuss theory, research, developmental stages, instructional strategies, and methods of assessment associated with them. The book views the development of literacy skills (reading, writing, and oral language) as concurrent and interrelated: the development of one enhances the development of the others. Furthermore, the theories, stages, acquisition, and strategies associated with each are similar, and it is difficult to separate them entirely. To make the volume more readable, however, I have treated the different areas of literacy in different chapters.

Chapter 9 discusses the preparation and organization of an environment that will help the teacher take all of the components presented earlier and implement them in a successful program. This chapter emphasizes the interrelatedness of the several areas of literacy and describes how they can be integrated into the entire school day within content areas. Separate chapters have not been devoted to assessment nor to addressing children with special needs. These topics are integrated into most chapters throughout the book.

Each chapter begins with questions to focus on while reading the text. Each chapter ends with suggested activities and questions and an idea for the classroom, and a case study activity to be used by preservice and inservice teachers. The appendixes list materials that parents and teachers may use in carrying out a successful program to develop literacy.

Acknowledgments

I want to thank many individuals who helped in the preparation of the first and second editions of this book. Thank you to past and present students: Patricia Addonizio, Susan Burks, Kathleen Cunningham, Katie Farrell, Donna Fino, Mary Ann Gavin, Laura Labarca, Tricia Lyons, Melody Olsen, Michele Preole, Mary Joyce Santoloci, Sari Schnipper, and Karen Szabo. Thank you to the teachers and administrators who helped: Maxine Bell, Karen Buda, Pat Burton, Barbara Callister, Tom DelCasale, Fran Diamente, Arlene Hall, David Harris, Lori Harrje, Noreen Johnson, Sheryl King, Penelope Lattimer, Nancy Mason, Joyce McGee, Carna Meechem, Dennis Monaghan, Stephanie Moretti, Joyce Ng, Ellen O'Connor, Lucy Oman, Barbara Oxfeld, Mary Payton, Tammye Pelovitz, Cynthia Peters, John Quintaglie, Robert Rosado, Sonia Satterwhite, Joyce Schenkman, Linda Schifflette, and Patty Thaxton. Thank you to Andrea Shane for taking many of the photographs and to Pamela Cromey for drawing the illustrations. Thank you to R. A. and L. K. for your continual guidance. Thank you to Carol Wada for supporting this book while it was a part of Prentice Hall and to Sean Wakely and Carol Chernaik, at Allyn and Bacon, who guided me through the revision of this book. Thank you to Allyn and Bacon reviewers who provided helpful comments.

Thank you, in particular, to the children I have taught, my college students, and the excellent teachers I have observed—from whom I've learned so much. Thank you to the researchers in early literacy who have provided exciting information in this field.

Thank you to those who reviewed the first edition of the book with positive comments and to the many college professors, college students, teachers, and parents who purchased the book and demonstrated their support for the publication. The second edition was made possible by you.

Thank you to my parents, Mary and Milton Mandel, who provided a rich literacy environment for me; thank you to Frank Morrow, my companion and computer consultant; and thank you to Stephanie Morrow, my friend and daughter for demonstrating the validity of many of the concepts expressed in the book.

L. M. M.

Foundations of Early Literacy Development

QUESTIONS TO FOCUS ON AS YOU READ THE CHAPTER

- Which educators, theorists, philosophers, and psychologists influenced early childhood education, and what was each one's unique contribution to instructional strategies used in classrooms for young children?
- What have been the different approaches to literacy learning from the early 1900s through the 1960s?
- How is the term *reading readiness* defined in relation to literacy instruction?
- What practical applications has the research on oral language, early reading and writing, and rich literacy environments at home had on early literacy instruction in the classroom?
- What concepts reflect the whole language orientation?
- What is meant by thematic unit instruction?
- What is portfolio assessment?
- What knowledge about child development is important to literacy learning and why?
- Who are children with special needs? What implications for instruction do special needs children present in the classroom?

What a dangerous activity reading is: teaching is. All this plastering of foreign stuff. Why plaster on at all when there's so much inside already? So much locked in? If only I could draw it out and use it as working material. And not draw it out either. If I had a light enough touch, it would just come out under its own volcanic power.

—SYLVIA ASHTON-WARNER

Spinster

Four-year-old Shane and his mother were driving in the car to do some errands. They approached the mall and Shane popped up in a loud voice and said, "Look Mommy, I can read those letters. S . . . E . . . A . . . R . . . S. Those letters spell Macy's." Shane's mother smiled and praised him. "That was great Shane. You got every letter right. Now I'll read the sign for you; it says SEARS. This is another department store like Macy's. You did some good thinking when you tried to read that word."

Not too long ago we would have laughed at Shane's remarks as cute but incorrect. Today we realize that Shane is demonstrating a great deal of literacy knowledge that needs to be recognized. First, he knows what letters are and can identify the ones in the sign. Next, he knows that letters spell words. He knows that words are read and have meaning. Although he did not read the word correctly, he made an informed guess. Shane was aware that this building was a department store, but he had never been to this one, so he called the new store by the name of the one with which he was already familiar. Shane was trying some of his literacy knowledge out on an adult who he knew was interested and willing to interact positively with him. His mother offered positive reinforcement for what he did know and support by modeling the correct response when he needed some help.

Babies begin to acquire information about literacy from the moment of birth. They continue to build on their knowledge of oral language, reading, and writing as they go through early childhood. Recently a great deal of attention has been focused on literacy development in early childhood, an area somewhat neglected in the past. Teachers, parents, and administrators tended not to perceive preschoolers as readers or writers. They emphasized oral language development and preparation for reading. Because of increased research, thinking about early literacy has changed: very young children are now viewed as individuals with literacy skills. The literacy skills of preschoolers and kindergartners are not those of older children or adults, but youngsters do acquire literacy traits that must be acknowledged and that have implications for instructional practice.

Over the past few years, research on literacy development in early childhood has burgeoned. That research not only has introduced new information, it has also raised concerns about certain common practices in early childhood literacy instruction and an awareness of the need for change. Like a child's first words and first steps, learning to read and write should be an exciting, fulfilling, and rewarding experience. Unfortunately, it sometimes is not. This book draws on the newer research and blends it with theory and practice that have proved successful. It presents a program for developing literacy in children from birth to seven years. It is based on the following rationale (IRA, 1985):

1. Literacy learning begins in infancy.
2. Parents need to provide a rich literacy environment to help children acquire literacy skills.
3. School personnel must be aware that children come to school with prior knowledge of oral and written language.
4. Early reading and writing experiences at school should build upon that existing knowledge.
5. Learning requires a supportive environment that builds positive feelings about self as well as about literacy activities.
6. Adults must serve as models for literacy behavior, by demonstrating an interest in books and print.
7. During their literacy experiences, children must interact within a social context so that they can share information and learn from each other.
8. Early literacy experiences should be meaningful and concrete and should *actively* involve the child.
9. A literacy development program should focus on holistic approaches, utilizing functional experiences that include the use of oral language, listening, writing, and reading.
10. Differences in cultural and language backgrounds must be acknowledged and addressed.

This book incorporates the work of learning theorists, philosophers, educators, psychologists, and researchers who have described how young children learn. It builds on the implications their work holds for instruction and reflects the newer attitudes toward literacy development in early childhood. Throughout, it emphasizes development of literacy through the teaching of language, listening, reading, and writing in coordination with other content areas across the curriculum. Though some of the chapters

Learning requires a supportive environment that builds positive feelings about self and literacy activities.

concentrate on language, reading, or writing, the major concern at all times is the integration of all four dimensions of literacy.

Literacy development early in life must focus on both learning and teaching. The teacher prepares an environment rich in literacy materials and activities from which children can choose; the children are encouraged to be actively involved in learning with other children, with materials, and with the teacher. A major focus of the book is how to provide an environment that will encourage children to take an interest in reading, to associate it with pleasure, and ultimately to read by choice.

Learning Theories That Have Shaped Practices

Several important philosophers, theorists, educators, and psychologists have addressed learning in early childhood, including the issue of appropriate educational practice. Many of their ideas support the newer research in early childhood literacy or are reflected in newer practices. These ideas also represent varying responses to the question of whether learning is primarily a matter of the *nature* or the *nurture* of the child.

In the eighteenth century Rousseau (1762) strongly suggested that a child's early education be natural. That is, children should not be forced to learn things for which they are not developmentally ready. Rousseau advocated abandoning the contrived imposition of instruction on children and instead allowing children to grow and learn with the freedom to be themselves. Education follows the child's own development and readiness for learning. According to Rousseau, children learn through curiosity; forcing education upon them interferes with their learning and development. He believed that individual children had ways of learning peculiar to themselves, ways that formal instruction should not tamper with. Rousseau's philosophy suggests that the role of the educator is to use strategies that mesh with the child's readiness to learn. Rousseau strongly emphasized as little intervention by an adult as possible. He believed a child's learning "unfolds" naturally.

Pestalozzi (Rusk & Scotland, 1979) was influenced by Rousseau's emphasis on natural learning, but he added a dimension to it. He started his own school and developed principles for learning that combined natural elements with informal instruction. He found it unrealistic to expect children to learn totally on their own initiative. Although he felt that children may be able to teach themselves to read, for example, he also felt that it was necessary for teachers or parents to create the climate and conditions in which the reading process grows. The natural potential of a child develops, he believed, through sensory manipulative experiences, so he designed lessons that involved manipulating objects and learning about them through touch, smell, language, size, and shape.

Froebel's (1974) approach was similar in some ways to those of his predecessors. Like Rousseau, he believed that the adult responsible for the education of a child needs to be concerned with the child's natural unfolding. He also followed Pestalozzi's ideas and provided plans for instructing young children. But he is best known for emphasizing the importance of play in learning. He specified, however, that realizing the fullest benefits of playing-to-learn requires adult guidance and direction and a planned environment. Froebel saw the teacher as a designer of activities and experiences that facilitate learning. On this premise he designed a systematic curriculum for young children involving objects and materials that he called *gifts* and *occupations*. In handling and playing with these objects and materials, children not only use psychomotor skills but learn about shape, color, size, measurement, and comparison as well. It was Froebel who coined the word *kindergarten*, which means "children's garden." The phrase illustrates his basic philosophy that children, like plants, will grow to fruition only if they are tended and cared for. He often referred to the child as the seed being cared for by the gardener, or teacher.

Froebel was the first educator to design an organized curriculum for young children, and many of his strategies are evident in preschools and kindergartens today. Most significant among his strategies was his emphasis on guided play as a method for learning, the learning of certain concepts through manipulative materials that utilize the senses, and *circle time*—an opportunity to sing songs and learn new ideas through discussion.

John Dewey's (1966) views were not unlike Froebel's. His philosophy of early childhood education led to the concept of the child-centered curriculum or progressive education as it was often called. Dewey believed that the curriculum should be built around the interests of children. He agreed with Froebel that children learn best through play and in real life. He maintained that social interactions encourage learning and that interests are the vehicles for learning information and skills. He rejected the idea of teaching skills as an end unto themselves. He also believed that learning is maximized through the integration of content areas.

Froebel and Dewey have significantly influenced programs in American preschools and kindergartens throughout the twentieth century, and especially from the 1920s through the 1950s. During those decades, preschools and kindergartens typically had different areas for different activities. Shelves in a "block corner" held various sizes and shapes of blocks, small cars, trucks, and wooden figures of people. An art area contained easels with watercolors, crayons, paper, paste, scissors, construction paper, clay, and scraps of interesting materials such as fabric, plastic foam, and pipe cleaners for making collages. The dramatic-play corner was set up like a kitchen, with sink, oven, refrigerator, empty food boxes, table and chairs, telephone, mirror, dolls, and some clothing for dressing up. Still another area held manipulative toys that teach concepts about color, shape, and size. A science area revealed a water-play table, shells, interesting rocks, plants, a class animal, magnets, and magnifying glasses. The music area usually had a piano, rhythm instruments, and a record player. Sometimes there was a rug for children to sit on when they came to sing by the piano. One corner of the room had a shelf of children's literature and, depending on the teacher, soft pillows to lie on when looking at books.

The daily routine was similar in most of these settings. As children entered the classroom, they played with quiet toys. The teacher then called them to circle time to talk about the weather and the calendar. Conversation soon focused on a topic in social studies or science—animals or community helpers, for instance—with perhaps a song in keeping with the theme. Circle time was commonly followed by a long period called free play in which children could use the materials in the different areas of the room. There was minimal guidance during free play; children could explore and experiment with the materials. A snack, sometimes followed by a rest period, was an integral part of the daily routine. The day might also include a special lesson in art, social studies, or science appropriate to the unit being studied. Outdoor play allowed children to run, climb, play in sandboxes, and use riding toys. The teacher read a story daily, probably at the end of the day, often relating it to the topic being studied.

Reading and mathematics were not taught formally. Instead, the teacher might ask a child to count out enough cookies for all the children in the class, to name the date on the calendar, or to compare the sizes of different children. There were no workbooks or commercial reading materials. Teachers led some informal activities that could eventually lead to reading, but they did not attempt to teach children to read. The letters of the alphabet might be found strung across the wall, the days of the week pointed out on a calendar, children's names written on their cubbies, and some other items in the room labeled with words. The general atmosphere was relaxed. The goal was to accustom children to school routines and make them comfortable in the school environment. The focus was on social, emotional, and physical development. There was no place in these programs for formal reading and writing instruction.

Maria Montessori (1965) departed from the educators and philosophers mentioned thus far. Although she believed in the use of the senses to promote learning, her emphasis on the senses was not based on the natural unfolding of the child, the child's interests, or play. Believing that children needed early, orderly, systematic training in mastering one skill after another, she supplied her teaching environment with materials for learning specific concepts in order to meet specific objectives. The materials provided the source of learning for the child. Children educated themselves by using these manipulatives, and because the materials were self-

According to the concepts of Pestalozzi, Froebel, Dewey, Piaget, Vygotsky, and other philosophers and theorists, learning in early childhood will take place when youngsters have the opportunity to explore, experiment, play at real-life experiences, and manipulate materials. They need to do this sometimes by interacting with adults or other children and sometimes by working alone.

correcting, the children could determine their own errors and make corrections independently.

Montessori referred to this type of learning as *auto-education.* Like Froebel and Pestalozzi, she spoke of *sensitive periods*, when children are better able to learn certain things than at other times. It is the role of the parent or teacher to watch for these periods and take advantage of them by preparing the environment with appropriate materials and experiences for learning. In short, according to Montessori, the teacher is a guide who prepares an environment for learning. But unlike the educators already discussed, Montessori carefully designed learning materials to teach specific skills. In Montessori's curriculum, children's natural curiosity and their propensity for exploration are of less concern than their ability to work with specific materials to achieve a specific goal. Play is not as important as work because it might waste precious opportunities for goal achievement during sensitive periods for learning. Although some of her ideas are not relevant to the new thrust in early literacy, her emphasis on learning rather than teaching; her concerns about independent learning, sensitive periods for learning, and respect for the child; and her insistence on organization and a prepared environment hold implications for today's instruction.

Psychologist Jean Piaget (Piaget & Inhelder, 1969) has had a particularly strong impact on early childhood education. In describing the stages of cognitive development, he recognized that children at certain stages are capable of only certain types of intellectual endeavors. Trying to involve children in abstract experiences during the preoperational stages of their early childhood, for instance, is considered inappropriate. Piaget did not advocate Montessori's systematic approach, nor did he believe in maturation as a completely natural unfolding. He believed, rather, that a child acquires knowledge by interacting with the world. Educators who have applied his theories involve children in natural problem-solving situations where they can assimilate new experiences into their existing knowledge. Children are active participants in their own learning, constantly changing and reorganizing their own knowledge.

Piaget stressed that learning takes place when the child interacts with peers and adults in a social setting as they act upon the environment. Educators who have incorporated Piaget's theories in curricula for early childhood education have designed programs that look very much like what Pestalozzi or Froebel might have created: a setting with many real-life materials, including the opportunity to play, explore, and experiment. Piaget agreed that young children should use their curiosity, inquisitiveness, and spontaneity to help themselves learn. In addition, a Piagetian preschool curriculum emphasizes decision making, problem solving, self-discipline, goal setting, planning one's own activities, and cooperating with teachers and peers in evaluating learning.

Vygotsky's (1981) general theory of intellectual development also has implications for learning in early childhood. Vygotsky believes that mental functions are acquired through social relationships. Children learn by internalizing activities conducted in the world around them. Children emulate behaviors and incorporate them into their existing structure of knowledge when they are exposed to new situations in which they can actively interact with others.

The learning theories of the individuals discussed have contributed to the way we look at literacy development in early childhood education. Their ideas are the basis for early literacy instruction as it is described in this book. Particularly applicable among their concepts are these:

1. Concern for a child's level of development—physical, social, emotional, and intellectual—when preparing a learning environment for that child
2. Concern for prepared environments in which learning can take place
3. Emphasis on learning rather than teaching
4. The learner's need for social interaction with supportive adults and other children
5. Focus on learning through real experiences in meaningful and natural settings rather than by imposed, contrived objectives or techniques
6. An awareness that children must actively participate in their own learning by engaging in manipulative experiences that are both functional and interesting

Practices in the Past

Judging from the professional literature of the early 1900s, little attention was paid to a child's literacy development before he or she entered school. Apparently it was generally assumed that literacy began with formal instruction in first grade. Wielding a strong influence on reading instruction, developmental psychologists such as Gesell (1925) advocated maturation as the most important factor in learning to read. Reading instruction was frowned on until the child was ready to read. Preschool and kindergarten teachers generally ignored or avoided reading instruction. But they did follow some of the teachings of Pestalozzi and Froebel. Typically, they read to children often; encouraged play, exploration, and problem solving; and led songs and discussions in circle times. Methods were child-centered, teaching units were interdisciplinary, and learning environments and instructional strategies were appropriate to the child's development.

Influenced by the climate of the times, Morphett and Washburne (1931) supported the postponement of reading instruction until a child was developmentally "old enough." Their study concluded that children with a mental age of six years six months made better progress on a test of reading achievement than younger children. But whereas many educators held fast to the concept of natural maturation as the precursor of literacy, others grew uncomfortable with simply waiting for children to become ready to read. They did not advocate formal reading instruction in early childhood, but they did begin to provide experiences that they believed would help children become ready for reading.

The growing popularity of testing during the 1930s and 1940s helped these educators in this effort and affected the next several decades of early childhood reading instruction. Generally, the standardized tests served the prevailing concept of maturation by indicating if a child had reached the maturity he or she needed to be able to learn to read. The tests usually included sections on specific skills. Unfortunately, those skills came to be seen as elements on which to base experiences that would help children to become ready to read. The term **reading readiness** came into popular use during these decades and is still with us. Instead of waiting for a child's natural maturation to unfold, educators focused on nurturing that maturation through instruction in a set of skills identified as prerequisites for reading. The concept gained strength when publishers of basal readers capitalized on the idea of readiness skills and began to prepare materials for preschool and kindergarten that would make children ready to read. Skills associated with reading readiness include *auditory discrimination*, the ability to identify and differentiate familiar sounds, similar sounds, rhyming words, and the sounds of letters; *visual discrimination*, including color recognition, shape, and letter identification; *left to right eye progression* and *visual motor skills*, such as cutting on a line with scissors and coloring within the lines of a picture; and such *large motor abilities* as skipping, hopping, and walking on a line.

Early childhood literacy instruction based on the reading readiness model implies that one prepares for literacy by acquiring a set of prescribed skills. These skills are taught systematically on the assumption that all children are at a fairly similar level of development when they come to preschool or kindergarten. The system does not consider experiences or information that a child may already have about literacy, and it focuses narrowly on a set of skills perceived as those needed for learning to read. Ironically, those skills stray from the original intent of the people who were concerned with maturation. They do not reflect the developmentalist's description of children's growth during the stages of early childhood. They do not encourage activities that are meaningful or interesting to a child, nor do they capitalize on what children know about literacy from the reading and writing they experience in their social and cultural environments.

Research findings about literacy in early childhood are beginning to challenge the deep-rooted practices in reading readiness that have been evident since the 1950s. Teale (1982, p. 567) argues that the typical literacy curriculum with its progression from part to whole and its hierarchy of "skills" does not reflect the way children learn to read:

> *The belief is that literacy development is a case of building competencies in certain cognitive operations with letters, words, sentences, and texts, competencies which can be applied in a variety of situations. A critical mistake here is that the motives, goals, and conditions have been abstracted away from the activity in the belief that this enables the student to "get down to" working on the essential processes of reading and writing. But . . . these features are critical aspects of the reading and writing themselves. By organizing instruction which omits them, the teacher ignores how literacy is practiced (and therefore learned) and thereby creates a situation in which the teaching is an inappropriate model for the learning.*

Teale's words bring back memories of the days when reading readiness instruction flourished in kindergarten programs. Froebel's and Dewey's influences diminished in programs because of the mandate for teaching skills. I questioned the relevance of some of the readiness activities for young children. The children were interested in looking at books, reading familiar words, and copying words that interested them. They approached the beginnings of literacy in ways that were meaningful, pleasurable, or functional. They carried out the reading readiness activities willingly, but it was obvious that they had no idea why they were doing them or how they were related to reading at all. This became even clearer to me in a conversation with Eric, who had chosen a worksheet identifying initial consonant sounds.

"I see you are practicing your reading, Eric," I said.

He looked up at me and said "No, I'm not. I'm practicing my sounding."

I then said, "Right, sounding is practicing reading."

Eric looked up at me and said rather emphatically, "I'm not practicing reading, I am practicing sounding."

"But Eric," I said, "sounding is reading."

Even more annoyed, Eric responded, "Now let's get this straight: reading is reading and sounding is sounding."

That little interchange left a strong impression on me and launched my general questioning of the importance and relevance of the reading readiness program. In my observations of early childhood classrooms, I found that many teachers no longer schedule play time. Block corners and dramatic-play areas have disappeared from many rooms. Interdisciplinary units in social studies and science have been replaced with units on such skill instruction as learning the letter *t*. Classrooms are not relaxed, nor are they child-centered. Children spend most of their time working on one skill worksheet after another. Social, emotional, and physical development are no longer a major concern.

Influences for Change in Early Literacy Practices

Researchers investigating early childhood literacy development are bringing about changes in theory and practice. Generally, they base learning and instructional strategies on what is known about cognitive development. They use varied research methodologies for data collection, including interviews, observations, and case studies in various cultural and socioeconomic settings. The research is field-based, taking place in classrooms and homes rather than in laboratories.

Research on Oral Language Development

The first challenge to the attitudes rooted in the 1930s through the 1950s came in the 1960s and 1970s in studies of how children learn oral language. Although language acquisition is based somewhat on developmental maturity, much of the research concluded that children play an active role in their acquisition of language by constructing language. They imitate the language of adults and create their own when they do not have the conventional words they need to communicate their thoughts. Their first words are usually functional words, and they are motivated to continue generating language when their attempts are positively reinforced. Children who are constantly exposed to an environment rich in language and who interact with adults using language in a social context develop more facility with oral language than children lacking these opportunities (Bloom, 1972; Brown, 1973; Brown & Bellugi, 1964; Brunner, 1975; Cazden, 1972; Chomsky, 1965; Halliday, 1975; Lennenberg, 1967; McNeil, 1970; Menyuk, 1977). Findings from research on language acquisition motivated investigators to carry out similar studies of how reading was acquired. Because reading involves the use of language, many believed that the acquisition of oral language and reading might share some similarities.

Research about Literacy Development in the Home

Other studies investigated homes in which children learned to read without direct instruction before coming to school (Durkin 1966; Heath, 1980; Holdaway, 1979; Morrow, 1983; Ninio & Brunner, 1978; Taylor, 1983; Teale, 1984). Such homes provide rich reading environments that include books and other reading materials from which children are free to select. These family members serve as models of involvement in literacy activities. For example, they answer children's questions about books and print. They read to children frequently and reward them for participating in literacy activities. The description of homes in which children seemed to learn to read quite naturally greatly interested those who saw in them possible implications for early literacy instruction in schools.

The phrase *learning to read naturally* is a bit misleading. It paints a picture of a child suddenly picking up a book and reading it, with no instruction in reading at all. Actually, a great deal is happening in homes where children learn to read "naturally," without formal instruction. These homes are rich in the supportive and interactive behaviors conducive to learning to read. Specific studies of home storybook readings have provided us with information on the kinds of interaction that encourage literacy development. Analysis of the recorded questions and comments of children during shared book experiences at home have given us information on what children already know about books and print and what they are interested in finding out (Flood, 1977; Heath, 1980; Morrow, 1988a; Ninio & Brunner, 1978; Roser & Martinez, 1985; Yaden, 1985). The results of these home studies hold strong implications for change in classroom instruction.

Research on the Development of Early Reading

In her research with preschool and kindergarten children, Yetta Goodman (1984) found that many already knew certain things necessary for reading. These children knew the difference between letter characters and pictures in books, how to handle a book, and how to turn pages, and they knew that books are sources of meaning through printed words. Her work also concerned children's awareness of environmental print in familiar contexts and suggested that literacy-rich environments can make learning to read as natural as language acquisition.

Other researchers have looked at the acquisition of reading in early childhood from a developmental point of view. They have studied children's knowledge and acquisition of the function, form, and structure of print (Clay, 1972; Ehri, 1979; Gibson & Levin, 1975; Mason, 1980, 1982; Mason & McCormick, 1981). The work of these researchers reinforces many of the ideas found in the studies of oral language and home literacy. These authors advocate early childhood reading instruction, but not instruction that emulates first-grade practice. Rather they suggest more informal strategies similar to those discovered in homes where children learned to read without direct instruction. They also encourage activities that enhance language development and experiences in problem solving, listening to stories, and, writing stories.

Research on Writing Development

Another area of research in early childhood literacy is the burst of investigations on writing. Studies of children's first attempts to make marks on paper have made us aware that youngsters try to communicate in writing at a very early age. Through sample analysis of children's first attempts at writing, it is clear that they have an interest in writing, that they model adult writing

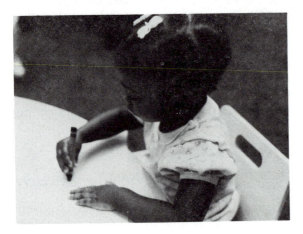

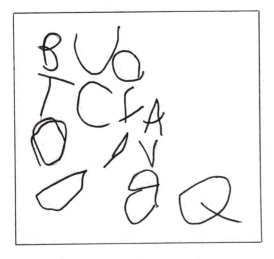

Tamika's early writing, attempts consisting of a mixture of letterlike forms and some real letters, need to be encouraged and positively reinforced.

behaviors, and that their scribbles, drawings, random letters, and invented spellings are early forms of writing (Clay, 1975). Many researchers now prefer to speak of reading and writing development as virtually one process. They view reading and writing as skills that build upon each other; when they are cultivated concurrently, each adds to proficiency in the other. Because it was traditionally perceived as developing after the ability to read, writing is an area that has certainly been missing from the early childhood curriculum. Research in early childhood writing has changed attitudes and promises dramatic implications for instruction. Encouraging writing in preschool and kindergarten and praising children's first attempts to write are becoming standard practices in early childhood classrooms.

The research and theories reviewed here have enabled us to understand better the processes involved in becoming literate. Certain levels of maturity are required for a child to reach specific levels of ability. To acquire skill in oral language, writing, and reading, children need models to emulate and the freedom to create their own forms of reading, writing, and speaking. They must be positively reinforced and guided so that they will continue in their development.

We have come to realize that literacy development does not begin with formal instruction when children enter school. Children bring with them to school many concepts about literacy and

Children need to be exposed to literacy early in life in the form of books and writing. Early attempts at literacy actively need to be encouraged and rewarded.

certain competencies in oral language, writing, and reading. They have some command of their language and have internalized many of its rules and some of the processes for learning more about it. Many children know the difference between drawing and writing and can imitate writing in invented ways. Many children have developed reading vocabularies from such environmental print sources as road signs, food packages, and store displays. Children know that books are for reading and expect that they will be able to read books in the early stages of schooling. We cannot, therefore, rationally view literacy in early childhood as something achieved by drilling children in specific contrived skills. Rather, we need to build on children's existing knowledge of literacy and help their literacy evolve.

Research tells us that children learn best in situations that are meaningful and functional. Children have developed their levels of literacy in social and cultural contexts and through interaction with adults and other children. The instruction they receive should reflect to a certain extent the natural and meaningful way in which they have learned what they already know. Problems arise when the developmental, social, and natural environments in which literacy flourishes are exchanged for a systematic presentation of skills that do not reflect a child's stage of development socially, emotionally, physically, or intellectually. The chapters that follow address each of the areas involved in the process of becoming literate. They reflect both old and new ideas that have made us aware of needed changes in our approaches to early literacy instruction. Based on theory derived from recent research, they focus on oral language, writing, and reading and on how these are acquired. They also reflect the development of the child.

The Whole Language Movement

One cannot review theory, philosophies, and research that have influenced changes in early literacy practices without a discussion of whole language. It is so difficult to describe the whole language orientation because it has been defined in so many different ways and, therefore, there is the risk of misinterpreting one theorist's perception or leaving out some idea related to the concept. In spite of this, the whole language orientation is having a strong impact on early literacy instruction and throughout the grades. The premises that this movement is based upon are not new. Many of its beliefs are drawn from the theorists of the past discussed in this chapter.

Whole language advocates support the natural approaches to learning fostered by Rousseau, Pestalozzi, and Froebel. Pestalozzi and Froebel added other dimensions with their concern for active learning through sensory experiences with materials.

Dewey's progressive education contributed to the philosophy with its child-centered approach that integrated the learning of information and literacy skill development into content area themes that were of interest to children. The influence of Piaget and Vygotsky is certainly seen in whole language through their emphasis on active learning and the adult as a facilitator of learning by guiding experiences in a social context.

From a content analysis of sixty-four professional articles related to whole language, Bergeron (1990) composed this definition:

> *Whole language is a concept that embodies both a philosophy of language development as well as the instructional approaches embedded within, and supportive of, that philosophy. This concept includes the use of real literature and writing in the context of meaningful, functional, and cooperative experiences in order to develop in students motivation and interest in the process of learning. (p. 319)*

Like so many others, after reading the literature, I have come up with my own definition of whole language. The ideas presented here may not be shared by all.

Whole language is a philosophy concerning how children learn, from which educators derive strategies for teaching. Some of its concepts and their implications for instruction follow.

Literacy learning is child centered because it is designed to be meaningful and functional for children. The function and meaning are drawn from the child's life experiences at home or those created in school. For example, if a beehive is discovered at school and removed by an exterminator, children may be interested in discussing, reading, or writing about bees. Although it is not built into the prescribed curriculum, the teacher allows this spontaneous interest to be pursued.

Literacy activities are purposefully integrated into the learning of content area subjects such as art, music, social studies, science, math, and play. The use of social studies and science themes, such as the study of ecology, links the content areas and literacy experiences. Equal emphasis is placed on the teaching of reading, writing, listening, and oral language, because all help to create a literate individual. In the past, this has been referred to as *an integrated language arts approach.* Varied genres of children's literature are the main source of reading material for instruction. This is called *literature-based instruction.* Classrooms must be rich with literacy materials for reading and writing throughout the room and also housed in special literacy centers. This is often called *the rich literacy environment.*

In a classroom that uses holistic strategies, more emphasis is placed on learning than on teaching. Learning is self-regulated and individualized, with self-selection and choices of literacy activities. Rather than only lessons in literacy, teachers provide models of literacy activities for children to emulate. There is adult and peer interaction as children observe each other and adults engaged in literacy acts. There is the opportunity for peer tutoring and collaboration with each other in active literacy experiences. There is the opportunity to learn through practice by engaging in long periods of independent reading and writing and sharing what is learned—by reading to others and presenting written pieces to an audience. Literacy learning is an active, interactive social process. The foremost objective for literacy instruction is the development of a desire to read and write.

Skills are taught in classrooms that use holistic approaches when they are relevant and meaningful—for example, when studying a theme such as dinosaurs, the teacher may focus on some of the letters and sounds in the initial consonants found in the names of dinosaurs.

In a whole language approach, assessment is continuous and takes many forms: teachers collect daily performance samples of work; they observe and record children's behavior; they audio- and videotape them in different situations; and they build a portfolio filled with information about each youngster. The evaluation process is for both teacher and child, and conferences are held to discuss progress.

In a whole language orientation, teachers along with children are the decision makers about instructional strategies, the organization of instruction, and instructional materials used. Commercial materials do not dictate the instructional program although they may be used if desired.

Literacy learning is consciously embedded throughout the curriculum in the whole school day. Large blocks of time are needed for process projects. There will be whole-group, small-group, and individualized instruction, and children will have time to read and write independently for long periods of time.

Whole language can be implemented in many different ways, based on the needs and interests of those involved. There is no one right way because different teachers and children make up the population in schools. One program could not satisfy everyone's needs. Those involved in whole language should feel comfortable with what they are doing and help with the decisions about how to proceed. Change should be slow and include appropriate information for individuals unfamiliar with the techniques. Regardless of what strategies are used, teachers must understand the processes involved in literacy development.

Throughout this book, whole language strategies will be included. Two strategies already mentioned that emerge from the whole language movement will be discussed in more depth here because they are referred to in several chapters throughout this volume.

Thematic Instruction

In the definition of whole language, I mentioned that literacy instruction should be meaningful and taught in combination with other content areas. Themes create meaning for children. In an *integrated language arts classroom* (a term used prior to the whole language movement), literacy is not taught as a subject, but as a mechanism for learning in general. Literacy learning becomes meaningful when it is consciously embedded into the study of themes.

Thematic units take several shapes; however, the main goal is to teach literacy skills in an interesting way. Thematic units may revolve around the exposure to certain types of children's literature, such as the study of fables, fairy tales, informational books, and so on. In this type of unit, a child would be exposed to one type of children's literature. The teacher would read several samples of the genre or children would read them to themselves if they were able. There would be discussions about the style of the works. Children would then have the opportunity to engage in writing their own stories that followed the genre being discussed.

Another type of thematic unit involves the selection of a topic that usually has a science or social studies thrust, such as the farm, and the identification of several pieces of children's literature about the topic as the source of reading instruction. All writing activities would revolve around the topic and would be driven by the children's literature. There could be art and music activities as well, but they would evolve from and revolve around the stories being read. For example, if the theme were the farm and one of the stories used in the unit were *The Little Red Hen,* some related activities might be to bake some bread, role-play the story, or write another version of the story in which the animals are all helpful in making the bread. One problem with using literature to drive the unit is that one piece may be overused for general activities and skill development. This practice could ruin the pleasure that can be received from the book. In addition, the literature often restricts the extension of ideas that could be generated.

The third type of thematic unit is one that utilizes a science or social studies topic and consciously integrates literacy into all content area lessons, including music, art, play, math, social studies, and science. Many selections of children's literature are used as a major part of the unit; however, the literature does not drive the unit—the topic of the unit is the main focus. In this type of unit, the classroom centers are filled with materials that relate to the topic, and literacy materials are placed in all of them to encourage reading and writing. In all science and social studies lessons, reading and writing are purposefully incorporated. Skills are taught when they seem appropriate—for example, in the unit on the farm, when the class hatches baby chicks in an incubator, journals will be kept on the progress of the chicks, and the digraph *ch* could be emphasized. Unit topics are incorporated into the entire school day in all content areas. Topics may be predetermined by the teacher, selected by the children and teacher, or decided upon spontaneously based on something of interest that occurs in the school, in someone's home, or in the world. Section 21 in Appendix A provides a list of popular early childhood unit topics with related selections of children's literature to use when studying those topics.

Portfolio Assessment

The emergent literacy and whole language movements, with their concern for children's interests, learning styles, and individual levels of ability, have made us begin to take a closer look at our methods for assessing performance. It has become apparent that the standardized group paper-and-pencil test is not sensitive to strategies drawn from emergent literacy constructs or the whole language philosophy. In addition, it has become quite apparent that one measure cannot be the main source for evaluating a child's progress. Rather than testing children, we need to assess their performance for growth in many areas and under many conditions. Assessment should help the teacher, child, and parent determine a child's strengths and weaknesses and plan appropriate instructional strategies. Assessment should match educational goals and practices. To meet the needs of the different populations in our schools, assessment measures need to be diverse, because there are children who perform better in some situations than in others.

In the International Reading Association's Policy Statement on Early Literacy Development (1985), the following recommendation was made: "Use evaluative procedures that are developmentally and culturally appropriate for the children being assessed. The selection of evaluative measures should be based on the objectives of the instructional program and would consider each child's total development and its effect on reading performance."

To accomplish the goals set forth by the International Reading Association, tests must be frequent and of many types. As a result, the volume of materials collected on a child in a given year needs to be stored in some type of portfolio to be passed on as the child proceeds through the grades.

Every chapter in this book that deals with literacy skills contains a section with suggestions related to portfolio assessment. The types of materials that teachers will be collecting about children include the following:

- **Daily performance samples.** These are samples of the child's work in all content areas that are done on a daily basis. Various types of samples should be collected periodically. Samples of writing, art work, and science and social studies reports can be collected throughout the school year.
- **Anecdotes of observations.** Anecdotes of observations can be used for many different purposes. Teachers will want to write down interesting, humorous, and general comments about the child's behavior in the classroom. Observations, sometimes called *running records*, could focus on one particular aspect of the child's performance, such as oral reading, silent reading, behavior while listening to stories, or writing.
- **Audiotapes.** Audiotapes are another form of assessment that can be used to determine language development and to analyze progress in oral reading. They can also be used in dis-

cussion sessions related to responses to literature to help understand how youngsters function in a group, the types of responses they offer, and so on.

- **Videotapes.** Videotapes relate similar information as audio-tapes with the additional data that can be gained by seeing the child in action. Because writing is not an auditory activity, videotapes of children in writing situations would be useful for assessment purposes. Audio- and videotapes are methods teachers can use for assessing their own performance.
- **Conferences.** Conferences allow the teacher to meet with a child on a one-to-one basis to assess skills in certain areas, such as reading aloud, to discuss his or her progress, to talk about steps to improve, to instruct, and to prescribe activities. Children should take an active role in evaluating their progress.
- **Surveys.** These can be prepared by teachers to assess children's attitudes about how they think they are learning or what they like or dislike in school. Surveys can be in the form of questionnaires or interviews with written or oral answers.
- **Teacher-prepared pencil-and-paper tests.** These tests will probably match instruction better than measures designed by commercial companies. Teachers need to provide this type of experience for children.
- **Standardized tests.** As long as standardized measures are a fact of life, children need to learn how to take them. Instruction should not be affected by the results of these measures— they are but one form of assessment among many others. As professionals, we need to minimize their importance and improve their contents so that they match instructional procedures. As teachers, we need to see that children are familiar enough with their format, so that they can take them to the best of their ability.

Throughout the chapters of this book, assessment will be discussed at the end of sections that deal with specific skill development. Multiple measures will be offered as suggestions to make up a portfolio of assessment materials for children that should help teachers create appropriate instructional strategies, help parents understand their child's development, and make the child aware of his or her strengths and weaknesses and how he or she can improve.

Understanding and Addressing Differences and Special Needs of Children in Our Schools

Many of the theoretical, philosophical, and psychological perspectives presented in this chapter discuss the necessity for meeting the individual needs of children. Early childhood educators have always been child centered and concerned about the social, emotional, physical, and intellectual needs of children. In early childhood, every youngster is seen as a unique individual with his or her own special needs. There is, however, greater diversity than ever in our classrooms today, and there are more and more individual needs to meet.

Frequently texts such as this will devote a separate chapter to a discussion about meeting individual needs. Because I view all children as special with individual needs, I would like to bring this issue to your attention in most of the chapters in the book, instead of just one. In addition, we have become aware that appropriate instructional techniques for all children will probably be appropriate with some modifications for special needs children.

Identifying special needs is the first step in dealing with them. Identification makes us more aware that they exist and then helps us determine the educational implications for instructional programs.

Children with Physical Impairments

Physical impairments refer to visual or hearing impairments, communication disorders, and orthopedic impairments. Children with minimal problems in these areas will be in the regular classroom. Others will be mainstreamed for portions of the day. *Mainstreaming* means that children who are in special classes will be integrated into regular classrooms for part of the school day.

Children with *visual impairments* are legally blind, have no useful vision, or have low vision with very limited sight. For these children, strategies that include auditory and tactile experiences are important. There are learning materials available in large print for the low-vision children. Children with no vision will need to learn to read through the use of Braille, a system of reading for the blind consisting of characters represented by raised dots on paper. These materials are available in basal readers from the American Printing House for the Blind (Ward & McCormick, 1981).

For the most part, only children with minimal visual problems will be present in the regular classroom.

Hearing impaired children are completely deaf or have some useful limited hearing. Some hearing impaired youngsters can be helped through the use of a hearing aid, which amplifies sounds for them. Hearing impaired children who are likely to be mainstreamed into regular classrooms or are in regular classrooms will be those with some hearing ability. Visual and tactile methods for learning are encouraged with these youngsters. Those who are deaf or have very limited hearing may use sign language to communicate. Some knowledge of signing would be helpful for classroom teachers.

Orthopedic impairment in this context refers to handicaps that are often congenital or acquired during childhood through such diseases as cerebral palsy, muscular dystrophy, spina bifida, and rheumatoid arthritis. Children who suffer from these problems to a severe degree are not in regular classrooms; however, those with mild cases may be in the classroom or mainstreamed in. Children with these problems may have normal intelligence but often need help with mobility. Learning strategies will be similar to those used with all children. If the ability to use fine motor control is compromised, alternative methods for writing need to be found, such as using a computer or having a teacher or peer take dictation. Youngsters with orthopedic problems may need more time to complete assignments, not necessarily because of their intellectual ability, but because of motor coordination problems. Because their disability is more obvious than others, an important goal with these youngsters is helping non–special needs children feel more positively toward them so that all are comfortable in each other's presence. Discussing the problems, how they occurred, and how everyone feels about them, will often help.

Children with *communication disorders* are likely to be a part of the regular classroom. These are children who have speech or language difficulties. Speech impairments include problems in articulation, voice disorders (abnormal loudness, pitch, or voice quality) and fluency disorders such as stuttering.

Children with *language disorders* have difficulty acquiring and using language. Delayed language children are significantly behind their peers in both the production and comprehension aspects of language development. These children will go to special classes for help with their problems. For the most part, strategies that are appropriate for all children will be appropriate for these youngsters in the regular classroom. Chapter 3, which deals with language development, discusses instructional contexts appropriate for children with minimal language problems.

Special Learning Situations: The Learning Disabled and the Gifted

Gifted youngsters are those who develop academic or other skills such as playing a musical instrument at an ability level far above that expected of a same-age child. These special talents need to be encouraged, but not at the expense of recognizing the social, emotional, and physical needs of the child. Differentiating assignments to make them more challenging for the ability levels of these children will accommodate their special talents.

Learning disabled youngsters are those who perform at a level below what is expected for their age or grade. Children are learning disabled for a variety of reasons, including mental retardation, emotional problems, and neurological problems. Only those youngsters with minimal learning disabilities are likely to be in regular classrooms. These children are often easily distracted and have a short attention span. Techniques for instruction need to be concrete and include active involvement. Helping these youngsters stay on task is an important goal. Activities that will grasp their attention are those that are most likely to be successful. Working with them on an individual basis is crucial to finding out the best ways for these children to learn. As with the gifted child, differentiating regular classroom activities to meet their ability levels will accommodate their needs.

Cultural and Language Differences

As time goes on, we find that classrooms are more and more diverse, with children from different language and cultural backgrounds. In the early 1900s, diversity was disregarded, and children were expected to ignore their cultural backgrounds and language differences and to learn the English language and American customs. Today we are more sensitive toward cultural and language differences and recognize that children can and should maintain their cultural heritage and that they can still be considered Americans and learn English without abandoning their native language (Templeton, 1991).

Cultural diversity should be welcomed in the school. It adds a richness to the classroom and to topics of study. By recognizing students' diverse backgrounds, we will enhance their self-image. Differences can become the norm rather than the exception. Differences in cultural backgrounds often provide explanations of why children behave as they do. Behaviors that are acceptable in one culture might be thought of as disrespectful in another.

Language differences vary. There are children who do not speak any English and are often classified as English-as-a-second-language (ESL) learners. These children come from homes where English is not spoken at all. There are children with very limited English proficiency who are often referred to as *bilingual*. The English proficiency of these youngsters varies. Many of them are more proficient in their home language than in English. The goal is for them to become truly bilingual—that is, equally proficient in English and their home language.

Children also come to school speaking different dialects. A *dialect* is an alternative form of one particular language used in different cultural, regional, or social groups (Leu & Kinser, 1991). These differences can be so significant that an individual from one region with one English dialect may have difficulty understanding someone from another region since the pronunciation of letter sounds is so different. Dialects are not inherently superior to one another; however, one dialect typically emerges as the standard for a given language and is used by the more advantaged individuals of a society. Teachers must be aware of different dialects and help youngsters with the comprehension of standard dialects. Children are not to be degraded or viewed as less intelligent for speaking different dialects. Although it is important for children to achieve a level of standard English to help them succeed in society, emphasizing the need to become a standard English speaker before learning literacy is inappropriate and likely to create more difficulties for the children by slowing their literacy development. Chapter 3 will discuss strategies for dealing with language differences and also provides an outline of language development from birth through eight years of age.

The regular classroom teacher will not have to deal with many of the special needs discussed. The youngsters with severe problems need special attention from individuals who are specifically trained to handle them. A variety of theoretical, educational, philosophical, and psychological perspectives for instruction have been presented in this chapter. Special needs are accommodated by finding that perspective that best suits the problem and child at hand. Classroom teachers must deal with children from diverse cultural and language backgrounds, students who have minimal learning disabilities and minimal physical impairments, as well as those who are gifted. Generally, good teaching strategies adapted to specific problems are those that work best. Where appropriate, reference to youngsters with special problems with implications for instruction will appear throughout the book. Children's literature can be helpful in dealing with special needs, whether they be physical disabilities or cultural differences. Section 22 in Appendix A presents a list of books that deal with cultural diversity and Section 23 lists books that discuss physical disabilities, learning disabilities, communication disorders, and the gifted.

Stages of Child Development

Knowing what children are like developmentally, what they are capable of doing, and what they already know is important when preparing instructional environments. This knowledge will also help to determine if children have special needs related to learning disabilities, giftedness, or communication disorders. The following description of the developmental characteristics of children from birth through eight years (Seefeldt & Barbour, 1986, pp. 63–69) is provided here to be used as a reference throughout the volume. (A fuller description of language development is found in Chapter 3.)

BOX 1–1 • *Developmental Characteristics of Children*

Infancy (birth through twelve months)

Physical
Develops rapidly.

Changes from waking because of hunger and distress to sleeping through the night with two naps during the day.

Changes eating patterns from every three hours to regular meals three times a day.

Develops control of muscles that hold up the head. By four months enjoys holding up head.

Focuses eyes and begins to explore the environment visually.

Begins to grasp objects at about sixteen weeks. Can grasp and let go by six months.

Rolls over intentionally (four to six months).

Holds own bottle (six to eight months).

Continued

BOX 1–1   *Continued*

Shows first tooth at about six months. Has about twelve teeth by age one.
Sits well alone, can turn and recover balance (six to eight months).
Raises body at nine months. May even pull self up to a standing position.
Starts to crawl at six months and to creep at nine or ten months.
May begin walking by age one.

Social

Begins to smile socially (four or five months).
Enjoys frolicking and being jostled.
Recognizes mother or other significant adult.
Notices hands and feet and plays with them.
By six months likes playing, alone or with company.
Begins to be wary of strangers.
Cooperates in games such as peekaboo and pat-a-cake.
Imitates actions of others.

Emotional

Differentiates crying according to specific discomforts, such as being hungry, cold, or wet.
Shows emotions by overall body movements such as kicking, arm waving, and facial expressions.
Begins to show pleasure when needs are being met.
By six months shows affection by kissing and hugging.
Shows signs of fearfulness.
Pushes away things not liked.

Cognitive

First discriminates mother from others; later, discriminates familiar faces from those of strangers.
Explores world through looking, mouthing, grasping.
Inspects things for long periods.
As a first sign of awareness, protests disappearance of objects.
Discovers how to make things happen and delights in doing so by repeating an action several times.
Between six and twelve months becomes aware of object permanency by recognizing that an object has been taken away and by looking for a hidden object.
Begins intentional actions by pulling at an object or removing an obstacle to get at an object.
Becomes increasingly curious about surroundings.

BOX 1–1 *Continued*

Toddlers (one and two years)

Physical

Begins to develop many motor skills.

Continues teething till about eighteen months, develops all twenty teeth by two years.

Develops large muscles. Crawls well, stands alone (at about a year), and pushes chair around.

Starts to walk at about fifteen months; may still be wobbly at eighteen months.

Places ball in and out of box.

Releases ball with thrust.

Creeps down stairs backwards.

Develops fine motor skills. Stacks two blocks, picks up a bean, and puts objects into a container. Starts to use spoon. Puts on simple things—for instance, an apron over the head.

By end of eighteen months, scribbles with a crayon in vertical or horizontal lines.

Turns pages of book.

During second year, walks without assistance.

Runs but often bumps into things.

Jumps up and down.

Walks up and down stairs with one foot forward.

Holds glass with one hand.

Stacks at least six blocks and strings beads.

Opens doors and cupboards.

Scribbles spirals, loops, and rough circles.

Starts to prefer one hand to the other.

Starts day control of elimination.

Social

At age one, differentiates meagerly between self and other.

Approaches mirror image socially.

By eighteen months, distinguishes between terms *you* and *me*.

Plays spontaneously; is self-absorbed but notices newcomers.

Imitates behavior more elaborately.

Identifies body parts.

Responds to music.

Develops socialization by age two. Is less interested in playing with parent and more interested in playing with a peer.

Continued

BOX 1–1   *Continued*

Begins parallel play, playing side by side, but without interaction.

By age two learns to distinguish strongly between self and others.

Is ambivalent about moving out and exploring.

Becomes aware of owning things and may become very possessive.

Emotional

At age one is amiable.

At eighteen months is resistant to change. Often suddenly, won't let mother out of sight.

Tends to rebel, resist, fight, run, hide.

Perceives emotions of others.

At age one, shows no sense of guilt. By age two, begins to experience guilt and shows beginnings of conscience.

Says no emphatically. Shows willfulness and negativism.

Laughs and jumps exuberantly.

Cognitive

Shows mental imagery: looks for things that are hidden, recalls and anticipates events, moves beyond here and now, begins temporal and spatial orientation.

Develops deductive reasoning: searches for things in more than one place.

Reveals memory: shows deferred imitation by seeing an event and imitating it later. Remembers names of objects.

Completes awareness of object permanence.

By age two or three distinguishes between black and white and may use names of colors.

Distinguishes one from many.

Says "one, two, three" in rote counting, but not often in rational counting.

Acts out utterances and talks about actions while carrying them out.

Takes things apart and tries to put them back together.

Shows sense of time by remembering events. Knows terms *today* and *tomorrow*, but mixes them up.

Preschoolers (three to four years)

Physical

Expands physical skills.

Rides a tricycle.

Pushes a wagon.

Runs smoothly and stops easily.

Climbs jungle gym ladder.

BOX 1–1 *Continued*

Walks stairs with alternating feet forward.

Jumps with two feet.

Shows high energy level.

By four can do a running broad jump.

Begins to skip, pushing one foot ahead of the other.

Can balance on one foot.

Keeps relatively good time in response to music.

Expands fine motor skills for dressing. Manipulates zippers, maybe even buttons.

Controls elimination at night.

Social

Becomes more social.

Moves from parallel play to early associative play. Joins others in activities.

Becomes aware of racial and sexual differences.

Begins independence.

By four shows growing sense of initiative and self-reliance.

Becomes aware of basic sex identity.

Not uncommonly develops imaginary playmates (a trait that may appear as early as two and a half).

Emotional

Begins enjoying humor. Laughs when adults laugh.

Develops inner control over behavior.

Shows less negativism.

Develops phobias and fears, which may continue until age five.

At four may begin intentional lying but is outraged by parents' white lies.

Cognitive

Begins problem-solving skills. Stacks blocks and may kick them down to see what happens.

Learns to use listening skills as a means of learning about the world.

Still draws in scribbles at age three, but in one direction and less repetitively.

At age four, drawings represent what child knows and thinks is important.

Is perceptually bound to one attribute and characteristic. "Why" questions abound.

Believes everything in the world has a reason, but the reason must accord with the child's own knowledge.

Continued

BOX 1–1 *Continued*

Persists in egocentric thinking.

Begins to sort out fantasy from reality.

Early Primary (five and six years)

Physical

Well controlled and constantly in motion.

Often rides a bicycle as well as a tricycle.

Can skip with alternating feet and hop.

Can control fine motor skills. Begins to use tools such as toothbrush, saw, scissors, pencil, hammer, needle for sewing.

Has established handedness well. Identifies hand used for writing or drawing.

Can dress self but may still have trouble tying shoelaces.

At age six begins to lose teeth.

Social

Becomes very social. Visits with friends independently.

Becomes very self-sufficient.

Persists longer at a task. Can plan and carry out activities and return to projects next day.

Plays with two or three friends, often for just a short time only, then switches play groups.

Begins to conform. Is very helpful.

By age six becomes very assertive, often bossy, dominating situations and ready with advice.

Needs to be first. Has difficulty listening.

Is possessive and boastful.

Craves affection. Often has a love–hate relationship with parents.

Refines sex roles. Has tendency to type by sex.

Becomes clothes-conscious.

Emotional

Continues to develop sense of humor.

Learns right from wrong.

At age five begins to control emotions and is able to express them in socially approved ways.

Quarrels frequently, but quarrels are of short duration.

At age six shifts emotions often and seems to be in emotional ferment.

New tensions appear as a result of attendance at school all day. Temper tantrums appear.

Giggles over bathroom words.

BOX 1–1 *Continued*

At age five develops a conscience, but sees actions as all good or all bad.
At age six accepts rules and often develops rigid insistence that they be obeyed.
May become a tattletale.

Cognitive
Begins to recognize conservation of amount and length.
Becomes interested in letters and numbers. May begin printing or copying letters and numbers. Counts.
Knows most colors.
Recognizes that one can get meaning from printed words.
Has a sense of time, but mainly personal time. Knows when events take place in his or her day or week.
Recognizes own space and can move about independently in familiar territory.

Late Primary (seven and eight years)

Physical
Great variation in height and weight, but rate of growth slows.
Masters physical skills for game playing and enjoys team sports.
Is willing to repeat a skill over and over to mastery.
Increases in fine-motor performance—can draw a diamond correctly and form letters well.
Has sudden spurts of energy.
Loss of baby teeth continues and permanent teeth appear.
Physique begins to change. Body more proportionately developed and facial structure changes.

Social
Beginning to prefer own sex—has less boy/girl interaction.
Peer groups begin to form.
Security in sex identification.
Self-absorption.
Begins to work and play independently.
Can be argumentative.
Seven still not a good loser and often a tattle teller.
By eight plays games better and not as intent on winning.
Conscientious—can take responsibility for routine chores.
Less selfish. Able to share. Wants to please.
Still enjoys and engages in fantasy play.

Continued

BOX 1-1 *Continued*

Emotional

Difficulty in starting things but will persist to end.

Worries that school might be too hard.

Beginning of empathy—sees other's viewpoint.

Sense of humor expressed in riddles, practical jokes, and nonsense words.

Discriminates between good and bad, but still immature.

Is sensitive and gets hurt easily,

Has sense of possession and takes care of possessions (makes collections).

Cognitive

Attention span is quite long.

Can plan and stay with a task or project over a long period.

Interested in conclusions and logical ends.

Aware of community and the world.

Expanding knowledge and interest.

Some sevens read well and by eight really enjoy reading.

Can tell time—aware of passage of time in months and years.

Interested in other time periods.

Conscious of other's work and their own. May comment "I'm good at art, but Sue is better at reading."

Differences in abilities widening.

Reprinted by permission of Charles E. Merrill Publishing Co. Figure 2-1, pp. 63 to 69 in Seefeldt and Barbour, *Early Childhood Education: An Introduction.*

AN IDEA FOR THE CLASSROOM

The following experience was created by an early childhood teacher for the children in her classroom. You may find this idea useful for your teaching.

Preschoolers Go Restaurant Hopping

As part of a unit dealing with nutrition, I have individual conferences with my preschoolers to help them create their own restaurant menus to be used during dramatic play. The children can either write their menus themselves (any form of early writing will be accepted—from drawing a picture, scribble writing, to random letters), or if they prefer they can dictate their menus and I will write them down. Their menus contain such savory items as fried chicken on the bone; apple juice; pink ice cream with sprinkles, whipped cream, and chocolate sauce; and cherry tacos. The children decorate covers for their menus and choose a name for their restaurant. The children have the opportunity to discuss and share their menus with the class during our "Morning Message" time.

The next step is to transform our housekeeping area into a restaurant. The play food and utensils are already there. We add items such as a tablecloth, serving trays, and small writing pads and pencils for taking orders. I've made large signs with every child's restaurant name on it. I rotate the names so that each child has a chance for his or her restaurant to be the restaurant of the day. When the children come to school, the first thing they do is rush over to the play area to see whose restaurant sign is posted.

During a typical play time, a great deal of literacy behavior occurs. Children read menus and take orders. They discuss the specials of the day and how the food tastes and pay the check. This science unit on good nutrition is conducive to providing meaningful literacy experiences for young readers and writers.

Meeting with each child on a one-to-one basis in a conference allows me to identify and deal with his or her individual needs. The needs span from finding strategies for early reading and writing that suit his or her learning style to realizing that he or she can share his or her diverse background. For example, in addition to traditional hamburger and pizza places, we had a Japanese restaurant, one that featured Hispanic delicacies, and a Jewish deli.

Marcia Wesalo, Teacher
Play and Grow Nursery School
Somerset, NJ

ACTIVITIES AND QUESTIONS

1. Answer the focus questions at the beginning of the chapter.

2. Using one of the literacy skills (reading, writing, speaking, listening), create an experience for an early childhood classroom that reflects the doctrines of Piaget. Repeat for Froebel, Montessori, and Dewey. In other words, teach the same lesson four different ways.

3. In the section of the chapter entitled "Influences for Change in Early-Literacy Practices," research and theory are described that have implications for new strategies in early literacy. Most of this book is devoted to describing these strategies. Try and predict one strategy for each of the literacy areas discussed (oral language, reading, and writing) that reflects the theory described. After you have read the entire book, come back to your answer and see how well you did.

4. Observe an early childhood classroom (preschool through second grade). Decide which theoretical influences have determined the type of practices carried out. Document your findings with specific anecdotes illustrating the theory.

5. We are aware that classrooms serve children with special needs. Special needs include children with language differences (those with dialects or those who are non–English speaking or have limited English proficiency), children with learning differences (gifted, learning disabled), children with physical impairments (visual, hearing, orthopedic, communication disorders), and children from different cultural backgrounds. Select a special need and describe a theory that you feel has implications for instructional strategies appropriate for a child with that special need. Outline the strategy.

Case Study Activity

Refer back to "An Idea for the Classroom." This experience was created by an early childhood teacher for the children in her classroom. After reading the vignette, identify the theories and research discussed in this chapter that influenced the strategies used. Describe what accommodations this teacher has made for meeting the special needs of her children. In addition to the special needs she has dealt with, what others could be addressed in the situation provided?

CHAPTER TWO

The Home and Family Literacy Development

QUESTIONS TO FOCUS ON AS YOU READ THE CHAPTER

- List and discuss three factors described by Leichter that help to promote rich family literacy environments in the home, thus making the home conducive to literacy development.
- What reading and writing materials should be present in a home, and where should they be placed to help promote children's literacy development?
- What reading and writing activities can families involve their children in to help promote literacy development?
- How can school personnel help to heighten parents' awareness of their role in the literacy development of their children?

You may have tangible wealth untold:
Caskets of jewels and coffers of gold.
Richer than I you can never be—
I had a Mother who read to me.

—STRICKLAND GILLILAN
"The Reading Mother"
from *Best Loved Poems of the American People*

Mrs. Feller spread the newspaper out on the floor as her two girls (Alice, 6 and Janet, 4), started to put down the paint jars, water can, brushes, and paper to paint. She always spread newspaper out to protect the floor when the girls would do something messy. As she spread the paper, she said, "Now let's see what section of the newspaper we have out on the floor today." "Oh look Mommy," said Alice, "It's the sports section. Some team won that baseball game 7 points to 0." "That's right," said Mrs. Feller, "the Mets beat the Dodgers 7 to 0." Mrs. Feller always made a point of having the girls look at the contents of the newspaper they spread on the floor. Her children would often continue to investigate the newspaper and almost forget their clay or paint. Sometimes they would paint about what they had just read. Mrs. Feller was taking advantage of the print in her environment that was a familiar part of her children's lives and was making it a pleasurable experience that would enrich their literacy knowledge.

Parents are the first teachers children meet. They are also children's teachers for the longest periods. Beginning at birth, children's experiences affect their success in becoming literate individuals. The success of the school literacy program frequently depends on the literacy environment at home. Studies carried out in homes have been a major catalyst for the new look in early literacy strategies. Because many children come to school already reading and writing, apparently without formal instruction, investigators began to study the characteristics of those children and of their homes. Such children were said to have "learned to read naturally," a phrase that suggests that their ability to read evolved like their acquisition of language or their learning to walk.

This line of investigation has been extremely helpful from two points of view. First, the findings reveal home practices that could be successful in school settings. Second, they provide information on the crucial role a family plays in the development of their children's literacy and on how they can help. The school can disseminate this information to parents.

I can attest to the vital role of the home in the development of early literacy. From the day of our daughter Stephanie's birth, my husband and I read to her. I read to her daily while she sat on my lap, always in the same chair. We looked at books. I talked about the pictures and read the stories. By five months, Stephanie would listen as we read to her. We chose mostly cardboard picture storybooks with only a few words on each page. From time to time her eyes focused intently on the brightly colored pictures. First she would be serious; next she would break into a broad smile. Sometimes she reached out to touch the book. Occasionally she made pleasant sounds that seemed attempts to imitate my reading voice. Because the experience was daily and positive, she became familiar with story readings and welcomed them.

As Stephanie grew older, her responses to the readings increased. Before she could talk, she pointed to pictures and made sounds as if naming objects or characters. As she acquired oral vocabulary, she labeled things in the book as I read. Quite naturally I responded with pleasure, reinforcing her attention and understanding of the concepts. Often I explained things beyond the words in the book. Both of us looked forward to these times we shared. They were relaxing, warm, and pleasurable. The practice has been referred to as the lap technique in storyreading (McCracken & McCracken, 1972).

By the time she was fourteen months old, Stephanie could often be found sitting on the floor reading a book—that is, reading as a fourteen-month-old can. She knew how to hold the book right side up, she knew which was the beginning of the book and which was the end, and she knew how to turn the pages. She looked at the pictures and chanted in tones similar to the sound of my reading. Except for a word here and there, most of her language was not understandable, but from a distance one might think that this baby was reading. Actually she was—not in the conventional manner, but by demonstrating early literacy behavior.

Books were all around the house. Stephanie had an accessible shelf of books in her room. We kept a crate of books with her toys on the floor of a closet, and she was free to use them at all times. There were books in the kitchen, the bathroom, and play areas. My husband and I had many books of our own, and we read a lot, both professional literature and recreational materials such as novels, magazines, and newspapers. Stephanie saw her parents reading frequently. At times she joined us with her own books just to feel like part of the group.

In addition to books, Stephanie had access to pencils, crayons, and markers, along with large supplies of different kinds of paper. Before three years it was quite natural for her to pick up a pencil and a sheet of paper, sit down and draw a picture, and even write about it. I could not identify what Stephanie had drawn, but she would talk about it. She was well aware of the difference between drawing and writing, and the squiggles of "print" looked different from the scribbles of the drawing. Although not yet capable of either drawing or writing in the conventional sense, she attempted to do both and differentiated between them.

In the house and on trips to the supermarket or post office, environmental print surrounded her as it does other children. Cognizant of its importance in the development of early literacy, I pointed out STOP signs at street corners and asked her to name as many signs as she could as we drove along. At home we read cereal boxes, directions for assembling new toys, and letters that came in the mail. As a result, her awareness of the print around her and of its functions was heightened. She quite naturally learned to ask what labels said and looked to print for information.

When she was three and four, our story readings became more interactive. Stephanie asked questions and commented about pictures and episodes. I responded with answers and comments that expanded the discussion. She began to narrate familiar stories with me as I read. Occasionally she asked what certain words were as her attention focused more and more on print as well as on pictures.

Stephanie was sitting in the back seat of the car on the way home from our weekly trip to the library. She was looking through one of the books she had selected and began reading it out loud. It was a humorous story called *Ten Apples Up on Top* (LeSieg, 1961). The book used a limited number of words, repetitive vocabulary, and rhyme. The attractive illustrations reflected the text. As she read, I first assumed that the book was one we had read together. Suddenly I realized it wasn't. I pulled to the side of the road and with great excitement confirmed what I thought was true. Stephanie was reading, actually reading on her own! She had made the transition from part-reading, part-narrating stories to reading each word.

Stephanie had reached this point in her literacy development quite gradually and naturally, unaware that her reading at four-and-a-half was unusual. I had offered no formal reading instruction, nor was there any such instruction in her nursery school. Because of her constant exposure to books and print from birth, she had developed a large sight vocabulary as well as a number of reading skills. Her ability to read, in other words, did not just happen. Rather, it developed in a natural way within a rich literacy environment and through the guidance, modeling, and encouragement of supportive adults.

Factors That Promote Literacy Development in the Home

According to Leichter (1984), families influence literacy development in three ways: (1) interpersonal interaction, (2) physical environment, and (3) emotional and motivational climate. *Interpersonal interaction* consists of the literacy experiences shared with a child by parents, siblings, and other individuals in the home. The *physical environment* includes the literacy materials available in the home. The *emotional and motivational climate* comprises the relationships among the individuals in a home, especially as reflected in the parents' attitudes toward literacy and their aspirations for their children's literacy achievement.

Various researchers have studied homes in which children read and write early without direct instruction (Briggs & Elkind, 1973; Clark, 1976; Durkin, 1966; King & Friesen, 1972; Morrow, 1983; Plessas & Oakes, 1964; Teale, 1978). The results have consistently established that certain characteristics are common to these children and their homes. The IQ scores of early readers are not consistently high; they range from low-average to above average. Early readers can accomplish Piagetian concrete operational tasks and are interested in pencil-and-paper activities, letters, and words. Their parents read to them, readily help them with writing and reading, and often read themselves. These parents read a great variety of material, including novels, magazines, newspapers, and work-related information. They own or borrow books, both for themselves and for their children. Reading and writing materials can be found throughout their homes, in living rooms, bedrooms, family rooms, playrooms, kitchens, and bathrooms. Parents in these homes often take their children to libraries and bookstores (Morrow, 1983). The homes hold ample supplies of books and writing materials, and reading and writing are generally valued as important activities. Books are associated with pleasure, and literary activities are rewarded. The homes are well organized, with scheduled daily activities, rules, and designated responsibilities for family members. They provide a setting where interactions between adults and children are socially, emotionally, and intellectually conducive to literacy interest and growth (Holdaway, 1979).

Children in these homes are also offered many experiences that broaden their background information. They go to the post office, the supermarket, parks, museums, and the bank. Talk surrounds their daily excursions, which enhances language development.

The families of early readers and writers tend to be small. Many of the parents have college educations, but Hansen (1969) argues that it is a literacy-rich environment, not parents' education, occupation, or socioeconomic level, that correlates most highly with children's early literacy ability. Children with an early interest in reading and writing tend to spend playtime at home writing and drawing with paper and crayons or looking at books. They watch television and use video games fewer hours a week than children who do not show an early interest in literacy. Parents in these homes enforce rules for selecting and limiting television viewing (Whitehead, Capey, & Maddren, 1975). These children are rated by their teachers as higher than average in social and emotional maturity, work habits, and general school achievement. They also perform well on standardized readiness tests (Morrow, 1983).

Durkin (1966), Holdaway (1979), Taylor (1983), and Teale (1984) describe home environments in which the ability and desire to read and write develop quite naturally. These homes provide rich literacy environments that include reading and writing materials from which children are free to select. They offer social contexts in which children are actively involved with others who serve as models of involvement in literacy activity. The adults reinforce the interest of children in reading and writing by cooperating with them in literacy activities.

Parents frequently ask teachers what they can do at home to help their children learn to read and write. In the past teachers suggested that parents drill children on the alphabet or help them with the sounds of letters. Many parents became convinced that formal teaching of skills would help their children get a head start. The newer research on early literacy suggests otherwise. When parents provide a rich literacy environment at home, teaching reading and writing becomes easier for both the teacher and the child at school. Because most children do not enter public school before age five and nursery school before age three, if at all, schools need to take responsibility for disseminating information in the community that parents can implement at home. Such information follows.

Materials to Read in the Home

Durkin (1966), King and Friesen (1972), and Morrow (1983) found that books were readily accessible to children who read early. Parents can provide library corners for their children, preferably in their bedrooms; even a little space is sufficient. Two cinder blocks and a piece of wood make a fine bookshelf, low enough for a child to reach. Books can be placed in a cardboard box or plastic crate with their spines showing, to serve as a bookshelf. In addition, books can be made available all around the house. Kitchens and bathrooms are important, because children spend considerable time in both places. If there is a playroom or a place for toy storage, it should contain books. Virtually every room can hold books that are visible and accessible. Before babies are crawling or walking, books can be brought to them in cribs and playpens; waterproof books are available for bathtubs.

A variety of books should be selected for the home. For babies up to eighteen months, brightly colored concept books with cardboard, plastic, or cloth pages are appropriate. They must be safe, with rounded edges, and sturdy enough to withstand chewing and other rough treatment. As the child becomes a toddler, preschooler, and then kindergartener, nursery rhymes, fairy tales, folktales, picture storybooks, realistic literature, informational books, picture books, alphabet books, number books, poetry, books related to favorite television programs, and easy-to-read books (those with limited vocabularies, large print, and pictures closely associated with the text) should be made available. (See Appendix A for a list of books for children, Appendix B for children's book clubs, publishers of children's books, and awards for children's books.) Children's magazines offer attractive print material for children and are a special treat if they come in the mail. In addition to children's literature, print material for adults, including books, magazines, newspapers, and work-related material, should be obvious in the home.

Reading as a Home Activity

Research indicates that children who are read to regularly by parents, siblings, or other individuals in the home, and who have parents who are habitual readers themselves, are the youngsters who become early readers and show a natural interest in books (Briggs & Elkind, 1973; Clark, 1976; Durkin, 1966; King & Friesen, 1972; Plessas & Oakes, 1964; Teale, 1978). That is not surprising. Through frequent story readings, children become familiar with book language and realize the function of written language (Smith, 1971). Story readings are almost always pleasurable, which builds a desire and interest in reading (Arbuthnot & Sutherland, 1977; Cullinan, 1977; Huck, 1976; Smith & Parker, 1977; Stewig & Sebesta, 1978). Continued exposure to books develops children's vocabulary and sense of story structure, both of which help them learn to read (Chomsky, 1972; Cohen, 1968; Mandler & Johnson, 1977; Morrow, 1985).

It is quite clear that verbal interaction between adult and child during story readings has a major influence on literacy development (Cochran-Smith, 1984; Flood, 1977; Ninio, 1980). Such interaction offers a direct channel of information for the child and thus enhances literacy development (Heath, 1982; Morrow, 1987a; Ninio & Brunner, 1978). It leads children to respond to story readings with questions and comments. These responses become more complex over time and demonstrate more sophisticated thinking about printed material. Research on home storybook readings has identified a number of interactive behaviors

Print materials such as books and magazines need to be readily available for children to use at a very young age.

that affect the quality of read-aloud activities. Those behaviors include questioning, scaffolding (modeling dialogue and responses), praising, offering information, directing discussion, sharing personal reactions, and relating concepts to life experiences (Applebee & Langer, 1983; Cochran-Smith, 1984; Flood, 1977; Roser & Martinez, 1985; Taylor & Strickland, 1986). Many parents engage their children in such interactive behavior rather naturally.

The following transcription from the beginning of a story reading between a mother and her four-year-old son Ian (Morrow, 1986a) illustrates how the adult invites and scaffolds responses, answers questions, offers positive reinforcement, and responds supportively to the child's questions and comments. As a result of the prompts, information, and support, Ian pursues his questions and receives additional information.

Mother: Are you ready for our story today, Ian? This is a new book. I've never read it to you before. It's about a mother and her baby bird.

Ian: (points to the title on the front cover) Hey, what's this for?

Mother: That's called a title. It says "Are You My Mother?" That's the name of the book. See, it's right here, too: "Are You My Mother?"

Ian: (long pause, then points to the words) "Are You My Mother?"

Mother: Right, you read it. See, you know how to read.

Ian: It says "Are You My Mother?" (points again with finger)

Mother: You read it again. Wow, you really know how to read!

Ian: Um, now read the book and I'll read it, too.

Ian's mother read the story. Each time they came to the words *Are You My Mother?*, she paused and looked at Ian, pointed to the words, and exaggerated her reading of the sentence. After two such episodes, Ian no longer needed prompting and simply read along each time they came to the phrase.

Research findings suggest that teachers should encourage parents to read to their children daily. Reading can begin the day a child is born. It must be recognized, however, that an infant's ability to listen attentively is generally limited and varies from one reading to the next. An infant may prefer to chew on the book or pound it rather than listen to it. However, babies read to from birth begin very early to be attentive in story reading situations.

*The interactive behavior between parent and child during
storybook reading involves negotiating, mediating, and
constructing meaning related to the print.*

From birth to three months, a child's attention to book reading is erratic. The baby who stares at the pictures and seems content and quiet can be considered receptive. If the baby wiggles, shows discomfort, or cries, the adult might just as well stop reading until the next time.

From three to six months, babies become more obviously involved in book readings. They begin to focus on pictures and to listen. Often, they will grab for the book, pound it, and try to put it in their mouth. As long as they seem content, they are probably involved with the reading.

Six- to nine-month-olds can be purposefully involved in story readings. They might try to turn pages. They might respond to changes in the reader's intonation or make sounds and movements to demonstrate involvement and pleasure. They sometimes begin to show preferences for books that have been read to them before.

Babies approaching one year show strong involvement in being read to. They might take a leadership role in turning pages, or babble along in tones that sound like reading. They actively look in the book for familiar things that they remember from other readings.

By six months the baby can be purposefully involved in story readings, pointing to pictures and demonstrating interest and pleasure.

By one year to fifteen months, babies who have been read to can tell which is the front and which is the back of a book and if the book is right side up or not. They begin to identify and name characters in the book. They take an active part in reading along with the adult, verbalizing a great deal (Schickedanz, 1986).

Fathers, mothers, grandparents, baby-sitters, and older siblings should all read to younger children. Let reading become a ritual, done at the same time and in the same place each day. Bedtime is a favorite time and bedtime stories are a good reading habit to establish. Both child and parent look forward to it as a time to share at the end of the day. Reading before children go to sleep has a calming effect; it establishes a routine for the children, who will eventually read by themselves before going to bed.

Spontaneous readings are encouraged as well, and if a parent finds it easier to read at different times of the day, it is certainly more desirable to do this than not to read at all. Reading to babies requires that the infant be held in the parent's arms. When the youngster is able to sit up alone, parent and child should be close to each other, preferably with the child on the adult's lap. The book with its pictures and print must be visible to the child. Children should be considered active participants in the story reading. Their comments and questions should be encouraged and acknowledged. Parents should relate comments about the story to

Fathers, mothers, baby-sitters, grandparents, and older siblings should read to children.

life experiences whenever possible and question children about familiar things in a relaxed manner to encourage their involvement.

Reading to children does not end when they begin to read themselves. This is a crucial time to continue to support and guide them in this activity. When children are able to read, the bedtime story tradition can change to the child's reading to the parent. Or it can continue with the parent's reading books above the reading level of the child. Six- to eight-year-olds are often interested in books with chapters and are not yet ready to read them themselves. Parents can take this opportunity to share more grown-up pieces of literature with these youngsters to encourage their interest. Another important parent motivation is making sure that children have new material to read that is always accessible and of interest to them. Keep track of what your youngster has read and if he or she needs new things. Sometimes we must continually put new books right in their hands even as they grow older and seem to have the reading habit established. As soon as we stop our interest in their reading, their reading interest is apt to wane.

Parents also need to read themselves. Children learn by emulating adult behavior. It has been found that children whose parents read at home become avid readers themselves. The parents become models for reading behavior that the child is likely to emulate.

In addition to reading to their children and reading themselves, parents should make a point of providing time for the family to read together. Sitting all together around the kitchen table or in the living room, each member of the family reading his or her own book, makes for a pleasant, rich literacy activity. Talking about what each family member is reading is an important part of the experience.

Materials for Writing in the Home

Some of the researchers who reported characteristics of early readers also found that these children spend a great deal of time and show a great deal of interest in pencil-and-paper activities (Clark, 1976; Durkin, 1966; Morrow, 1983; Plessas & Oakes, 1964). The parents of many such children reported that the interest in writing began with scribbling in babyhood. Certain scholars have suggested that writing develops naturally before reading. Many children, they point out, invent writing systems of their own that seem to have meaning for them (Read, 1971). Whether reading comes before writing or writing before reading is an unsettled issue. What we have come to recognize, however, is that learning to read is enhanced by concurrent experiences with writing and that the development of writing is facilitated by experiences with reading.

One implication of these findings is that writing materials should be made available for children at home. A variety of sizes of unlined white paper is preferable, especially for babies. As children get into their preschool years and kindergarten, smaller sheets can be added to the household supply. A child approaching kindergarten might like lined paper as well. Pencils, crayons, colored pencils, a chalkboard and chalk, and markers are appropriate home writing tools. Manipulatives such as magnetic, felt, or wooden letters are also useful. Children should be exposed to them early and have free access to them. Typewriters and home computers encourage writing and are appropriate for preschoolers. (A list of computer software for young children can be found in Appendix E.)

As with book reading, youngsters need to see their parents involved in writing activities. Parents should communicate with their children through writing as often as possible. When children begin preschool, notes can be placed in lunch boxes that say simply, "Hi! Love, Mommy and Daddy." Notes on pillows can say "Good night" or "Good morning."

As with reading, make writing a family event whenever possible. Ask your child to help you write a thank you note or a letter to his or her teacher. Fill out school forms with them or make up the family grocery list together. Children will emulate parents who take opportunities to communicate through writing.

Responsive Adults Encourage Literacy

Studies of early readers reveal that the adults in their environment tended to be receptive and responsive to their interest in literacy activities (Clark, 1976; Durkin, 1966; King & Friesen, 1972; Plessas & Oakes, 1964). Parents answered children's questions about books and print, offered information, provided experiences that enhanced literacy development, and praised children for participating in literacy behaviors. Such channels of information and support systems in the home naturally encourage the development of reading. Durkin (1966) found that parents who attempted to teach children more formally were not as successful as parents who simply responded to children's requests for information about reading.

Responsiveness between parent and child needs to begin with babies and be cultivated. Responsive adults respond in many ways. Language provides a primary opportunity for developing this behavior. Responsive adults not only answer questions, they initiate activities that promote literacy. While dressing, diapering, or feeding an infant, for instance, a parent can talk, sing, recite nursery rhymes, and tell stories. The baby responds by smiling, cooing, and moving, encouraging the parent to continue, and a cycle of mutual responsiveness develops.

Environmental print surrounds children and holds meaning for them. This natural source of reading material offers a way into literacy through things whose function children are already familiar with (Downing, 1970). Children begin to read and ask about environmental print probably before they are interested in the print found in books. Parents who are aware of the importance of environmental print can point out familiar labels and other information on cereal boxes, vitamin bottles, detergent containers, and food packages. Children are naturally interested in telephone books, cookbooks, television guides, advertisements, and mail. They are particularly interested in personal letters, fliers, greeting cards, bills, catalogs, and magazines. The outside world presents a wealth of environmental print: road signs, street signs, and the names of fast food restaurants, gas stations, and other well-known chains. Parents note the environmental print that is meaningful to children and encourage children to do the same, pointing out specific letters in these familiar words and even sounding the letters. This gamelike involvement in skills has been found to promote early literacy (Tobin, 1981).

In addition to responding to requests about books and print, parents of early readers generally respond to the need to provide varied experiences for their children. They take them to libraries and bookstores. They talk to them a great deal, which builds the children's vocabulary. Trips to zoos, fire stations, airports, and parks all foster literacy growth if they are accompanied by oral language and positive social interactions. It should be emphasized that a trip not only broadens a child's experience but allows verbal interactions between parent and child before, during, and after. Those interactions include providing the child with background about the place to be visited and the things to be seen, answering questions about the experience, offering information, reading stories related to the experience, and discussing the trip afterwards so that new ideas are absorbed. Suggesting that the child record the experience by drawing a picture about it and dictating a story for the parent to write will further expand literacy growth.

Television is part of our lives and definitely here to stay. To make the most of TV viewing, parents should watch some programs with their youngsters, posing questions, raising critical issues, and changing passive viewing into responsive interaction. Choose programs for which parallel books are available, such as "Sesame Street," "Reading Rainbow," and "Mister Rogers." When specific stories are scheduled on television, such as *How the Grinch Stole Christmas* (Seuss, 1957), borrow or purchase the book. (Books associated with TV shows are listed in Appendix D.)

In a series of interviews with parents whose children were early readers (Morrow, 1980), it became apparent that literacy was embedded in daily activities that were meaningful, functional, and part of the mainstream of their lives. Various print materials were visible in the homes. Language was used interactively and frequently, in all its forms and in a positive emotional climate. There was praise for literacy activity and pleasure and joy in reading and writing. When asked what they believed helped their children become literate so early, the parents found it difficult to answer because they had not viewed the experiences they offered their children as attempts to promote reading and writing. Most of these activities had other functions, such as keeping the house running smoothly. Many of the experiences had social objectives—to promote positive interpersonal relationships and to teach responsibility and manners, for example. Here are some anecdotes related by some of these parents:

> "I started a baby book for each of my children from the day they were born, with information about their weight and height, and I included pictures. I made sure to report major events, such as first words, first steps, likes and dislikes concerning food, and events of interest to me. I found myself looking at the book frequently and my toddler snuggling beside me showing great interest. I've continued the books and as the children are getting older they add to them and read them over and over. They are without a doubt among their favorite books."

> "Long trips can be tedious with young children in the car. To make the time pass we play games. Some games that are fun in the car are trying to rhyme words, reading road signs, and reading letters and numbers on the license plates of cars."

> "As a grandfather I don't get to see my grandchildren as frequently as I would like. In order to keep close contact, I often send them things through the mail. I'll enclose games cut from the children's section of the newspaper which I'll ask them to complete. I send them pictures of famous people and ask them to call and tell me who they think they are. Sometimes I include questions and tell them it is a contest for which they can win a prize if all their answers are correct."

> "From the time they were very young, my children were required to write thank you notes for gifts received. At first they

dictated them and I wrote down what they said. Later they were able to write simply 'thank you.' One good incentive for the task was to allow them to choose their own stationery for note writing."

"The public library has provided many fine experiences for my children. One in particular is to help prepare them for experiences to come and allow them to relive experiences they have. Before we went to the circus, we took a circus story out of the library in preparation for our trip. After seeing the circus we enjoyed another circus story from the library. No one's home library could ever be as complete as the public library and going to the library for books is such a good habit to get into."

"I started leaving notes for my children in surprise places before they could read. Somehow they managed to find out what the notes said, even at the pre-reading stage. Now I put messages in their lunch boxes. The notes often just say 'hello.' Sometimes I'll write a riddle or a joke, and sometimes the note may require an answer. This has become a family tradition and lately I find surprise notes addressed to me left in the most unusual places."

"The amount of TV viewing by our three- and four-year-old children was a source of aggravation to us. To make the experience a more meaningful one, we read the television program guide to decide on what programs to watch and to limit the number of selections that the children are allowed to make in one day. We try to watch at least some programs with them and ask who, what, when, and where questions to elicit recall of facts. We also ask why questions to encourage more interpretive responses."

"I've always kept a journal recording my daily experiences. My four-year-old found me writing in it one day and asked about what I was doing. She wanted to do the same thing, so we started a joint journal. I'd write things that happened to me during the day and she'd tell me what to write for her. Soon she was able to do her own writing. Sometimes I'd ask her questions about what she'd written. I did this by writing in the journal, of course, and she would have to answer. The *journal had no formal format, except that each of us wrote about an event of the day, and we would share the same journal page."*

Researchers have found that home environments possessing the characteristics described here will generally instill an interest in reading and writing, a desire to read and write, and the ability to read and write early. It should be noted that most of the data from the investigations that provided this information were correlational. Therefore, it is difficult to draw conclusions about cause and effect. There are children from homes that display all of the characteristics described who are not early readers and writers and have difficulty learning to read and write. There are early readers and writers from environments lacking the characteristics described. Obviously there are factors other than the environment that affect successful literacy development. But it has been demonstrated that environmental factors do play a strong role in fostering literacy. A rich literacy environment at home gives children a better chance to learn to read and write easily and to enjoy reading and writing as well.

School personnel should inform parents of the school's program in literacy development through orientation programs and regular newsletters. In multicultural settings where English is not spoken or read, materials need to be in both English and the language used at home. The letter can tell parents what is being studied, include samples of children's work, and offer suggestions for enriching the child's experience at home. Anecdotes concerning promoting literacy at home such as those just cited can be solicited from parents. Parents should be given lists of quality children's literature related to what is being studied and suggestions for toys that promote literacy. A list of suggested books is found in Appendix A, which also includes multicultural selections as well as children's literature published in Spanish. Finally, parents can be invited to school to help with such literacy activities as reading to children, taking story dictations, and helping with bookbinding projects.

The school also needs to take on the responsibility of getting information to homes about the need for rich literacy environments even before children enter school. Information can be disseminated at special meetings for expectant parents, in hospital maternity wards, in obstetricians' and pediatricians' offices, and through churches, synagogues, and community agencies. A succinct handout such as the one that follows will be a helpful start. (Books and pamphlets on the development of literacy at home can be found in Appendix C.)

BOX 2–1 • *Parents' Guidelines for Promoting Early Literacy at Home*

    Your youngster's ability to read and write depends to a great extent upon the things you do at home from the time he or she is born. As a parent you can do many things to help that will not take much of your time. The rewards from these activities will be enormous in terms of your child's reading and writing. The following list suggests materials, activities, and attitudes that are important for promoting literacy at home.

Materials

1. Have twenty-five children's books available at home and add to the collection regularly.
2. Subscribe to a children's magazine.
3. Place some of your child's and some of your own books, magazines, and newspapers in various rooms throughout your home to encourage spontaneous reading in spare moments.
4. Provide materials that will encourage children to tell or create their own stories, such as puppets, feltboard and felt story characters, story records, tapes of stories, and a tape recorder.
5. Provide materials for writing, such as crayons, felt-tip pens, pencils, and plenty of white paper of different sizes.

Activities

1. Read or look at books with your child daily and talk about the stories.
2. If your child is able, have him or her read along with you or to you.
3. Visit the library at least once every two weeks.
4. Tell stories to each other.
5. Talk about things you've read.
6. Provide a model for your child by reading yourself.
7. Provide a model for children by writing.
8. Heighten your child's awareness of the function and uses of print by pointing out words, written notes, and other print used in your daily life. Read environmental print such as words on cereal boxes, other food packages, and road signs. Occasionally communicate through written messages.

Continued

BOX 2–1 *Continued*

Fostering Positive Attitudes

1. Reward your child's attempts at reading and writing by offering praise.
2. Answer your child's questions about reading and writing.
3. Let reading and writing be enjoyable experiences so that children associate them with pleasure.

Seek Help from School If You Need It

1. If you have concerns about your child's literacy development, consult us at school anytime.
2. If you feel your child has any special problems with his or her vision, hearing, or schoolwork in general, consult us at school anytime.
3. If you need help because the language you speak at home is not English, consult us at school anytime.
4. If you want to discuss how you can help and how we can help you, consult us at school anytime.

Broad Perspectives Concerning Family Literacy

In this chapter family literacy has been approached from the perspective of parents helping children to support their reading and writing development. In our country today we must recognize that many families do not speak English and therefore are not able to help their children in the ways that schools have suggested. In addition there are many parents who have limited literacy ability and although eager to help, cannot do so in the mainstream approach. In some cases the parent is a teenager who has dropped out of school. Therefore, when we speak of family literacy, in many situations we need to recognize that it must be an intergenerational matter in which environments are created to enable adult learners to enhance their own literacies, and at the same time promote the literacies of their children. It has been generally accepted that poverty and illiteracy are linked. However, there is evidence that many low-income, minority, and immigrant families cultivate rich contexts for literacy development. Their efforts are, however, different from the school model we are accustomed to. We must learn from and respect parents and children from cultures in which no books exist, yet there is evidence of literacy activity, such as storytelling.

The intention of family literacy programs is to arrest what is perceived as a cycle of illiteracy. We must include in this effort perspectives on family literacy that begin within the family itself. Such perspectives acknowledge the complexities of literacy activities and environments within families that are often described as "illiterate," and in doing so emphasize that the "illiteracy" within a culture is not necessarily an all-or-nothing state, but rather a function of individual interactions with print within a multidimensional range of literacy and personal experiences. Such accounts go beyond definitions of literacy that are related only to schooling; in this broader definition, literacy is seen as woven through the whole of the social fabric. Family literacy must be approached to avoid cultural bias and ethnocentrism.

Examples of Family Literacy Programs

A variety of family literacy programs exists. Projects are often in partnerships with varied organizations, and may be spearheaded by public schools, adult literacy programs, communitybased groups, government agencies, or any combination thereof.

Three types of programs seem to emerge. There are those that focus on *Bringing the Adult and Child Together.* These initiatives spend equal amounts of time with the adult and child. There are separate activities and instruction for both parents and their children, as well as group activities. Programs are structured and occur over a long period of time. *Parents and Literacy* (PALS) is one such effort, originating in Tucson, Arizona, which involves adults with limited education and their preschool children, both attending a public school for literacy instruction. The parents are given an adult curriculum focusing on oral language development, book sharing, reading, writing, mathematics, life skills and parenting skills. At the same time, teachers work with the preschool children doing tasks that are coordinated with the parents' curriculum. Parents also visit regular classrooms in the school for "book sharing" in Spanish and English to learn to use with their own children.

A second type of program has its *Focus on the Adult.* Adults receive literacy instruction, English as a Second Language instruction, and instruction in how to read to children including the modeling of appropriate strategies. An adult-focused program,

Bookmates: Family Literacy Project in Winnipeg, Canada, promotes the literacy development of inner-city preschoolers by providing direct instruction to immigrant parents regarding why, what, and how to read to their children. Parents are taught to use children's literature and environmental print in reading activities. It also involves teaching parents how to encourage their children to write.

The third type of program is called *Focuses on the Child.* In these programs there is direct instruction with children only, and parents are asked to assist at home, but do not receive training. This type of program reflects the suggestions made earlier in this chapter. *Books and Beyond,* originating in Solano Beach, Calif., seeks to increase students' recreational reading at home. Children, parents, and administrators participate in a *Read-A-Thon,* which involves recording numbers of books read, and time spent reading.

Models need to be developed that view family literacy as activities that promote parent/child interaction in a wide range of literacy events, and that view participating families from the perspective of the richness of their experiences and heritage, rather than from the perspective of their deficits and dilemmas.

Educators are recognizing that the family is the key to successful literacy development for both children and their parents. Policymakers from a wide range of agencies need to collaborate and form partnerships in their efforts to create and support effective and strong family literacy programs. Literacy programs in school will only be successful if they have home support; therefore family literacy programs are crucial for literacy development.

AN IDEA FOR THE CLASSROOM

A newsletter follows that is to be sent to parents describing a unit that their children are involved in entitled *Life on the Farm.* A similar newsletter can be sent with every unit taught during the school year. This gives parents information about the unit and asks for their participation by working with their child at home and sending materials to school or coming to school to make presentations. This newsletter will heighten parents' awareness of activities to do at home that correspond with what their children are doing at school. It also makes parents active participants in school experiences.

Life on the Farm Newsletter
Message to Parents

Dear Parents:

This month your child is participating in an exciting unit about farm life. This unit includes the study of people and the jobs they do on farms, farm animals and their babies, farm machinery, farm buildings, and products that come from farms.

The unit is organized so that all subject areas, social studies, science, math, art, play, reading, and writing, are incorporated within the farm theme. Reading and writing will have a special emphasis in all activities including those in art, music, and so on.

We would like to ask you to participate in the farm unit and feel that each and every one of you can help in some way. If you have any pictures, materials, or personal experiences to talk about related to the topic, please let me know and come to school to share them with us. There are a wide variety of topics dealing with the farm, and I'm sure each of you would have something to share. The topics following would be appropriate:

Jobs on the farm (growing plants, caring for animals, selling products, equipment), farm animals and their babies (cats, dogs, and their care, etc.), farm machinery (tractors, trucks, plows, etc.), farm buildings (barns, animal housing), the products that come from farms (corn, wheat, cotton, wool, fruit, vegetables, meat, milk, etc.), the preparation of food from farm products (apple pie, cheeses, etc.) and the preparation of other items from farm products (goose down pillows, wool sweaters, etc.). We always need help with projects in class so please volunteer to help at school one day regardless of whether you have a farm idea to share or not.

Featured Farm Activities in School

In school, your child will participate in the following experiences:

- *In science, the children will learn to keep a journal to record the growth of their very own lima bean plants.*
- *In social studies, we will discuss cooperation when we read and act out the story of* The Little Red Hen.
- *In the dramatic-play area, we will learn about care of animals and the role of doctors and nurses by setting up a veterinarian's office that has prescription forms, books and magazines in a waiting room, and stuffed animal patients.*

Materials in this area encourage reading and writing as children role-play.

- *In the Library Corner, we will add books, poems, and songs about the farm to read to your children. Some of the titles are:*

  1. Petunia *by Roger Duvoisin*
  2. Over in the Meadow *by Ezra Jack Keats*
  3. Go Tell Aunt Rhody *by Marcia Brown*
  4. Rosie's Walk *by Pat Hutchins*
  5. Ask Mr. Bear *by Marjorie Flack*

Things to Do at Home with Your Child about the Farm

- *Ask your child about the activities he or she is doing in school. Some of them have been mentioned, and you can focus on those. Ask your child to draw a picture about the farm and write about it also.*
- *Try and get some of the books we are reading in school from your local library and reread the stories to your child. Ask your youngster to retell the story using the pictures if necessary. Talk about the issues discussed in the stories.*
- *The unit focuses on cooperating with others while doing a job. To reinforce this idea, encourage your child to help you with any household tasks or with the care of a pet or plant.*
- *When you prepare food at home, point out the products that come from the farm. Notice newspaper or magazine articles that relate to the farm and read and discuss them together.*
- *If possible, visit a farm, a petting zoo that has farm animals, a pet store, a plant nursery, or the supermarket where you can look at and talk about the products that come from the farm.*

*   *   *

THANK YOU VERY MUCH FOR YOUR INTEREST AND ENTHUSIASM WHICH WE APPRECIATE AND WHICH ARE GREATLY APPRECIATED BY YOUR CHILD.

I will be happy to answer any questions you may have about this unit and your child's development. I hope to hear from you.

Sincerely,

Susan Burks

Susan Burks
Teacher—North Plainfield, NJ

ACTIVITIES AND QUESTIONS

1. Answer the focus questions posed at the beginning of the chapter.

2. Interview members of your family or friends who are parents. Ask them to relate specific activities they have done with their children to promote literacy with natural events that arose from daily living. Collect ideas from all members of the class and put them together in a newsletter or pamphlet format to distribute to parents of early childhood youngsters.

3. Using the memories of your own home when you were a young child or the home of a friend or family member who is a parent of a young child, observe the physical characteristics and record activities done with children that promote literacy development. Determine elements that could improve the richness of the literacy environment you analyzed.

4. The characteristics of homes of early readers are influencing practices in early childhood literacy development. Describe a portion of an early childhood literacy program in school, including materials, activities, and teacher behaviors, based on the characteristics of homes where children are found to read early.

Case Study Activity

Refer back to the "Ideas for the Classroom" section. This newsletter was created by an early childhood teacher for the parents in her classroom. After reading the newsletter, consider the following: David Hernandez will take the newsletter home to his mother who does not speak any English but is literate in Spanish, and Tiffany Jones will take the newsletter home to her mother who has minimal literacy skills. What is likely to be the response to the newsletter in each of these homes?

Review the newsletter as if for a journal that focuses on literacy development. Concentrate on the following: What are the most important items included in the newsletter? What is missing? Present those ideas you feel are missing. This newsletter was written for kindergartners or first graders. What changes would you make for second and third graders?

What accommodations has this teacher made for meeting the needs of all the children and parents in her classroom? What else could she have included to accommodate special needs better? Present those ideas you feel are missing.

CHAPTER THREE

Language and Literacy Development

QUESTIONS TO FOCUS ON AS YOU READ THE CHAPTER

- According to the different theorists described in the chapter, how is language acquired?
- What are the general stages of language development that a child progresses through from birth to age eight?
- What do we mean when we speak of children with language differences?
- What are the objectives for language development in early childhood?
- What strategies can teachers and parents carry out to encourage language development from birth to age two?
- What strategies can teachers and parents carry out to encourage language development from preschool through second grade?
- What techniques can be used for starting a portfolio of materials that assesses children's language development?

"The time has come," the Walrus said,
"To talk of many things:
Of shoes and ships and sealing-wax,
Of cabbages and kings. . . ."
—LEWIS CARROLL
"The Walrus and the Carpenter"

The kind of talking to which Lewis Carroll refers in his poem is very much the language babies need to hear in their first steps toward literacy. From the moment of birth, the infant is surrounded by oral language. The development of language is one of the child's first steps toward becoming a literate individual; it helps to make reading and writing possible. Using newer research methods that involve close observation of children, investigators have been able to describe the strategies by which youngsters learn and use language. Among the many things these researchers have observed is that children are active participants in their learning of language. In order to learn, children involve themselves in problem solving, first creating hypotheses based on background information that they already have and then interacting with those individuals around them who are generating language. These strategies have implications for initial instruction in early literacy.

A parent of a child in one of my kindergarten classes related an anecdote concerning a conversation she had had with her daughter Arielle. Mrs. Vogel said they were outside looking at the sky one evening, and she noticed that the moon was full. She said to her daughter, "Look Arielle, the moon is full tonight." Arielle looked up at the moon with a slightly confused expression on her face and said, "Why is it full Mommy, did the moon eat too much for dinner?" Arielle used her background language information to help her understand her mother. Until this time the word *full* meant filled up, and Arielle made sense of the discussion with what she knew. Her mother went on to explain what she meant by a full moon and that different words can have different meanings depending on the situation in which they are used.

Children do not learn language passively; they actually construct—or reconstruct—language as they learn.

We were talking about what the children in my classroom wanted to be when they grew up. It was Michael's turn. He started by telling us that his dad is a doctor and recently he had taken him to see the operating room where he works. Michael said, "I liked the people and all the machines that my Daddy uses and so when I grow up, I want to be an *operator,* just like my Daddy."

Michael constructed a word for the situation that made wonderful sense under the circumstances. This illustrates the construction of language previously mentioned.

The discoveries of how language is acquired laid the foundation for a new way of looking at how early reading develops. Researchers realized that because reading is a language process, it must be closely associated with oral language.

Language Development and Reading

Now that language processes are commonly recognized as the basis for learning to read, *language learning* is considered an important part of *learning to read.* Ruddell (1971) defines reading as the use of one's language ability to decode and comprehend. Goodman (1967) calls it the interaction between the reader and the written language. He states that reading is the attempt by a reader to reconstruct the author's message, that the graphic sequences and patterns that appear as print represent the oral sequences of language. In the process of reading, we look and listen for recognizable grammatical sequences and patterns that trigger appropriate phrasing. Using what we already know of language structure, we then test how each word fits into the context of what we are reading. Lennenberg and Kaplan (1970) tend to agree with Goodman's view. They see the reader as continually assigning tentative interpretations to the text and then checking those interpretations. As readers, we use syntactic and semantic cues that enable us to predict what comes next. Our skill in processing semantics (meaning) and syntax (language structure) makes us more adept readers. As Athey (1971) points out, the reader who encounters unfamiliar language structures and unfamiliar concepts in material to be read has difficulty understanding it. Familiarity with both syntax and semantics enables even the very young reader to anticipate the format and content of sentences in print. Past theory held that it was our accumulation of letters and words that led to competent reading. Now we realize that our ability to understand what we are reading is based on our *reconstruction* of the meaning behind a printed word. Such reconstruction is based on our previous experience with the topic, our familiarity with its main concepts, and our general knowledge of how language works.

The relationship between reading and language is evident in studies of children who are early readers. It has been found, for instance, that early readers score higher on language screening tests than children who were not reading early. Early readers come from homes where rich language and a great deal of oral language are used (Snow & Perlmann, 1985). When interviewed, parents of early readers revealed that their children tended to use very descriptive language and sophisticated language structures. The youngsters invented words, used humor, and talked a lot. The mother of a four-year-old early reader reported that while watching the first snowfall of the year, her youngster said, "The snow is swirling down and looks like fluffy marshmallows on the ground." One spring day a few months later, the same child noted, "Look, Mommy, the butterflies are fluttering around. They look like they are dancing with the flowers."

Halliday (1975) notes that among other functions, language helps children learn how to ascertain meaning from the world around them. Early readers demonstrate an awareness of story language (Snow, 1983). They can retell stories using such literary conventions as "Once upon a time" and "They lived happily ever after." When telling stories they tend to use delivery and intonation like those of an adult reading aloud. Cazden (1972) suggests that such "book language" takes children beyond their own language patterns and is distinctively characteristic of early readers.

How Children Acquire Language

Although we do not have all the answers about language acquisition, there are many theories that help explain how babies learn to speak. Knowing how language is acquired has strong implications for providing environments that promote language development. It also implies how reading and writing skills develop.

The *behaviorists* have influenced our thinking about how language is acquired. Although behaviorism does not present the total picture, it still offers ideas about language acquisition that ought to be considered for instruction. Skinner (1957) defined language as the observed and produced speech that occurs in the interaction of speaker and listener. Thinking, he said, is the internal process of language; both language and thought are initiated through interactions in the environment—such interactions as those between a parent and a child, for instance. According to behaviorists, adults provide a language model that children learn through imitation. The child's acquisition of language is enhanced and encouraged by the positive reinforcement of an adult.

The behaviorist description of language acquisition is incomplete, but it is evident that children imitate adult models and are motivated to continue using language because of positive reinforcement. Children surrounded by rich language begin to use the language they hear, even though imitation sometimes occurs with erroneous comprehension or no comprehension at all. A child can imitate the sounds of the "words" of a familiar song, for instance, with no concern at all for meaning. A three-year-old girl sang "My country 'tis of thee" as "My country tis a bee." A four-year-old sang "Torn between two lovers" as "Torn between two mothers." Both children were imitating what they heard and were thus acquiring language. But when they came upon unfamiliar words in context, both substituted similar-sounding words that had meaning for them from their own experiences.

In most environments early attempts at language are rewarded. When newborns coo or make other verbal sounds, most parents are delighted and respond with gentle words of encouragement. The infant, in turn, responds to the positive reinforcement by repeating the cooing sounds. As babies get older and are able to formulate consonant and vowel sounds, they try them out. It is not uncommon to hear a six-month-old playing with sounds such as *ba, ba, ba,* or *ma, ma, ma.* The responsive parent perceives such sounds as the child's first words and assumes that the child's *ma-ma* means *mommy.* The delighted adult says more warm and loving things to the baby and adds hugs and kisses. The parent might say, "Come on, now say it again, ma, ma, ma." The baby is pleased with the warm reception and tries to repeat the sounds in order to receive additional reinforcement.

As a child builds an oral vocabulary, he or she tries words more frequently. Children will point to a toy and name it. While playing with a ball, a child may say the word *ball* over and over again. The attentive parent now reinforces the child's words by expanding and extending the original language (Cazden, 1972). After the child says *ball,* the parent may say, "Yes, that is a nice, big, round, red ball." Through such expansion and reinforcement of words by the adult, the child acquires new language. The adult often extends upon the baby's words by asking questions, for instance, "Now what can you do with that nice red ball" Such extension requires the child to think, understand, and act. Positive reinforcement encourages practice, which helps continue language development.

Unfortunately, the converse is also true. If a baby's babbling is considered annoying, if the parent is aggravated by the sound and responds with negative reinforcement by telling the baby in harsh tones, "Be quiet and stop making so much noise," the child is less likely to continue to explore the use of language.

Chomsky (1965), Lennenberg (1967), and McNeil (1970) have described the *nativist* theory of language acquisition. They contend that language develops innately. Children figure out how language works, say the nativists, by internalizing the rules of grammar, which enable them to produce an infinite number of sentences. They do so even without the practice, reinforcement, and modeling offered by adult language, which are considered necessary by the behaviorists. The ability to learn language must be innate to humans, the nativists believe, because almost all children develop and use language in the first few years of their lives. Language growth depends on maturation: as children mature, their language grows. Children learn new patterns of language and unconsciously generate new rules for new elements of language. The child's rule system increases in complexity as he or she generates more complex language. Lennenberg (1967), an extreme nativist, finds nothing in the child's environment to account for language development. Rather, language acquisition is motivated *inside children;* learning language is a natural ability. Although maturation does play a role in language development, newer theories offered by Piaget and Vygotsky have come to be the more accepted ideas concerning language acquisition.

Piaget's theory of *cognitive development* is built on the principle that children develop through their activity. Children's realization of the world is tied to their actions or their sensory experiences in the environment. According to this theory, children's first words are egocentric, or centered in their own actions. Children talk about themselves and what they do. Their early language as well as their general development relates to actions, objects, and events they have experienced through touching, hearing, seeing, tasting, and smelling (Piaget & Inhelder, 1969).

Vygotsky's theory of *basic learning* also has implications for language development. According to Vygotsky, children learn higher mental functions by internalizing social relationships. Adults initially provide children with names of things, for instance; they direct youngsters and make suggestions. Then, as children become more competent, the adults around them gradually withdraw the amount of help they need to give. Vygotsky (1978) describes a *zone of proximal development*, a range of social interaction between an adult and child. Theoretically, the child

*Children learn language from soc'al
interaction with a responsive adu t who
provides a language model and positive
reinforcement for the child's early language
attempts.*

can perform within that range, but only with adult assistance. Proximal development ends when the child can function independently. The implications for language instruction are clear: to promote language development, adults need to interact with children by encouraging, motivating, and supporting them (Sulzby, 1986a).

Brown, Cazden, and Bellugi-Klima (1968), Halliday (1975), and Smith (1973) follow the *constructivist* theory of language development. They all describe the acquisition of language as an active process. The child creates and constructs language, often making errors. But making errors is a necessary part of learning how language works (Harris & Smith, 1980), and we tend to accept language errors quite readily in a child' first years. The implications are important for early literacy development. Even though language development charts tell us when to expect certain stages of language development on average, we do not discipline babies who have not uttered their first words at eight months or their first complete sentences by two-and-a-half years. Sometimes we even find their errors cute. We seem to respect their individuality and their right to grow at their own pace. Yet when children enter school, we neglect to recognize developmental differences; we prescribe tasks based on a curriculum, not on the child.

The process of acquiring language is continuous and interactive; it takes place in the social context of the child's interacting with others. Children also learn by playing with language themselves. They try out new words, involve themselves in monologues, and practice what they have learned. The acquisition of language varies from child to child, depending on his or her social and cultural background (Jagger, 1985). Their remarks illustrate that children do not *simply* imitate adult language. It is as if children need to express themselves but do not have sufficient conventional language to draw upon, so they create their own based on their backgrounds and their awareness of semantics and syntax.

A three-year-old saw a freckled youngster for the first time and said, "Look, Mommy, that little girl has *sprinkles* on her nose." A four-year-old observed an elderly man with deep wrinkles and said, "I wonder why that man has *paths* all over his face." A father and his three-year-old daughter were toasting marshmallows; the little girl said, "Mmmm, I can smell the taste of them." After a quick summer rain, a three-year-old boy observed the sun returning to the sky and the water evaporating all around him. "The sun came out and ate up all the rain," he observed. Toward the end of the winter as the snow was melting, a four-year-old girl observed, "See how the grass is peeking out from underneath the snow."

Halliday's Theory of Language Development

Halliday (1975, p. 7) describes language development as a process by which children gradually "learn how to mean." According to his theory of developmental language, what a child can do during interactions with others has meaning, and meaning can be turned into speech. In other words, children's initial language development is based on function: what can be said reflects what can be done. Halliday (1975, pp. 19–21) identifies seven functions evident in the language of young children:

1. *Instrumental:* children use language to satisfy personal needs and to get things done.
2. *Regulatory:* children use language to control the behavior of others.
3. *Personal:* children use language to tell about themselves.
4. *Interactional:* children use language to get along with others.
5. *Heuristic:* children use language to find out about things, to learn things.

6. *Imaginative:* children use language to pretend, to make believe.
7. *Informative:* children use language to communicate something for the information of others.

The several theories just discussed help us to understand how language is acquired. Each has something to offer but by itself does not present a complete picture. We *do* know, however, that children's language grows according to their need to use it, their interests, and the meaning it has for them. In other words, according to Halliday (1975), what can be said reflects what can be done. Children's language is acquired through exploration and invention and is controlled by their own maturity, the structure of the language, and its conventions.

Stages in Language Development

Children acquire language by moving through predictable stages. In doing so, they discover the rules that govern the structure of language—specifically, those of phonology (sound), syntax (grammar), and semantics (meaning).

There are forty-four separate sounds, or *phonemes* in English. With them we produce oral language. Children who grow up in a language-rich environment can learn these sounds quite easily. They learn appropriate articulation, pronunciation, and intonation. *Intonation* involves pitch, stress, and juncture. *Pitch* refers to how high or low a voice is when producing a sound, *stress* to how loud or soft it is, and *juncture* to the pauses or connections between words, phrases, and sentences (Hittleman, 1983).

Syntax refers to the rules that govern how words work together in phrases, clauses, and sentences. Internalizing the syntactic rules of our language helps children understand what they hear and what they read. Syntax includes rules for forming basic sentence patterns, rules for transforming those patterns in order to generate new sentences, and rules for embedding, expanding, and combining sentences in order to make them more complex. Brief examples follow:

1. Some Basic Sentence Patterns
   a. Subject–verb: *The girl ran.*
   b. Subject–verb–object: *The girl ran the team.*
   c. Subject–verb–indirect object–direct object: *Susan gave Lynn a dime.*

    d. Subject–to be–noun or adjective or adverb complement: *Tom was the captain. He was happy. He was there.*

    e. Subject–linking verb–adjective: *Jane is tall.*

2. Some Basic Sentence Transformations

    a. Question

        (1) kernel: *Jim went to the store.*

        (2) transformation: *Did Jim go to the store?*

    b. Negative

        (1) kernel: *Jane is a cheerleader.*

        (2) transformation: *Jane is not a cheerleader.*

    c. Passive

        (1) kernel: *Jennifer gave Lisa some bubble gum.*

        (2) transformation: *Some bubble gum was given to Lisa by Jennifer.*

3. Some Embeddings (sentence expansion and combination)

    a. Adding modifiers (adjectives, adverbs, adverbial and adjective phrases)

        (1) kernel: *The boy played with friends.*

        (2) transformation: *The boy in the red pants played with three friends.*

    b. Compounding (combining words, phrases, or independent clauses to form compound subjects, verbs, etc.)

        (1) kernel: *Jane ran. Jane played. Jack ran. Jack played.*

        (2) transformation: *Jane and Jack ran and played.* (Morrow, 1978)

Semantics deals with the meaning that language communicates, both through content words and through function words. It largely governs vocabulary development. *Content words* carry meaning in themselves. *Function words* have no easily definable meanings in isolation, but they indicate relationships between other words in a sentence. Function words include prepositions, conjunctions, and determiners (Pflaum, 1986).

Although we have identified stages of language growth, the pace of development may differ from child to child. An individual child's language development also tends to progress and then regress, so that the stages of growth are not always easily recognized. However, language development has been studied to the extent that it can be described generally (Grieve & Hoogenraad, 1979).

From Birth to One Year

In the first few months of infancy, oral language consists of a child's experimenting or playing with sounds. Infants cry when they are uncomfortable and babble, gurgle, or coo when they are happy. Parents are able to distinguish cries. One cry is for hunger and another is for pain, for instance. Infants learn to communicate specific needs by producing different cries. They communicate nonverbally as well by moving their arms and legs to express pleasure or pain.

When a baby is about six months old, its babbling becomes more sophisticated. Children at that age are usually capable of combining a variety of consonant sounds with vowel sounds. They tend to repeat these combinations over and over. As mentioned earlier, it is at this stage that parents sometimes think they are hearing their child's first words. The repeated consonant and vowel sounds, such as *da, da, da,* or *ma, ma, ma,* do sound like real words, ones that the parents are delighted to hear. Most parents tend to reinforce the child's behavior positively at this stage. Repetition of specific sounds and continued reinforcement lead the child to associate the physical mechanics of making a particular sound with the meaning of the word the sound represents.

From eight to twelve months, children increase their comprehension of language dramatically; their understanding of language far exceeds their ability to produce it. They do, however, tend to speak their first words, usually those most familiar and meaningful to them in their daily lives: *Mommy, Daddy, bye-bye, baby, cookie, milk, juice,* and *no,* for instance. As they become experienced with their first words, children use holophrastic speech—one-word utterances that express an entire sentence (Smith, 1972). For example, a baby might say "cookie," but mean "I want a cookie," "My cookie is on the floor," or "I'm done with this cookie."

From One to Two

A child's oral language grows a great deal between one and two. Along with one-word utterances, the child utters many sounds with adult intonation as if speaking in sentences. These utterances are not understandable to adults, however. Children begin to use telegraphic speech from twelve months on—the first evidence of their knowledge of syntax. Telegraphic speech uses content words, such as nouns and verbs, but omits function words, such as conjunctions and articles. In spite of the omissions, words are delivered in correct order, or syntax: "Daddy home" for "Daddy is coming home soon," or "Toy fall" for "My toy fell off the table."

Language grows by leaps and bounds once the child begins to combine words. By eighteen months most children can pronounce four-fifths of the English phonemes and use twenty to fifty words (Biehler, 1976).

From Two to Three

This year is probably the most dramatic in terms of language development. Typically, a child's oral vocabulary grows from 300 words to 1000. The child can comprehend, but cannot yet use, 2000 to 3000 additional words. Telegraphic sentences of two or three words continue to be most frequent, but syntactic complexity continues to develop, and the child occasionally uses such functional words as pronouns, conjunctions, prepositions, articles, and possessives. As their language ability grows, children gain confidence. They actively play with language by repeating new words and phrases and making up nonsense words. They enjoy rhyme, patterns of language, and repetition (Brown, 1973). Consider the following transcription of Jennifer's dialogue with her dog. Jennifer was two years ten months at the time. "Nice doggie, my doggie, white doggie, whitey, nicey doggie. Good doggie, my doggie, boggie, poggie. Kiss doggie, kiss me, doggie, good doggie." Jennifer's language is repetitive, playful, silly, and creative, demonstrating some of the characteristics of language production typical for a child her age.

From Three to Four

A child's vocabulary and knowledge of sentence structure continue to develop rapidly during the fourth year. Syntactic structures added to the child's repertoire include plurals and regular verbs. Indeed, children of this age are prone to overgeneralization in using these two structures, mainly because both plural formation and verb inflection are highly irregular in our language (Jewell & Zintz, 1986). Four-year-old Jonathan illustrated both problems when he had an accident in class and came running over very upset. He said, "Mrs. Morrow, hurry over, I knocked over the fishbowl and it broked and all the fishes are swimming on the floor." Jonathan knew how to form the past tense of a verb by adding *ed*, but he didn't know about irregular verbs such as *broke*. He also knew about adding an *s* to form a plural but again was unaware of irregular plural forms such as *fish*.

As they approach age four, children *seem* to have acquired all the elements of adult language. They can generate language and apply the basic rules that govern it. However, although their ability with language has grown enormously and they sound almost as if they are using adult speech, they have really acquired only the basic foundations. Language continues to grow throughout our lives as we gain new experiences, acquire new vocabulary, and find new ways of putting words together to form sentences. At the age of three to four, children talk about what they do as they are doing it. They often talk to themselves or by themselves as they play. It seems as if they are trying to articulate their actions (Seefeldt & Barbour, 1986). While painting at an easel, four-year-old Christopher said to himself, "I'm making a nice picture. I'm making colors all over. I'm painting, pit, pat, pit, pat. I'm going back and forth and up and down. Now I'm jumping as I paint." He carried out this monologue while painting this picture. As he talked and painted, he did exactly what he said, words and actions coinciding.

From Five to Six

Five- and six-year-olds sound very much like adults when they speak. However, their vocabularies are always increasing, and so is the syntactic complexity of their language. They have vocabularies of approximately 2500 words, and they are extremely articulate. Many, however, still have difficulty pronouncing some sounds, especially *l*, *r*, and *sh* at the ends of words. They become aware that a word can have more than one meaning. When they are embarrassed or frustrated at misunderstanding things, they say something silly or try to be humorous. They also tend to be creative in using language. When they do not have a word for a particular situation, they supply their own. Adults often find the language used by children of this age to be amusing as well as delightful and interesting (Seefeldt & Barbour, 1986):

> *Benjamin ran into school very excited one morning. "Mrs. Morrow," he said, "you'll never believe it. My dog grew puppies last night!"*

My husband and I were going to a formal dance one evening. My five-year-old daughter had never seen us dressed up like this before. When I walked into the room wearing a long gown and asked Stephanie how I looked, she said, "Mommy, you look soooo pretty. What is Daddy's costume going to be like?"

Escorted by her mother, Allison was on her way to her first day of kindergarten. She seemed a little nervous. When her mother asked her if she was okay, Allison replied, "Oh, I'm fine, Mommy. It's just that my stomach is very worried."

There are other characteristics of kindergarteners' language. Kindergarteners have discovered bathroom talk and curse words, and they enjoy shocking others by using them. They talk a lot and begin to use language to control situations. Their language reflects their movement from a world of fantasy to that of reality.

From Seven to Eight

By the time children are seven years of age and continuing on to eight and older, they have developed a grammar that is almost equivalent to that of adults. Of course they do not use extensive numbers of grammatical transformations found in adult language nor do they have the extent of vocabulary found in adult speech. Seven- and eight-year-olds are good conversationalists who talk a lot about what they do.

Recognizing Language Differences in Young Children

A major instructional concern in early childhood literacy programs is the varied language backgrounds of the many children who come to day-care centers, preschools, kindergartens, and first and second grades. Any given group may contain children using words, syntax, and language patterns quite different from those of standard English. Particularly in the United States, there are many different forms of English usage. There are, for example, distinct grammars in rural New England, Appalachia, and in some black communities, There are children whose families have immigrated from Latin America, the Middle East, or Asia. Foster (1982, p. 14) compiled six categories that represent the diverse language abilities of young children:

1. Recent immigrants with little or no English.

2. Children whose home language is something other than English, but who are themselves likely to know at least some English because of their experiences with television and their contacts outside the home.

3. Children who speak both English and another language fluently. Such children are usually easily assimilated into the majority group. Often English becomes the major language with which they communicate. They then risk losing the advantages that fluent bilingualism gives them.

4. Children who speak mainly English but who have poor skills in their parents' or family's language. Often these children speak English at home, but their parents speak to them in another language. Children in this group sometimes deny their heritage and are ashamed of the cultural differences between themselves and their majority classmates at school.

5. Children who speak nonstandard English because the English spoken at home is nonfluent or a dialect. Although they need to learn a more standard English at school, they must not be made to feel that their home language is inferior.

6. The vast majority of children, those who are monolingual in a pluralistic society. Their "understanding and appreciation of the various cultures in America," said Foster, "would be greatly enhanced through study in another language besides English."

All six categories represent major concerns because a firm base in oral language bears a strong relationship to literacy development. A child fluent in any form of nonstandard English may have difficulty reading and writing without some proficiency in standard English. Along with this concern for skill development are affective concerns. Unfortunately, teachers have been known to look down on children with language differences and to classify them as students with potential learning problems. We have come to realize, however, that differences do *not* mean deficits. Linguists have found, for example, that black English is a systematic, rule-governed dialect that can express all levels of thought (Robinson, Strickland, & Cullinan, 1977). Teachers must be sensitive to the differences in language among youngsters in their classrooms. Children must not be embarrassed or made to feel inferior because they do not speak standard English. Teachers need to respect language differences and help children take pride in their backgrounds. Diversity in language and heritage should be shared in classrooms to enrich the classroom experience.

Pragmatically, children must become somewhat fluent in the language used at school. If they are expected to read standard English, they need a foundation in speaking standard English. According to Pflaum (1986), young children do not have a great deal of difficulty acquiring new language. She suggests that the typical preschool seems to provide a linguistic environment that enables young children to learn standard English if they are encouraged to speak it. An environment that provides varied experiences and opportunities to converse helps the child acquire the ability to speak the language. Children who speak nonstandard dialects, such as black English, need the opportunity to use their own dialects in school during creative dramatics or in storytelling and discussions. Any child given the opportunity to use language frequently and effectively, even if it is not standard English, will be receptive to language learning in general (Robinson, Strickland, & Cullinan, 1977). Frequent opportunity to use language in varied situations will help children become more fluent. As Gonzales-Mena (1976, p. 14) has pointed out:

1. Children are eager to learn English or any other new language when there is an openness and an acceptance of them, their culture, and their native language.
2. Language should not be taught in isolation from any of the other basic school activities, but as a part of the total, integrated program, which includes a focus on language development. Listening, speaking, reading, and writing are all a part of math, social studies, art, and science.
3. Children learn through their senses, including their muscles. Concepts as well as new words and phrases are learned better when children can participate in some action. They need to examine and explore real objects and act out new expressions. Pictures can help, but action imprints the message in a stronger fashion.

The strategies discussed on the following pages to help develop young children's language will also be successful with children who have language differences or special language needs.

Strategies for Language Development

The review of theory and research suggests how we can help children acquire and develop language pleasantly, productively, and appropriately. Children acquire language by emulating adult models and experiencing positive reinforcement for their efforts. If language is innate, it can develop naturally as individuals pass through common stages of development at certain times in their lives. As children mature, they become capable of generating ever more complex language structures. They learn language by doing, by acting upon and within familiar environments. Their first spoken words are those that are meaningful for them within their own experiences. Their earliest language is an expression of needs. They learn language through social interaction with individuals more literate than they, whether adults or older children. Children also create their own language, play with it, and engage in monologues.

Using what we know of language acquisition and developmental stages as guidelines, we can begin to create and prepare appropriate materials, activities, and experiences in a suitable atmosphere to nurture a youngster's language development. The following objectives are formulated for a program fostering language development in children from birth to age seven.

Objectives for the Development of Receptive Language

1. Children will be provided with an atmosphere in which they will hear language frequently.
2. Children will hear language associated with pleasure and enjoyment.
3. Children will be given opportunities to discriminate among sounds heard.
4. Children will be exposed to rich sources of new words.
5. Children will be given opportunities to listen and comprehend what others say.
6. Children will be given opportunities to learn to follow directions.

Objectives for the Development of Expressive Language

1. Children will be given opportunities to use their own language freely at any stage of development. Their desire to communicate will be encouraged, accepted, and respected.
2. Children will be encouraged to pronounce words correctly.
3. Children will be given opportunities to increase their speaking vocabularies.
4. Children will be encouraged to speak in complete sentences at appropriate stages in their development.

5. Children will be given opportunities to expand their use of various syntactic structures, such as adjectives, adverbs, prepositional phrases, dependent clauses, plurals, past tense, and possessives.
6. Children will be encouraged to communicate in such a way that they are understood by others.
7. Children will be given opportunities to use language socially and psychologically by interpreting feelings, points of view, and motivation and by solving problems by generating hypotheses, summarizing events, and predicting outcomes.
8. Children will be given opportunities to develop language that involves mathematical and logical relations, such as describing size and amount, making comparisons, defining sets and classes, and reasoning deductively.

Language is best learned when it is integrated with other communication skills and other content-area subjects in a meaningful environment. Isolating that objective and trying to teach that skill to a child does not promote the development of lifelong literacy. For growth, natural settings are optimal. Teachers need to be accepting of language differences and help those youngsters with special needs to acquire better skills.

Strategies for Language Development from Birth to Two

"Hi, Michael. How's my great big boy today? Let's change your diaper now, upsy-daisy. My goodness, you're getting heavy. Now I'll put you down right here on your dressing table and get a nice new diaper for you. Here, want this rubber ducky to hold while I change you? That's a good boy. You really like him. Let's clean you up now. This is the way we clean up Michael, clean up Michael, clean up Michael. This is the way we clean up Michael, so he'll feel so much better. You like that singing, don't you. I can tell. You're just smiling away, and cooing. Want to do that again? This is the way we clean up Michael, clean up Michael, clean up Michael. This is the way we clean up Michael, so he'll feel so much better. Wow, you were singing with me that time. That's right, ba-ba-ba-ba, now do it again. Mmmmm, doesn't that smell good? The baby powder is so nice and smooth."

Michael was four months old when his mother's conversation with him was taped. Here in print, it reads like a monologue; in reality it was not. Michael was a very active participant in the conversation. He stared intently at his mother's face. He cooed, he waved his arms, he smiled, he became serious. His mother was providing a rich language environment for her baby. She encouraged his participation in the dialogue and acknowledged his responsiveness in a positive way. She provided him with the environmental stimuli necessary for his innate language ability to flourish. She engaged him in this type of conversation during feedings and while changing, bathing, and dressing him. She talked to him even when he was in his crib and she in another room or while in the same room but involved in other things. The baby knew that communication was occurring because he responded to the talk with body movements, coos, babbles, and smiles. When he responded his mother responded in turn; response brought response, back and forth.

Infants need to be surrounded by the sounds of happy language. Whether from mother, father, care giver at home, or teacher or aide in a day-care center, sounds and interaction should accompany all activities. Adults responsible for babies from birth through the first year need to know nursery rhymes, chants, finger plays, and songs. It is important for children simply to hear the *sounds* of language as well as the meanings. Thus, adults can make up their own chants to suit an occasion, as Michael's mother did when she spontaneously adapted "Here We Go Round the Mulberry Bush" to the situation at hand. Such experiences make the baby conscious of the sounds of language. Children learn that they can have control over language and that oral language can be a powerful tool as well as fun.

In addition to the conversation of nearby adults, infants should experience other sounds and other voices: soft music from a radio, record player, or music box. They need to hear the sounds of "book language," which differs in intonation, pitch, stress, juncture, and even syntax from normal conversation. They need familiarity with language in all its variety so they can learn to differentiate among its various conventions and patterns. Speaking to infants, singing to them, reading to them, and letting them hear the radio and television provide sources of language that help their own language grow. In addition, there are sounds in the immediate environment that need no preparation and are not the sounds of language but that provide practice in auditory discrimination—the ringing of the doorbell, the hissing of the teapot, the chimes on the clock. the hum of the vacuum cleaner, a dog barking, a bird singing, a car screeching, and so on. Bring them to the baby's attention, give them names, and heighten the child's sensitivity to them.

In addition to hearing a variety of sounds, the baby needs objects to see, touch, smell, hear, and taste. They should be placed in the baby's immediate environment—the crib or playpen. They will stimulate the baby's activity and curiosity and become the meaningful things within the environment from which language evolves. Some of the objects should make sounds or music when pushed or touched. They can have different textures and smells. They should be easy to grab, push, kick, or pull. They can be placed so they are visible and within the child's reach, and at least one item should be suspended overhead: stuffed animals, rubber toys, music boxes made of soft material, plastic or wooden mobiles that can be kicked or grasped, mechanical mobiles that hang from the ceiling and rotate by themselves, and books with smooth edges. Books can be propped open against the side of the crib or playpen when the baby is lying on its back, or against the head-

Reading to young children provides book language—a source of new vocabulary and new sounds with different stress, pitch, and intonation.

board when the baby is on its stomach. Certain familiar objects should always remain, and new objects frequently made available. In addition to allowing the child to play independently with these objects, the adults in charge need to talk about them, name them, occasionally join the child in playing with them, and discuss their characteristics and what they are capable of doing. Objects should have different textures and scents, make different sounds, and provide different visual effects. Some should be chewable.

From three to six months the baby gurgles, coos, begins to laugh, and babbles. Recognize an infant's sounds as the beginning of language. Reinforce the infant positively with responses aimed at encouraging the sounds. When the baby begins to put consonants and vowels together, again reinforce the behavior, imitating what the baby has uttered and urging repetition. When the baby becomes aware of the ability to repeat sounds and control language output, he or she will do these things. Babies will also begin to understand adult language, so it is important to name objects, carry on conversations, and give the baby directions. At the end of its first year, assuming he or she has experienced appropriate sounds of language as well as encouragement and pleasant interaction, the baby will be on the verge of extensive language growth during its second year.

Through the second year of a child's life, the adults in charge need to continue the same kinds of stimulation suggested for developing oral language during the first year. However, because the baby is likely to develop a vocabulary of up to 150 words and to produce two- and possibly three-word sentences during the second year, additional techniques can be used to enhance language growth. As described earlier, one- and two-word utterances by children at this age usually represent sentences. When a twelve-month-old points to a teddy bear and says "bear," the child probably means "I want my bear." Parents and care givers at home or in day-care centers can begin to expand and extend the child's language at such times by helping to increase the number of words the child is able to use in a sentence or by increasing the syntactic complexity of their own utterances.

One method for helping a child develop ability with language is a kind of modeling called *scaffolding* (Applebee & Langer, 1983). In scaffolding, an adult provides a verbal response for a baby who is not yet capable of making the response itself. In other words, the adult provides a language model. When the baby says "bear," for instance, the adult responds, "Do you want your teddy bear?" or "Here is your nice, soft, brown teddy bear." In addition to expanding on the child's language, the adult can extend it by asking the youngster to do something that demonstrates understanding and extends his or her thinking. For example, "Here is your nice, soft, brown teddy bear. Can you hug the teddy? Let me see you hug him." In addition to questions that require action , the adult can ask questions that require answers. Questions that require answers of more than one word are preferable—for example, "Tell me about the clothes your teddy is wearing." *How, why,* and *tell me* questions encourage the child to give more than a yes/no answer and more than a one-word response. *What, who, when,* and *where* questions, on the other hand, tend to elicit only one-word replies. As the child's language ability develops, the adult provides fewer and fewer such "scaffolds"; the child learns to build utterances along similar models.

Select songs, rhymes, and books for one- to two-year-olds that use language they can understand. They are capable of understanding a great deal of language by now, and the selections should help expand and extend their language. Both vocabulary and conceptual understanding are enhanced by experiences. For the one- to two-year-old, frequent outings are desirable. Visits to the post office, supermarket, dry cleaners, and park provide experiences to talk about and new concepts to explore. Household tasks taken for granted by adults are new experiences that enrich children's language. Involve them in activities. For example, an eighteen-month-old can put a piece of laundry into the washing machine or give one stir to the bowl of gelatin or some other food that is being prepared. During such daily routines, surround the activity with language, identifying new objects for the baby and asking for responses related to each activity.

As the child becomes more verbal, the adult sometimes wants to correct the child's mispronunciations or overgeneralization of grammatical rules. The child who says, "Me feeded fishes," for instance, has simply overgeneralized the rules for:

- Forming most past tenses (*feeded* for *fed*)
- Using pronouns (objective *me* for subjective *I*) and
- Forming most plurals (*fishes* for *fish*)

Children can also overgeneralize concepts,. A child who has learned to associate a bird with the word *bird* might see a butterfly for the first time and call it a bird, thinking that anything that flies is a bird. Correcting such an overgeneralization is best done positively rather than negatively. Instead of saying, "No, that's not a bird," simply refer to the butterfly as a *butterfly*, commenting on its beauty, perhaps, and thus expanding the child's verbal repertoire. Eventually, with positive reinforcement and proper role models in language, the child will differentiate between birds and butterflies as well as between regular and irregular grammatical conventions and forms.

Correcting overgeneralizations negatively as absolute error, on the other hand, is not likely to help young children understand the error or use proper tense and plural forms the next time. Rather, it is likely to inhibit the child from trying to use language. In learning, children need to take risks and make mistakes. Hearing good adult models will eventually enable them to internalize the rules of language and to correct their errors themselves. At least until age five, the child should be allowed to experiment and play with language without direct concern for 100 percent correctness in syntax and pronunciation. The English language is extremely complex and irregular in many of its rules; in time, the child will master these rules in all their complexity and nuance, given good adult models and plenty of verbal interaction. At the same time, encouraging "baby talk" simply because it is cute, for instance, is likely to inhibit growth because children will use whatever language they believe will please the adults around them.

Materials for the one- to two-year-old should be varied and more sophisticated than those in the first year. Now that the baby is mobile in the home or day-care center, books need to be easily accessible to the child. Toys should still include items of various textures, such as furry stuffed animals and rubber balls. Other toys should require simple eye–hand coordination. Three-to-five–piece puzzles, trucks that can be pushed and pulled, dolls, a child-size set of table and chairs, crayons and large paper, and puppets are examples. Choose objects that require activity, for activity encourages exploration, use of the imagination, creation, and the need to communicate.

Strategies for Language Development in Early Childhood Classrooms

From three to seven a great deal of language development occurs. Children should continue to hear good models of language. They need continued opportunities to use language in social situations with adults and other children. Their oral language production must be reinforced positively. They must be actively involved in meaningful experiences that will expand their knowledge and interest in the world around them. Language should be purposeful and its development integrated with other subjects rather than taught separately as a content area unto itself.

To accomplish these continuing goals, early childhood teachers provide an environment in which language will flourish. They organize centers of learning, one for each content area, that include materials for encouraging language use. A science center, for instance, can include class pets such as a pair of gerbils. Gerbils are active, loving animals, fun to watch and handle. Children surround the cage often and generate talk just from watching the animals. Gerbils reproduce in twenty-eight–day cycles. When litters arrive, the birth process can be observed. The new babies cause a great deal of excitement and generate questions, comments, and unlimited conversation.

In my own classroom, our parent gerbils reproduced a second litter twenty-eight days after the first and before the first babies had been weaned. The mother looked tired and thin from feeding and caring for ten baby gerbils. One morning one of the children noticed that the mother was not in the cage. We couldn't imagine what had happened to her. A few days later, having almost given up hope, we found her hiding behind the refrigerator in the teachers' room. We never figured out how she got out of the cage, but we hypothesized all kinds of possibilities, and there was a great deal of discussion about why she left. No teacher alone could provide a lesson in which language flourished and grew the way it did during that incident, simply because gerbils were part of the classroom.

Here are some examples of centers of learning and appropriate materials in early childhood classrooms that will help to generate language:

Science: aquarium, terrarium, plants, magnifying glass, class pet, magnets, thermometer, compass, prism, shells, rock collections, stethoscope, kaleidoscope, microscope, informational books and children's literature reflecting topics being studied, and blank journals for recording observations of experiments and scientific projects.

Social studies: maps, a globe, flags, community figures, traffic signs, current events, artifacts from other countries, informational books and children's literature reflecting topics being studied, writing materials to make class books or your own books about topics being studied.

Art: easels, watercolors, brushes, colored pencils, crayons, felt-tip markers, various kinds of paper, scissors, paste, pipe cleaners, scrap materials (bits of various fabrics, wool, string, and so forth), clay, play dough, food and detergent boxes for sculptures, books about famous artists, books with directions for crafts.

Music: piano, record player and records, tape recorder with musical tapes, rhythm instruments, songbooks, books of songs that have been made into books, and photocopies of sheet music for songs sung in class.

Mathematics: scales, rulers, measuring cups, movable clocks, stopwatch, calendar, play money, cash register, calculator, dominoes, abacus, number line, height chart, hourglass, numbers (felt, wood, and magnetic), fraction puzzles, geometric shapes, math workbooks, children's literature about numbers and mathematics, writing materials for creating stories, and books related to mathematics.

Literacy: children's literature, tape recorder, headsets and taped stories, pencils, writing paper, stapler, construction paper, three-by-five cards for recording words, hole punch, letter stencils, typewriter, computer, puppets, storytelling devices such as felt-board and roll movies, stationery with envelopes, letters (felt, wood, and magnetic), sets of pictures for different units (Halloween, seasons, animals, and so on), rhyme games, color games, cards for associating sounds and symbols, alphabet cards, pictures and words representing out-of-school environmental print (*Burger King, Dairy Queen, Exxon*). (The literacy center also includes a library corner, a writing center, oral language materials, and language arts manipulatives, all of which are described in later chapters.)

Dramatic play: dolls, dress-ups, telephone, stuffed animals, mirror, food cartons, plates, silverware, newspapers, magazines, books, telephone book, class telephone book, cookbook, note pads, cameras and photo album, table and chairs, broom, dustpan, child-size kitchen furniture such as refrigerator, sink, ironing board, and storage shelves. (The dramatic-play area can be changed from a kitchen to a grocery store, beauty shop, gas station, business office, or restaurant with the addition of appropriate materials.) Include appropriate materials for reading and writing related to the theme of the dramatic-play area.

Block area: blocks of many different sizes and shapes and figures of people, animals, toy cars, trucks, items related to themes being studied, paper and pencils to prepare signs and notes, and reading materials related to themes.

Workbench: wood, hammer, screwdriver, saw, pliers, nails, worktable.

Experiences in science lead to new discoveries, new vocabulary, and reasons to talk and discuss.

Varied art experiences with different media encourage descriptive language and develop the manual dexterity needed for writing.

Outdoor play: sand, water, pails, shovels, rakes, gardening area and gardening tools, climbing equipment, riding toys, crates, playhouse, balls, tires, ropes.

Children need opportunities to use such areas for interacting with each other and the teacher, and they should be given enough time to touch, smell, taste, listen, and talk about what they are doing. Exploring and experimenting with the materials in the centers are creative, imaginative, problem-solving, decision-making experiences in which children use language and thereby give it the opportunity to grow. The opportunity to *use* language is one of the key elements in language development.

Some materials remain permanently in the centers; others are replaced or supplemented from time to time so that new items of interest become available. Materials added to the centers are often coordinated with thematic units of instruction. For example, if a unit on Indians is introduced, Indian dolls and artifacts are added to the social studies center, and books about Indians to the literacy center. The different content-area centers provide sources for language use and development; the literacy center is devoted *primarily* to language development. Thematic units of instruction that integrate all areas make learning more meaningful and expand concepts. (Interdisciplinary instruction is described more fully in Chapter 9.)

Each new unit of instruction offers specific language experiences that expand vocabulary, syntax, pronunciation, and the ability to understand others and be understood. Again, these experiences should incorporate all content areas and make use of the senses. The suggestions that follow can be used each time a new theme is initiated. They reflect or describe activities designed

Playing with puppets will encourage children to tell stories and create their own. Participating in dramatic play will stimulate language from real life.

to aid language growth in early childhood classrooms. For purposes of illustration, assume that the topic throughout these suggestions is *winter.* (Virtually any other topic can be substituted.)

1. Hold discussions about the unit topic. What is the weather like in winter? What kind of clothing do the children need to wear in winter? What fun things can they do in winter that they can't do at other times of the year? What problems does winter bring? What is winter like in different parts of the country, for example, New York, Florida, Chicago, California, and so on.

2. Ask the children to name every word they can that makes them think of winter. Your list might eventually include: *snow, ice, cold, white, wet, freezing, sleds, snowman, mittens, scarf, hat, slush, skiing, ice skating, snowballs, fireplace,* and *snowflakes.* Classify the words on the list into how winter feels, looks, smells, sounds, and tastes, or what you can and cannot do in winter. List the words on a chart, and hang the chart in the room. Leave the chart hanging when you go to the next unit. When the wall gets too crowded, compile the charts in a class book.

3. Provide pictures of winter scenes for discussion, each depicting different information about the season.

4. Hold a sharing period during which children bring things from home related to the topic. Give all the children an opportunity to share if they wish, but assign different children for different days, because sharing by more than five or six children in one period can become tedious. Sharing objects from home is an important activity. It gives children confidence because they are talking about something from their own environment. Even the shyest children will speak in front of a group if they have the security of sharing something familiar from home. Encourage children to relate the items to the unit topic, if they can. Model language for children to encourage them to speak in sentences. Coordinate the activity with parents, informing them of their children's scheduled sharing and the general topic under discussion.

5. Carry out a science experiment related to the topic being studied. Involve the children actively. Discuss the purpose and hypothesize what is likely to happen. Encourage children to discuss what they are doing while they are doing it. When the experiment is complete, discuss the results with the class. (Example: Allow water to freeze, then melt. In warm climates use the refrigerator for freezing the water.)

A Winter Experience.
We mixed Ivory
Snow with water.
We spread it with
our hands on blue
paper. It felt:

sticky   soft
gluey   slimy
smushy   icky
yucky   mushy
gooky   warm
gushy

We did this because
it's winter, and it's
snowy, and Ivory
Snow and real
snow are
white.

Experiences related to topics of study generate oral language that can be written down and then read.

6. Carry out an art activity related to the topic; the activity should be process-oriented rather than teacher-directed. Allow children to create their work rather than making them follow specific directions that yield identical results from child to child. Discuss the project and the available materials before the activity. Provide interesting materials and encourage children to touch, describe, and compare them. While children are creating, it is natural for them to converse about what they are doing. Encourage such conversation. For example, provide blue construction paper, tin foil, white doilies, cotton, wool, tissue paper, and chalk for a winter collage. Discuss why these colors and objects were selected. What is there about them that makes people think of winter? Suggest creating a picture that makes someone think of winter. Discuss the textures of the materials and what can be done with them.

7. Sing songs about winter, such as "It's a Marshmallow World in the Winter." Music is enjoyable and lyrics help build vocabulary and sensitivity to the sounds and meanings of words. Listen to music without words, music that creates images concerning the topic. Ask the children for words, sentences, or stories that the music brings to mind.

8. Prepare food related to the unit. Make hot soup, flavored snowballs, or popcorn. Discuss food textures, smells, taste, and appearance. Do they change during preparation? Follow directions and recipes, developing sequence as well as quantitative sense. Allow children to help prepare the food, then enjoy consuming it together, encouraging discussion and conversation throughout about the activity. Food preparation can be a source of new vocabulary, especially because many of its terms take on special meanings—*stir, blend, boil, measure.*

9. Add items related to the topic to the dramatic-play area— mittens, hats, scarves, boots for dress-up—to encourage role-playing and language about winter. Introduce them by placing each in a separate bag and asking a child to reach in, describe what it feels like, and identify it without peeking. The sense of touch elicits descriptive language.

10. Encourage spontaneous language and frequent problem-solving situations during outdoor play. For example, provide snow shovels, sleds, pails, and cups during playtime in the snow. Discuss outdoor play before going out, and again after coming in.

11. Discuss weather and dates during daily opening exercises. Encourage children to talk about news concerning them-

selves: a new pair of boots for the snow, a grandparent's visit, a birthday party. Make plans for the school day.

12. Take the class on a trip, bring in a guest speaker, or show a film. All three activities can generate language and encourage its use.

13. Read stories to the children on the topic under study. Books such as *Katy and the Big Snow* (Burton, 1943) enhance information and expand vocabulary.

14. Provide the children with a title, such as "The Big Winter Snowstorm," and let them think of a story about it.

15. Encourage children to retell stories. This activity, of course, encourages them to use book language and incorporate it into their own. Retelling is not always an easy task for young children, so props can be very helpful—puppets, felt-boards and felt characters, roll movies, and pictures in a book. With these same props, children can be encouraged to make up their own stories as well.

16. In any of these activities, children should be encouraged as often as possible to select their favorite Very Own Words about winter. Favorite Very Own Words can be selected from discussions, art lessons, science experiments, songs, books, poems, cooking experiences, or any other activity. Early in the school year, encourage children to collect their favorite Very Own Words. After a particular experience, ask them to name a favorite word. Record children's favorite Very Own Words for them on three-by-five cards and store them in each child's own file box or on a binder ring. When children are capable of recording their own words, assist them with spelling when they ask for help. Favorite Very Own Words enhance vocabulary and are a source for reading and writing development.

17. Summarize the day's events at the end of the school day, encouraging children to tell what they liked, did not like, and want to do the next day in school.

Among more general suggestions, select and offer children's literature that represents varieties of language and experience. Some children's books feature the sounds of language; they aid auditory discrimination or incorporate additional phonemes into a child's language repertoire—for example, *Too Much Noise* (Mc-Govern, 1967). Others help develop the syntactic complexity of a child's language through embeddings and transformations and the use of numerous adjectives and adverbs—for example, *Swimmy* (Lionni, 1963). Craft books require children to follow directions. Wordless books encourage them to create their own stories from the pictures. Concept books feature words such as *up, down, in, out, near,* and *far,* or involve children in mathematical reasoning. Realistic literature deals with death, divorce, loneliness, fear, and daily problems. Discussion of such themes leads to sociopsychological language, interpretation of feelings, sensitivity to others, and problem solving. Books of riddles, puns, jokes, and tongue twisters show children how language plays on meaning in certain situations. Poetry introduces children to rhyme, metaphor, simile, and onomatopoeia and encourages them to recite and create poems. (Children's books are listed by these and other categories in Appendix A.) When children hear and discuss the language of books, they internalize what they have heard; the language soon becomes part of their own language. Research studies have found that children who have had stories read to them frequently develop more sophisticated language structures and increased vocabulary (Chomsky, 1972; Cohen, 1968).

Two anecdotes illustrate how children incorporate into their own language the language of books that have been read to them. My kindergarten class was playing on the playground one early spring day. A few birds circled around several times. Melissa ran up to me and said, "Look, Mrs. Morrow, the birds are fluttering and flapping around the playground." Surprised at first by Melissa's descriptive and unusual choice of words, I thought for a moment, then remembered. The words that Melissa was using came directly from a picture storybook we had read shortly before, *Jenny's Hat* (Keats, 1966). In the book, birds *flutter* and *flap* around Jenny's hat. Melissa had internalized the language of the book and was able to use it in her own vocabulary.

One day after a big snowstorm, my daughter asked, "Mommy, can I go out and play? I want to build a smiling snowman." I was surprised and pleased with this sophisticated language being uttered by my four-year-old. *Smiling snowman,* after all, represents a participle in the adjective position, a syntactic structure usually not found in the language of children before the age of seven or eight. Then I noticed that Stephanie had a book in her hand, *The Snowy Day* (Keats, 1962). In it Peter goes outside and builds a *smiling snowman.* Stephanie had used the book's language and made it her own.

The activities just suggested can be repeated throughout the school year with each new theme that is studied. Such adaptation and repetition make it possible to introduce children to hundreds of new vocabulary words, concepts, and ideas. They will assure children of opportunities to participate in new kinds of spontaneous language as topics and structured experiences change. Word lists and other materials produced during each unit can be maintained and made available for review and reuse.

Most of the suggestions can be followed at home as well as at school. Parents should not be expected to create elaborate centers or carry out units of instruction. But, daily living offers holidays, seasons, family events, and other topics and events of special interest. Parents can tap such meaningful occasions for their potential enhancement of language development. They can discuss events, list words, help children collect favorite Very Own Words, involve children in cooking and household chores, take trips, read stories, sing songs, and generally encourage the use of language as a pleasurable activity and a useful skill.

In the learning environment described throughout this chapter, language development is spontaneous and also encouraged. Modeling, scaffolding, and reinforcement make this environment interactive between child and adult, and they guide and nurture language development to an extent that children are not likely to achieve on their own. The strategies discussed are appropriate for children who have language differences and minimal language disorders. These youngsters, however, may need additional attention on a one-to-one basis from the classroom teacher or a resource room teacher.

Portfolio Assessment of Children's Language Development

It is important to assess children's language to determine if it follows expected stages of development. Assessment also determines how much a child has progressed. The word *assessment* suggests several rather frequent measures by which to judge progress. Assessment should reflect instructional objectives and strategies. It should include evaluation of a wide range of skills used in many contexts. A certain child, for example, may perform better in an interview than on a pencil-and-paper test. Both kinds of evaluation, therefore, should be used. Literacy includes a wide range of skills; it is important to evaluate a child for as many as possible to determine strengths and weaknesses. Unfortunately, many assessment instruments are quite narrow in scope and frequently do not tap a child's total abilities (Glazer & Searfoss, 1988; Teale, Heibert, & Chittenden, 1987).

There are several ways to measure children's language development in early childhood. *Checklists* are practical because they provide concise outlines for teachers and appropriate slots for individual children. They are most effective if used periodically over the school year. Three to four evaluations during the year can provide sufficient data to determine progress. Program objectives offer criteria to include on checklists.

Checklist for Assessing Language Development

	Always	Sometimes	Never
Makes phoneme sounds			
Speaks in one-word sentences			
Speaks in two-word sentences			
Identifies familiar sounds			
Differentiates similar sounds			
Understands the language of others when spoken to			
Follows verbal directions			
Speaks to others freely			
Pronounces words correctly			
Has appropriate vocabulary for level of maturity			
Speaks in complete sentences			
Uses varied syntactic structures			
Can be understood by others			

Teacher Comments:

Anecdotal records are another form of language assessment. They tend to be time-consuming but can reveal rich information. Loose-leaf notebooks and file cards offer two means for keeping anecdotal records. These records require no particular format. Rather, the teacher or parent simply writes down incidents or episodes on the days they occur. Samples of a child's language and situations involving language can be recorded. Like checklists, anecdotal samples are necessary periodically to determine growth over a school year.

Tape recordings are another means of evaluating language. The process can take the form of an open interview or a hidden recording. (Videotaping equipment can serve the same purpose but may not be readily available in most early childhood classrooms.) Children who are unaware that their conversation is being recorded are likely to be more spontaneous and uninhibited (Genishi & Dyson, 1984). It is often difficult, however, to place a tape recorder where it will record language clear enough to transcribe and analyze. Interviews with children become more natural when an adult familiar to the child does the interviewing. Allow the tape recorder to become such a familiar tool in the classroom that the child uses it often in the language arts center. Under such circumstances the machine is not threatening when used in an assessment interview. Children become accustomed very quickly to using tape recorders.

To record samples of natural language, discuss the child's experiences. Ask about home, favorite games or toys, TV programs they like to watch, brothers and sisters, trips they have taken, or birthday parties they have recently attended. What you are hoping to collect is a corpus of spontaneous language that provides a typical sample of the child's ability with language.

Tape assessment samples three or four times a year. Let children hear their own recorded voices, enjoy the experience, and learn a bit about themselves. Then, for assessment purposes, transcribe the tapes and analyze them on such items as numbers of words uttered and numbers of words spoken in a single connected utterance (for example, "Tommy's cookie" or "Me want water"). The lengths of such utterances can be averaged to determine mean length. Length of utterance is considered a measure of complexity (Brown, 1973). When children begin to speak in conventional sentences, such as "That is my cookie," measure the length of the t-units. A *t-unit* is an independent clause with all its dependent clauses attached, assuming it has dependent clauses. It can be a simple or a complex sentence. Compound sentences are made up of two t-units. Length of t-units, like length of utterances, is a measure of language complexity. It typically increases with the user's age, and usually the more words per unit, the more complex the unit (Hunt, 1970).

Further analysis of taped utterances and t-units can determine which elements of language a child uses—number of adjectives, adverbs, dependent clauses, negatives, possessives, passives, plurals, and so on. The more complex the transformations, embeddings, and syntactic elements used, the more complex the language overall (Morrow, 1978). Data from several samples over the course of a year can be most revealing.

I have discussed oral language separately from the other communication skills in this chapter in order to describe its developmental stages and the theories of how it is acquired. This separation is somewhat artificial, however, because oral language is as important to literacy development as are reading and writing. The whole language approach to early literacy has demonstrated that communication skills develop concurrently, each helping the growth of the others. Coordination and integration of the several communication skills in a single program are described in Chapter 9.

AN IDEA FOR THE CLASSROOM

The following experience was created by an early childhood teacher for the children in her classroom. You may find this idea useful for your teaching.

The Five Senses and a Fall Theme Generate Language

My first grade class had been studying the five senses. Since it was October, I decided to associate the five senses with the fall season to try and generate vocabulary and increased language complexity. I asked the children to bring in fall things that you can taste, touch, smell, look at, and listen to. Children were asked to select a sense category, about five children to each, and they were to get into their groups to discuss what each one might bring so as not to overlap. A great deal of excitement occurred within the groups as children collaborated with each other trying to figure out five different things that they could bring related to the season of fall and to the sense they had selected. In addition to bringing in the materials, the children were to describe what they had brought, with as many interesting words as they could think of. They could also tell how they decided what to bring and where they located their object.

On the day the materials were brought to school, before getting together with the whole class, the children were to have group meetings to show what they had brought and help each other with descriptions.

When we came together as a class, we wrote the names of the five senses, each on a separate piece of experience chart paper. The groups displayed their objects and they were to talk about each item with as many descriptive words as possible. The items were listed on the appropriate sense chart with the descriptive words written under each.

Many rich ideas were generated, related to the fall materials and the five senses. The children talked about the sound of crunchy dry leaves that were crushed under their feet as they walked on them; they described the shape of acorns and how they looked like tiny elves with lumpy hats on their heads. They discussed the slimy texture of seeds inside the pumpkin and the stringy nature of its pulp. They took deep breaths as they discussed the fresh scent of the pine cones and their mouths watered as someone described the juicy, tart apples that made their lips pucker.

Everyone in the class had an opportunity to describe what he or she had brought. I helped some children who were at a loss for words by scaffolding some descriptions to get them started. This form of the old show-and-tell format attached to themes that we were studying proved to be a rich source for language development.

Jane Roosa
First Grade Teacher
MacAfee School
Franklin Township, NJ

ACTIVITIES AND QUESTIONS

1. Answer the focus questions at the beginning of the chapter.

2. Select an objective for language development listed in the chapter. Prepare a lesson that will help a child achieve the goal. Identify the theories of language acquisition used in your lesson.

3. Begin a portfolio for assessment materials that you will continue as you read this book. Collect one language sample from a child age two through seven. Elicit the language by

showing a picture to discuss or asking the child to talk about favorite TV shows, pets, friends, family members, or trips. Tape-record the sample and transcribe it.

   a. Check the characteristics of the child's language development according to the descriptions in this chapter and decide if the child is above, below, or at a level appropriate to his or her age. Have different members in the class study different age groups and compare them.
   b. Divide your language sample into t-units and determine the average length per t-unit; then count the number and type of syntactic elements used. Compare your sample to someone else in the class who is working with a child of a different age.
   c. Collect three additional language samples for the same child at different times in the year. Evaluate the new samples as you did the first time and check for growth.

4. Tape-record children at play or working in a group. Identify which characteristics of their language can be described by various theories of language acquisition. For example, imitation could be explained by the behaviorist theory.

5. Begin a thematic unit that you will continue as you read this book. Select a social studies or science topic. Select three objectives for language development and describe three activities that will satisfy each of the objectives using your theme. An example follows:

   Content Area: Science
   Theme: Creatures That Live in the Sea
   Objective for Language Development: Develop new vocabulary
   Activity: Read *Swimmy* by Leo Lionni. Ask the children to remember two new words they hear in the story. After reading, list words that the children mention on a chart and discuss their meaning.

6. Observe in a preschool, kindergarten, or first or second grade class for about three hours. Note the amount of time children are given to talk, the amount of time the teacher talks, and the amount during which there is no verbal interaction. Compare the three figures. Then classify talk in the classroom into the following categories:

   a. questions and answers
   b. whole-class discussion

    c. small-group discussion

    d. interactive discussion among children

    e. interactive discussion between teacher and children

Based on the results of this ministudy, determine how often we allow children to use language, and in how many different contexts or situations.

Case Study Activity

Refer back to the "Idea for the Classroom" section. Read it again and identify the theories of language acquisition that the teacher is incorporating. Has she made any accommodations for children with language differences? If yes, how? If not, how could she do so?

CHAPTER FOUR

Reading and Literacy Development

QUESTIONS TO FOCUS ON AS YOU READ THE CHAPTER

- Define the term *emergent literacy.*
- How does the emergent literacy approach to literacy instruction differ from reading readiness?
- Based on emergent literacy concepts, what are the ways in which reading is acquired?
- Describe Holdaway's theory of developmental learning.
- Describe the importance and benefits of small-group collaborative learning.
- What stages of development do children go through as they learn to read?
- What are the major objectives for emergent literacy development?

Thomas Jefferson articulated three fundamental beliefs about literacy and education that have become part of our national ethos: (1) the ability of every citizen to read is necessary to the practice of democracy, (2) it is therefore the duty of the general public to support the teaching of reading for all youngsters, and (3) reading should be taught during the earliest years of schooling. Among the reasons he cited, "none is more important, none more legitimate, than that of rendering the people safe, as they are the ultimate guardians of their own liberty."

—THOMAS JEFFERSON
The Life and Selected Writings of Thomas Jefferson

Three-year-old Colleen was playing house in the dramatic-play area. She was the mommy and she asked Kevin to be the daddy. They had a doll in the cradle. Colleen got a book and sat in the rocking chair facing the doll and Kevin. She pretended to read *The Three Bears*, although that was not the book she was holding. She rocked and turned the pages while telling the story.

Colleen was engaged in attempted reading behavior that she modeled or emulated after a real-life experience. She was a youngster who was read to regularly by her mother and father. In addition she was read to daily in her preschool classroom. Being read to made her enjoy and be familiar with the act of reading; therefore, she found it quite natural to engage in the activity. It was a social activity with another child who took the role of the father.

Mrs. Schenkman created a restaurant in the dramatic-play area of her kindergarten with menus, play money, uniforms, a cash register and an OPEN and CLOSED sign. Ricky turned the sign to read OPEN and began preparing burgers. Steven joined Ricky and seemed upset. He said, "See that sign, now that says OPEN." He flipped it over. "We're not opened. Now it says CLOSED. We need to clean up the place first before we can open."

In this situation, which is socially interactive, the literacy that takes place is functional. It is something that children had the opportunity to observe and then model. In this play situation, children get to practice and perform literacy skills with each other—all a part of literacy learning.

The examples provided here represent a new perspective in literacy development. Teachers provided materials and modeled behavior for children to observe and emulate. In addition, they provided real-life situations to encourage literacy learning in a social and cooperative manner.

As noted in Chapter 1, early developmentalists believed in the natural unfolding of the child. At a certain level of maturity, they felt, a child was ready to read, instruction was then appropriate, and the child would learn to read. Some educators became impatient with the notion of simply waiting for maturation, even though they held to the idea that certain levels of maturation were necessary before reading could be taught formally without detriment to the child. This attitude led to instructional programs in reading readiness.

In general, reading readiness programs view getting ready to read as a set of social, emotional, physical, and cognitive competencies. If a child possesses these competencies, adherents say, formal reading instruction can take place. Conversely, a child who has not mastered particular tasks is not considered ready for reading instruction. Strategies for readiness instruction depend on lists of skills in the four areas of development. Typically, these lists include characteristics such as the following, on which children are tested:

1. *Social and Emotional Development:* The child
   a. Shares
   b. Cooperates with peers and adults
   c. Demonstrates confidence, self-control, and emotional stability
   d. Completes tasks
   e. Fulfills responsibilities
2. *Physical Development:* The child
   a. Demonstrates large motor control by being able to run, hop, skip, trot, gallop, jump, throw, and walk a straight line
   b. Demonstrates fine motor control by being able to hold a pencil properly, color within lines, and cut with scissors
   c. Demonstrates eye–hand coordination
   d. Can write name, copy letters, draw a human figure
   e. Is generally healthy and vigorous
   f. Shows no visual or auditory defects
   g. Has established dominance (hand, eye, foot)
3. *Cognitive Development:* The child
   a. Demonstrates auditory discrimination by identifying familiar sounds, differentiating sounds, recognizing rhyming words, identifying initial and ending consonant sounds, and possessing an auditory memory
   b. Demonstrates visual discrimination by understanding left to right eye progression, recognizing likenesses and differences, identifying colors, shapes, letters, and words, possessing visual memory, and showing a sense of figure–ground perception

Many such lists go on and on, and often it is assumed that a child must master all behaviors on the list before entering formal reading instruction. There are sad stories of kindergarten teachers who have retained children who were unable to master skipping, trotting, or galloping. Parents have become frantic and children brought to tears by teachers' insistence on mastery of motor skills. It still is not uncommon to see classes of kindergarten children undergoing skipping lessons to the teacher's cadence of "step-hop, step-hop, step-hop, step-hop."

At least two misguided assumptions lie behind such an approach: (1) children know nothing about literacy before coming to school; and (2) they therefore need an instructional program in readiness. In actuality, some of the listed competencies are irrelevant and inappropriate for early literacy development. Many lists do not include awareness of book and print characteristics that are necessary and important for reading. Instructional practices motivated by the readiness-skills approach abstract activities away from the act of reading. There have been reports of children who had accomplished few of the tasks on a list of reading readiness skills but were nonetheless already reading. Their ability to read went unrecognized by their teachers because reading readiness tests and activities never do ask children to read. There are also children who can carry out the tasks on a list and still experience difficulty learning to read.

Research in cognitive development, language acquisition, early readers, and what children learn before school about books, print, and writing which has been cited in the book thus far has changed attitudes and ideas about early childhood instructional strategies and literacy development. Until recently, reading, writing, listening, and speaking were thought of as separate skills taught independently of one another. Our teacher education programs have tended to separate courses in the teaching of reading from those in language arts. We now realize, however, that literacy involves all of the communication skills and that each skill enhances the other as they are learned concurrently.

Although some of the skills associated with reading readiness are important to literacy learning, new concepts are replacing the reading readiness approach to literacy development. The phrase **emergent literacy,** first used by Marie Clay (1966), has caught the attention of educators interested in early literacy. Emergent literacy assumes that the child acquires some knowledge about language, reading, and writing before coming to school. Literacy development begins early in life and is ongoing. There is a dynamic relationship between the communication skills; each influences the other in the course of development. Development occurs in everyday contexts of the home and community. Children at every age possess certain literacy skills, though these skills are not fully developed or conventional, as we recognize mature reading and writing to be (Teale, 1986). Emergent literacy acknowledges as rudimentary writing a child's scribble marks on a page, even if not a letter is discernible. The child who knows the difference between such scribbles and drawings certainly has some sense of the difference between writing and illustration. Similarly, when a child narrates a familiar storybook while looking at the pictures and print and gives the impression of reading, we acknowledge the activity as legitimate literacy behavior, even though it cannot be called reading in the conventional sense.

Emergent literacy constructs are sensitive to children with special needs because they look for strengths youngsters have rather than weaknesses. Literacy development approached in this manner accepts children at whatever level of literacy they are functioning and provides a program for instruction based on individual needs.

Theories on the Acquisition of Reading

To speak of the acquisition of reading apart from that of writing and speaking is somewhat artificial if literacy is viewed as the concurrent development of communication skills. In this text, however, the several communication skills are addressed in separate chapters, primarily because much of the relevant research discusses them rather discretely. Their concurrent development and integration in pedagogy are addressed in Chapter 9.

Reading Is Acquired Through Social, Collaborative Interaction

Teale (1982) views literacy as the result of children's involvement in reading activities mediated by literate others. It is the social, collaborative interaction accompanying these activities that makes them so significant to the child's development. Not only do interactive literacy events teach children the societal function and conventions of reading, they also link reading with enjoyment and

Interactions during literacy events play a significant role in learning to read. The interaction can occur between adult and child or between children.

satisfaction and thus increase children's desire to engage in literacy activities. Teale's emphasis on the social aspects of reading development reflects Vygotsky's (1981) more general theory of intellectual development. Vygotsky suggests that higher order thinking occurs as a result of social relationships that have been internalized. This movement from interpsychological learning to intrapsychological learning is apparent as children become increasingly able to engage independently in reading activities that previously required interaction with more literate others. This time period has been referred to by Vygotsky as the *zone of proximal development* (see Chapter 3). It is that moment when the child becomes capable of participating in a particular literacy activity alone and the adult assistance is no longer necessary.

Collaboration plays an important role in the acquisition of reading among small groups of children in different settings. Studies dealing with student cooperation in academic tasks conclude that such cooperation promotes achievement and productivity and yields strong social and attitudinal benefits (Sharon, 1980; Slavin, 1977; Yager, Johnson, & Johnson, 1985). Researchers propose that the positive effects observed are due to the dynamics of cooperative learning, which include a great deal of oral interaction between students and the heterogeneous nature of the groups. Yager, Johnson, and Johnson (1985) found that passive learners particularly benefit from small-group dialogue and interaction. They suggest that cooperative learning succeeds because it allows children to explain material to each other, to listen to each other's explanations, and to arrive at joint understandings of what has been shared. In addition, young children use language and nonverbal signals that other children understand easily.

Dewey (1966) argued that children who engage in task-oriented dialogue with peers can reach a higher level of understanding than that attained by students who listen to a teacher's didactic presentation of information, and Piaget and Inhelder (1969) suggested that childhood peers can serve as resources for one another in their cognitive development.

Learning in small groups can be accomplished with or without adults. The previous discussion referred to the benefits for learning when children worked together without an adult present. A number of researchers have explored the value of small-group instruction when an adult plays an active role in the setting. It has been found that the interactive dialogue between adults and children and between children in small groups improves children's comprehension and oral language (Applebee & Langer, 1983; Palincsar, Brown, & Martin, 1987). Cochran-Smith (1984) and Morrow and Smith (1990) found that transcripts of story readings to groups of three children included more participation by children and more complex discussion in the small groups than transcripts of readings to larger groups.

This review of research suggests the importance of small-group situations for learning in general and for literacy learning in particular. The small-group instruction can be with or without the teacher and should occur both ways. When the teacher is present, he or she needs to allow for interaction to take place between adult and child and between children. There are several formats for learning situations without the teacher. In one, a task is assigned by the teacher; in another, the children decide what they will do when there are several choices involved. The latter situation can take place in independent reading and writing periods when children have the opportunity to make choices. This setting is described in Chapter 5 and is appropriate for children from preschool through the early childhood and elementary grades. Another situation in which literacy learning can occur when children interact and collaborate in small groups is dramatic-play time.

Early childhood educators have recognized the value of play for social, emotional, and physical development. The use of play to promote literacy development, however, is at an earlier stage. The prevalent concept of reading readiness as a set of abstract skills taught in a formal pencil-and-paper setting assigns no role to play, especially free-choice cooperative play.

Recently, play has attracted greater importance as a medium for literacy development. It is recognized now that literacy develops in meaningful, functional social settings. Literacy development involves a child's active engagement in cooperation and collaboration with peers, builds on what the child already knows, and thrives on the support and guidance of others. Play provides this setting. During observations of children at play, one can observe the functional uses of literacy that children incorporate into their play themes. Children have been observed to engage in attempted and conventional reading and writing in collaborations with other youngsters (Morrow, 1990; Neuman & Roskos, 1990).

To demonstrate the importance of the social, collaborative, and interactive nature of literacy development, I take you into a classroom where the teacher, Mrs. Schifflette, has designed a veterinarian's office to go along with their animal theme with a concentration on pets. The dramatic-play area was designed with a waiting room; chairs; a table filled with magazines, books, and pamphlets about pet care; posters about pets; office hour notices; a "No Smoking" sign; and a sign advising visitors to "Check in with the nurse when arriving." A nurse's desk carried patient forms on clipboards, a telephone, an address and telephone book, appointment cards, and a calendar. Offices contained patient folders, prescription pads, white coats, masks, gloves, cotton swabs, a toy doctor's kit, and stuffed animals for patients.

Mrs. Schifflette guided students in the use of the various materials during free-play time in the veterinarian's office, for example, by reminding the children to read to pets in waiting areas, fill out forms with prescriptions or appointment times, or fill out forms with information about a patient's condition and treatment. In addition to giving directions, Mrs. Schifflette also modeled behaviors by participating in play with the children when the materials were first introduced. The following anecdotes relate the type of behavior that was witnessed in this setting—a setting that provided a literacy-rich environment with books and writing materials; modeled reading and writing by teachers that children could observe and emulate; the opportunity to practice literacy in real-life situations that had meaning and function; and children socially interacting, collaborating, and performing reading and writing with peers.

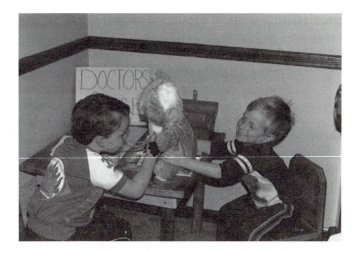

DOCTOR	SERVICE	ROOM	
DATE		Note progress of case, complications, consultations, change in diagnosis, condition or discharge, instructions to patient.	

Preston examined a teddy bear and wrote out a report in the patient's folder afterward. He read his scribble writing out loud and said, "This teddy bear's blood pressure is 29 points. He should take 62 pills an hour until he is better and keep warm and go to bed."

Jessica was waiting to see the doctor. She told her stuffed animal dog Sam not to worry, that the doctor wouldn't hurt him. She asked Jenny who was waiting with her stuffed animal cat Muffin, what the kitten's problem was. The girls agonized over the ailments of their pets. After a while they stopped talking and Jessica picked up a book from the table and pretended to read Are You My Mother? to her pet dog Sam. Jessica showed Sam the pictures as she read.

Jennie ran into the doctor's office shouting "My dog got runned over by a car." The doctor bandaged the dog's leg; then the two *children decided that the incident must be reported to the police. Before calling the police, they got out the telephone book and turned to a map to find the spot where the dog had been hit. Then they called the police on the toy phone to report the incident.*

Preston examined Christopher's teddy bear and wrote out a report in the patient's folder. He read his scribble writing out loud and said, "This teddy bear's blood pressure is 29 points. He should take 62 pills an hour until he is better and keep warm and go to bed." At the same time that he read, he showed Christopher what he had written so he would understand what to do.

In my discussion of play, I have concentrated on cooperative learning to encourage literacy development. Play is typically thought of as a preschool and kindergarten activity; however, this type of setting could and should be utilized with first and second grades as well. Older children engage in more sophisticated literacy behaviors when participating in play. In Chapter 5, the section "Independent Reading and Writing Periods" discusses opportunities for collaborative, social, and interactive learning that can be provided for the first and second grade child.

Children Acquire the Ability to Read as a Result of Life Experiences

Some children already have considerable information about reading and writing before they enter school for formal instruction. Some are reading before they come to school; others have had little exposure to literacy at all. Even though children's strengths in literacy vary with the individual, most children have a general command of their language and a sizable vocabulary and have internalized rules of language. They know the difference between drawing and writing and they associate books with reading. They can read environmental print and they realize the functional purposes of reading. Because their knowledge about literacy to this point is based on meaning and function, they expect that reading will be an activity that makes sense.

Research since the 1960s has made us aware of early childhood competencies and literacy skills. Studies such as those by Clark (1976), Durkin (1966), Krippner (1963), and Torrey (1969) have revealed that many children read early—that is, before starting school and without formal instruction. Investigations have also revealed how the environment supports literacy development. Children as young as three are able to read such common words in their environment as *Burger King, McDonald's, Exxon,* and *Sugar Pops* (Goodman & Altwerger, 1981; Harste, Woodward, & Burke, 1984; Hiebert, 1986; Mason, 1980; Ylisto, 1967). The results of these investigations indicate that very young children are aware of print, letters, and words, and that their ability to identify familiar printed symbols constitutes the beginning of reading. According to Goodman (1984), the "roots of literacy" are established in early childhood by most children in literate societies. Environmental print helps children discover how print is organized and used as well as what it is used for. Young children also demonstrate such knowledge of books and book handling as (1) where to begin reading, (2) the difference between pictures and print, (3) awareness of the left-to-right progression of print, (4) the difference between the beginning and the end of the book, and (5) how to turn pages (Wiseman & Robeck, 1983). Efforts to expand their reading abilities into reading fluency need to build on their strengths and on what they already know and expect of reading (Jewell & Zintz, 1986).

The psycholinguistic definition of reading is based on this last premise. It strongly recommends capitalizing on children's prior strengths, knowledge, and past experiences. Goodman (1967) described reading as a psycholinguistic "guessing game" in which the child attempts to reconstruct, in light of his or her own knowledge, what the author has to say. Young children bring to school concepts and understanding from past experiences. Their awareness and use of oral language are particularly helpful. When they read, they anticipate what the written message is likely to say. Reading is an active process. Children search the printed page for cues based on what they already know. They search for *graphic* cues, or cues about print—whether a squiggle is a letter or a word. There are *syntactic* cues such as *The boy ran down the* _____. The child's internalized knowledge of syntax indicates that the word in the blank must be a noun such as *hill, stairs,* or *street.* A verb would make no sense: *The boy ran down the jumped.* From *semantic* clues, children know which words make sense in the slot and which do not. Few if any would guess that the sentence reads *The boy ran down the sky,* for example. Using these graphic, syntactic, and semantic cues, children predict, guess, expect, make associations, and correct themselves to derive meaning from the printed page. The meaning comes from what they know about language and from their own experiences. The most meaningful cues are those in whole pieces of print, rather than in isolated words. All the processes of reading are brought to bear at once within the reader.

It is difficult for us as adults to understand and appreciate the various processes involved in learning to read because we have been reading for so many years. To understand better the nature of learning to read, put yourself in the place of the learner. With a contrived alphabet called the Confusabet, I have taken college students back to when they were five and six and first taught to read. Whole words are introduced in the unfamiliar alphabet, accompanied by picture clues and context clues. They are reinforced with worksheets. After being introduced to about twenty-five words, the students are given a book containing pictures and stories that use these words. They are called upon to read just as they were in a reading group in an early childhood classroom.

After the lesson we discuss how they have just learned to read with the Confusabet. Students consistently report similar strategies: they try to relate information they already know about reading to the situation. They realize quickly that Confusabet words have the same number of letters as words written in our regular alphabet, and their knowledge of words in general helps them make sense of Confusabet words. Certain similarities in letter forms help them figure out words. They use context and picture clues as much as possible. Their knowledge of syntax (language structures) and the meanings of words surrounding an unknown word helps them determine words they cannot otherwise identify. They skip around within a sentence looking for words they might know. Some rely on the first letter of a word to identify it. Many try to memorize words by the "look–say" method. Most agree that words with unusual shapes or lengths are easy to identify. They acknowledge that to learn they have to involve themselves actively in the reading process. In short, they guess, make mistakes, and correct themselves.

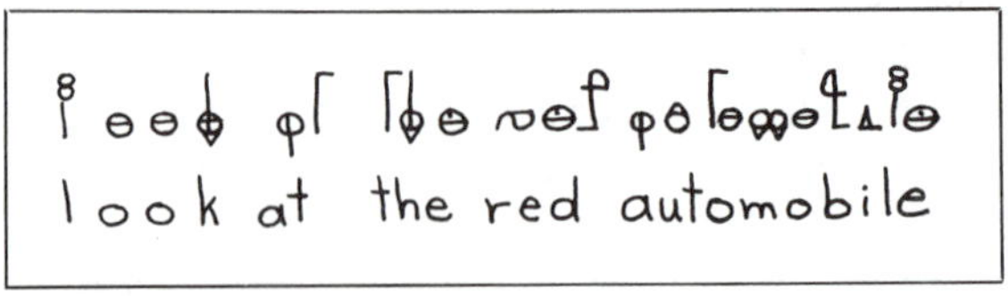

FIGURE 4–1 · *Illustration of the Confusabet.*

My observations of their behavior also reveal that they look to others for help and share successes and failures with those around them. It is not unusual to see a student who has grasped the ability to read the Confusabet material, peer tutoring someone having difficulty. Cooperation and collaboration seem to occur quite naturally. They agree that such social interaction and collaboration are important parts of their learning. They demonstrate a natural curiosity as they flip eagerly through new materials. In their descriptions of how they have learned to read material written in the Confusabet, the students define the psycholinguistic nature of the reading process. In all cases they sought meanings. They approached a printed message as a whole and not by segmenting it into little parts. Granted, these college students draw on many more experiences and associations with print and reading than can the typical kindergarten child or first grader, but this only indicates more emphatically how important it is for initial reading experiences to be based on meaning and function.

Children Acquire Reading Skills When They See a Purpose and a Need for the Process

Children are more likely to become involved in formal reading if they have seen reading, writing, and speaking as functional, purposeful, and useful. Studies of early reading behaviors clearly illustrate that young children acquire their first information about reading and writing through their functional uses (Goodman, 1980; Heath, 1980; Mason, 1977; Mason & McCormick, 1981; Taylor, 1983). Grocery lists; directions on toys, packages, household equipment, and medicine containers; recipes; telephone messages; school-related notices; religious materials; menus; environmental print inside and outside the home; mail; magazines; newspapers; storybook readings; TV channels; telephone numbers; conversation among family members; and letters represent but a sample of the functional literacy information with which a child comes in contact daily. Children are familiar with such forms of literacy, they participate in them, they pretend to use them at play, and they understand their purpose. Parents and day-care, preschool, and kindergarten teachers need to provide experiences with reading similar to experiences children have already had. Children expect learning to read to be meaningful and functional.

Being Read to Plays a Role in the Acquisition of Reading Skills

Research indicates that reading to a child benefits the child's acquisition of reading ability. It provides a model for children to emulate, aids development of literacy skills, increases interest in books and in learning to read, enhances background information and sense of story structure, and familiarizes children with the language of books as opposed to oral language (Chomsky, 1972; Cohen, 1968; Cullinan, 1977; Huck, 1976; Morrow, 1985). A well-structured story has a *setting* (a beginning, time, place, and introduction of characters), a *theme* (the main character's problem or goal), *plot episodes* (a series of events in which the main character tries to solve the problem or achieve the goal), and a *resolution* (the accomplishment of the goal or solving of the problem and an ending). From hearing many well-formed stories, children can predict what will happen next in an unfamiliar story on the basis of their awareness of its structural elements (Morrow, 1985). That the language of books is different from oral language is quite evident in such passages as these from two picture storybooks:

One bad day a tuna fish, fierce, swift and very hungry, came darting through the waves. (Lionni, Swimmy, *1963)*

The wild things roared their terrible roars, gnashed their terrible teeth, and rolled their terrible eyes. (Sendak, Where the Wild Things Are, *1963)*

This next piece is from E. B. White's *Charlotte's Web* (1952) and is appropriate to be read to first and second graders.

At last Wilbur saw the creature that had spoken to him in such a kindly way. Stretched across the upper part of the doorway was a big spiderweb, and hanging from the top of the web, head down, was a large grey spider. She was about the size of a gumdrop. She had eight legs, and she was waving one of them at Wilbur in friendly greeting. "See me now?" she asked.
"Oh, yes indeed," said Wilbur. "Yes indeed! How are you? Good morning! Salutations! Very pleased to meet you. What is your name, please? May I have your name."
"My name," said the spider, "is Charlotte."

Often, children benefit in terms of comprehension skills from their assimilation of and familiarity with vocabulary and syntactic structures in books that have been read to them. Children who have been read to frequently and early tend to read earlier than others and to learn to read more easily (Clark 1984; Durkin, 1966; Hiebert, 1981; Schickedanz, 1978). Furthermore, as pointed out earlier, reading to children at school or at home generally leads them to associate reading with pleasure and provides them with models for reading. In fact, when children begin to read on their own, they often choose books read to them earlier. After I had read *The Little Engine That Could* (Piper, 1954) to a four-year-old, she said to me, "Show me where it says 'I think I can, I think I can.' I want to see it in the book." When I showed her the words, she repeated them while pointing to them and then asked to see them again in another part of the book. She proceeded to search through the rest of the book, reading with great enthusiasm each time she found the line "I think I can, I think I can."

Researchers have found that reading to children enhances the development of reading in many ways. Repeated reading of the same story is an important strategy as well (Morrow, 1986a; Sulzby, 1985; Yaden, 1985). Smith (1978) suggests that reading to children gives them an understanding of the functions of print, a sense of how print is used and of what people are doing when they are reading. Children with storybook experience learn how to handle a book and are sensitive to its front-to-back progression; a story's beginning, middle, and end; and the concept of authorship (Clay, 1979a; Torvey & Kerber, 1986). Mason (1980) found not only that reading to children contributes to their awareness of the functions, form, and conventions of print, but that children develop metacognitive knowledge about how to approach reading tasks and how to interact with teachers and parents. *Metacognition* is one's own awareness of how learning is taking place; it thus nurtures one's own learning.

Children who are read to develop positive attitudes toward reading. The warmth that accompanies storybook readings by a caring adult lasts beyond the experience. It involves ritual, sharing, and mutual good feelings. Certain books take on special meanings between an adult and child through repetition or because they are favorites of the one or the other. My daughter and I have had a special relationship with the book *Alexander and the Terrible, Horrible, No Good, Very Bad Day* (Viorst, 1972). I first read it to Stephanie when she was four, and whenever things seemed to go wrong for her I found myself saying, "I guess you're having

*Being read to plays an important role in the
acquisition of reading skills.*

a terrible, horrible, no good, very bad day." Soon, when things
were not going well for me, Stephanie would say, "I guess you're
having a terrible, horrible, no good, very bad day."

One day, when she was in the seventh grade, Stephanie came
home from school looking terrible. She was wearing only one
sneaker, her hair was not combed, and she looked generally
distraught.

"What's the problem?" I asked.

"Someone stole one of my sneakers, I got yelled at for talking
when my friend asked me a question in class and I answered her,
I have tons of homework, and I lost my assignment notebook."

"I guess you're having a terrible, horrible, no good, very bad
day," I said.

She smiled and said, "You're right. I think I'll go to Australia."

"Some days are like that, even in Australia," I replied.

We both laughed. The familiar words of a familiar book have
created a special ritual between us by which one tries to cheer the
other. Good feelings gained in story readings transfer to the act of
reading itself (Hiebert, 1981; Taylor, 1983).

Children who have been read to often begin to concern themselves with strategies for independent reading. It is not just the
reading itself but the interaction between adult and child that
motivates the interest. Studies carried out in school settings illustrate that active participation in literacy experiences enhances
comprehension of story and sense of story structure. Role-playing

stories they have heard, retelling them, and reconstructing them through pictures enable children to relate parts of a story, integrate information, and interact with teachers and other children (Brown, 1975; Morrow, 1985b; Pellegrini & Galda, 1982).

Studies of home read-aloud sessions clearly illustrate that active social interaction between parents and children during these sessions is a major factor in literacy development. This interaction offers a direct channel of information for the child. Initially, children are interested in the illustrations and label items pictured or repeat words said by the adult who is reading the story (Yaden, 1985). Such interactive behavior leads children to respond with questions and comments, which become more complex over time and demonstrate more sophisticated thinking about printed material. Eventually, children's remarks about story content reflect interests in narration, evaluation, interpretation, association, prediction, information, and elaboration. These remarks focus sometimes on title, setting, characters, and story events (Morrow, 1988a; Roser & Martinez, 1985), and at other times on print characteristics, including names of letters, words, and sounds.

One of the primary goals of reading aloud is the reconstruction of meaning through the interaction between adult and child. The adult helps the child understand and make sense of the text through their cooperative personal interpretation of the written language based on their experiences and beliefs (Atwerger, Diehl-Faxon, & Dockstader-Anderson, 1985). Particularly helpful behavior includes prompting children to respond, scaffolding responses for children to model when they are unable to respond themselves, relating responses to real-life experiences, answering questions, and offering positive reinforcement for children's responses. (See Chapter 2.) We often stop reading to children as they begin to read themselves, usually during first grade. It is crucial to continue reading to youngsters throughout the grades. Reading to children as they grow older continues to enhance skills already learned and to motivate interest in the books featured in the classroom.

The emphasis thus far is on the child's understanding of whole concepts, not isolated reading skills such as letter–sound relationships and decoding. The development of such specific skills has been overemphasized and pursued almost exclusively in recent decades. Their overemphasis has often led to inappropriate home and classroom practices. Yet, we cannot ignore them because research supports their role in literacy development. For instance, children who are taught letter–sound relationships have been found to get off to a better start in learning to read than other children (Adams, 1990; Baumann, 1984; Chall, Conrad, & Harris-Sharples, 1983; Williams, 1985). On the other hand, there is evidence that teaching many phonic rules does not greatly help most youngsters learn to read, because most of these rules are irregular. Rather, only the most regular letter–sound relationships should be taught. Once those are clear to a child, the best way to refine and extend them is to give the child repeated opportunities to read. What needs to be stressed is that the teaching and learning of the alphabet, letter–sound relationships, and decoding skills are only a small part of reading instruction. The time spent on them should be minimal, and the strategies selected for instruction appropriate for young children.

Reading Is Acquired Through the Direct Instruction of Skills

The emphasis in whole language and emergent literacy constructs concerning literacy development is learning through meaning and function and in settings that deal with real life. If children have an interest in reading because it means something to them, they will want to learn and consequently will learn more efficiently and effectively than if meaningless sets of abstract skills are imposed on them. However, one must always take into account that in these natural settings for learning literacy, many children may need additional help, with a focus on one particular skill or another. Therefore, there still is the need for the direct instruction of skills for many youngsters. Early in the emergent literacy and whole language movements, direct instruction was looked upon as the skill, drill, teach, test approach and had no place within whole language or emergent literacy classrooms. As we have spent a few years exploring these new ideas, we have come to realize that some of the old can blend and is needed along with the new. Direct instruction is important for most children. However, this type of instruction needs to be directed at the needs of individuals and to be a small part of the literacy program. Direct instruction can take place on a one-to-one basis and in small groups. The groups form and disband as needed. Chapter 9 deals with organizational strategies for literacy instruction and discusses direct instruction for both groups and individual conference settings. Without this direct instruction component, some children would miss learning many important skills that would reflect poorly upon the emergent literacy and whole language philosophies and could cause their demise. It is crucial that teachers be aware of the individual needs of their children and accommodate those needs with appropriate instructional strategies, which might mean direct instruction for the purpose of promoting skill development.

Holdaway's Theory of Literacy Development

Holdaway's (1979) theory of literacy development provides a summary concerning how reading is acquired:

> *The way in which supportive adults are induced by affection and common sense to intervene in the development of their children proves upon close examination to embody the most sound principles of teaching. Rather than provide verbal instructions about how a skill should be carried out, the parent sets up an emulative model of the skill in operation and induces activity in the child which approximates towards use of the skill. The first attempts of the child are to do something that is like the skill he wishes to emulate. This activity is then "shaped" or refined by immediate rewards. . . . From this point of view, so called "natural" learning is in fact supported by higher quality teaching intervention than is normally the case in the school setting.*

Holdaway contends that this form of "developmental" teaching is appropriate for school-based literacy instruction. Characterized by self-regulated, individualized activities, frequent peer interaction, and an environment rich with materials, Holdaway's model is derived from observations of home environments where children have learned to read without direct instruction, homes such as those described in Chapter 2.

Holdaway (1986) explains four processes that enable children to acquire reading ability. The first is *observation* of reading behaviors—being read to, for example, or seeing adults reading themselves. The second is *collaboration* with an individual who interacts with the child, providing encouragement, motivation, and help when necessary. The third process is *practice*. The learner tries out alone what has been learned—role-playing, for instance, or other reading activities—and experiments without direction or adult observation. Practice gives children opportunities to evaluate their performances, make corrections, and increase skills. In the fourth process, *performance*, the child shares what has been learned and seeks approval from adults who are supportive, interested, and encouraging. The ideas expressed by Holdaway (1986) are also articulated in work on literacy development by Calkins, 1983; Clark, 1976; Read, 1975; and Smith, 1983.

Stages of Reading Development

The concept of emergent literacy suggests that one does not suddenly learn to read; rather, becoming literate is a process that begins at birth and continues throughout one's lifetime. Children differ in their rates of literacy achievement; they must not be pressured into the accomplishment of tasks or placed on a predetermined time schedule. Stages in reading development are not as precise as we might like them to be. Certain traits of literacy do seem to be acquired by many youngsters before others, but the dividing lines among traits and among youngsters are not always distinct. Different children pass through stages at different levels of maturity. Although it is helpful to recognize the various stages and to monitor a child's progression through them, we must not be trapped into believing that all children must pass through all stages or all at the same time and in the same order. In planning for instruction, we must never presume that the stages are fixed, or that a child cannot operate at a "later" stage before an "earlier" one.

Mason (1980, 1984) suggests that there are three strands of reading behavior that develop separately but concurrently—attention to the *functions, forms,* and *conventions* of print, with the first of these predominating in initial reading development. Other researchers, too, have found that children learn how print *functions* as a first step toward reading (Goodman, 1984; Smith, 1971). Often, the first words a child reads are those with meaning and purpose in the child's life—family names, food labels, road signs, and names of fast food restaurants. It is this stage of development that Goodman (1984) referred to as the "roots of literacy." In the second stage, the learner is concerned more with the *forms* of print. Details about names, sounds, and configurations of letters and words serve the child's learning more than does observation of how print functions. The third stage, identifying and using *conventions* of print, involves the recognition that print is read from left to right, that punctuation serves certain purposes in printed material, that spaces serve to demarcate letters and words, and so forth. In other words, although recognition of the functions of print dominates the first stage of reading development in early childhood, the child is at the same time, but to a lesser degree, acquiring notions about the form and conventions of print (Mason, 1984). As the child matures as a reader, the form of print becomes more important in reading development, and finally the conventions of print become a focus.

Sulzby (1985) found developmental trends in two- to five-year-olds in her work on attempted reading of familiar storybooks. Children's first attempts at "reading" familiar stories were governed by pictures, their stories were not well formed, the children sounded as if they were telling a story rather than reading, and they paid no attention to print. In later attempts, the children approached conventional reading behaviors. They attempted to read the print, their stories were well formed, and their language sounded as if they were reading.

In a study of what children know about reading and of their skill in letter and word recognition, McCormick and Mason (1981) established three developmental levels in word recognition. Children first identified words through context, then used letter–sound cues, and finally relied on sounding out words.

Studies of young children's responses to story readings also reveal developmental trends that follow Mason's basic three-strand paradigm. Children's initial questions and comments during story readings are related to the pictures and the meanings of the stories. As they gain experience with story readings, their questions and comments begin to concern the names of letters, the reading of individual words, or attempts to sound out words (Morrow, 1987a; Roser & Martinez, 1985; Yaden, 1985). Again, the function of print dominates early responses; the form of print becomes more important in later responses.

Judging from the research, then, there seem to be categories of reading development in early childhood. Yet reading is obviously a complex process, and individual case studies vary between children. One must never forget that each child is an individual developing at his or her own pace.

Strategies for Reading Development

According to Teale (1987), studies on emergent literacy suggest that to become literate young children must learn about the functions and uses of literacy, conventions of written language, decoding and encoding strategies, and comprehending and composing strategies. They must also develop positive attitudes toward reading. From the theories on reading acquisition and the categories of reading development, we can formulate four objectives for emergent readers from birth to seven:

1. Develop positive attitudes toward reading
2. Develop concepts about books
3. Develop comprehension of story
4. Develop concepts about print

These objectives are intended simply as basic guidelines for helping teachers design strategies for instruction.

The instructional strategies described in the next three chapters are designed to serve these objectives. Chapter 5 emphasizes the use of children's literature and concentrates on the first objective. Chapter 6 deals with the second and third objectives, and Chapter 7 with objective four. In all of the chapters, the strategies will be guided by the theories of reading acquisition just discussed.

AN IDEA FOR THE CLASSROOM

The following experience was created by an early childhood teacher. You may find this idea useful for your teaching.

A Bakery in the Dramatic-Play Area

In coordination with a unit on Community Helpers, we set up a bakery in the dramatic-play area. Materials included a baker's hat and apron; cookie cutter; rolling pin; mixing bowls; measuring spoons; and trays and boxes with labels for baked goods, such as donuts, cookies, cakes, pies, and so on. Some classroom recipes that had already been made were hung in the area; a file box with old recipes and blank cards for new recipes was available; and pens and pencils and books with recipes for baking were also placed in the area.

For the purpose of buying and selling baked goods, which were actually made, there was an ordering pad, a cash register, receipts for purchases, number tickets for standing in line, and name tags for the baker and salesperson.

To guide the children in their play, on different days, I modeled the behavior for a salesperson, a customer, and the baker. This was a popular play area in which a great deal of literacy behavior occurred. For example, the salesperson took orders on the phone and in person and wrote them down; the bakers followed recipes in the cookbook and on the wall; and the customers counted out money and read the labels naming the baked goods. Children participated in behaviors that I modeled and generated their own ideas when participating in play in the bakery.

Joyce C. Ng
Kindergarten Teacher
Livingston, NJ

ACTIVITIES AND QUESTIONS

1. Answer the focus questions at the beginning of the chapter.

2. Describe how the emergent literacy approach to literacy development is more sensitive to children with special needs than the reading readiness approach.

3. Reading is acquired through a child's (a) social and collaborative interaction with adults and other children, (b) association of print materials with real-life experiences, (c) awareness that there is a purpose for reading, (d) the development of a desire to read that comes as a result of being read to, and (e) interaction with a teacher in direct instruction of skills when additional help may be needed. Briefly discuss each of these five areas related to reading acquisition. Then,

   a. Create a learning situation for each of the five categories mentioned.

   b. Observe in a preschool, kindergarten, first, or second grade for a few hours and record literacy activities observed. Classify the literacy activities into the categories previously mentioned.

4. Observe a preschool, kindergarten, first, or second grade. List those activities that seem characteristic of an emergent

literacy approach to instruction and those that seem characteristic of a reading readiness approach.

5. Observe a child between the ages of three and seven. Identify his or her emergent reading behaviors or reading developmental characteristics.

Case Study Activity

Review the "Idea for the Classroom" and identify the theories of reading acquisition that exist in the learning setting described. Would this be an activity that accommodates children with special needs? If yes, explain how; if no, suggest what might be done within this activity to accommodate such children better.

CHAPTER FIVE

Developing Positive Attitudes Toward Reading Through the Use of Children's Literature

QUESTIONS TO FOCUS ON AS YOU READ THE CHAPTER

- What does research have to say about the benefits of voluntary reading and exposure to children's literature in relation to specific aspects of literacy development?
- What are the physical characteristics of well-designed literacy centers and the benefits of having these centers in classrooms?
- Name and define different genres of children's literature.
- Describe strategies that can be used by teachers to facilitate interest in reading.
- Describe the organization of an independent reading and writing period and the type of activities children participate in during this time.
- What characteristics of the literature experiences described in this chapter seem to be appropriate for children with special needs?
- What objectives help guide the development of positive attitudes toward reading, and how can we assess children's attitudes?

Children who read only when in a reading group are not being taught a love of reading. The best index of the success of reading instruction is the eagerness with which children approach reading.
  Love of reading is not taught, it is created.
  Love of reading is not required, it is inspired.
  Love of reading is not demanded, it is exemplified.
  Love of reading is not exacted, it is quickened.
  Love of reading is not solicited, it is activated.
                                              —RUSSELL STAUFFER
                                              Wilson Library Bulletin

During an independent reading and writing period, Tesha and Jamin chose a felt story of the book *Are You My Mother?* The following transpired as they worked together reading the story and manipulating the felt characters:

Jamin: Can I read the story?

Tesha: O K.

Jamin: (Begins reading with enthusiasm and Tesha works the felt pieces on the board.) The baby bird asks the cow, "Are you my mother?"

Tesha: (Puts the cow on the felt-board.) Mooooooo

Jamin: Moooooooo (Jamin continues to read the book.)

Tesha: Look at this picture. (She points to the baby bird. Both start to giggle. They continue along in the story.)

Jamin: Here I am Mother! (He read in a high-pitched voice.) Here comes the funny part. (He points to a picture of the mother bird in a red scarf and both children giggle. Jamin again does the bird-pitched voice.) Mother, mother, here I am!

Tesha: I like it when he says to the tractor, You are my mother, Snort, Snort.

Jamin: Snort, Snort!

Tesha: Snort, Snort!

Jamin: I thought I had a mother. (He puts his hand to his head as he says this using a baby bird voice and swaying back and forth pretending he is crying.)

Tesha: (imitates Jamin by putting her hands on her hips) I thought I had a mother!

Jamin: (pointing to the felt-board) Can I do this now and you read? (They trade places and Tesha starts reading. She speaks in a loud dramatic voice and has voices for the two birds. Tesha is reading the story too fast for Jamin to put the characters up on the board.)

Jamin: Wait, wait, will you wait a minute Tesha. (He puts the dog on the felt-board and Tesha continues.) Wait, Wait, Wait! (He puts the mother bird on the felt-board.)

The teacher asks everyone to put all work away because independent reading and writing time is over. Both children are disappointed that they have to put the materials away and suggest they will continue tomorrow.

This dialogue was between two second-grade children engaged in an independent reading and writing period in which they had the opportunity to choose whom they would like to work with and what they would like to do that involves literacy behavior. The

Two second graders reading and performing a felt story together.

children have the opportunity to practice literacy to become proficient, the classroom atmosphere is relaxed, and a desire to read and write has been created through teacher modeling of pleasurable literacy activities. Because children can select what it is they want to do, and whom they do it with, the motivation and desire to read and/or write are high. The atmosphere promotes cooperative and collaborative behavior.

Becoming a Nation of Readers (Anderson, Hiebert, Scott, & Wilkinson, 1985) states, among other things, that learning to read requires (1) the motivation and desire to read, (2) practice to the point of proficiency, and (3) continuous and lifelong involvement so that fluency is maintained. One of the first goals in early literacy development is the nurturing of positive attitudes toward reading. Those attitudes usually result in voluntary readers. If children learn to read but have little desire to use their ability, we have not accomplished much (Spiegel, 1981). In a 1984 report to Congress entitled *Books in Our Future,* Daniel Boorstin, then Librarian of Congress, warned that *aliterates*—individuals who can read but choose not to—constitute as much of a threat to our democratic tradition as illiterates. Voluntary reading, or the lack of it, he wrote, "will determine the extent of self-improvement and enlightenment, the ability to share the wisdom and delights of our civilization, and our capacity for intelligent self-government" (p. iv).

Unfortunately, substantial numbers of children and adults read neither for pleasure nor for information. Greaney (1980) found that 22 percent of the fifth-grade students he surveyed chose not to read at all, and that those who did read spent only 5 percent of their leisure time at it. Morrow (1982) and Morrow and Weinstein (1982) observed that few primary children chose books during free-choice time in school. A Gallup survey revealed that 80 percent of the books read in the United States were read by only 10 percent of the population; half the adults sampled had never read a book all the way through (cited by Spiegel, 1981). An extensive investigation by the Book Industry Study Group (1984) indicated that the number of young people under twenty-one identified as readers dropped from 75 percent In 1976 to 63 percent in 1984.

One reason for such distressing reports may be that most instructional programs in reading have been skills-oriented, providing little opportunity for students to read for enjoyment (Lamme, 1981; Spiegel, 1981). Children's reading habits develop early in life (Bloom, 1964). If schools do not deliberately and thoughtfully entice children to read during their early years, the desire and motivation to learn to read and to acquire the reading habit may never develop.

Apart from the common belief that voluntary reading is desirable, there is considerable empirical evidence that it correlates with success in school. Children identified as voluntary readers in elementary and middle grades demonstrated high levels of reading achievement in comprehension and in vocabulary development (Anderson, Wilson, & Fielding, 1985; Greaney, 1980; Taylor, Frye, & Marugama, 1990; Whitehead, Capey, & Maddren, 1975). Morrow (1983) found that in comparison with children whose interest in books was low, kindergarteners who demonstrated a strong interest in books scored significantly higher on standardized reading readiness tests and were rated higher by teachers on work habits, general school performance, and social and emotional development. Chomsky (1972) found that children who are introduced to literature at an early age tend to develop sophisticated language structures. Cohen (1968) concluded that the language structures and vocabulary children gain from early exposure to literature correlate with their subsequent success in learning to read. Both vocabulary and language structures can be improved significantly in youngsters by regular listening to stories read aloud. Children who experience literature early accumulate background knowledge, appreciate books, and show increased interest in learning to read. As we saw in previous chapters, they often begin to read early or learn to read more easily (Durkin, 1966). Bissett (1970) contends that discussing books provides a foundation for comprehension skills because of the language development, background knowledge, and sense of story structure acquired thereby.

Researchers have repeatedly stressed the importance of providing children with daily opportunities to experience literature pleasurably; to discuss stories through literal, interpretive, and critical questioning; to relate literature activities to content-area learning; and to share the books they read or look at (Arbuthnot & Sutherland, 1977; Cullinan, 1977, 1987, 1989; Huck, 1976; Smith & Parker, 1977; Stewig & Sebesta, 1978.) More recent research (Morrow, 1987b; Morrow & Weinstein, 1982, 1986) has shown that children's use of literature increases dramatically when teachers incorporate enjoyable literature activities into the daily program and design attractive classroom library corners.

The information in Chapter 2 for parents of infants and toddlers focuses on techniques and practices to develop positive attitudes toward books that are appropriate as well for aides and professionals in day-care centers. For that reason, the discussion in this chapter focuses on techniques for use with two- to eight-year-olds (much of this information is applicable to younger children, too).

As you read the chapter, think about the characteristics of the strategies presented that would be particularly effective with children from diverse backgrounds.

Strategies for Promoting Positive Attitudes Toward Reading

The information presented in this chapter is based on investigations revealing classroom practices that seem to promote positive attitudes toward reading and consequently increase children's voluntary reading. Investigators have observed and described such strategies, correlated use of literature to materials in classrooms and activities carried out by teachers, and intervened with programs to see if changes in attitudes toward reading, demonstrated by increased use of books, were possible. The programs or strategies are based on the following objectives to guide the development of positive attitudes toward reading and increased use of children's literature:

1. Children will be provided with an environment that is rich in literacy materials.
2. Children will be provided with models of literacy behavior to emulate.
3. Children will be given the opportunity to participate voluntarily in literacy activities during independent reading and writing periods.
4. Children will have the opportunity to select the literacy activities in which they will participate.
5. Children will have the opportunity to work alone or in cooperation and collaboration with others.
6. Children will have the opportunity to listen to stories read by their teachers and peers in a pleasant, relaxed atmosphere.
7. Children will have the opportunity to respond to stories through discussion, role-playing, the use of puppets to retell stories, and so on.
8. Children will have the opportunity to take books from the classroom literacy center home to read.
9. Children will be exposed to varied genres of children's literature to help them find those that are most appealing to them.

Preparing a Literacy-Rich Environment

Before planning instruction that will entice children to books, the teacher must prepare appropriate materials and a physical setting that sets the stage for pleasurable literacy experiences. As Plato said, "What is honored in a country will be cultivated there." Teachers who honor the development of literacy demonstrate that attitude by providing within their classrooms a rich environment where the use of books can be cultivated. Their students honor literacy development by assimilating the attitudes and atmosphere presented by the teacher.

A classroom literacy center is essential for children's immediate access to literature (Beckman, 1972). Bissett (1969) found that children in classrooms with literature collections read and looked at books 50 percent more often than children in classrooms without such collections. Coody (1973) and Huck (1976) both report that the efforts spent in creating an inviting atmosphere for a classroom literacy center are rewarded by increased interest in books. Studies by Morrow and Weinstein (1982, 1986) and Morrow (1987b) showed that well-designed classroom literacy centers significantly increased the number of children who chose to participate in literature activities during free-choice periods. Morrow (1982) observed literacy centers in nursery schools, kindergartens, and first and second grades and identified specific design characteristics that correlated with children's use of the centers during free-choice periods. Conversely, Morrow (1982), Rosenthal (1973), and Shure (1963) found that poorly designed literacy centers were among the least popular areas during free-choice periods in early childhood rooms. Suffice it to say, the physical features of a classroom literacy center can play an important role in enticing children to use the corner voluntarily.

Features of Well-Designed Literacy Centers

A classroom literacy center should be a focal area, immediately visible and inviting to anyone entering the classroom. To provide privacy and physical definition, it should be partitioned on two or three sides with bookshelves, a piano, file cabinets, or freestanding bulletin boards. The dimensions of the literacy center will vary with the size of the classroom. Generally, it should be large enough to accommodate five or six children comfortably (Figure 5–1).

FIGURE 5–1 • *Morrow Literacy Center.*

Well-designed literacy centers have two kinds of bookshelves. The first houses the bulk of the books, which are shelved with the spines facing out. The other type is open-faced, allowing the covers of the books to be seen, which is important for calling attention to special books. Featured books, changed regularly, are placed on the open-faced shelves for easy access. An alternative to open-faced shelving is the circular wire rack, commonly found in bookstores.

Books in the collection should be shelved by category and color-coded according to the type of book. Identify all animal books, for example, by placing blue dots on their spines and clustering them on a shelf marked *Animals,* with a blue dot next to the label. Another color might distinguish books about holidays, a third color poetry, and so on. Color coding introduces children to the idea that books in libraries are organized so as to be readily accessible.

The literacy center should be furnished with an area rug and pillows or beanbag chairs because much of the activity there takes place on the floor. If possible, it should also include a small table and chairs where children can use headsets to listen to taped stories and make their own books. A rocking chair allows comfortable reading, a place for teachers to read to children and children to read to other children.

Children are given little privacy in the typical school. It has been found that many children relish privacy. Because it is partially partitioned from the rest of the room, the literacy center provides some privacy. Listening to recorded stories on headsets offers even more privacy, and an oversized carton, painted or covered with contact paper, makes a cozy private reading room. Children have been found reading in coat closets and under shelves.

Attractive posters that encourage reading are available from the Children's Book Council (67 Irving Place, New York, NY 10003) and the American Library Association (50 East Huron Street, Chicago, IL 60611). Stuffed animals also belong in a literacy center, especially if they are related to books available in the corner—a stuffed rabbit next to *Peter Rabbit* (Potter, 1902), for instance. Children enjoy reading to stuffed animals or simply holding them as they look at books. A felt-board, with figures of story characters from favorite books, is one of the more heavily used materials in a literacy center, as are roll movies. A roll movie consists of a box with a picture window cut out that makes it look like a television. A dowel is inserted at the top and bottom of the

The library corner is a cozy place where children can relax and read, sitting on a rug, leaning on soft pillows, and hugging stuffed animals.

box. Shelving paper is written on and illustrated and attached to the dowels for presentation (see photograph on page 149.) Viewmasters with story wheels are a source of literature for young children, and puppets aid the acting out of stories. The center should also include materials from which children can make their own books, felt stories, and roll movies.

Huck (1976) recommends five to eight books per child in a classroom library. Books are not difficult to accumulate. They can be purchased very inexpensively at flea markets. Teachers can borrow as many as twenty books a month from most public libraries, ask for book donations from parents, and hold fund-raisers for book purchases. Children's paperback book clubs offer inexpensive books and free bonus books for bulk purchases.

Children's magazines and newspapers belong in the classroom library even if they are not current. For the cost of mailing and shipping, some publishers and local magazine agencies will donate outdated periodicals to schools.

Children should be involved in the planning and design of a literacy center. They can develop rules for its use, be in charge of keeping it neat and orderly, and select a name for it, such as Book Nook.

To ensure continued interest in the literacy center, the teacher must introduce new books and materials and recirculate

others. Approximately twenty-five new books should be introduced every two weeks, replacing twenty-five that have been there
for a while. In this way, "old" books will be greeted as new friends
a few months later. Recirculation compensates limited budgets.

Books from the literacy center should be available for students to check out and take home for a week at a time. The
check-out system should be simple. At specified times during the
school day, children might bring the books they want to borrow to
the teacher, who notes the date, the child's name, and book title.
Some kindergarten children have been taught to check out books
themselves by copying titles and recording dates on five-by-eight
cards filed under their own names. Other youngsters enjoy keeping track of books borrowed by recording titles and dates on
three-by-five cards hung on curtain-rod hooks or key rings
mounted on a bulletin board, one hook or ring per child.

Books and other materials selected for the center should
appeal to a variety of interests and span a range of grade levels. It
is advisable to stock multiple copies of popular books. Children
sometimes enjoy reading a book because a friend is reading it
(Morrow, 1985a). Several types of children's literature should be
represented:

Picture concept books are appropriate for the very young
child who cannot yet read. Most picture concept books do not have
story lines, though they often have themes, such as animals or
toys. Each page usually carries a picture identified by a printed
word. Many picture books are made of cardboard, cloth, or vinyl
to withstand rigorous handling. Alphabet and number books are
also considered picture concept books.

Traditional literature includes nursery rhymes and fairy
tales, familiar stories that are part of our heritage and originated
in the oral tradition of storytelling. We assume that children are
familiar with *Goldilocks and the Three Bears* (Izawa, 1968a) and
The Three Little Pigs (Brenner, 1972), yet many youngsters have
not been exposed to these traditional stories. Children who *do*
know the stories welcome them as old friends.

Picture storybooks are most familiar to us as children's
literature. Their texts are closely associated with their illustrations. Picture storybooks are available on a wide range of topics,
and many are known for their excellence. The Caldecott Medal is
awarded annually to the author or illustrator of an outstanding
picture storybook. Many of these books have become classics and
their authors renowned—Robert McClosky, Dr. Seuss, Ezra Jack

Keats, Tomie DePaola, Maurice Sendak, and Charlotte Zolotow, to name just a few. Every child should be given the benefit of hearing some of these books read. In particular, the earliest emergent readers will often find the vocabulary and syntax too sophisticated to read them on their own.

Realistic literature—really a category of picture story-books—deals with real-life issues. *Bedtime for Frances* (Hoban, 1960), for example, is about the fears and concerns a child faces when told to go to sleep, and *Peter's Chair* (Keats, 1967) handles the problems that arise with a new baby in the house. Some touch on very sensitive issues, such as divorce and death. Many can be read to the entire class if they address issues that all share. Teachers can also recommend specific titles to parents of children who face particular problems.

Easy-to-read books are designed to be read by emergent readers themselves. They have limited and repeated vocabularies, and many of them rhyme, which makes them predictable and aids independent reading. Because of their limited language, few easy-to-read books rate as quality literature, but many preschool and kindergarten children begin to read independently with them.

Fables and folktales retell many of the myths and traditional stories that are available in picture-book style for the younger child. Many of these stories originate in other countries and cultures and therefore broaden a child's experience and knowledge base.

Informational books offer nonfiction for emergent readers. There are books about holidays, plants, animals, foreign countries, communities, dinosaurs, and famous people. They broaden a child's background information, explore new ideas, and often stimulate deep interest in particular topics.

Wordless books carry definite story lines, but use no words. They are often thought appropriate for very young children and are confused with picture books. They are designed not for babies but for children three and older. The child creates the story by reading the pictures, some of which are intricate.

Poetry is too often forgotten in collections of children's literature at home and in school. Many themed anthologies have been compiled for young children, and they are an important part of the literacy center.

Novels are longer books with chapters. We can begin reading novels to young children to expose them to the genre. They are often quite attracted to them and eager to begin to read them. Children often call novels chapter books.

Biography is another genre appropriate for young children. There are simple biographies of historical figures, as well as popular figures in sports and on television.

Big Books are usually large versions of smaller picture storybooks. They can also be original stories. They are oversized books that rest on an easel in order to be read. The purpose of the Big Book is for children to be able to see the print as it is being read, to make the association between oral and written language, and to see how the print is read from left to right across the page.

In addition to these categories of books, young children enjoy joke and riddle books; participation books, which involve them in touching, smelling, and manipulating; books in a series built around a single character; and books related to television programs appropriate for their age. Children particularly enjoy literature that is predictable, because it helps them to understand the story line more easily and enables them to read along with the individual reading to them. Predictable literature contains rhyme; repetition; catch phrases; conversation; familiar sequences, such as days of the week or numbers; cumulative patterns, in which events are repeated or added on as the story continues; stories about familiar topics; familiar or popular stories; books with uncluttered illustrations that match the text; and stories that have well-developed story structures (setting, theme, plot, episodes, and resolution). (Selected children's books are listed in Appendix A, including books for children with special needs and books that are multicultural. Children's book clubs and publishers of children's literature are listed in Appendix B, and television programs that feature children's literature are in Appendix D.)

The *Author's Spot* is an integral part of the literacy center. It usually consists of a table and chairs with various writing materials available, such as colored felt-tip pens, crayons, and lined white paper ranging from 8 1/2 × 11 inches to 24 × 36 inches. If possible, include a typewriter or a computer. Materials for making books should also be present, including colored construction paper for covers, plain white paper for inside pages, a stapler, and scissors. (The Author's Spot will be described more thoroughly in Chapter 8.)

Teachers and children had the following reactions to literacy centers that I designed in their classrooms: teachers said they were concerned that there wasn't enough space in their classrooms for literacy centers and were surprised that all the materials could fit. As time went on, teachers themselves provided more space for the literacy centers. Teachers commented that the physical presence of the literacy center made a statement to the children that literacy was so valued that space was taken from the classroom to make room for the area. Teachers agreed that children were attracted to the area by the manipulative materials in the center, such as the felt-board stories and puppets. They found that the elements of comfort, such as the rocking chair, rug, pillows, and stuffed animals made the center relaxing and comfortable for reading:

> *The literacy center became a place where children of all reading and writing abilities mingled. . . . This social context seemed to provide an atmosphere for cooperative learning. The children looked forward to their time there each day.*

A child commented:

> *I liked to cuddle up on the pillows with a book, or crawl into a private spot, or rock in the rocking chair and read. You get to take books home right from the classroom center.*

Children referred to the center as a special place. They felt that the literacy center could be improved by adding more space, more books, more time to use it, and a snack bar with food they could eat while reading.

The Teacher as Facilitator

The teacher plays a critical role in influencing children's attitudes toward voluntary reading.

> *If children live associating reading only with repetition of skill, drill, teach, and test, they will never reach for a book on their own. If, on the other hand, children live in an environment that associates reading with pleasure and enjoyment as well as with skill development, they are likely to become voluntary readers. How children live and learn at home and in the classroom ultimately determines whether they will live their lives as literate or aliterate individuals. (Morrow, 1985a, p. 20)*

Chapter 2 dealt with literacy activities appropriate for home use and was intended primarily to provide parental models for literacy behavior and to help children associate reading with pleasure. The school must follow a similar agenda.

One of the clear points to emerge from research into reading failure is that there was no association between reading and pleasure. . . . The role of teachers in stimulating voluntary reading among children and young people is . . . potentially the most powerful of all adult influences upon the young. (Irving, 1980, p. 7)

Programs that incorporate pleasurable experiences with literature create interest in and enthusiasm for books that in turn increase children's voluntary use of books (Morrow, 1982, 1983, 1987b; Morrow & Weinstein, 1982, 1986). Among other specific activities in early childhood classrooms, teachers should read or tell stories to children daily. Interest heightens when stories are discussed both before and after being read, especially if they are related to issues that reflect children's real-life experiences or current school topics. Literal, inferential, and critical questions can be introduced even at the preschool level. Skill development can easily be incorporated into storybook reading activities in pleasurable and meaningful ways. The following example describes a discussion about *Goldilocks and the Three Bears* where inferential and critical comprehension is being developed.

I recently led a discussion with four-year-olds after reading *Goldilocks and the Three Bears.* I asked who were the good and the bad characters. Hands waved in the air and Jennifer answered, "Goldilocks was good and the bears were bad." When I asked Jennifer why she thought that, she said, "Well, the bears scared Goldilocks."

Another hand went up and Tim said, "No, that's not right. The bears are good and Goldilocks is bad. Goldilocks went into the bears' house when they weren't home. She ate their food and didn't even ask."

"That's right," said Megan, "and she broke their chair and went to sleep in their bed and didn't even ask if it was okay."

Chris chimed in, "Yeah, Goldilocks was really bad. She did a lot of bad things because she didn't ask if she could."

"Would you go into a stranger's house and do the things Goldilocks did?" I asked. The whole group called out in unison "Nooooo." I asked why not. Sara answered, "Because that is bad. It's like stealing. She was naughty. If the cops found out, I bet they will arrest her."

Discussion about authors and illustrators also arouses interest. Reading different stories by the same author or a series of books about the same character, such as Madeline (Bemelmans,

1939) or Curious George (Rey, 1941), increases interest as well. Read different kinds of literature to the class and as often as possible coordinate stories with topics being discussed. If the topic is spring, bring a cocoon to class, discuss the life cycle of a butterfly, and follow the discussion with *The Very Hungry Caterpillar* (Carle, 1969), the story of the caterpillar's transformation to a butterfly. Read and recite poetry together regularly. Recruit older children, the principal, the custodian, the nurse, the librarian, parents, and grandparents to read to classes, to small groups, and to individuals. Encourage children to share books with one another. Books from home should be shared with the group and children encouraged to take books home from school.

Many popular folk songs have been made into picture storybooks, such as *Go Tell Aunt Rhody* (Quackenbush, 1973) and *Old MacDonald Had a Farm* (Quackenbush, 1972). These books are particularly good to read to children because the children are familiar with the words and very much want to pretend to read the books themselves and to another person. Cooking is another pleasurable activity that can be related to literature. Many picture storybooks feature food—*Blueberries for Sal* (McCloskey, 1948) and *Bread and Jam for Frances* (Hoban, 1964) for instance. After such stories have been read, the class can make blueberry muffins or bread and jam or whatever food is appropriate. Art activities can also be motivated by story readings. After reading *The Snowy Day* (Keats, 1962), have the children create a winter collage from blue construction paper, white cotton, wool, doilies, chalk, and silver foil. After reading *Where the Wild Things Are* (Sendak, 1963), ask kindergarteners and first graders to think of a wild thing and draw a picture of it. Gather their pictures into a class book. Class books become favorites and are read frequently by children. Children also enjoy filmstrip and movie stories, which motivate their interest in reading the associated book.

Making Story Reading Pleasurable

To make story readings as enjoyable and pleasurable as possible, select good pieces of literature—well-structured stories with well-delineated characters, clear and uncluttered illustrations, catch phrases, rhyme, and repetition. Read to youngsters in a relaxed atmosphere in a location designated for such readings. Each day let a different child sit close to you while you are reading, with the other children in a semicircle. If the children are on the floor, sit on a low chair. If they are sitting on chairs, you can sit on your own-size chair. Because children enjoy seeing illustrations in books during story readings, hold the book so it faces the group or turn the book at appropriate pauses so its pictures can be seen. Before reading a story to a group, practice reading it aloud to yourself.

Be expressive in your reading, change your voice when a different character speaks, and highlight special events. Use facial expressions. A story reading is like a dramatic presentation. Read slowly and with a great deal of animation. Record or videotape your readings to improve your technique. Begin a story with an introduction such as, "Today I'm going to read a story about a little girl who wanted to get a present for her mother's birthday. She can't think of anything and asks a rabbit to help her. The title of the story is *Mr. Rabbit and the Lovely Present* [Zolotow, 1962]. The author's name is Charlotte Zolotow and the illustrator is Maurice Sendak. While I read the story think of which part of the present you like the best." When you have finished reading the story, begin a discussion with a question such as "Who would like to tell me which part of the present you liked best?"

Storytelling: Some Creative Techniques

Storytelling strongly attracts children to books (Morrow, 1982; Morrow & Weinstein, 1982, 1986). It has a power that reading stories does not, for it frees the storyteller to use creative techniques. It also has the advantage of keeping him or her close to the audience. The storyteller establishes direct eye contact with the group. Telling a story produces an immediate response from the audience and is one of the surest ways to establish rapport between the listeners and the storyteller. Long pieces of literature can be trimmed so that even very young children can hear whole stories in one sitting. Considered an art, storytelling can be mastered by most people.

It is not necessary to memorize a story, but be sure you know it well. Use all the catch phrases and quotes that are important to the story. Use expression in your presentation, but don't let your dramatic techniques overshadow the story itself. Look directly at your audience and take their attention into consideration. Storytelling allows you to abridge stories as you go if attention spans seem to grow short. It is important to have the original book at hand when you have finished telling a story so that the children can see it and enjoy it again through its pictures and printed text.

Creative techniques help storytelling come alive. They excite the imagination, involve the listeners, and motivate children to try storytelling themselves and create their own techniques. Take clues for creative techniques from the story. Some stories lend themselves to the use of puppets, others are perfect for the felt-board, and still others can be worked up as chalk talks.

Felt-boards are a popular and important tool in a classroom. You can make characters or purchase them commercially. Prepare your own with construction paper covered with clear contact or laminate. Attach strips of felt or sandpaper to the backs of the cutouts so they cling to the felt-board. Stories that lend themselves to felt-board retelling are those with a limited number of characters who appear throughout the story—*Ask Mr. Bear* (Flack, 1932), for example, or *Caps for Sale* (Slobodkina, 1947).

Prop stories are quite easy to develop. Simply collect stuffed animals, toys, and other articles that represent characters and objects in a story. Display the props at appropriate times during the storytelling. Three stuffed bears and a yellow-haired doll aid in telling *Goldilocks and the Three Bears* (Izawa, 1968a), several toy trains in *The Little Engine That Could* (Piper, 1954).

Stories strong in dialogue are best suited to the use of **puppets.** There are many kinds of puppets, including finger, hand, stick, and face puppets. Shy children often feel secure telling stories with puppets. Such stories as *The Gingerbread Boy* (Holdsworth, 1968) and *The Little Red Hen* (Izawa, 1968b) are appropriately told with puppets because they are short, have few characters, and repeat dialogue.

Another technique that attracts the listener is the **chalk talk.** The storyteller draws the story while telling it. Chalk talks are most effective when done with a large chalkboard so that the story can keep going in sequence from beginning to end. The same technique can be carried out on mural paper hung across a wall. The storyteller simply uses crayons or felt-tip markers instead of chalk. The chalk talk technique can also be adapted to easel and chart paper or an overhead projector. Choose a story with simple illustrations. Draw only a select few pictures as you tell the story. There are stories that have been written as chalk talks, including an entire series, *Harold and the Purple Crayon* (Johnson, 1955).

Sound-story techniques allow both audience and storyteller to provide sound effects when they are called for in a plot. The sounds can be made with voices, rhythm instruments, or music. When preparing to tell such a story, first select those parts of the story for which sound effects will be used. Then decide on each sound to be made and who will make it. As the story is told, students and storyteller chime in with their assigned sounds. Record the presentation, then leave the recording in the literacy center with the original book. Among books that adapt easily to sound-story techniques are *The Noisy Book* (Brown, 1939), *Too Much Noise* (McGovern, 1967), and *Mr. Brown Can Moo: Can You?* (Seuss, 1970).

Other creative techniques, plus the opportunity to create your own, offer endless possibilities for storytelling (Morrow, 1981). By serving as a model of creative storytelling, you can excite children about literature and motivate them to try their own creative storytelling as well.

I had the opportunity to work with several first- and second-grade teachers concerning sharing literature with children in pleasurable ways. The teachers practiced reading and telling stories and made manipulatives for storytelling to use in their classrooms. These teachers incorporated many of the strategies discussed earlier and one of them commented about their use:

> *The children enjoy being read to and they never grow tired of this activity. I thought that in second grade, reading to youngsters was not that important anymore; however, the benefits of read aloud sessions became quite evident as I involved my children in them more and more. The stories generated sophisticated discussion; we'd relate them to the students' own life experiences. We discussed authors, illustrations, and elements of story structure. Through these story readings and discussions, I found that my students seemed to appreciate literature more, they became more aware of the different genres of children's literature that exist, and vocabulary and comprehension were enhanced as well. I realized how important it was for me to model reading to children and in many different ways. I read using felt characters, roll movies, chalk talks, and so on. I learned how to make reading more appealing for the children. Consequently I saw an increased desire in my children to read as they modeled my behavior in reading stories I had read to them and using the storytelling props.*

Second graders who participated in the program were asked what they learned and liked. They commented:

I like it when the teacher reads to you. . . . She uses such good expression, you can learn to read better yourself by listening to her. . . . The teacher reads and tells stories in many different ways so it is always interesting, and you can learn to do it the way she does. . . . You learn about authors and illustrators and that they are people like you and you think that you could be one.

One day during a story reading session in a second-grade class with a focus on making comparisons between styles of illustrators, Ms. Payton told the children that she was going to read two picture storybooks that they had heard before. She asked the children to concentrate on the pictures or illustrations as she read the stories, to note their styles so they could describe them. After the stories were read, she asked if the children thought that the books were illustrated by the same individual. They all said no because they looked very different. Ms. Payton identified the illustrators of the books who were also the authors, Ezra Jack Keats for *Peter's Chair* and Dr. Seuss for *Green Eggs and Ham.* Then she asked the children to describe the illustrations for each book.

Tamika said, "Well in *Peter's Chair* the illustrations look like a painting. They are made like they are real. I think that Ezra Jack Keats is a very good drawer, I like the colors he uses."

Ms. Payton went on to explain that not only does Mr. Keats paint his pictures but he uses collage as a technique as well. When you look closely at his illustrations, you see bits of wallpaper, newspaper, doilies and so on blended into his pictures.

Ms. Payton asked if someone would like to describe the style of the other book. Marcel raised his hand.

He said, "Dr. Seuss is very different from Keats; he uses lots of lines and sort of fantasy little shapes. He uses colors on people and things that aren't what we usually expect. His drawings look like cartoons and the other ones look like real things."

The discussion was followed by the children's illustrating stories they had written. They were told that their illustrations could be their own original styles or that if they wished they could use the style of an illustrator in a storybook that they knew. Ms. Payton walked around to talk about the work the children were doing. Magda decided to make her drawings similar to those of Dr. Seuss and Ms. Payton said to her, "Magda, if Dr. Seuss came through our door he would think that he illustrated your story, your work looks so much like his."

Magda is a child with limited English proficiency. The positive reinforcement in this situation started a conversation about her work with the teacher.

Independent Reading and Writing Period

Once the environment, materials, and activities are designed and implemented to draw children to literature, the children need time to look at books and become immersed in literature independently during the school day. In the past, such periods have been called *sustained silent reading (SSR)*.

Sustained silent reading has generally been defined as quiet time, with little socialization and little student choice beyond selection of the particular book the child chooses to read. If we expect them to become interested in reading, young children (and perhaps older children as well) require more options and greater flexibility than have been characteristic of SSR periods. Setting aside fifteen to thirty minutes three to five times a week for looking at books as well as for engaging in other activities related to literature allows the variety, free choice, social interaction, and flexibility children need if they are to be enticed into voluntary reading. Research has indicated that children of different ability levels worked together during independent reading and writing periods. It was also found that although many options were available, including felt-boards, roll movies, and taped stories, 70 percent of the free-choice activities selected by children involved the reading of books. Other materials and options attract children into a free-choice literacy area, but they lead children to choose books (Morrow & Weinstein, 1982, 1986).

Here are some ways you can help children function effectively during independent reading and writing periods:

1. Introduce the materials in the literacy center to the children. You might do so by drawing on different materials for each day's lesson, then placing those materials in the literacy center for the children's further use.
2. Discuss the care of the books and other materials and indicate where everything belongs so that children can find and return whatever they want. Instill the Montessori concept of building respect for the materials (Morrison, 1984).

3. Ask children to decide beforehand what they will do during each independent reading and writing period. Let children change activities, but only after they have replaced materials they have already been using.
4. Allow children to work alone or with other children, and let them take materials out of the literacy center to other parts of the room if they want.
5. Point out that the independent reading and writing period is generally a quiet time because some classmates are reading and looking at books or listening to stories, but that quiet talk and some movement are okay.
6. All manipulatives should have books associated with them that the children should use.
7. Although there are choices and the materials encourage active involvement, on-task behavior is the goal.

These rules are based on Montessori's instructional procedures. Children as young as two are able to assimilate them and work well within the structure they establish. The rules allow freedom of choice in activities while defining limits for working with materials.

When children first begin to participate in independent reading and writing periods, it is the teacher's responsibility to circulate among them to see what they are doing and to help them become involved, if help is needed. Once the children have become familiar with the procedures and can work independently, the teacher can also participate directly in independent reading and writing activities. It is most desirable for teachers to model behavior by reading and writing themselves. The independent reading and writing period exposes children to reading in many forms and gives them the opportunity to make choices. It is a positive approach toward activating interest in voluntary reading. Because of the choice, there seems to be something for everyone, even children with different ability levels and children with special needs.

I visit classrooms on a regular basis and work with teachers who are implementing some of the strategies discussed in this book. Mrs. Oman has a second-grade class in an inner-city district, and I visited her room the last day of school to say good-bye to the children I had grown to know so well. Mrs. Oman and I shared a sense of pride while observing the children in their last independent reading and writing period for that year. We saw some children curled up on a rug or leaning on pillows in the literacy center with books they had selected themselves. Louis and Ramon were squeezed tightly into a rocking chair, sharing a book. Marcel, Patrick, and Roseangela snuggled under a shelf—a "private spot" filled with stuffed animals. They took turns reading.

Tesha and Tiffany were on the floor with a felt-board and character cutouts from *The Gingerbread Boy*, alternately reading and manipulating the figures: "Run, run as fast as you can! You can't catch me, I'm the Gingerbread Man!"

Four children listened on headsets to tapes of Maurice Sendak's *Pierre*, each child holding a copy of the book and chanting along with the narrator, "I don't care, I don't care." Yassin and Shawni were writing a story together and bouncing ideas back and forth.

Tyrone had a Big Book and gave several other children copies of the same story in smaller format. Role-playing a teacher, he read to the others, occasionally stopping to ask who would like to read.

Leon asked Tamaika if she would like to hear a story he had written. She agreed and he read it to her. When he finished, she suggested acting out Leon's story with puppets, which they did. Throughout the dramatization, Leon behaved like the director of a play. He knew his story and his characters and wanted them to act in a manner that reflected his intent.

Much of the information discussed here represents the results of studies that involved classroom observation and intervention in kindergarten through second grade. Children in these classrooms participated in literacy programs that included activities that have been described in this chapter. These youngsters scored significantly better on tests of reading comprehension, the ability to retell and rewrite stories, and the ability to create original oral and written stories by including elements of story structure than children in classrooms that did not participate in the program. Children in the treatment rooms also showed significant improvement in use of vocabulary and language complexity (Morrow, 1990; Morrow, O'Connor, & Smith, 1990).

Teachers and children were interviewed to determine their attitudes toward the independent reading and writing period and the program in general. Teachers commented that the children particularly like the independent reading and writing periods because they were able to:

- Choose activities they want to do
- Choose the books they want to read
- Choose to work alone or with others
- Choose manipulatives such as puppets and roll movies

Headsets with taped stories and the accompanying storybooks provide a good reading model for children.

Teachers also said that children enjoyed the independent reading and writing period because everyone participated, and there were few discipline problems.

During independent reading and writing periods, children may choose to tell a roll movie story or a felt-board story. All activities are literature-related and are accompanied by the original book.

Teachers said that children learned the following in the program:

- To work together and cooperate with each other
- To be independent and make decisions

- A sense of story structure from the stories they listened to and read, improved comprehension, and vocabulary development
- An appreciation for books and knowledge of different genres of children's literature
- The names of authors and illustrators and an increase in their general knowledge from the amount of reading being done
- That their peers could teach them and were willing to do so
- To like to read and write

By participating in the program teachers said they learned that:

- The social family atmosphere created by the independent reading and writing period was conducive to learning.
- Children are capable of cooperating and collaborating independently in reading and writing activities and learning from each other.
- When there was choice of activity and person to work with, children of all ability levels chose to work together.
- There was something for everyone in this program, advanced and slower children alike.
- The program made me more flexible and spontaneous and a facilitator of learning rather than always a teacher.
- Children who don't readily participate in reading and writing did so during independent reading and writing. I think it is because they are the ones making the decisions about what they do.

In the student interviews, children were asked what they learned in the literature program, and they answered:

- You learn that reading can be fun.
- You learn to read and write better because you read a lot and you read real books.
- You learn to understand what you are reading and you learn a lot of new words.
- You get to learn how to read better if you don't read real good because kids who know how to read good help you.
- You learn about authors and illustrators and that they are people like you and you think that you could be one.

What do you like about the literature program?

- It makes you want to read; it's fun and makes you feel happy.
- You can choose what you want to read, like long books or short books, or hard books or easy books.
- You can write stories.
- You can do felt stories, tape stories, chalk talks, and roll movies, which are all fun, and they have books with them too.
- During independent reading and writing, the teacher reads to you, and she never does in regular reading.
- During the literature program, the teacher talks to you one at a time like a friend; in regular reading she talks to you all together.

It became apparent when speaking with teachers that children's special needs were attended to in this program. Mrs. Bell described an incident about a child who went to the resource room daily, because her reading skills were far below grade level. According to Mrs. Bell, Charlene never read aloud. One day Mrs. Bell noticed her reading aloud to a rag doll as she sat in the rocking chair. Mrs. Bell offered positive reinforcement to Charlene, and the reading aloud continued daily during independent reading and writing.

Mrs. Meechem described another situation with a bilingual youngster who had limited ability in English. This child would not speak in class at all. During an independent reading and writing period, Mrs. Meechem observed Tasha acting as a teacher with a group of children she had organized. She had each one taking turns reading.

Marcel was a gifted child in a classroom with mostly low achievers. He was alone all the time. About two months after independent reading and writing was initiated in his classroom, he found himself able to participate with other children in literacy activities. The first time I observed him with others, he was reading the newspaper and checking out the weather in other parts of the country. Patrick asked Marcel if he could look too. Marcel was pleased and then David joined them. Together they read and discussed how hot and cold it was in Florida, Colorado, and so on.

There were numerous anecdotes from the independent reading and writing period describing how children were able to find a way to participate in spite of special problems. One teacher commented, "There seems to be something that every child can find to do during independent reading and writing and do it well."

The recommendations in this chapter for developing positive attitudes toward reading incorporate Holdaway's (1979) developmental approach to literacy. This approach highlights less teaching and more learning, learning that is self-regulated rather than regulated by adults. It has been suggested here that the teacher provide an environment rich with materials and activities from which children are invited to select, plus a social context in which children are actively involved with other children, with the teacher, and with materials. The environment is emulative rather than instructional, providing lively examples of reading skills in action. Teachers present themselves as models involved in literary activities. They serve as sources of support and positive reinforcement for appropriate behavior patterns in the child. Through regularly scheduled literary activities and ready access to attractive and comfortable classroom literacy centers stocked with books and materials that inspire interest and active participation, children associate reading with pleasure and develop an appreciation for books. Given time to use the literacy center and participate in independent reading and writing activities, children reinforce their learning of skills through enjoyable, self-selected practice. The outcome can only be children who not only learn to read, but who choose to read voluntarily.

Portfolio Assessment of Children's Attitudes Toward Books

Direct observation of children's behavior while they are listening to stories, reading, or looking at books independently is probably the most effective method for assessing their attitude toward books. How much attention do they give to the books they are looking at or reading? Do they simply browse? Do they flip through the pages quickly, paying little attention to print or pictures? Do they silently study the text, sustaining attention to pictures and print throughout (Martinez & Teale, 1988)? The teacher should also note how frequently children select looking at books when faced with other options. In occasional interviews with individual children, asking what they like to do best in school and at home might reveal interest in reading. During conferences, ask parents if their children voluntarily look at books or pay close attention when they are read to. At the same time, ask parents how often

**Checklist for Assessing Attitudes Toward Reading
and Amount of Voluntary Reading**

	Always	*Sometimes*	*Never*
Voluntarily looks at or reads books			
Asks to be read to			
Listens attentively while being read to			
Responds with questions and comments to stories read to him or her			
Takes books home to read			
Reads voluntarily at home			

they read to their children. Gather facts about the home literacy environment that will help you understand the child's attitude toward books.

AN IDEA FOR THE CLASSROOM

I created the following experience when I was teaching children in a mixed-age grouping primary classroom. You may find this idea useful for your teaching.

I wanted to introduce my children to the use of the felt-board as a means for retelling stories and creating their own original stories with characters. I selected a story that was easy to illustrate, had a theme that would generate conversation, and encouraged the opportunity to write additional episodes for it. The name of the story was A Bunny Called Nat, *an anonymous tale that I found in a resource book many years ago. The story is about "a bunny named Nat, who was funny and fat, and he could change his color, just like that." This was the repetitive rhyme in the story and at the end of the rhyme, fingers are snapped. The bunny in the story is a gray bunny who doesn't like his color because it is so plain. He is able to change his color and each time he does, he has an unpleasant adventure. For example, Nat changed himself to blue and when he was blue he was blue like the water and blue like the sky. He went down to the pond to admire his reflection in the water. He bent over so far while looking that he fell into the pond and he couldn't swim. He yelled for help, but no one could see him because he was blue like the water. Luckily a turtle came by and pulled him out. Nat said, "Not much fun being blue, but, I'm a bunny named Nat, I'm funny and fat, and I can change my color, just like that." After trying out four different colors, Nat realizes that it's not so bad being just what he was and that's the way he stayed.*

When I introduce the story to the children, I ask them to listen for the different colors that Nat becomes and the problems he faces each time. I then tell the story, using the different colored bunny characters on the felt-board to help. When the story is over we discuss Nat and his different colors. We also discuss the ending of the story and its meaning, trying to relate it to the experiences of the children. We discuss if they ever wanted to be anyone other than themselves and why and would it really be better.

After the discussion, I ask the children to think of another color that Nat could become with an adventure attached to it as in the real story. I then ask them to write their story and draw and color a bunny to add to the felt story we already have. The bunnies are made of construction paper and felt strips are glued onto the back to make them stick to the felt-board.

Seven-year-old Lindsey wrote the following:

"I'm a bunny named Nat, I'm funny and fat, and I can change my color just like that." And suddenly Nat was a red bunny. Red like an apple, red like a cherry, and red like a fire truck. Suddenly a group of bees was coming. They saw Nat in the red color and they were thinking that Nat was an apple. The group of bees was going where Nat was sitting, they wanted to eat him. Then Nat saw the bees. He ran and ran but the bees followed him. So he said as he ran, "Being red is not so good, but I'm a bunny called Nat, I am sassy and fat, and I can change my color, just like that."

In this activity, children were given the opportunity to participate in a pleasurable experience with literature. They were actively involved in the discussion and the creation of a story, using the one below as a model. The underlying theme of this story concerning one's self-image is an important topic for conversation and can help children understand each other's strengths, weaknesses, and special needs.

The story of A Bunny Named Nat *and a pattern for the bunny follow:*

SAMPLE FELT-BOARD STORY

A Bunny Called Nat

(adapted version of an anonymous tale)

(As the story is being told, hold up and then place a new colored bunny on the felt-board as each bunny is named.)

Materials—*Five bunny characters drawn the same but in the following colors: gray, blue, green, yellow, and orange. The bunny pattern is found at the end of the story.*

Once upon a time there was a little gray rabbit and his name was Nat. One day he looked around and saw that all his brothers and sisters, cousins and friends were gray, too. He thought he would like to be different from them. So he said:

> I'm a bunny called Nat,
> I'm funny and fat,
> And I can change my color
> Just like that. (Snap your fingers.)

And suddenly Nat was a blue bunny. He was blue like the sky and blue like the sea. He was blue like the twilight and blue like the dawn. It felt nice and cool to be blue. He decided to take a look at himself in the pond. He hurried to the edge and admired his reflection in the water. He leaned over so far that SPLASH! he fell into the pond. Nat fell deep into the blue water and he couldn't swim. He was frightened. He called for help. His friends heard him, but when they came to the pond they couldn't see him because he was blue just like the water. Fortunately a turtle swam by and helped Nat get safely to shore. Nat thanked the turtle. He decided that he didn't like being blue. So he said:

> I'm a bunny called Nat,
> I'm funny and fat,
> And I can change my color
> Just like that. (Snap your fingers.)

*And this time, what color did he change himself
to? Yes, he was yellow—yellow like the sun, yellow like
a daffodil, yellow like a canary bird. Yellow seemed
like such a happy color to be. He was very proud of his
new color, and he decided to take a walk through the
jungle. Who do you think he met in the jungle? He met
his cousins the lion and the tiger. The lion and the tiger
looked at Nat's yellow fur and said, "What are you
doing in that yellow coat? We are the only animals in
this jungle that are supposed to be yellow." And they
growled so fiercely that Nat the bunny was frightened
and he ran all the way home. He said:*

> *I'm a bunny called Nat,*
> *I'm funny and fat,*
> *And I can change my color*
> *Just like that. (Snap your fingers.)*

*And this time what did he change his color to?
Yes, he was green. He was green like the grass and
green like the leaves of the trees. He was green like a
grasshopper and green like the meadow. As a green
bunny, Nat thought he'd be the envy of all the other
bunnies. He wanted to play with his other bunny
friends in the meadow. Since he was the color of the
grass in the meadow, he could not be seen and his
friends just ran and jumped about him not seeing him
at all or mistaking him for a grasshopper. So Nat the
bunny had no one to play with while he was green.
Being green wasn't much fun. So he said:*

> *I'm a bunny called Nat,*
> *I'm funny and fat,*
> *And I can change my color*
> *Just like that. (Snap your fingers.)*

*And what color was he then? Right, he was or-
ange. He was orange like a carrot, orange like a sun-
set, orange like a pumpkin—he was the brightest color
of all. He decided he would go out and play with all his
brothers and sisters and friends. But what do you
suppose happened? When his friends saw him, they
all stopped playing and started to laugh, "Ha-ha, who-
ever heard of an orange bunny?" No one wanted to
play with him. He didn't want to be orange anymore.
He didn't want to be a blue bunny because if he fell
into the pond no one could see him to save him. He*

didn't want to be a yellow bunny and be frightened by the lion and the tiger. He didn't want to be a green bunny because then he was just like the meadow and none of his friends could see him. And so he said:

> *I'm a bunny called Nat,*
> *I'm funny and fat,*
> *And I can change my color*
> *Just like that. (Snap your fingers.)*

Do you know what color Nat the bunny changed himself into this time? Yes, you're right. He changed himself back to gray. And now that he was gray all of his friends played with him. No one growled or laughed at him. He was gray like a rain cloud, gray like an elephant, gray like pussy willows. It felt warm and comfortable being gray. From that time on, Nat the bunny was always happy being a gray bunny, and he decided that it's really best being just what you are.

ACTIVITIES AND QUESTIONS

1. Answer the focus questions at the beginning of the chapter.

2. Select a piece of children's literature and choose a creative storytelling technique that seems appropriate for the story

(e.g., felt characters, chalk talk, sound story, etc.). Create materials for the story and tell it to a group of children or to your peers. Evaluate your performance according to the criteria for storytelling discussed in the chapter.

3. Evaluate the literacy center in an early childhood classroom. List all the characteristics of the center that reflect criteria described in this chapter. List items that need to be included.

4. Observe in an early childhood classroom on three different occasions. List all the literacy activities carried out by the teacher that you believe contribute to developing positive attitudes toward reading.

5. Continue your portfolio assessment for the child you selected to assess for language development in Chapter 3. Observe the child using the assessment checklist provided in this chapter concerning the evaluation of his or her attitudes toward reading and voluntary reading behavior.

6. Continue the thematic unit that you began in Chapter 3. Select three objectives for building positive attitudes toward reading and describe three activities using your theme that will satisfy each of the objectives.

Case Study Activity

Refer back to "An Idea for the Classroom." Read it again and describe how you think it is enhancing children's interest in books. How has the activity made accommodations for children with special needs? What special needs could apply here?

CHAPTER SIX

Developing Concepts about Books and Comprehension of Text

QUESTIONS TO FOCUS ON AS YOU READ THE CHAPTER

- What are the concepts about books that are important for young children to know?
- What experiences enhance a child's concepts about books?
- What are the objectives for comprehension development for young children?
- Define the following: directed listening and thinking activity, directed reading and thinking activity, shared book experiences, repeated storybook readings, story retellings, mapping, and webbing.
- List and define the structural elements in a good story.
- Define what is meant by comprehending materials in a literal, interpretive, and critical manner.

*Few children learn to love books themselves. Someone must
lure them into the wonderful world of the written word, someone must show them the way.*

—ORVILLE PRESCOTT
A Father Reads to His Child

For several months, Mrs. Johnson has been discussing different authors and illustrators with the children in her first-grade
class. The class has a chart on which their favorite authors and
illustrators are listed. Today she asked them to add names to the
list because they had recently read stories by authors and illustrators who were new to them. First she asked for authors and the
following names were generated: Ezra Jack Keats, Leo Lionni,
Robert McClosky, and Arnold Lobel. Next she asked if they could
name some illustrators, and the following names were mentioned
and written next to the authors: Maurice Sendak, Dr. Seuss, Eric
Carle, and Crockett Johnson. Jamie raised her hand and said,
"Hey something weird just happened. I noticed that all of the
authors named are also illustrators and all of the illustrators are
all authors too." Christopher raised his hand and said, "That's not
so weird, I know a bunch of people who are authors and illustrators at the same time. There's me, and Josh, Jennifer, and Patrick." Christopher was looking around the room and naming all
the children in the class. When he finished naming his classmates, he continued, "We're all authors and illustrators. We all
write books and illustrate them. They are published and they are
in our classroom library. How could we forget that?"

Investigators have found a number of instructional strategies
that nurture children's concepts about books and help them to
comprehend text. Those practices include children's role-playing,
retelling, and reconstructing with pictures stories that have been
read to them. They also include discussions concerning the parts
of books, how to handle books, and who authors and illustrators
are. The active involvement of children in experiences with literature enhances their comprehension of stories, their sense of story
structure, and their language development. Through experiences
with literature, young children integrate information and learn the
relationships among a story's various parts (Brown, 1975; Morrow, 1985b; Pellegrini & Galda, 1982). The fact that interactive
behavior plays a leading role in such learning seems to reinforce
a model of generative learning: the reader or listener understands
prose by actively engaging in construction of and relationships

with the textual information he or she hears or reads (Linden & Wittrock, 1981; Wittrock, 1974, 1981).

Teale (1984) has utilized Vygotsky's (1978) definition of higher mental functions as internalized social relationships and applied it to literacy. Literacy develops, according to Teale, from children's interactions with others in specific environments of which reading and writing are a part. Holdaway's (1979) model of developmental teaching, derived from observations of middle-class homes, indicates that a child benefits when early experiences with storybooks are mediated by an interactive adult who provides problem-solving situations. The child is asked to respond and the adult offers information when necessary. In such situations, children and adults interact to integrate, construct, and make relationships with printed text. The strategies to be described in this chapter follow the theory, research, and models just outlined.

Activities That Develop Concepts about Books and Comprehension of Text

The many benefits of reading to children have been discussed throughout this volume. Strategies for reading to infants and toddlers that are applicable in the home and in day-care centers have been described, as have techniques for reading stories to children that will arouse their interest and entice them to books. The following sections suggest strategies for using children's literature to develop children's concepts about books and the meanings to be found in books.

Activities That Emphasize Concepts about Books

A child who has a good concept of books:

1. Knows that a book is for reading
2. Can identify the front and the back of a book as well as the top and the bottom
3. Can turn the pages of a book properly
4. Knows the difference between print and pictures
5. Knows that pictures on a page are related to what the print says
6. Knows where one begins reading on a page
7. Knows what a title is

8. Knows what an author is
9. Knows what an illustrator is

Adults take such concepts for granted. To many two- to-six-year-olds, however, those concepts are totally unfamiliar. To help children master them, point them out at every opportunity when you read to children. You can introduce a story reading, for instance, by pointing appropriately as you say, "The title of the story that I'm going to read is *Mr. Rabbit and the Lovely Present* [Zolotow, 1962]. This is the title on the front of the book. The author of the book, the person who wrote it, is Charlotte Zolotow. Here is her name. And the illustrator, the person who drew the pictures, is Maurice Sendak. Here is his name. All books have titles and authors, and if they have pictures they also have illustrators. The next time you look at a book, see if you can find the title. It is always on the front cover."

The repetition of such dialogue familiarizes a child with the concepts, which they assimilate easily. Similar dialogues explain other concepts. Point to a picture, then to print. Identify each, then ask, "Which do we read, the picture or the print?" As you get ready to read to them, ask children to point out the top and bottom of the book, the title, and where you should begin reading on a page. Not only will you give the children the opportunity to learn the concepts, you can at the same time determine which children have the concept and which need help. These activities and dialogues can be carried out during story readings to small groups or to individual students. A child's independent exploration of books will reinforce what the teacher has pointed out or explained.

Big Books have become an important part of early literacy instruction. They are oversized picture storybooks that measure from 14 × 20 inches up to 24 × 30 inches. Holdaway (1979) suggested that the enlarged print and pictures in these books help to get children involved with concepts about books, print, and the meaning of text. Big Books are appropriate from preschool through third grade, and because they are used mostly in small to large group situations, active involvement by the group is encouraged. When using a Big Book, a teacher places it on a stand because it is hard to handle otherwise. An easel is usually used for a Big Book stand and makes the print and pictures visible for the children. Class Big Books can be made as well as purchased. When they are made, children become even more aware of book concepts because they are engaged in creating a book. Box 6–1 provides directions for making a Big Book.

Children learn concepts about books when they are read to by adults who point out features such as the print and the pictures.

Children learn concepts about books by interacting with other children as they browse through the pictures and by looking at books themselves.

Big Books are quite effective for developing concepts about books mainly because of their size. As the teacher reads the book and tracks the print from left to right across the page, children see

---

BOX 6–1 · *Instructions for Making a Big Book*

Materials

- 2 pieces of oak tag for the cover (14 × 20 to 20 × 30)
- 10 pieces or more of tagboard or newsprint the same size as the oak tag used for the cover to be used for the pages in the book
- 6 looseleaf rings (1 1/4 ")
- Holepunch

Directions

- Punch three sets of holes in top, middle, and bottom of the cover and paper that is to go inside of the book.
- Insert a looseleaf ring in each hole. The Big Book should have a minimum of ten pages.
- Print should be 1 1/2 to 2 inches high

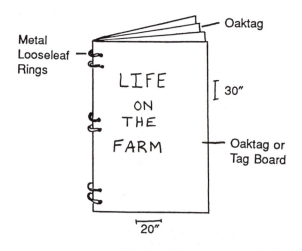

---

that books are for reading and where one begins to read on a page. They also learn to differentiate the print from the pictures. The connection is made that the oral language they hear from their teacher is being read from the print on the page in the book. The correct way to turn pages is easy to see with Big Books because they are so enlarged. The title of the book is prominently displayed on the front of the book and on the title page, as is the name of the author and illustrator.

In addition to using the Big Book to emphasize the concepts of author and illustrator, feature different authors and illustrators on a special bulletin board or in book displays. Carry out discussions about their work. Don't forget to refer to the children in your class as authors and illustrators as they write stories and draw pictures about text.

In Mrs. Johnson's room, children are encouraged always to read the title of a book and the name of the author and illustrator prior to starting to read the text. One day during an independent reading and writing period, Jonathan placed the Big Book *Chicken Soup with Rice*, on the Big Book stand. He had gathered three children to sit in front of him to read to. He started by saying, "The title of the book I'm going to read is *Chicken Soup with Rice*." He turned the first page and began reading the text. Patrick popped up and said, "Jonathan, you can't read the book yet; you forgot to read who the author and illustrator are." Jonathan pounded his fist to his forehead, looked somewhat annoyed with himself, and said, "How could I forget that. Let's see, the author of this book is Maurice Sendak and he is the illustrator too."

Understanding what is read, or comprehending text, is one of the major goals for reading instruction. The English poet Samuel Taylor Coleridge wrote the following short piece entitled *On Reading Comprehension*:

> There are four kinds of readers. The first is like an hour glass, and their reading being as the sand, it runs out, and leaves not a vestige behind. A second is like the sponge, which imbibes everything and returns it in nearly the same state, only a little dirtier. The third is like a jelly bag, allowing all that is pure to pass away, and retaining only the refuse and drugs. And the fourth is like the workers in the diamond mines of Colconda, who cast aside all that is worthless and retain only pure gems.

How do we get children to cast aside unnecessary information and retain only the pure gems when reading or listening to a passage?

Recent definitions of comprehension emphasize that it is an active process. In this process, the reader or listener interprets and constructs meaning about what he or she reads or listens to based on what he or she already knows about the topic, thereby making connections between the old and the new (Pearson & Johnson, 1978). This concept arises from research on schema theory that suggests that we have a schemata (background knowledge) for certain information based on prior experience with a given topic. That schemata is never complete because more can always be learned about a subject. For example, if someone told us something about the circus that would give us one bit of information, if we saw pictures of the circus we would have additional information, and if we went to see the circus we would have even more. Then when we read about the circus or listen to a story about it, the new information would expand and refine what we already know. Comprehension of a story that is read or listened to involves a child's integration of his or her prior knowledge concerning a topic with the new text to create new knowledge (Johnston & Pearson, 1982). With that background, we can begin to discuss objectives and activities for the development of comprehension.

Activities That Develop Comprehension of Text

A child is developing comprehension of text when he or she:

1. Attempts to read well-known storybooks that results in the telling of a well-formed story
2. Participates in story reading by saying words and narrating stories as the teacher reads to him or her
3. Retells a story without the help of the book
4. Includes elements of story structure in story retellings: setting (beginning, time, place, characters), theme (main character's problem or goal), plot episodes (events leading toward a solution of the main character's problem or attainment of his or her goal), resolution (problem solution, goal achievement, ending)
5. Responds to text after reading or listening with literal questions and comments about details, sequence, main idea, and following directions
6. Responds to text after reading or listening with interpretive questions and comments that predict outcomes, infer feelings and ideas, and recognize cause and effect
7. Responds to text after reading or listening with critical questions and comments that analyze information; draw conclusions; distinguish fact, fantasy, and opinion; and apply information
8. Uses reference materials such as the dictionary, encyclopedia, and magazines to find information; uses study aids in materials such as the table of contents, the index, titles, subtitles, charts, and so on

Children's Literature as a Source for Developing Comprehension and Concepts about Books

Children's literature is especially appropriate for developing a child's sense that print conveys meaning. The stories are attractive; they relate well to a child's real-life experiences; and they are typically well structured, containing clearly delineated settings, themes, plot episodes, and resolutions. Furthermore, the use of children's literature offers ample opportunity for developing such traditional comprehension skills as literal, inferential, and critical thinking. Children exhibit literal understanding when they recall details of a story, recognize its sequences and the main idea, or follow directions. Inferential and critical skills enable a child to recognize cause and effect, predict outcomes, make associations, relate story episodes to life experiences, analyze information, make generalizations, and apply information.

Children's literature is particularly appropriate for first experiences with books because it is likely that youngsters have had some exposure to this material. The following pages will discuss strategies for comprehension development, which also include learning concepts about books and print. In these activities, children play active roles as they respond to literature in many different ways. I begin with an early experience for the emergent reader and continue with experiences that are appropriate for the emergent as well as the conventional reader.

Favorite Storybook Readings

To study emergent reading behaviors, Sulzby (1985) observed children from ages two to six attempt to read favorite storybooks. Although they were not yet readers in the conventional sense, the children were asked, "Read me your book." Sulzby found that in their "reading," the children produced speech that could indeed be categorized as a first act of reading; that the speech they used as they "read" was clearly different in structure and intonation from their typical conversation; and that different developmental levels could be observed in these "oral readings." Sulzby's Simplified Classifications Scheme for Children's Emergent Reading of Favorite Storybooks follows (Sulzby, 1987; adapted by permission):

1. *Attending to pictures but not forming stories.* The child "reads" by labeling and commenting on the pictures in the book but does not "weave a story" across the pages.

2. *Attending to pictures and forming oral stories.* The child "reads" by following the pictures but weaves a story across the pages through wording and intonation like those of someone telling a story. Often, however, the listener too must see the pictures in order to understand the story the child is "reading."

3. *Attending to a mix of pictures, reading, and storytelling.* The child "reads" by looking at the pictures. The majority of the child's "reading" fluctuates between the oral intonation of a storyteller and that of a reader.

4. *Attending to pictures but forming written stories.* The child "reads" by looking at the pictures. The child's speech sounds like reading, both in wording and intonation. The listener rarely needs to see the pictures in order to understand the story. With his or her eyes closed, the listener would think the child was reading print. The "reading" is similar to the story in print and sometimes follows it verbatim.

5. *Attending to print.* This category has four divisions: (a) exploring the print, as evident in such strategies as refusing to read for print-related reasons; (b) using only some of the aspects of print; (c) reading with imbalanced strategies; and (d) reading independently, or "real" reading.

From children's attempts at storybook reading, then, we can determine stages of development. Because the activity is developmental and leads to literacy, teachers should ask children to participate in it, either to evaluate their ability or simply to encourage their emergent literacy.

Directed Listening-Thinking and Reading-Thinking Activities

When children read themselves or are read to, there should always be a purpose, in addition to pleasure, that complements content-area learning or develops specific concepts about books. The format of the directed listening-thinking activity (DLTA) and the directed reading-thinking activity (DRTA) can be internalized with frequent use by the child and transferred when new material is presented (Anderson, Mason, & Shirley, 1984; Morrow, 1984; Stauffer, 1980). Whatever a DLTA's or DRTA's specific objective, its framework offers the listener or reader a direction and strategy for organizing and retrieving information from the text. In the following outline for *The Little Red Hen* (Izawa, 1968b), there are two main objectives: to emphasize the sequence of events and to involve children in making inferences and judgments from the text. The following outline follows a DLTA or DRTA format. With the DLTA, the child listens to the story; with the DRTA, the child reads the story.

A. *Prepare for listening or reading with prequestions and discussion.*

1. Build a background by introducing the story: "Today I'm going to read a story (or, you will be reading a story) entitled *The Little Red Hen.* Let's look at the pictures to see if you can tell what the story is going to be about." Encourage children to respond as the pages of the book are turned. After they have offered their ideas say, "The story is about a hen who wants to bake some bread and asks her friends for some help."

2. Ask prequestions that build additional background that sets a purpose for listening or reading. Relate the questions to real-life experiences whenever possible: "Have you ever asked people for help? What kind of help? Did they help you? Has anyone ever asked you for help? What kind of help? Were you able to help the person? How? While I'm reading (or, while you are reading), try to decide if you think the little red hen did the right thing with her bread at the end of the story, and why. Try also to remember what happened first, second, third, and at the end of the story."

3. When the children have gained enough experience with your prequestions, you can ask them to think of their own: "Now that I've told you a little about the story, what do you want to find out when I read it to you (or, when you read it)?" When prequestioning, show the pictures in the book to the children as further preparation for their listening or reading.

B. *Reading the Story.*

1. Be sure to show the children the pictures as you read the story. Stop a few times for reactions, comments, or questions from the children. If the children are reading the story, remind them to

study the pictures. Model or scaffold responses to guide them in their thinking, keeping in mind the objectives for this particular DLTA or DRTA: "Can you remember what help the little red hen has asked for so far? How have the other animals acted about giving help?" If the children do not respond, scaffold or model responses by changing questions to statements: "These animals aren't very helpful to the little red hen. Each time the hen asks for their help, the animals all answer, 'Not I.'" Also ask for children's predictions of what will happen next. If the children are reading silently, assign stopping points for discussion. If there is oral reading, only stop in a few places.

C. *Have a discussion after reading.*

1. The postdiscussion should be guided by the objectives set for listening and reading: "What did the little red hen want help with first? second? and so on." Ask children to retell the story; retelling will demonstrate their knowledge of sequence. Allow children to use the pictures in the book to help them follow sequence. Finally, focus on the second goal, making inferences and judgments: "What would you have done if you were the little red hen? What lesson can we learn from this story?"

A DLTA or DRTA can have many different objectives. The framework, however, is always basically the same: (1) preparation for listening or reading—prequestions and discussion; (2) reading the story; and (3) discussion after the reading. All three steps are focused on the DLTA's or DRTA's specific objectives. A DLTA or DRTA can focus on literal responses (such as recall of facts and sequencing), inferential responses (such as interpreting characters' feelings, predicting outcomes, and relating the story to real-life experiences), and critical responses (such as evaluating, problem solving, and making judgments). It can focus on elements of story structure, such as setting (introduction, time, place, characters); theme (the goal or problem faced by the main character), plot episodes (events leading to solution of the problem or achievement of the goal), resolution (problem solution or goal achievement, story ending). It helps youngsters draw meaning from the print. Research has demonstrated that a DLTA can increase the story comprehension of young listeners (Morrow, 1984), just as a DRTA can increase the story comprehension of young readers (Danford, 1973; McGraw & Groteleuschen, 1972; Pearson, Hansen, & Gordon, 1979; Richards, 1979).

Small-Group and One-to-One Story Readings

Although teachers share literature with children most commonly by reading to whole classes, the importance and benefits of reading to small groups and to individuals must not be overlooked. Too often considered impractical in school settings, one-to-one and small-group readings yield such tremendous benefits that they must be incorporated into school programs. The most striking benefit of one-to-one story readings at home is the interactive behavior it involves, along with the direct channels of information it gives the child. It also provides the adult with insight into what children already know and want to know. In one study (Morrow, 1988a), it was determined that similar readings in a school setting had similar positive results with preschoolers from lower socioeconomic

---

BOX 6–2 • *Guidelines for Teacher Behavior During Storybook Reading*

1. *Manage*
   a. Introduce story.
   b. Provide background information about the book.
   c. Redirect irrelevant discussion back to the story.

2. *Prompt Responses*
   a. Invite children to ask questions or comment throughout the story when there are natural places to stop.
   b. Scaffold responses for children to model if no responses are forthcoming. ("Those animals aren't very nice. They won't help the little red hen.")
   c. Relate responses to real-life experiences. ("I needed help when I was preparing a party, and my family shared the work. Did you ever ask for help and couldn't find anyone to give it to you? What happened?")
   d. When children do not respond, ask questions that require answers other than yes or no. ("What would you have done if you were the little red hen and no one helped you bake the bread?")

3. *Support and Inform*
   a. Answer questions as they are asked.
   b. React to comments.
   c. Relate your responses to real-life experiences.
   d. Provide positive reinforcement for children's responses.

From Morrow, 1988a.

backgrounds, even though the youngsters had little previous experience interacting with adults. Teachers in the study practiced the same interactive behaviors identified by researchers who had studied home storybook readings (Applebee & Langer, 1983; Cochran-Smith, 1984; Flood, 1977; Heath, 1980; Ninio & Brunner, 1978; Roser & Martinez, 1985; Teale, 1981). These teacher behaviors follow:

Frequent readings by teachers who followed these guidelines increased the number and complexity of the children's responses. The youngsters offered many questions and comments that focused on meaning. Initially, they labeled illustrations. Later, they gave increased attention to details, their comments and questions became interpretive and predictive, and they drew from their own experiences. They also began narrating—that is, "reading" or mouthing the story along with the teacher. As the program continued, some children focused on structural elements, remarking on titles, settings, characters, and story events. Eventually, after many readings, the children began to focus on print, questioning names of words, letters, or sounds. They also began to recognize letters and words and read them as they were able (Morrow, 1987a). Compared with one-to-one readings, reading to small groups of children seems to encourage more and earlier responses. Children tend to repeat one another's remarks, and they are motivated to respond to and elaborate on what their peers have said.

The following segments from transcriptions of small-group story readings illustrate the various questions and comments children make when they are involved in the activity, and the wealth of knowledge and information they receive from the responding adult. The transcriptions also illustrate what the children already know and what their interests are, which helps us design instruction.

Story: *The Very Hungry Caterpillar* (Carle, 1970) (questions about a part of the book)

Jerry: (pointing to the picture on the front of the book) Why does it have a picture on it?

Teacher: The cover of the book has a picture on it so you will know what the story is about. Look at the picture. Can you tell me what the book is about?

Jerry: Ummm, I think that's a caterpillar. Is it about a caterpillar?

Teacher: You're right, very good. The book is about a caterpillar, and the name of the story is *The Very Hungry Caterpillar.* When you look at the pictures in a book, they help you find out what the words say.

Story: *Caps for Sale* (Slobodkina, 1947) (asks for a definition)

Teacher: I'm going to read a story today called *Caps for Sale.*

Jamie: What are caps?

Teacher: A cap is a little hat that you put on your head. See, there is a cap in the picture.

Jamie: I never knew that before. I knew about hats, but I never heard about caps.

Story: *Chicken Soup with Rice* (Sendak, 1962) (attends to print)

Chris: Wait, stop reading. Let me see this again. (He turns back to the page that talks about the month of June.) How come they're the same? (He refers to the words of *June* and *July.*)

Teacher: What do you mean?

Chris: Look at the letters, J–U, J–U . . . They look alike.

Teacher: Look more closely at the ends of the words. Are they the same?

Chris: Ohh, nooo, just the front part.

Story: *Caps for Sale* (Slobodkina, 1947) (predicts)

Colleen: I wonder why those monkeys took the caps?

Teacher: I don't know. Can you think why?

Colleen: Well, the peddler was sleeping and those monkeys looked at the caps, and and maybe they think they're for them. Or, I know! Maybe they're cold so they want a cap.

Teacher: Those are good ideas, Colleen.

Story: *Madeline's Rescue* (Bemelmans, 1953) (relates to real-life experience)

Jamie: What's the policemen going to do?

Teacher: He's going to help Madeline. Policemen are nice; they always help us.

Jamie: Policemans aren't nice. See, my daddy beat up Dominic and the policeman came and took him away and put him in jail for no reason. And my Daddy cried. I don't like policemans. I don't think they are nice.

Segments such as these reveal children's understandings. Do their comments and questions relate to literal meanings? Do they raise interpretive and critical issues by associating the story with their own lives, make predictions of what will come next in a story, or express judgments about characters' actions? Do comments or questions relate to matters of print, such as names of letters, words, and sounds? The same types of questions and comments occur when small groups of children read together without the presence of a teacher. Recording and then analyzing one-to-one and small-group story readings reveal what children know and want to know (Morrow, 1987a). The coding sheet that follows (p. 177) aids such analysis.

Although whole-class readings are more practical and have tremendous value in simply exposing children to literature, the interactive behavior between adult and child in one-to-one readings and small-group readings does not occur in the large group setting. If we review transcripts of story readings in all three settings, several things become apparent. In whole-group settings, no one child can ask questions or comment repeatedly throughout the story without interfering with the story line for the other children. The teacher might never get through a coherent reading. Dialogue that does occur is managed by the teacher to such an extent that the teacher often says more than the children. A truly interactive situation does not exist due to the size of the group. In small-group and one-to-one readings, by contrast, a teacher may initially do a lot of managing and prompting, but only to encourage and model responses for children. In a short time the roles reverse: most dialogue is initiated by children through questions and comments, and the teacher offers positive reinforcement and answers questions posed by the children (Morrow, 1987a).

Children who come from homes that do not offer them one-to-one readings are at a disadvantage in their literacy development. It is necessary to carry out such strategies in school to compensate for what is not provided at home as well as to provide the other benefits. Gains both in literacy skills and in positive attitudes toward books can occur. To learn to associate books with

---

BOX 6–3 • *Coding Children's Responses During Story Readings*

Child's name_____ Date_____

Story_____

(Read one story to one child or a small group of children. Encourage the children to respond with questions and comments. Tape record the session. Transcribe or listen to the tape, noting each child's responses by placing checks in the appropriate categories. A category may receive more than one check, and a single response may be credited to more than one category. Total the number of checks in each category.)

1. Focus on Story Structure
   a. setting (time, place)   _____
   b. characters   _____
   c. theme (problem or goal)   _____
   d. plot episodes (events leading toward problem
      solution or goal attainment)   _____
   e. resolution   _____

2. Focus on Meaning
   a. labeling   _____
   b. detail   _____
   c. interpreting (associations, elaborations)   _____
   d. predicting   _____
   e. drawing from one's experience   _____
   f. seeking definitions of words   _____
   g. using narrational behavior (reciting parts
      of the book along with the teacher)   _____

3. Focus on Print
   a. questions or comments about letters   _____
   b. questions or comments about sounds   _____
   c. questions or comments about words   _____
   d. reads words   _____
   e. reads sentences   _____

4. Focus on Illustrations
   a. responses and questions that
      are related to illustrations   _____

---

warmth and pleasure, children who have not had the benefit of the lap technique at home can experience it at school. It is difficult to provide one-to-one readings in school because of time limitations and the number of children, but asking aides, volunteers, and older children to do so helps solve the problem. So does reading to small groups of youngsters from time to time, perhaps replacing some of the traditional instruction in reading groups. Many school districts have federal funding for work with young children identified as having potential learning problems. Ratios in such programs may be as low as five children per teacher. Certainly those settings allow one-to-one readings as part of a literacy development program.

Shared Book Experiences

Shared book experiences (Holdaway, 1979) are usually a whole-group approach, although they may be carried out in small groups as well. In one way or another, they enable children to participate in the reading of a book. They also help develop listening skills, for children must listen attentively in order to participate.

Predictable stories are ideal for shared book experiences because they allow children to guess what will come next, thereby encouraging participation. Predictability takes many forms. The use of catch phrases, such as "'Not I,' said the dog," "'Not I,' said the cat," and so on, in *The Little Red Hen* (Izawa, 1968b), encourages children to chant along. Predictable rhyme enables children to fill in words, as in *Green Eggs and Ham* (Seuss, 1960). Cumulative patterns contribute to predictability. New events are added with each episode, for example, then repeated at the next, as in *Drummer Hoff* (Emberley, 1967). *Are You My Mother?* (Eastman, 1960) repeats phrases and episode patterns as its central character, a baby bird, searches for his mother by approaching different animals and asking the same question. Conversation can contribute to predictability, as in *The Three Billy Goats Gruff* (Brown, 1957) or *The Three Little Pigs* (Brenner, 1972). All stories become predictable as children become familiar with them, so repeating stories builds up a repertoire for shared book experiences. Fairy tales are already familiar to most children and therefore often predictable to a group. Books that carry familiar sequences, such as days of the week, months of the year, letters, and numbers, are predictable—*The Very Hungry Caterpillar* (Carle, 1970), for instance. Books gain predictability through good plot structures and topics familiar to children. Books in which pictures match text page by page tend to be predictable to children, especially if everyone in the group can see the pictures as the story is being read.

Shared book experiences involve the children in some way during the story reading. Often Big Books are used so that they can be seen easily by all and children can see the print as the teacher reads and points to it.

Predictable books are excellent for emergent and conventional readers in shared book experiences as well as in independent reading. They allow the child's first experience with reading to be enjoyable and successful with minimal effort. Such immediate success encourages the child to continue efforts at reading. (A list of predictable books is provided in Appendix A.)

One shared book technique involves reading from a Big Book (Scholastic, 1986) or a similar book made by the class or the teacher. Such a book is designed so that everyone in the group can see the pictures and the words of the story clearly while it is being read. If the book is a new one for the class, the children are asked to listen during the first reading. If it is being read for the second time or is otherwise already familiar, immediate participation is encouraged. Often the teacher uses a pointer during the reading to emphasize left-to-right progression and the correspondence of spoken and written words. The teacher encourages participation by stopping at predictable parts and asking children to fill in words and phrases. As the children become more and more familiar with the books, they begin to know them by memory, which enables the children to begin to associate words as they say them with the printed words the teacher points to on the page. Big Books and regular-size copies of the same book should be available for children to use independently after a first Big Book reading.

Shared book experiences can involve children in dramatizations of a story, art activities, or other extended experiences after the story has been read. Shared book experiences can be recorded and made available in the listening station. So can tapes of teachers' readings and commercially recorded tapes. These will provide fluent models with good phrasing and intonation for children to emulate. Shared book experiences can easily be adapted to the DLTA format, as long as it is emphasized that shared book experiences are to be pleasurable, relaxed, participatory, and enjoyable read-aloud events.

Repeated Story Readings

Children enjoy repetition, as we all do. Being familiar with an experience is comfortable, like singing a well-known song. Besides offering the pleasure of familiarity, a repeated story helps develop concepts about words, print, and books. One study (Morrow, 1987a) compared responses of two groups of four-year-olds. One group listened to three readings of each of three stories, the other group a different story at each of nine sessions. The repeated-reading group increased the number and kind of their responses, and their responses differed significantly from those of the different-story group. Their responses became more interpretive, and they began to predict outcomes and make associations, judgments, and elaborative comments.

They also began to narrate stories as the teacher read (their first attempts at reading) and to focus on elements of print, asking names of letters and words. Even children of low ability seem to make more responses with repeated readings than with a single reading (Roser & Martinez, 1985).

We can see that repeated readings are important to youngsters, because they engage in the activity frequently on their own. Children who are able to read themselves or engage in pretend reading behaviors will often select the same book to look at or read over and over again. This is an activity they obviously enjoy, and learn from and from which they experience success. In addition to repeated readings of stories by the teacher to the children, teachers should encourage youngsters to read stories more than once and carry out discussions about books that have been read and discussed previously.

The following dialogue is taken from a transcription of a child's responses to a third reading of *The Little Red Hen.* For the sake of brevity, this excerpt includes primarily the child's comments and questions and the teacher's responses; most of the story text has been omitted.

Teacher: Today I'm going to read the story, *The Little Red Hen.* It is about a hen who wanted some help when she baked some bread. (The teacher begins to read the story.) . . . Who will help me to cut this wheat?

Melony: "Not I," said the cat. "Not I," said the dog. "Not I," said the mouse.

Teacher: That was good, Melony. You are reading. (The teacher continues reading.) . . . Who will take this wheat to the mill to be ground into flour?

Melony: "Not I," said the cat. "Not I," said the dog. "Not I," said the mouse with the whiskers.

Teacher: Very nice, Melony. (The teacher continues to read.)

Melony: I want to read that part, but I don't know how.

Teacher: Go ahead and try. I bet you can. I'll help you: The cat smelled it.

Melony: The cat smelled it and she said *umm* that smells good, and the mouse smelled it, and it smelled good.

Teacher: (continuing reading) . . . Who will eat this cake?

Melony: The mouse, the doggy, the kitty!

Teacher: You're right again, Melony. (The teacher reads to the end of the story.) Did you want to say anything else about the story?

Melony: He was bad so he couldn't have no cake. (Melony searches through the pages.) That's the wrong part.

Teacher: Show me the part you are talking about.

Melony: There it is, almost at the end. She's going to make a cake and she'll say who's going to bake this cake for me. And the cat says, "Not I," the dog says, "Not I," the mouse says, "Not I." And then when she's cooking it they smell a good thing and then they wanted some, too, but they didn't have any, 'cause they didn't plant the wheat.

Teacher: You're so right. They didn't help do the work, so they didn't get to eat the cake.

Melony: Where does it say "Not I"? Show me the words in the book.

Teacher: Here it is. Can you find it again?

Melony: (flipping through the pages) I'm looking for where she bakes the cake. Here it is. Yea. And he smelled it. And he smelled it. And the mouse smelled it. (She turns pages.) They're going in the kitchen. And she said, "All by myself, I cut the wheat. All by myself, I took it to the mill to get it into flour. All by myself I baked the cake. All by myself I'm going to eat it."

Teacher: That's terrific, Melony. That's what the hen said.

Melony: (pointing to the dog) The dog was not happy. Where does it say *dog?*

Teacher: You're right. He doesn't look happy. Here is where it says dog (pointing).

Melony: There's the word, *dog, dog, dog.* How does that dog look?

Teacher: He looks hungry and mad because he can't have any bread.

Melony: You're right. But it's his fault. He didn't help. And that's the end. (Morrow, 1987a)

Besides illustrating the value of repeated readings in the responses generated by the child, this exchange demonstrates the encouragement, reinforcement, and rapport that can evolve from one-to-one storybook sessions.

Story Retelling and Rewriting

Letting a listener or reader retell or rewrite a story offers active participation in a literacy experience that helps a child develop language structures, comprehension, and sense of story structure (Morrow, 1985b). Retelling, whether it is oral or written, engages the child in holistic comprehension and organization of thought. It also allows for personalization of thinking as children mesh their own life experiences into their retelling. Retelling contrasts with the more traditional piecemeal approach of teacher-posed questions that require a child to recall bits of information (Gambrell, Pfeiffer, & Wilson, 1985). With practice in retelling, children come to assimilate the concept of story structure. They learn to introduce a story with its beginning and its setting. They recount its theme, plot episodes, and resolution. In retelling stories, children demonstrate their comprehension of story details and sequence, organizing them coherently. They also infer and interpret the sounds and expressions of characters' voices.

Retelling is not an easy task for children, but with practice they improve quickly. To help children develop the practice of retelling, tell them before they read or listen to a text or story that they will be asked to retell or rewrite it (Morrow, 1985b). Further guidance depends on the teacher's specific purpose in the retelling. If the immediate intent is to teach or test sequence, for instance, the children should be instructed to concentrate on what happened first, second, and so on. If the goal is to teach or assess the ability to integrate information and make inferences from text, children should be instructed to think of things that have happened to them like those that happen to characters in the story. Props such as felt-board characters or the pictures in the text itself can be used to help the students retell the story. Pre- and postdiscussion of the story, help to improve retelling ability, as well as the teacher's modeling a retelling for children (Mitchell, 1984; Morrow, 1985b). The following procedure is helpful in guiding a child's oral or written retelling. With written retellings, teachers may prefer to have the child write the entire piece first and then conference with him or her afterward using the following guide:

1. Ask the child to retell the story. "A little while ago, I read the story [name the story]. Would you retell the story as if you were telling it to a friend who has never heard it before?"

2. Use the following prompts only if needed:

   a. If the child has difficulty beginning the retelling, suggest beginning with "Once upon a time," or "Once there was . . ."

   b. If the child stops retelling before the end of the story, encourage continuation by asking, "What comes next?" or "Then what happened?"

   c. If the child stops retelling and cannot continue with general prompts, ask a question that is relevant at the point in the story at which the child has paused. For example, "What was Jenny's problem in the story?"

3. When a child is unable to retell the story, or if the retelling lacks sequence and detail, prompt the retelling step by step. For example:

   a. "Once upon a time," or "Once there was . . ."

   b. "Who was the story about?"

   c. "When did the story happen?" (day, night, summer, winter?)

   d. "Where did the story happen"

   e. "What was [the main character's] problem in the story?"

   f. "How did [he or she] try to solve the problem? What did [he or she] do first [second, next]?"

   g. "How was the problem solved?"

   h. "How did the story end?" (Morrow, 1985b, p. 659.)

Retellings can be used to develop many types of comprehension. The prompts should match the goals. In addition to its usefulness as a learning technique, retelling also allows adults to evaluate children's progress. If you plan to evaluate a retelling, let the child know during your introduction of the story you are about to read that he or she will be asked to retell it after the reading. During the evaluative retellings, do *not* offer prompts beyond general ones such as "Then what happened?" or "Can you think of anything else about the story?" Retellings commonly reveal a child's sense of story structure, focusing mostly on literal recall, but they also reflect the child's inferential and critical thinking ability. To assess the child's retelling for sense of story structure, the examiner should first parse (divide) the events of the story into four categories—*setting, theme, plot episodes,* and *resolution.* A guide sheet and the outline of the parsed text are then used to record the number of ideas and details the child includes within each category in the retelling, regardless of their order. *Do* credit a child for partial recall or for recounting the "gist" of a story event (Pellegrini & Galda, 1982; Thorndyke, 1977). Evaluate the child's sequencing ability by comparing the order of events in the child's retelling with the proper order of setting, theme, plot episodes, and resolution. The analysis indicates not only which elements a child includes or omits and how well a child sequences, but also where instruction might be focused. Comparing analyses of several retellings over a year will indicate a child's progress.

The following example uses a parsed outline of *Jenny Learns a Lesson* (Fujikawa, 1980). The story is about a little girl who likes to play "pretend games" with her friends. However, when her friends come to play, Jenny becomes bossy and tells everyone what to do, and her friends leave angry. After several such episodes, her friends leave and do not return. Jenny becomes lonesome and realizes her problem. She apologizes to her friends, invites them back to play, and promises not to boss them. They agree to play, and this time all do as they wish. The following parsed outline is accompanied by transcriptions of two children's retellings of the story. A retelling guidesheet follows with an analysis of the second transcription told by Beth (Morrow, 1985b).

Parsed Story

Setting
a. Once upon a time there was a girl who liked to play pretend.
b. Characters: Jenny (main character), Nicholas, Sam, Mei Su, and Shags, the dog.

Theme
Every time Jenny played with her friends, she bossed them.

Plot Episodes
First episode: Jenny decided to pretend to be a queen. She called her friends. They came to play. Jenny told them all what to do and was bossy. The friends became angry and left.

Second episode: Jenny decided to play dancer. She called her friends and they came to play. Jenny told them all what to do. The friends became angry and left.

Third episode: Jenny decided to play pirate. She called her friends and they came to play. Jenny told them all what to do. The friends became angry and left.

Fourth episode: Jenny decided to play duchess. She called her friends and they came to play. Jenny told them all what to do. The friends became angry and left.

Fifth episode: Jenny's friends refused to play with her because she was so bossy. Jenny became lonely and apologized to them for being bossy.

Resolution

a. The friends all played together and each person did what he or she wanted to do.
b. They all had a wonderful day and were so tired that they fell asleep.

Verbatim Transcriptions

(Beth, age five) Once upon a time there's a girl named Jenny and she called her friends over and they played queen and went to the palace. They had to . . . they had to do what she said and they didn't like it so then they went home and said that was boring. It's not fun playing queen and doing what she says you have to. So they didn't play with her for seven days and she had . . . she had an idea that she was being selfish, so she went to find her friends and said, I'm sorry I was so mean. And said, let's play pirate, and they played pirate and they went onto the ropes. Then they played that she was a fancy lady playing house. And they have tea. And they played what they wanted and they were happy. The end.

A retelling by five-year-old Beth when she was in the first part of her kindergarten year was just presented. To demonstrate how retellings can become more sophisticated and improve with practice and time, another retelling by this same child when she was at the end of her kindergarten year follows. The story is called *Under the Lemon Tree.* It is about a donkey who lives under a lemon tree on the farm and watches out for all the other animals. A fox comes in the night to steal a chicken or duck and the donkey hee-haws loudly to protect them. He succeeds in scaring the fox away and in addition wakes the farmer and his wife who never see the fox. This happens frequently until the farmer can no longer take the noise and moves the donkey to a tree far from the farm house where he is very unhappy. The fox comes back and steals the farmer's prize red rooster. The other animals quack and cluck

Sample Analysis

BOX 6–4 • *Story Retelling Evaluation Guide Sheet*

Child's Name_____ Beth _____ Age____ 5 ____
Title of Story_____ Jenny Learns a Lesson _____ Date_____

General directions: Give 1 point for each element included as well as
for "gist." Give 1 point for each character named as well as for such
words as *boy, girl,* or *dog*. Credit plurals (friends, for instance) with 2
points under characters.

Sense of story structure

Setting
    a. Begins story with an introduction   1
    b. Names main character   1
    c. Number of other characters named   2
    d. Actual number of other characters   4
    e. Score for "other characters" (c/d):   .5
    f. Includes statement about time or place   1

Theme
Refers to main character's primary goal or
problem to be solved   1

Plot Episodes
    a. Number of episodes recalled   4
    b. Number of episodes in story   5
    c. Score for "plot episodes" (a/b)   .8

Resolution
    a. Names problem solution/goal attainment   1
    b. Ends story 1   1

Sequence
Retells story in structural order: setting,
theme, plot episodes, resolution. (Score 2 for
proper, 1 for partial, 0 for no sequence
evident.)   1
Highest score possible: ___ 10 ___   Child's score   8.3

Checks can be used instead of numbers to get a general sense of elements children
include and progress over time. A quantitative analysis as shown above is optional.
Retellings can be evaluated for interpretive critical comments as well.

From Morrow, 1988b.

and finally wake up the farmer who chases after the fox. When the fox passes him, the donkey makes his loud noises again, frightening the fox, who drops the red rooster. The farmer realizes that the donkey has been protecting his animals and moves him back to the lemon tree where he is happy again.

Here is six-year-old Beth's retelling of *Under the Lemon Tree:*

Once upon a time there was a donkey, and he was in a farm. He lived under a lemon tree close to the animals on the farm. In the morning all the bees buzzed in the flowers under the lemon tree. He was next to the ducks, the chickens, and the roosters. It was night time. The red fox came into the farm to get something to eat. The donkey went "Hee-Haw, Hee-Haw" and then the chickens went "cluck, cluck" and the ducks went "quack-quack." . . . Then the farmer and his wife waked up and looked out the window and saw nothing. They didn't know what came into their farm that night. They said, "What a noisy donkey we have. When it gets dark we will bring him far away." So when it get darker and darker they brang the donkey over to a fig tree. And he had to stay there. He couldn't go to sleep alone. That night the red fox came into the farm again to try and get something to eat. All the ducks went quack-quack and the turkeys went gobble-gobble. The farmer and his wife woke up and said, "Is that noisy donkey back again?" They rushed to the window and saw the fox with their red rooster in his mouth and yelled, "Stop thief, come back." The fox passed the donkey and shouted "hee-haw, hee-haw." The red fox heard it and dropped the rooster and ran away. The farmer and his wife said, "Aren't we lucky to have the noisiest donkey in the whole world." And they picked up the rooster and put one hand around the donkey and they all went home together and tied the donkey under the lemon tree.

Retellings can be evaluated for many different comprehension tasks. The directions to students prior to retelling and the method of analysis should match the goal.

Webbing and Mapping

Webbing and mapping are graphic presentations for categorizing and structuring information. The strategy builds on a child's prior knowledge and makes children become active in the reading process. It helps the child to retrieve what is known about a topic, expand his or her knowledge, and use the information in reading and listening to text.

Webs and maps are diagrams that help students see how words and ideas are related to one another. They are visual representations of the relationships among ideas underlying a concept. Research has demonstrated that the use of webbing and mapping strategies is successful in the development of vocabulary and comprehension. This research has also demonstrated the effectiveness of the strategy with poor readers and minority and bilingual children (Karbon, 1984; Pittelman, Levin, & Johnson, 1985).

Webs and maps are virtually the same thing. Webs tend to be drawn in a spider-like effect, and maps may have boxes with labels in them that connect in different places.

When used to develop vocabulary concepts and definitions related to a word, the word is written on the board or chart paper. Children are asked to brainstorm ideas related to the word. For example, after reading *The Snowy Day* by Ezra Jack Keats, the teacher asks the children to provide words that describe what snow is like. The word *snow* is written in the center of the chart or chalkboard and the words given by the children are attached to it. A sample of a snow web done by a kindergarten class is shown in Figure 6–1.

Another web about the same story could generate the things that Peter did in the snow in the story and then other things that we can do in the snow. Figure 6–2 is such a web done by a first-grade class.

A map provides a different format for graphically presenting materials before and after listening to or reading a book. Maps

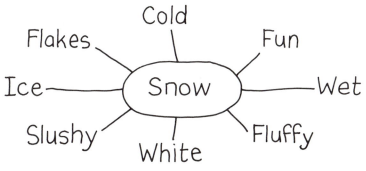

FIGURE 6–1

deal with more complex representations; therefore, boxes for different categories are needed to present the ideas graphically. Story structures can be mapped to help children learn about the structural elements in the text. Sequence of events can be mapped as well or studies of individual characters. Figure 6–3 is a map of the story *Mr. Rabbit and the Lovely Present* created by a second-grade class. The map illustrates the structural elements in the story.

In this chapter, several strategies have been discussed for developing concepts about books and comprehension of text. The strategies are appropriate for both emergent and conventional readers. Most of them can be used with children aged two through eight; however, it is the manner in which they are implemented and the children's literature used that will determine the appro-

FIGURE 6–2

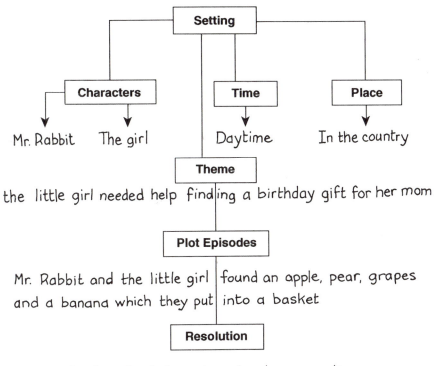

FIGURE 6-3

priate age group. With younger children, the teacher will have to do more modeling or strategies with the children. In grades one, two, and three, children are able to participate in some of them in a more independent manner.

Strategies such as the DLTA and DRTA are appropriate with all ages. It is the objectives set for them that will make the difference. Whole-group, small-group, and one-to-one literature sessions are active procedures for preschool through third grade. Shared book experiences, in which the group participates in the story reading as well as repeated readings of books, are appropriate for all early childhood youngsters. Story retellings are one of the most effective procedures for developing comprehension skills and take many forms for children two through eight. There are oral or written retellings, retellings through dramatic role-playing organized by the children, puppet shows, roll movies, chalk talk, and felt-story presentations. When children engage in these types of retellings, they must know the setting, theme, plot episodes, resolution, and story sequence. They infer how characters feel, sound, and act as they take their parts in role-playing stories. They make judgments and decisions about the responsibilities of everyone participating to make the best presentation. With all of these strategies for comprehension development, including mapping and webbing, children are active participants in their learning without the teacher's having to ask the typical comprehension questions, such as "How many pigs are in the story?" or "Which house did the wolf go to first, second, and third?" Children demonstrate that knowledge as they are actively engaged in the strategies previously discussed. They can engage in them whether in preschool or third grade—the difference is the sophistication of their involvement and the children's literature that is used.

The Value of These Strategies with Special Needs Children

Because many of these experiences involve the use of oral language, they are helpful in improving an ESL child's facility with English. The active participation is particularly appropriate for children from disadvantaged backgrounds because many of them have not had the opportunity to engage in literacy activities that require them to be quiet and listen. When they can be more active, they participate more readily.

Portfolio Assessment of Children's Concepts about Books and Comprehension of Text

The techniques described in this chapter are designed to develop concepts about books and comprehension of story through the use of children's literature. These skills listed in the Checklist for Assessing Concepts about Books and Comprehension of Text (p. 193) can be developed and assessed by a broad range of techniques used in various contexts. To determine how much children know about books, such as their front, back, top, and bottom; which part is print and which parts are pictures; how pages are turned; where reading begins; and what titles, authors, and illustrators are, one can observe regularly how youngsters handle books; hold one-to-one interviews with children; question

**Checklist for Assessing Concepts about Books
and Comprehension of Text**

	Always	Sometimes	Never
Concepts about Books			
Knows a book is for reading			
Can identify the front, back, top, and bottom of a book			
Can turn the pages properly			
Knows the difference between the print and the pictures			
Knows that pictures on a page are related to what the print says			
Knows where to begin reading			
Knows what a title is			
Knows what an author is			
Knows what an illustrator is			
Comprehension of Text			
Attempts to read story books resulting in well-formed stories			
Participation in story reading by narrating as the teacher reads			
Retells stories			
Includes story structure elements in story retellings:			
Setting			
Theme			
Plot Episodes			
Resolution			

Continued

	Always	Sometimes	Never
Responds to text after reading or listening with literal comments or questions			
Responds to text after reading or listening with interpretive comments or questions			
Response to text after reading or listening with critical comments or questions			

and otherwise encourage response in whole-group, small-group, or individual interaction; or use any of the several other techniques described in this chapter. Children's responses can be literal, interpretive, or critical. They can reflect simple recall, detail, sequence, association, prediction, judgment, and evaluation. Children's comprehension of story can be demonstrated and evaluated through their story retelling, story rewriting, attempted reading of favorite storybooks, role-playing, picture sequencing, use of puppets or felt-boards to reenact stories, and their questions and comments during storybook reading. When possible, keep periodic performance samples of activities, such as a story rewriting and audio- or videotapes of retellings.

AN IDEA FOR THE CLASSROOM

The following experience was created by a second-grade teacher in an inner-city school. You may find it useful for your teaching.

The experience was motivated by student's interest to create costumes they discovered in a craft book. I was quick to seize the opportunity to attach my youngsters' desire to design costumes and integrate it with a literature selection that I thought would work into a dramatization of a play. I had a collection of T. S. Elliot's poems in a picture storybook format. I decided to read Growl Tiger's Last Stand *to them and suggested that this might be a poem they could create costumes for and act out because there were several unusual characters. Some of the vocabulary in the poem was difficult for the children, and as I read, I needed to stop occasionally to discuss the meaning of certain words. The children became very engrossed when I read that the tiger was missing an ear and an eye. The children were sprawled on the floor listening, and they drew closer to me to see the pictures more clearly as the story ended.*

Immediately following the story, two boys (Yassin and James) took the lead in motivating the rest of the class to act out the poem and make costumes. The children flipped through the pages in order to reread certain lines so that costumes would be accurate. Roseangela decided that Lady Grittlebone must have gloves because this was a ladylike thing to do. There was a long discussion of how to make a costume for Growl Tiger who was missing an eye and an ear. A patch on one eye would be good for depicting the missing eye, but they couldn't figure out what to do about the ear.

During all of this, I was close at hand to facilitate ideas when necessary, or get the children back on track to help them accomplish their goal. Costumes were made and the poem dramatized. In this activity, I drew from the spontaneous interests of my children and created an experience that involved them in demonstrating literal, inferential, and critical comprehension skills. Youngsters had to know the details of the story to act it out and create costumes. They made many inferences about how the characters should act and sound. They engaged in critical thinking as they discussed costumes, roles, and scenery.

Following the project, David and Tamika became involved in a lively debate about whether T. S. Elliot was a boy or a girl. Obviously these youngsters were very much aware of the concept of author and had an interest in it as well.

This classroom experience is an example of one in which I utilized the interests of my children to create a learning experience. This was a comprehension activity in which youngsters were actively engaged, instead of a testing-type question-and-answer session without real child involvement.

Tammye Pelovitz, second-grade teacher
McKinley School
New Brunswick, NJ, Public Schools

ACTIVITIES AND QUESTIONS

1. Answer the focus questions at the beginning of the chapter.

2. Ask a two-, four-, and six-year-old to read their favorite stories using a storybook. Describe the reading behaviors they attempt. Are developmental differences evident among their performances?

3. Select a child between the ages of three and eight. Meet with the child three to five times, each time to let the child practice retelling a story. Tape and transcribe each session. Using the guidesheet provided in this chapter, analyze the tapes for the elements of story structure, details, sequence, and so on that the child includes in retelling. Are there developmental changes in the child's performance from session to session?

4. Select a piece of children's literature and prepare three literal, three interpretive, and three critical comprehension questions to test a child's knowledge of that story. Now take those questions and change them into activities (such as role-playing stories or creating chalk talks or felt stories) that enable the children to demonstrate their comprehension of the story.

5. Prepare two different directed listening-thinking and directed reading-thinking activities, including pre- and postdiscussions. Select different objectives for each DLTA or DRTA. Use your plans with small groups of children.

6. Continue your portfolio assessment for the child you selected to assess for language development in Chapter 3. Observe the child using the assessment checklist provided in this chapter concerning the evaluation of concepts about books and comprehension of text.

7. Continue the thematic unit that you began in Chapter 3. Select three objectives in the area of concepts about books and three in comprehension of text and describe three activities that will satisfy each of the objectives using your theme.

Case Study Activity

Two first-grade teachers have come to you as the reading specialist in the district for help with students in classrooms who have limited English proficiency. You are concerned about improving their ability in English and are also aware that they must learn about book concepts and strategies for comprehending text as well. You prepare a workshop to share strategies to help these teachers with these youngsters. You have decided to use children's literature as a resource. Describe the strategies you will be sharing with the teachers.

CHAPTER SEVEN

Developing Reading Through Learning about Print

QUESTIONS TO FOCUS ON AS YOU READ THE CHAPTER

- What are the concepts about print that are important for a young child to know?
- Define and describe how the use of the following strategies enhances a child's knowledge about print: (1) environmental print, (2) very own words, (3) language experience approach, and (4) context and picture clues.
- Define the following terms: (1) alphabetic understanding, (2) phonemic awareness, (3) phoneme–grapheme correspondence, (4) cryptanalytic intent, (5) digraphs, (6) consonant blends, (7) long and short vowel sounds, (8) hard and soft consonant sounds, and (9) phonics.
- Describe the characteristics of commercially prepared basal materials designed for literacy instruction.
- Describe the characteristics and concerns surrounding the composition and use of standardized tests.

First words must have an intense meaning.
First words must be already part of the dynamic life.
First books must be made of the stuff of the child himself, whatever
and wherever the child.

—SYLVIA ASHTON-WARNER
Teacher

Mrs. Satterwhite's class was studying nutrition. The dramatic-play area was set up like a supermarket with products displayed separately into food groups. There were the dairy products; breads and cereals; meat, poultry, and fish; and fruits and vegetables. To connect the learning of sound–symbol relationships and letter names with the unit, three letters were featured: *m* for meat, *f* for fish, and *d* for dairy. In addition to creating nonsense stories using the featured letters such as *Fanny the Fish was a Friendly Flounder who liked t) Flip her Flippers as she Fluttered through the waves,* the children collected things that began with the featured letters and placed them in boxes labeled with the appropriate symbol. These experiences caused them to talk about letters, sounds, and words in spontaneous play. Kathy and Kelly were pretending that they were shopping in the dramatic-play store. Kathy picked up a can of tuna fish and said, "Kelly, let's see how many foods we can find that begin with the letter *F.*" They looked around and Kathy found a box of Frosted Flakes and some French Fries. Kelly found a can of Fruit Cocktail, Fruit Loop cereal, and a container of Frozen Yogurt. The girls were excited when each found some food that began with the letter *f.* They said the word with a strong emphasis on the beginning *f* sound. They each decided to take a piece of paper and copy the names of the food that began with *f.* They decided to do the same thing for the other featured letters in the unit, *m* for meat and *d* for dairy.

The role that word recognition skill development plays in literacy instruction is being reevaluated. Word recognition skills, or knowledge about print, involve learning strategies that will help children become independent readers. Word recognition skills include the use of context and syntax to figure out an unknown word, the development of a sight vocabulary, the use of configuration or the shape of a word, structural analysis (attending to different parts of words such as prefixes, suffixes, or the root to decode), and the use of phonics that involves the learning of letter and combinations of letter sounds (referred to as *phonemes*) associated with their corresponding letter symbols (referred to as *graphemes*). One of the main problems with phonics is that the English alphabet has at least forty-four different sounds, and sound–symbol correspondence is not consistent—there are many irregularities and exceptions to most rules. Phonics is but one method for decoding and recognizing words to build independent readers. It is the concurrent use of a combination of several of the word recognition skills just mentioned that will create the most proficient reader.

Research concerning early literacy has made us aware of the importance of meaningful and natural experiences in early literacy instruction (Teale, 1982; Goodman, 1984). When this research was new, word recognition skill development, with an emphasis on decoding, was looked upon as a synthetic approach that lacked meaning for the young child. Now that we have dealt with many of the new ideas in early literacy instruction, skill development is receiving more attention to try and determine the appropriate way to handle this part of literacy development. This area of literacy instruction involves objectives that have existed for many years, including some of the reading readiness objectives that have dom-inated early literacy programs. Through the years, research has demonstrated that to become a proficient reader, language codes need to be learned. This is not only true in English-speaking countries. There is considerable evidence from both experimental and longitudinal studies from many countries that phonemic awareness and some knowledge of phonics are necessary for success at learning to read and write alphabetic languages (Adams, 1990; Blachman & James, 1985; Juel, Griffith, & Gough, 1986; Tunmer & Nesdale, 1985). According to Juel (1989), a child needs to have the following in order to learn to read proficiently: (1) alphabetic understanding (knowing that words are composed of letters); (2) phonemic awareness (knowing that words are com-posed of a sequence of spoken sounds that have no meaning and being able to hear those sounds); and (3) cryptoanalytic intent (knowing that there is a relationship between the printed letters and spoken sounds). These three elements are in some ways precursors to learning phonics. Therefore, the question no longer is do we deal with these skills in early literacy development; rather, it is exactly what skills are we talking about, when do we introduce them, how do we teach them, and how much time do we spend dealing with them?

Skills and Objectives for Learning about Print

Objectives concerning knowledge about print to enhance literacy development assume that the child:

1. Knows that print is read from left to right
2. Knows that oral language can be written down and then read
3. Knows what a letter is and can point to one on a printed page
4. Knows what a word is, can point to one on a printed page, and knows there are spaces between words
5. Is aware of print in the environment, knows that it has a message, and is capable of reading some of this print on signs and logos
6. Recognizes some words by sight
7. Can identify rhyming words they hear and can make up a rhyme
8. Can identify and name upper- and lowercase letters of the alphabet
9. Associates letters with their initial and final corresponding consonant sounds including sounds of the same letter (hard and soft) (c—cat, city; g—goat, George)
10. Associates letters with corresponding long and short vowel sounds (a—acorn, apple; e—eagle, egg; i—ice, igloo; o—oats, octopus; u—unicorn, umbrella)
11. Knows the consonant blends bl, cr, dr, fl, gl, pr, st, and so on (consonant blends are two or three letters that when placed together blend into one sound that represents both letter sounds)
12. Knows the consonant digraph sounds ch, ph, sh, th, and wh (digraphs are two letters that when placed together make a new sound unlike the sound of either letter)
13. Can blend and segment phonemes in words
14. Begins to use context, syntax, and semantics to identify words
15. Knows that words are made up of syllables
16. Attempts reading by attending to picture clues and to print
17. Guesses and predicts words based on some knowledge of phoneme–grapheme correspondence
18. Is aware of different structural elements of words such as prefixes, suffixes, adding -ing, -ed and -s at the end of a word, and contractions
19. Knows the following phonic generalizations:
    a. In a consonant-vowel-consonant pattern, the vowel sound is usually short (bat, bet, but, bit)
    b. In a vowel-consonant-e pattern, the vowel sound is usually long (cake, cute, bike)
20. When two vowels come together in a word, the first is usually long and the second is silent (train, receive, bean).

In the past, many of these skills were taught through the use of meaningless worksheets that involved mechanical responses on the part of the child. It was also believed that a child could not read until all of the skills were mastered. However, not all skills are necessary for all children. There are many ways for this information to be learned that are more meaningful for the child than methods used in the past. Less time is needed to deal with these skills than was thought in the past.

Instructional activities designed to help youngsters learn about the function, form, structure, and conventions of print should involve the same types of learning experiences as other skill areas dealt with in this book. Children need to be socially interactive when they are learning about print; they need models to emulate; and the learning must be through experiences that are meaningful and connected with real life and incorporate what children already know. If children see a need or usefulness attached to a reading skill, that skill will probably be learned without difficulty.

In the sections that follow, strategies will be described to help children learn about print in meaningful and functional ways. Each strategy is appropriate for youngsters from preschool through second grade—the teacher simply adjusts the activity to the age group he or she is working with. In the past, we selected the behavioristic approach for learning about print. Skills were taught through the use of drill with exercises and worksheets that had little meaning for the child. Learning these skills should be connected to content-area material and functional activities. Activities such as reading to children; pointing out words in the environment; noting their letters and sounds; taking a child's dictation; encouraging children to write in their own way; allowing youngsters to see the print as it is read from a Big Book and tracked from left to right across the page; and using predictable books that rhyme or have patterned language, where children can guess and share in the reading, all help youngsters to learn about print (Juel, 1989). Through these experiences, children are learning that print is read from left to right, that words in a book are oral language that has been written down and can be read, that letters have sounds, that letters make up words, that words have meaning, that pictures hold clues to what the print says, and that words can be predicted based on the meaning of the text. Some direct instruction of phonemic awareness, phonics, and alphabetic knowledge may be needed, which is acceptable as long as it does not dominate instruction. Children should be able to read several words and simple books through their knowledge of syntax, semantics, and acquired sight vocabulary before there is an emphasis on phonics. When youngsters have experienced success with reading, they will seek information about the forms of print since they will have a desire to read independently.

Environmental Print

Several researchers have found that children as young as two can read familiar environmental print (Goodman, 1980; Harste, Woodward, & Burke, 1984; Hiebert, 1978). Others, however, have shown that a child is often reading the sign rather than its print; when the print is separated from its familiar environmental context, the young child sometimes can no longer identify it (Dewitz & Stammer, 1980; Mason, 1980). Even so, when very young children associate the McDonald's logo with the word *McDonald's* and try to read it, they are learning that a group of letters make up a word that can be read and thus provide information. Reading environmental print also carries with it a sense of accomplishment and usually elicits positive reinforcement of the child's achievement by caring adults.

As noted earlier, parents can make children aware of environmental print from the first year of life. During daily routines, parents need to point out and read words and labels on food boxes, road signs, stores, and restaurants. The world is filled with environmental print. School, however, is not. With the exception of *Exit, Boys, Girls,* and special names such as *Library* and *Office,* few familiar words appear in the typical school building. Thus, environmental print needs to be brought into school from outside, and classroom teachers need to label items within the walls of their own day-care centers, nursery schools, kindergartens, and first and second grades. Such print, once familiar, becomes part of a child's sight vocabulary.

The environmental print that children tend to know best appears on food containers, especially those for cereal, soup, milk, and cookies, and on detergent boxes and bottles. Among common signs, they recognize fast-food logos, road signs, traffic signals, and names of popular store chains, supermarkets, and service stations. Collect such logos and trade names and make them available in your classroom by posting them on charts, pasting them onto index cards, and making up looseleaf books of environmental print. Most firms distribute various printed materials free,

Label the room with words representing topics of study.

complete with logos. Photograph examples of environmental print yourself to bring to your classroom. Suggest that children read such words and copy them, if they wish.

Fill your room with its own environmental print. Start at the beginning of a school year with only a few signs, such as children's names on their cubbies, and the word *block center* to identify that area of the room. Make labels with five-by-eight index cards and dark felt-tip markers. Begin each word with a capital letter and continue with lowercase manuscript, thus providing youngsters with configuration clues. Hang labels at heights easy for children to see. Point out the labels to the children, and suggest that they read them to friends and, if they wish, copy them. As the school year progresses and things you are learning about are added to the classroom, label these items as well. Refer to the labels as part of your normal routine so that they are used and will then add to the child's sight vocabulary. Label items because they are of interest to the class and serve a function such as identifying important classroom materials and learning centers. Use labels for relating messages such as **Wash Your Hands Before Snack.** Refer to the labels often so the children identify them as useful and functional.

Label items related to content area topics. If you are studying dinosaurs—a very popular topic in early childhood—display model dinosaurs and label each with its name. Even long, difficult words such as *brontosaurus* and *tyrannosaurus* immediately become sight words for many early childhood youngsters. It is not at all uncommon to observe preschool, kindergarten, first-grade and second-grade children reading labels to themselves or to each other. I observed a kindergarten class shortly after the teacher had put up two new labels in the science center, which featured a lesson on the sense of touch and focused on items that were hard and soft. I watched Josh take Jennifer by the hand and heard him say, "See, Jen. See this. This bunny is soft. This word says 'soft.'" Josh continued, "See this, Jen. This is a rock and this word says 'hard.' Touch it. It is hard." The two children stroked the bunny, pointed to the label, and said in unison, "soft"; they then touched the rock, pointed to the label, and said, "hard." They repeated the sequence several times.

Another way to make print part of the classroom environment is to communicate through print, even with children as young as two. Every day have messages and assignments for children. Select a permanent spot on the chalkboard. Use rebus or picture writing along with print to help children make sense of the message. For example:

Happy Birthday, Tyrone!
Happy Valentine's Day!
Read a book to a friend.
We are going on a trip to the town library today.

This routine will have children automatically looking at the chalkboard each day for a special message. They will learn that print carries meaning that is interesting and useful. Some teachers refer to this practice as the *Morning Message* and have formalized it into a lesson when the school day begins (Stewart, Benjamin, & Mason, 1987). Continue to communicate in print throughout the day whenever the opportunity occurs. Write at least some of the message with the children watching, so that you provide a writing model for them. Use the message to develop various concepts about print. Emphasize specific words or letters, pursue questions about meaning, or let children add sentences to the original message.

When working with seven- and eight-year-olds, the contents of the Morning Message and the environmental print displayed in the room will be more sophisticated than when working with younger children. They can be used to point out sound–symbol relationships or phonic generalizations that are appropriate to deal with in first and second grade. For example a Morning Message such as:

> Shelly is wearing *shiny* new *shoes* that *she* just bought yesterday.

is a perfect opportunity to point out the *sh* digraph. In another message such as the following:

> *Kate*'s Birthday *cake* was *made* in the *shape* of a *kite*.

There are five examples of the phonic generalization that in a vowel-consonant-*e* pattern, the vowel is usually long. This is a perfect opportunity to observe and discuss this letter–sound pattern.

Computers are a newer part of our print environment. They are now present in many of our homes and schools. Computer literacy is almost a must, and early childhood is the time to expose children to computers. Early exposure makes the computer a part

In our technological world, computers must become a part of literacy development, just as books, pencils, and paper are. Computers should be a part of early childhood equipment and provide a source for literacy development.

of the child's life rather than a threat. Many adults are intimidated by computers, especially because their introduction came after they were set in their ways. Many avoid using them or approach them with trepidation, but today's children must be made as comfortable with computers as their parents and grandparents have been with typewriters. Children as young as a year can sit on an adult's lap and use a keyboard. The computer places letters of the alphabet before the child and instant left-to-right progression on the screen as keys are pressed. The computer helps with knowledge about print as children compose narrative and expository text.

Many computer programs teach children literacy skills, some better than others. It is important to be selective when choosing software, because some of it is no more creative than the skills-oriented workbooks that have been criticized for years. Other programs, however, encourage active, creative participation rather than simply questions and answers. Selected computer software for children is listed in Appendix E.

Very Own Words for Developing Sight Vocabulary and Knowledge about Print

In *Teacher* (1963), Sylvia Ashton-Warner described Very Own Words as a method for developing sight vocabulary. She encouraged children to write their favorite words from a story or content-area lesson on three-by-five cards, each word on a separate card. Very Own Words are often from a child's home life—*Mommy, Daddy, Grandpa, Grandma, birthday*—they also reflect emotional feelings—*naughty, nice, good, no, punish.* After Very Own Words are recorded on index cards, they are stored in a child's file box, in a coffee can, a zip-lock baggie, or on a loose-leaf ring hung on a bulletin board. Teachers have devised many other methods for storing Very Own Words.

Helping children start their collections of Very Own Words is an exciting experience in school. Before an activity or exercise, let them know that at its completion you will ask them to name their favorite words from the activity. The activity should be a pleasant one that produces interesting language, perhaps popping corn or making play dough. It can also be a favorite word in a storybook or words generated from the study of social studies and science units. Soon children will request their Very Own Words without being asked.

*Very Own Words provide a source for a
personal sight vocabulary. Teachers provide
new Very Own Words and encourage
children to copy, write stories with, and read
them.*

Encourage children to do things with their words—to read
them to friends or to themselves, copy them, dictate them to the
teacher, and use them in sentences or stories. Because they are
based on a child's expressed interests in situations at home and
in school, the collection of Very Own Words is a powerful technique for developing sight vocabulary.

Seven- and eight-year-olds also enjoy and learn from collecting Very Own Words. They should alphabetize them and store
them in a file box. Teachers can encourage children to study the

letter patterns in their Very Own Words. They can discuss consonant and vowel sounds, blends, and digraphs when applicable,
and structural elements such as prefixes and suffixes, as well as
phonic generalizations that may be evident. When a child studies
letter patterns in words he or she has selected, it will mean more
than doing the same task with words selected by the teacher or a
textbook.

Very Own Words will be useful with bilingual children. The
index card will include a child's Very Own Word in English and
can have the word written in his or her native language as well.

The Language Experience Approach

The Language Experience Approach (LEA) has been used for many
years in reading instruction. Already tried and true for many
teachers, it encompasses in its techniques and suggestions the
newer theories of emergent literacy. It can help children associate
oral language with written language, teaching them specifically
that what is said can be written down and read. It illustrates the
left-to-right progression of our written language. In practice, it
demonstrates the formation of letters plus their combination into
words; it helps build sight vocabulary; it is a source for meaningful
teaching of phoneme–grapheme correspondence as well as other
knowledge about print; and it is based on the child's interest and
experiences.

Many educators have been associated with developing and
articulating the Language Experience Approach, among them
R. V. Allen (1976), M. A. Hall (1976), and J. Veatch et al. (1973).
The LEA is based on the following premises, all from the learner's
point of view:

> What I think is important.
> What I think, I can say.
> What I say can be written down by me or by others.
> What is written down can be read by me and by others.

The interests and experiences on which the LEA builds come
from children's lives both at home and at school. Home experiences, of course, tend to be spontaneous. In school, the teacher
needs to plan experiences—for example, class trips, cooking projects, use of puppets, guest speakers, class pets, plants, holiday
events—or the study of topics that are exciting to young children,

such as dinosaurs, outer space, and other cultures. The language experience lesson is usually carried out with an entire class, but it can also take place with a small group or an individual child.

An LEA lesson begins with oral language. A discussion is usually generated from an interesting or exciting class experience—a recent trip to the zoo, for instance, Halloween costumes, or the pet gerbil's new litter. To begin the discussion, ask open-ended questions that will encourage descriptive responses rather than yes/no answers. For example, if the topic is a trip to the zoo, ask children to name their favorite animal. Why was it their favorite animal? What did the animal look like? What did the animal do while the child was watching it at the zoo? It is important to accept all of the children's responses. Accept nonstandard English without correction, but provide a language model by using standard English to paraphrase what the child has said.

After a discussion has generated several ideas, write them down. With a large group of children, write the ideas on a large sheet of paper (approximately 24 by 36 inches), which becomes an experience chart. It can be taped to the wall or mounted on an easel. Print with a dark felt-tip marker of medium thickness, allowing ample spacing between words and between lines so that the chart is very readable. Use manuscript in upper- and lower-case letters, following the conventions of regular print and thus giving configuration to words that the use of uppercase alone cannot give. Word configuration aids children in word identification.

In recording language on experience charts, teachers should write quickly and legibly, providing good manuscript samples for children to read and copy. Not only is rewriting a chart time-consuming, but a rewritten chart is typically more difficult for children to read because they have not witnessed the writing of the chart firsthand. As you write what children dictate, use their language unless it is difficult for others to understand. When dictation is difficult to understand, ask a child to restate an idea or, if necessary, help the child restate it. It is important to include the comments of as many children as possible. When creating a new chart, try to remember which children have not contributed in the past, and encourage them to contribute to the new chart. It is a good idea to identify who said what. The chart is more interesting to youngsters whose names are included. For example: John said, "I liked the gorilla at the zoo. He jumped around and made funny faces." Jordanna said, "I liked the baby deer. They had big, bright, black eyes, wet black noses, and shiny brown fur." Try

The Language Experience Approach provides experiences that interest children, who in turn can write about, develop vocabulary from, and read about them. Experience charts, dictated by the children and written by the teacher, develop language and encourage reading and writing.

to accompany each sentence with an illustration; this will help children be able to read the charts.

Experience charts should not be very long. Charts dictated by two- and three-year-olds can simply be lists of words, such as names of animals with illustrations next to them. Used occasionally, lists of words make appropriate charts for older children as well. They are a quick way to record and reinforce vocabulary associated with topics being studied. Small-group and individual dictations of experiences can be made into books by the teacher or the child. While writing a chart, take the opportunity to point out concepts about print: "Now I am writing the word 'gorilla'— g-o-r-i-l-l-a. See, it begins here with a 'g' and ends here with an 'a.'" Mentally note which letters or sounds interest children. Ask children to point out on the chart where you should begin to write. Like the Directed Listening (or reading) Thinking Activity and the Morning Message, the LEA lesson can have a specific skill objective.

The last step in the LEA lesson is to read the chart back to the class. Use a pointer to emphasize left-to-right progression. Let the class read the chart in unison, or ask individual children who contributed different sentences to read them. Leave the chart in a visible spot in the room and encourage the children to read it and copy parts of it, copy words they like, or add to their Very Own Word collection from the chart. Vocabulary charts and experience charts representing the different topics discussed in school can be left hanging in the room as long as space permits, then made into Big Books for children to look at throughout the school year. If a laminating machine is available, it is wise to preserve charts. They can also be covered with clear contact paper to withstand handling by the children. Children's dictated stories can also be placed in the class library for others to read, as can books made by the entire class. Those made by the class often become the most popular books in the room. Class books can be made by having each child draw and write directly onto a duplicating master. This method allows easy production of multiple copies, one for each child.

The Language Experience Approach, which is appropriate throughout early childhood and beyond, can be used similarly to the Morning Message and Very Own Words for noticing phonic generalizations and sound–symbol correspondences. Learning about print in this situation is done with material that is familiar and meaningful. Occasionally prepare a chart in the language of bilingual children in your class. If necessary solicit help from bilingual parents or colleagues. This strategy will help the bilingual youngsters see that we respect their home or native language and will guide them in making connections between their language and English.

Although the Language Experience Approach has been used for many years, it has often been seen only as a program supplement. Skill drills and standard workbooks on letters and sounds have too often been given instructional priority. Yet, the LEA incorporates all the constructs that are sound principles in nurturing emergent literacy. LEA materials are inexpensive and easy to use. They include chart paper, markers, colored construction paper, white paper, index cards, scissors, staplers, pencils, and crayons. With directions from the teacher, these simple classroom materials record the precious words and pictures created by children from their own meaningful, real-life experiences. The LEA should be central, not supplemental, to literacy instruction in early reading programs.

Using Context and Pictures to Develop Reading

Experiences with literature can lead children to use contextual print and illustrations to recognize that words have meaning and help them decode words written on the printed page. Again, those experiences can take place in whole-class, small-group, or one-to-one settings and through such techniques as directed listening/reading–thinking activities, shared book experiences, and repeated readings of stories. For example, select a story that is predictable, in which the text and illustrations are closely related. Ask children to look at the pictures on a page before reading it to them. Ask them what they think the words will say. Then read the page to demonstrate that print and illustration are closely related and that the pictures provide information that can help the children as they read the story.

The syntax and semantics of a sentence (its grammatical structure and meaning) also help children to identify words. Encourage children to use these elements of written language by stopping your oral reading at predictable points in a story and asking them to fill in words. For example, when reading *The Little Engine That Could* (Piper, 1954), first read the repetitive phrase "I think I can" through, the second time say, "I think I _____," the next time "I think _____," and last "I _____." This technique is most effective with a Big Book because you can point to the words as the children say them. As the children begin to understand the concept of filling in words, choose more difficult passages for your pauses. Prepare charts and sheets with predictable text and leave out words to be filled in as you read. Children unconsciously use their prior knowledge of syntax and context in predicting words. They assimilate and use the strategy when they read themselves.

Identifying Letters of the Alphabet

Many children who cannot yet identify individual letters of the alphabet are able to read. As we have seen, they read sight words from environmental print, from classroom labels, and from Very Own Words lists. They learn other sight words from repeated readings and shared book experiences. It is obviously not necessary to be able to identify and name the letters of the alphabet in order to develop an initial sight-reading vocabulary. It is actually more desirable and easier for a young child *initially* to learn whole words already familiar through oral language, rather than learn abstract letters. Familiar words carry meaning for them whereas isolated letters do not.

Children do, however, need to learn the alphabet to eventually become independently fluent readers and writers. There is no evidence that alphabet identification ought to be treated as the first skill in early literacy; it makes more sense for children to learn to identify letters after they have learned a number of sight words. Traditionally, learning the alphabet has often been the first thing parents try to teach their children at home, and it is usually high on any list of reading readiness skills in preschool and kindergarten curricula. Because it is hard to depart from deeply rooted tradition, learning the alphabet will probably always be prominent in emergent literacy programs. The main concern is that it not be overemphasized in experiences provided for learning, in our expectations for the children's performance, and in terms of the time given to it.

Allow children to explore letters by using manipulative materials available in the literacy center. Be sure to have on hand alphabet puzzles, magnetic upper- and lowercase letters with an accompanying magnetic board, a set of wooden upper- and lowercase letters, tactile letters made of sandpaper, alphabet games, felt letters and an accompanying felt-board, letter stencils, alphabet flash cards, and a long alphabet chart posted along the wall of the classroom at the eye level of the children. In addition to these materials, a large supply of alphabet books and taped songs about the alphabet should be in the classroom library. Encourage children to explore these materials, first through play. Later, they will begin to identify the letters they are playing with, and teach letters they know to other children. Provide chalk and a chalkboard so they can make letters themselves. Children also enjoy finger-painting letters, painting them on easels, shaping them out of clay, and eating them in alphabet soup or as cookies or pretzels.

Systematic teaching of the alphabet, one letter per week, is not as successful as teaching children letters that are meaningful to them. Many teachers lead children to identify the letters in their own names first. When teaching thematic units, select a few letters to feature that are used in the context of the theme. For example, in a unit on transportation, feature *b* for boat and *t* for train. When children have learned to identify several different letters, ask them to look for the same letters in other contexts, such as magazines, newspapers, and books. Check children individually by using flash cards to determine just which letters they know and which they do not know. Ask children which letters they would like to learn next from their Very Own Words or other sources that allow them to decide for themselves. Give children flash cards of the letters they choose to learn and encourage them to use those letters in all of the activities just mentioned.

A prepared environment rich with alphabet materials to be explored and experienced will help children learn the letters of the alphabet. (Alphabet books are listed in Appendix A.)

Phonemic Awareness and Associating Letters and Sounds

We do have research that supports the importance of learning sound–symbol relationships, and there is no research that suggests we should ignore it in the development of emergent literacy (Adams, 1990). The newer research *does* suggest, however, that traditional early reading instruction ignores many important strategies and practices while abstracting discrete skills from the total act of reading. It suggests that the teaching of letter–sound association has dominated early childhood programs to the point of excluding other practices. As with teaching the alphabet, caution is proposed in the instructional strategies, time allocation, and performance expectations we bring to sound–symbol relationships in the early childhood classroom. Children who have already had substantial experience with books, who are firmly familiar with the structures and uses of language, and who have already acquired large sight vocabularies are perhaps ready to deal with sound–symbol relationships in preschool and kindergarten; children without those backgrounds are not. Like the letters of the alphabet, sound–symbol relationships are abstract and lack intrinsic meaning for children. Only a child who has assimilated concepts about books and print and has acquired a sight vocabulary begins to show an interest in trying to decode unknown words independently. Usually children ask about letters and sounds themselves when they see a need for this knowledge. Studies have demonstrated that children who are taught phonics as part of initial reading instruction do achieve better in the early grades than children who have not (Chall, Conrad, & Harris-Sharples, 1983; Williams, 1985). It must be remembered, however, that the goal of phonics is not to teach a set of rules, but to get across the alphabetic principle that there are systematic relationships between letters and sounds.

Phonemic awareness is a precursor to phonics and necessary for children to benefit from phonic instruction. Phonemic awareness is the knowledge that words are made up of a sequence of spoken sounds. To help children gain this awareness, we expose them to rhymes and jingles and carefully selected children's literature that features language play. Reading books such as *Green Eggs and Ham* (Seuss, 1960), *Goodnight Moon* (Brown, 1947), and *The Queen of Hearts* (Hennessy and Pearson, 1989) will help develop phonemic awareness. If you do introduce kindergarten children to sound–symbol relationships, deal with initial consonants, initial digraphs, and vowels. Although there does not seem to be a particularly appropriate sequence for teaching specific sounds, it does appear as if the letters used more often should be more familiar to children and therefore easier for them to learn—letters such as initial *s*, *t*, *p*, and *m*. After initial consonants, introduce the more familiar beginning digraphs, such as *sh*, *ch*, *th*, and *ph*. Then introduce vowels. Teach sounds in meaningful contexts rather than by isolating sounds from words. Using meaningful context tends to avoid the pedagogical distortion of sounds. Rather than asking a child, "Can you think of words that begin with the 'buh' sound?" ask the child to think of words that begin with the letter *b*, such as *baby*. Feature different letters and provide many experiences with the sound–symbol relationship of each letter.

Children need continual practice in order to learn sound–symbol relationships; rarely is a single lesson sufficient. Therefore, provide several experiences with each letter and review frequently, even after proceeding to new letter sounds. Incorporate experiences with sound–symbol association in all content areas whenever possible, and in situations that are meaningful to the child.

How might children be helped to recognize the sound–symbol relationships of consonants and vowels in a meaningful context.

Science and social studies themes lend themselves to featuring letters that appear in units. For example, when studying farm, pet, and zoo animals, feature the letter *p*, because it is used frequently within this context. The following types of activities can follow:

1. Read *The Pigs' Picnic* (Kasza, 1988), *The Pet Show* (Keats, 1972), and *The Tale of Peter Rabbit* (Potter, 1902) during the unit, and point out words that begin with the letter *p* in these books.
2. Make word charts using words from the books that begin with the letter *p*.
3. Make popcorn and bring peanuts to the zoo to feed the animals.
4. Make lists of animals that begin with the letter *p*.
5. Read the book *Animalia* (Base, 1987) and point out the *p* page, which says "Proud Peacocks Preening Perfect Plumage."
6. Collect sensory items about animals that begin with the letter *p*, such as Puppy Chow to smell, peanuts to eat and to feed to elephants when you visit the zoo, peacock plumes to touch, a purring kitten to listen to, and the book *Petunia* (Duvoisin, 1977) to look at and read.
7. List words from the unit that begin with the letter *p*.
8. Write an experience chart of activities carried out during the unit and highlight the letter *p* when it appears in the chart.
9. Ask children to add to their very own word collection with favorite words from the unit that began with the letter *p*.
10. Make a collage of pictures featuring things from the unit and mark those that begin with the letter *p*.
11. Print on a chart the song "Peter Cottontail." Sing the song and highlight the letter *p* when it appears.
12. Have children help you to make up nonsense rhymes for featured letters and chant them, such as:

   My name is Penelope Pig
   I pick petals off of petunias
   I play patty cake
   and eat pretzels with pink punch

13. Encourage children to write about their experiences in the units such as their visit to the zoo, the books they read, the songs they sang, etc. In their writing they will be using the letters emphasized and although their writing may not be conventional, through the use of their invented spellings they are indirectly enhancing their phonemic awareness. When

children write they have to face head-on the problem of mapping spoken language into written language. This can lead to an understanding of the structure of spoken language, and the more children write, the better they become at segmenting sounds in words. This is demonstrated in the following example of Zach's story about *The Pigs' Picnic* when he wrote, Pig wanted the picnic to be perfect, as follows:

Pg wtd tha pcnc to be prfkt

Children's literature is an excellent source for featuring letters attached to themes. Be careful not to abuse the stories by overemphasizing the sounds featured; however don't pass up the opportunity to feature letters in this natural book setting. For example in a unit on food, Ms. Fino a first-grade teacher featured the letter *b* and read *Blueberries for Sal* (McClosky, 1948), *Bread and Jam for Frances* (Hoban, 1964), and *The Berenstain Bears and Too Much Birthday* (Berenstain, 1987).

These and similar activities can be carried out for any initial consonant. Whenever letters being featured in a thematic unit appear in a language experience chart or a piece of children's literature, take the opportunity to point it out to the children. Alphabet books generally use sound–symbol relationships as they introduce each letter as do picture storybooks that use a particular letter prominently. (See section 18 in Appendix A for children's literature for building sound–symbol relationships.) For additional practice and individual exploration, include among the language arts manipulatives in the literacy center any materials that help children associate sounds and their symbols—materials in Lotto or Bingo formats, puzzles that require children to match pictures with initial consonants, felt pictures and letters, and boxes of objects representing initial consonant sounds.

When we read, we use several skills concurrently to decode and derive meaning from the printed page. We therefore need to encourage children to use multiple rather than isolated skills in their approach to reading. Children should be taught to use context clues and phonic clues simultaneously. One strategy that accomplishes this goal has already been suggested—reading a sentence in which you pause and leave a "blank" to be filled in by the child. For example, say, "The b_____ flew up to the tree and landed on a branch." Supplying the initial consonant for the word, either by sound or by sight, draws on a child's skills with phonics, context, syntax, and semantics.

It must be emphasized that many preschool, kindergarten, and first-grade children are not likely to associate the identification of sound–symbol relationships with reading. Many of them do seem to be able to name words beginning with specific consonants, but they will probably not relate that ability to reading until they approach the end of first grade. Very little time should be spent on such skills before then, and more time spent with the many other strategies already suggested. Although many more phonic rules have been identified, such as those involving final consonants, long and short vowels, and blends, early childhood classrooms should deal mostly with sound–symbol relationships of initial consonants and digraphs and perhaps rudimentarily with the most obvious vowel sounds. There are, however, some children who are capable of dealing with the more complicated skills.

There are several concerns with sound–symbol relationships and phonics generalizations. A major problem is that so many of the rules have exceptions. For example, the sound of *k* in the word *kite* is its usual sound, but when *k* is followed by *n* it becomes silent as in the word *knot*. It is the opinion of this author that we should teach fewer rather than more rules because the ability to apply them is so limited for young children. Many of the exceptions can wait until the children are older. Exceptions can be dealt with when they come up in print and sometimes treated as sight words when they occur infrequently. In early childhood, our main concern should be with sound–symbol relationships and generalizations that rarely have exceptions.

Another problem when dealing with sound–symbol relationships is dialects. If a teacher from New York taught in the South, he or she would teach long and short vowels with different sounds than those taught by a teacher who was from the South. Children in most parts of the United States are in communities that are made up of youngsters who speak many different dialects and attend the same school. These children may have difficulty dealing with sounds regardless of where their teacher is from.

In addition, there are different types of learners. There are auditory learners and visual learners. A child who is weak in auditory discrimination is not likely to master phonics and is best taught to his or her strength rather than to a weakness. We need to be cautious with sound–symbol relationships. The skills a child acquires as a result of being knowledgeable in this area are important toward becoming a proficient reader; on the other hand, it is just one strategy within the total picture of literacy development, and we need not overemphasize it.

As suggested, a section of the classroom literacy center should be set aside for general language arts manipulatives. This section will include the multipurpose materials preschools, kindergartens, and first and second grades characteristically use to develop eye–hand coordination and sharpen visual and auditory discrimination and memory. Such manipulatives include puzzles; pegboards; sewing cards; beads and string; materials that lace, button, or snap; construction toys such as Legos and Tinker Toys; picture collections for holidays and unit topics; materials for sorting and identification; games such as Concentration, Bingo, Lotto, and Candyland; and card games that involve such skills as use of the alphabet, rhyme, and letter–sound association.

Many of the materials for developing the skills just mentioned can be purchased from school supply companies. Teacher-made items increase the inventory and often suit children's needs better than purchased materials. They also add warmth and help personalize the classroom. Older children, parents, aides, and teachers can all contribute to the classroom inventory by making materials. (School supply companies that offer materials and resource books for making materials are listed in Appendix F.)

Whenever possible take advantage of spontaneous situations that grow out of daily experience to help children learn about print, such as the following example:

> *Christopher, a child in first grade, had just written his name on a picture he drew and exclaimed, "Wow, the word STOP is right in the middle of my name. See Christopher." He pointed to the letters in his name that spelled STOP. He continued, "But that doesn't make sense, then I should say my name Chri-STOP-her." The teacher immediately seized the opportunity to point out the ph digraph and explain to Christopher that the word STOP was in his name but when the letters p and h come together they make a new sound as heard in Christopher, like the sound of F. She mentioned other words such as photograph and phantom that illustrated the ph sound.*

Transitions

In the last three chapters dealing with reading development, theories and strategies for helping children develop the desire to read, comprehend written text, and learn about the features of print have been discussed. It is the opinion of the author that all the strategies are appropriate for preschool through second grade, with adaptations based on the particular age group. Teachers often want to know how children move from one level of reading ability to another or from attempted reading to conventional reading when children are attending to the print and not depending entirely on pictures and memory. It is a somewhat different process for every child, but trends do emerge. First and foremost we want to be sure that an atmosphere exists in which a child wants to read. Therefore, their attempts at reading at whatever level must be acknowledged and encouraged. Children who are reluctant to read because they think they can't, can listen to the attempts of their friends to see that unconventional reading is acceptable. We foster acceptance so that children will attempt reading. As youngsters learn more about phoneme–grapheme correspondence and the predictability of text based on the context and build sight vocabularies, they begin to realize that their attempted reading is not conventional. At this point they begin to ask for help with identifying words as they move into the conventional stage of reading. It may seem as if they are taking a step backward at this time because their reading is suddenly more labored as they try to sound out words rather than fill in words based on their memory or what seems to fit. Their concern for reading correctly has that effect on their performance. This will last for a short period of time as their skills for independent reading increase and they practice reading more and more. Conventional reading does not just occur one day; it is a gradual process in which a child goes back and forth from conventional to unconventional reading until sufficient proficiency is gained for the reading to be considered completely conventional.

Using Published Materials

Even in the mid-1960s, commercially prepared instructional materials for the development of early literacy were rare. Nursery schools and kindergartens, still very much directed by the doctrines of Pestalozzi and Froebel, used manipulative materials and real-life settings for the child's development. But the burgeoning concept of reading readiness brought with it commercial materials for developing those skills believed to be prerequisite to learning to read. Generally, the reading readiness materials were developed by the same publishers that had produced basal readers for primary grades. What they offered did not look very much like what had been used with children in preschool and kindergarten in the past. Rather, the materials were similar to those used by first, second, and third graders. They consisted mostly of workbooks accompanied by teacher's manuals.

Such materials are quite common and will probably continue to be, because they provide a complete package of materials for instruction and are revised to include new findings in early literacy development. Some general rules need to be applied to the selection and use of materials:

- Be sure to study the objectives for the published program and determine if they include those that incorporate the latest findings on strategies for nurturing early literacy.
- Be sure that the materials suit the needs of the children you teach. Urban and rural children may need materials different from those needed by children raised in suburban settings.
- Examine the materials for clarity, appeal to children, and durability.
- Analyze the teacher's editions for clarity of objectives, descriptions of plans, suitability of lesson content, and flexibility given to teachers in using the material.
- You, the teacher, should determine how the materials are to be used; materials should not dictate their use to you.
- Select sequences that seem most appropriate. You need not start at the beginning of a book and follow it page by page to the end.
- Eliminate sections that you feel are inappropriate for your children. On the other hand, material can be repeated if it is particularly good or if children have not grasped its content.

Remember at all times that you are the teacher and that you need to make critical decisions about your instructional program. Published materials are tools to be used by you. Often they are best used for reinforcing concepts. Published materials can also provide independent work for students when you need to work with individuals or small groups.

It is extremely important to realize that published materials are only one part of a program for early literacy development. What has been described thus far in this book is all but devoid of such programs. Many school districts require the use of published readiness and basal materials, and many teachers depend on them as organizational tools. When they are used, select them carefully for quality of content, use them as you see fit, and remember that they are just one part of a literacy program. As the teacher you must be a decision maker about the design of your literacy program, the materials you use, and how you use them.

Portfolio Assessment and Standardized Measures Concerning Knowledge about Print

Children's knowledge about print and the skills they have mastered in recognizing and using it can be evaluated best through portfolio assessment techniques such as running records of their behavior in frequent individual observations, collection of work samples, and personal interviews. Frequent checking and re-checking are required because young children are constantly learning and occasionally they forget. Standardized tests also measure some of the print concepts covered in this chapter. Because they are used to assess "readiness for reading" in most kindergartens and some preschools in the United States, those tests raise issues that need to be addressed.

There are a number of problems associated with standardized tests. First, we must recognize that they represent only one form of assessment; their use must be coordinated with that of other assessment measures. Second, some standardized tests for early literacy test only reading readiness skills. These tests evaluate children on skills different from those identified in this book as characteristic of emergent literacy. For the most part, they deal with skills abstracted from the reading process and then designated as precursors of reading. Those skills include such things as auditory memory, rhyme, letter recognition, visual matching, school language, and listening. By contrast, practices that nurture emergent literacy emphasize children's prior knowledge, book concepts, attitudes about reading, association of meaning with print, and characteristics of printed materials. One child might pass all portions of a standardized reading readiness test yet not be able to begin to read, whereas a second child might not pass any portion of the test but may already be reading.

Reading readiness training was a major emphasis in my first year of teaching. Imagine my surprise, then, when I saw some of my kindergarteners reading during free-choice time. I had no idea that any of them could read. The results of their reading readiness tests certainly gave no indication of this. I was so busy getting them ready to read that I never stopped to ask them if they could read or if they would read to me.

Hypothesized subtest profiles on three (3) kindergarten children achieving about the same Test Performance Rating

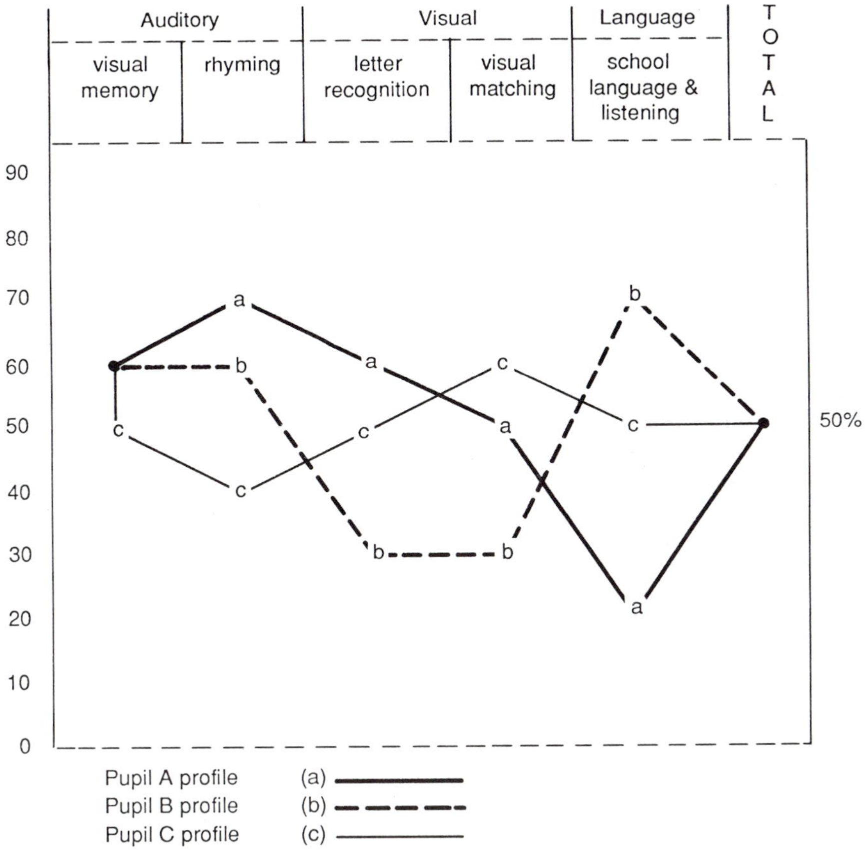

FIGURE 7–1

Some standardized tests may not match the instructional practices suggested by the latest research and theory on emerging literacy. This leads to a third problem. Unfortunately, because school districts are often evaluated on how well children perform on the standardized tests, teachers may feel pressured to teach for the test. Teachers who succumb to this temptation are likely to be using inappropriate strategies for teaching young children. In addition, such teachers spend an enormous amount of time preparing children for standardized tests by drilling them on sample tests similar to the real ones. The sample tests are graded, and instruction geared to remedy student weaknesses indicated by the test. If teachers do not prepare children for the test with practice sessions, and do not teach to the test, their children may not score well. Thus, teachers may feel they are putting their own jobs on the line if they refuse to teach to standardized tests. It is a frightening dilemma.

A fourth problem with standardized tests is that the results of such tests are commonly used in placing children in specific classrooms and reading groups. Once placed, a child is seldom shifted to a different group. Yet, the standardized tests on which placement decisions are based can yield information that is inaccurate. Figure 7-1 (p. 223) illustrates the subscores and overall percentile ranks of three kindergarten children on a typical standardized reading readiness test.

Child A scored well in auditory and visual discrimination skills, and poorly in language skills. The child's overall score is at the fiftieth percentile. Child B has good auditory skills, poor visual skills, and good language skills and also scored overall at the fiftieth percentile. Child C scored fairly consistently across visual, auditory, and language skills and likewise scored overall at the fiftieth percentile. All three children will go to the first grade and could be placed in the same reading group, even though child A has a possible language deficit and is missing one of the most important ingredients for reading success—a strong language base. These three children are quite different in ability yet have scored at the same overall percentile on a standardized test. It is very unlikely that the three will achieve similar success in reading, although they might be expected to on the basis of their test scores.

Yet another problem with standardized tests is bias. For example, standardized test scores are less reliable with younger children than with older children. Furthermore, some standardized tests are still biased in favor of white, middle-class children despite genuine attempts to alleviate the problem. Their use tends to place rural, black, and bilingual youngsters at a disadvantage. Prior knowledge plays a large role in how well children will do on the test. Children from white, middle-class homes tend to have experiences that lead to better achievement on the tests. In addition, following test directions such as "Put your finger on the star" or "Circle the goat that is behind the tree" is often a problem for the young child. Children who have never seen a goat may not circle anything, because the animal on the page might look to them like a dog.

The policy statement of the International Reading Association on *Literacy Development and Early Childhood (Preschool through Grade 3)* (IRA, 1985) suggests that evaluative procedures used

Checklist for Assessing Concepts about Print

	Always	*Sometimes*	*Never*
Knows print is read from left to right			
Knows that oral language can be written down and then read			
Knows what a letter is and can point one out on a page			
Knows what a word is and can point one out on a printed page			
Knows that there are spaces between words			
Reads environmental print			
Recognizes some words by sight			
Can name and identify rhyming words			
Can identify and name upper- and lowercase letters of the alphabet			
Associates consonants and their initial and final sounds (including hard and soft *c* and *g*)			
Associates consonant blends with their sounds (*bl, cr, dr, fl, gl, pr, st*)			
Associates vowels with their corresponding long and short sounds (*a*—acorn, apple; *e*—eagle, egg; *i*—ice, igloo; *o*—oats, octopus; *u*—unicorn, umbrella)			

Continued

	Always	Sometimes	Never
Knows the consonant diagraph sounds (*ch, ph, sh, th, wh*)			
Can blend and segment phonemes in words			
Uses context, syntax, and semantics to identify words			
Can count syllables in words			
Attempts reading by attending to picture clues and print			
Guesses and predicts words based on knowledge of sound–symbol correspondence			
Can identify suffixes and prefixes			
Demonstrates knowledge of the following phonic generalizations:			
a. In a consonant-vowel-consonant pattern, the vowel sound is usually short			
b. In a vowel-consonant-*e* pattern, the vowel is usually long			
c. When two vowels come together in a word, the first is usually long and the second is silent (train, receive, bean)			

with young children be developmentally and culturally appropriate and that the selection of evaluative measures be based on the objectives of an instructional program and consider each child's total development and its effect on reading performance. Various steps can be taken to remedy the abuse of standardized testing in early childhood education. First, administrators and teachers must understand the shortcomings of standardized tests. Second, the use of multiple assessment tools given frequently throughout the school year would tend to prevent undue emphasis on standardized test results. Third, tests that measure demonstrated characteristics of early literacy should be developed and used.

Finding suitable tests is a difficult task. However, some test makers are becoming aware of the discrepancies between new instructional strategies and the design of the present tests. There are tools for assessing many aspects of early literacy that acknowledge the newer theories and research findings and reflect the instructional strategies suggested in this book, specifically Marie Clay's (1979b) Concept about Print Test and the Early Reading Test (Mason, Stewart, & Dunning, 1986). The Early Reading Test examines such things as children's ability to read environmental print, their attempts to read predictable books, and their awareness of how they are learning to read. In addition to any standardized test, portfolio assessment measures such as interviews, anecdotal records, collection of work samples, and others described throughout the book should be used frequently.

AN IDEA FOR THE CLASSROOM

I created the following experience to try and help teachers incorporate concepts about print into thematic units carried out in early childhood classrooms. The purpose was to connect knowledge about print with content-area learning to make the information about print more meaningful. This was also a way to be sure that all letters in the alphabet were highlighted at some given point in the school year. The order in which the units are studied is not important, and it would be expected that even though a particular letter was featured in a given unit, it would be reinforced in other units when appropriate. You may choose to study unit topics that are not suggested here. If that is the case, try your hand at selecting appropriate letters to feature in other unit topics, making sure to include every letter in the alphabet as a featured letter at least once.

Refer back to this chapter to include as many strategies as possible to use in meaningful ways to feature the letters mentioned.

Unit Topics with Featured Letters and Words

All about Me—h *for home and* m *for mother*

Fall—a *for apples*, l *for leaves*, r *for raking leaves*

Learning about Different Cultures—ph *for photographs illustrating other lands*; f *for food represented in other cultures*; c *for clothing from different cultures*

My Five Senses—s *for sounds*, t *for touch*, q for quiet

Animals—p *for pets*, z *for zoo*, j *for jungle*

Winter—sh *for shoveling snow*, i *for ice*, g for gloves

Jobs in the Community—x *for X-ray*, n *for newspaper*, o *for office*

Nutrition—d *for dairy*, v *for vegetables*, e *for eggs*

Spring—y *for yellow flowers*, u *for umbrella*, k *for kite*

Transportation—w *for transportation that uses water*, b *for boats*, ch *for choo-choo*

ACTIVITIES AND QUESTIONS

1. Answer the focus questions at the beginning of the chapter.

2. Observe the environmental print in an early childhood classroom. Note what you think could be added to it, both from within the classroom and from the outside world.

3. Select three children from prekindergarten through second grade whose scores on standardized tests are available. Observe the children for oral language ability, competence in comprehension, and print knowledge. Compare what you observe concerning the children's literacy ability with their test results.

4. Write an experience chart dictated to you by children in an early childhood classroom. If you do not have access to children, do this in your college classroom with your peers dictating the contents for the chart. Critique the appearance of your chart and note problems you encountered while writing it. Use your self-evaluation for ideas for improvement.

5. Select five children at random from an early childhood classroom in which they have collected Very Own Words. List all of the words in the children's collections. Compare the list with the words found in basal reading material for the age children you selected. How closely do the basal words and the children's Very Own Words match each other?

6. Select three initial consonants other than *p*. Design classroom experiences that will illustrate and reinforce the sound–symbol relationships of each. Connect the letters to a thematic topic that is commonly studied in science or social studies in early childhood classrooms.

7. Continue the portfolio assessment for the child you selected to assess for language development in Chapter 3. Observe the child using the assessment checklist provided in this chapter concerning the evaluation of concepts about print.

8. Continue the thematic unit that you began in Chapter 3. Select three objectives in the area of concepts about print and describe three activities that will satisfy each of the objectives using your theme. (You dealt with sound–symbol associations earlier; select other concepts about print to emphasize.)

Case Study Activity

Standardized testing and the use of basal materials are being questioned in your district. Two committees are formed to deal with issues concerning each. Because you were recently promoted to the position of coordinator of language arts for the district, you are a member of both committees. The committee dealing with standardized tests is trying to decide whether or not to use them in early childhood classrooms. The committee is to write a statement supporting its position. If it decides to use standardized tests, the committee needs to continue that statement and describe how the results of the tests will be utilized.

The second committee is trying to decide whether or not to continue using basal readers, considering the strong emphasis on literacy instruction through the use of children's literature. If you decide to eliminate or maintain basals, provide a statement that supports your decision. If you decide to continue to use basals, continue your statement by describing just how these instructional materials will be used.

CHAPTER EIGHT

Writing and Literacy Development

ROBERT P. PARKER
LESLEY MANDEL MORROW

QUESTIONS TO FOCUS ON AS YOU READ THE CHAPTER

- How are reading and writing related?
- Describe theories concerning how early writing is acquired.
- Describe the six categories discussed in this chapter that reflect children's early attempts at writing.
- What objectives are appropriate for promoting writing development in early childhood?
- Describe strategies for writing development from birth to two years of age.
- There are many strategies for developing writing in preschool through second grade. Describe these strategies and be sure to include the writing center, independent writing periods, functional writing, journal writing, and writing motivated by children's literature.
- Describe the steps involved in the process approach to writing.

*Children want to write. They want to write the first day they
attend school. This is no accident. Before they went to school
they marked up walls, pavements, newspapers with crayons,
chalk, pens or pencils . . . anything that makes a mark. The
child's marks say, "I am."*

—DONALD GRAVES
Writing: Teachers and Children at Work

Mrs. Callister read the story *The Old Lady Who Swallowed a
Fly*. It is a nonsense tale that is read and also sung. The story is
composed of rhymes, and each segment is repeated to make it
quite predictable. A portion of the story follows:

*I know an old lady who swallowed a fly,
I don't know why she swallowed a fly, perhaps she'll die.
I know an old lady who swallowed a spider
That wiggled and giggled and tickled inside her,
She swallowed the spider to catch the fly,
I don't know why she swallowed the fly, perhaps she'll die.
I know an old lady who swallowed a bird,
How absurd to swallow a bird
(the refrain is repeated)
I know an old lady who swallowed a cat,
Now fancy that she swallowed a cat
(the refrain is repeated)
I know an old lady who swallowed a dog,
What a hog to swallow a dog
(the refrain is repeated and additional verses are chanted).*

After the story, Mrs. Callister suggested that the children
might think of additional rhymes for the story.

Tasha and Jason decided to work together. Tasha said, "I got
one, I know an old lady who swallowed a snake, ummm, ummm,
she got a big ache when she swallowed the snake." Jason said,
"How about what a mistake to swallow a snake." Tasha agreed she
liked that better. They tried another one. Jason said, "I know an
old lady who swallowed a frog, what a hog to swallow a frog."
Tasha said, "We can't do that, in the real story when she swallows
a dog, they say what a hog to swallow a dog." Jason thought and
said, "I know—she started to jog when she swallowed a frog."
"That's great," said Tasha.

The class came together to see what they had come up with.
Many of the rhymes were the same and many were different. There
were about ten to add to the story that they wrote out on an

experience chart and then chanted together. When they were done, Michael said, "You know, I think what we wrote is better than the original one." Everyone nodded and agreed.

Children love to play. Through play they develop socially and intellectually in fundamental ways. Especially in literate societies, children's play can take the form of making marks on paper. Children enjoy the act of making the marks, the social relationships they develop in the process, the sense of accomplishment mark making brings, and the products of the action. By writing messages, children achieve a sense of identity in their own eyes and in the eyes of others. The movement from playing with drawing and writing to communicating through written messages to writing narrative and expository text is a continuum that reflects the basic theories of emergent literacy (Dyson, 1985; Halliday, 1975; Parker, 1983; Sulzby, 1986a).

Relationships Between Reading and Writing

Some scholars view writing and reading as identical; others consider them unrelated. As Birnbaum and Emig (1983, p. 87) assert, "Both ultimate positions can be swiftly dismissed." In either process, they point out, readers and writers transform their experiences through verbal symbols. Writers reconstruct meanings by constructing texts; readers reconstruct texts by constructing anticipated meanings.

The parallels between writing and reading are more obvious for young children than for older children and adults. For example, children teach themselves to write in much the same way that they teach themselves to read: experimentally. Through personally motivated and personally directed trial and error—a necessary condition of their literacy development—they try out various aspects of the writing process. They invent and decorate letters, symbols, and words; they mix drawing and writing; they invent messages in various forms and shapes; and they often continue to use invented forms of writing after they have begun to master conventional ones (Figure 8–1).

More specifically, by experimenting with writing, children construct and refine the kind of knowledge about written language that makes reading possible. In Marie Clay's words:

*The child who engages in creative writing is manipulating the
units of written language—letters, words, sentence types—*

and is likely to be gaining some awareness of how these can be combined to convey unspoken messages. The child is having to perform within the directional constraints that we use in written English. The child is probably learning to generate sentences in a deliberate way, word by word. He makes up sentences which fit both his range of ideas and his written language skills. Fluent oral language may permit the young reader to depend almost entirely on meaning and the eye may overlook the need for discriminating details of letters and words. Creative writing demands that the child pay attention to the details of print. To put his message down in print, he is forced to construct words, letter by letter, so he becomes aware of letter features and letter sequences, particularly for the vocabulary which he uses in writing again and again. (1979a, p. 2)

In other words, as children write they integrate knowledge of reading with knowledge of writing. They need relatively little direct

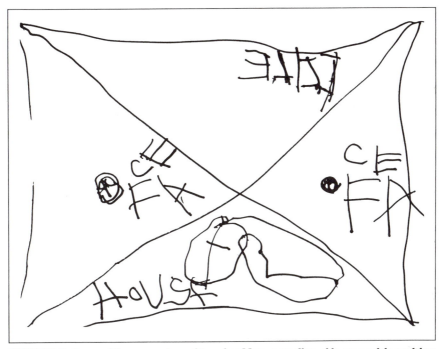

FIGURE 8–1 • *The sample written by Max, age five. He uses his writing almost as a decoration for the drawing.*

instruction to do so—just active models, supportive talk about writing and reading, and praise for their efforts.

How Early Writing Is Acquired

Children's early literacy experiences are embedded in the familiar situations and real-life experiences of family and community membership (Gundlach et al., 1985). In fact, ethnographers have discovered that because these literacy events are so natural, most parents simply do not know about many of their own children's writing and reading experiences until researchers point them out (Taylor, 1983). Many things that family members do, including the ways they relate to each other, involve literacy. They write each other notes, lists, holiday greetings, complaints, and directions. As Anderson and Stokes (1984) discovered in a study of working-class white, black, and Latino families, early literacy experiences and learning are not confined to middle- and upper-class families, even though such experiences may differ greatly from one another. "Literacy," they concluded, "is influenced largely by social institutions and not cultural membership" (p. 35).

As a process, early writing development is characterized by children's moving from playfully making marks on paper, through communicating messages on paper, to making texts as artifacts. Like Giti (Baghban, 1984), children are at first unconcerned about the products of their "writing"; they lose interest in them almost immediately. However, once Giti began to understand that the marks she made on paper "could be meaningful and [that] she enjoyed producing them, she was determined to learn how to write" (pp. 89–90). The description parallels Yetta Goodman's (1986) conclusions on children's earliest learning about writing and reading.

Children learn the uses of written language before they learn the forms (Gundlach et al., 1985; Rosen & Rosen, 1973; Taylor, 1983). In observing children scribbling and inventing primitive "texts," researchers have observed that children seem to know what writing is *for* before they know much about how to write in correct forms. The letters to friends or relatives, the greeting cards, and the signs they produce hardly resemble conventional forms. Yet, the children seem impelled by an understanding of the function of written texts. Teale (1986) draws a similar conclusion: "The functions of literacy are as much a part of learning to read and write as are the formal aspects of written language" (p. 9). (See Figure 8–2.)

FIGURE 8–2 • *Jay's early attempts at functional writing. When Jay, age five, was asked to write a letter, he chose to write to his friend Peter.*

Children's writing develops through constant invention and reinvention of the forms of written language (Dyson, 1986; Parker, 1983). Children invent ways of making letters, words, and texts, moving from primitive forms through successively closer approximations of conventional forms. As they reconstruct their abilities to produce messages and texts, they simultaneously reconstruct their knowledge about written language (Bissex, 1980; Read, 1975). Parents of preschool children who show great interest in writing typically accept and support their youngsters' production of the primitive forms, offering little or no criticism or correction. Just as children's early forms of oral language are sometimes called *proto-language*, their invented writing might be called *proto-writing*. No one teaches them the forms; they invent them from their observations of environmental print and their observing, modeling, and interacting with more literate individuals who write in their presence.

Children's involvement in written language, though typically embedded in social situations and interactions, is essentially self-initiated and self-directed. Most of the time, young children choose when to write, what to write, and how to do it. Parents, other adults, or siblings may encourage them to write, and certain situations (such as playing restaurant or waitress) may demand it, but most young children seldom write as the result of a direct order or as part of anything resembling an assignment. Tracing, copying, drilling—all such activities do not work well when given as external assignments. However, if a child voluntarily chooses to participate in such tasks, they can contribute to their writing development. Researchers such as Harste, Woodward, and Burke (1984) and Newman (1984) emphasize the importance of intent in children's early writing and learning. Children learn to expect written language to be meaningful, and they relate best to those situations in which writing occurs in that manner.

In writing, as in talking, story making is a primary impulse and activity. As humans, we share a deep and fundamental need to turn our experiences into stories (Hardy, 1968). Story making is a fundamental means by which we learn and by which we shape our intellectual development. Making and telling stories play central roles in the development of literacy and the growth of children's minds. Children often surprise us with the things they can do with written language and with what they know about it (Britton, 1982b). They seem to grasp important aspects of its functions and forms, using this imaginative awareness to produce primitive but extraordinary manifestations of language because they want to.

Children learn about writing by observing more skilled others and by participating with them in literacy events. People who are more proficient writers play an important modeling role in children's writing development (Birnbaum, 1981). Children need to observe adults participating in writing, and they must write having the guidance and support of the adult.

Children need to work independently on the functions and form of writing that they have experienced through interactions with literate others. Teale (1986) calls these activities *explorations* and claims they make it possible for children's literacy to come to "complete fruition." They may involve practicing or rehearsing aspects of writing—letter formation and differentiation, similarities or differences between drawing and writing, spelling, punctuation, and so forth. They are apparently linked to children's evolving knowledge *about* language—their *metalinguistic knowledge.* When children explore their emergent knowledge and their skill in writing independently, they become more conscious of what they know and more explicit. They may even develop language to talk about it (Goodman, 1986). The more they make their knowledge about language explicit, the more children are able to use that explicit knowledge to direct and control their own attempts at writing, and thus the forms and functions of writing.

Two points are important here. First, children practice what they learn about writing, but such practice is most helpful when self-initiated. Second, self-initiated practice contributes to what children learn consciously about writing, an evolving phenomenon that plays a fundamental role in the development of their writing abilities. (See Figures 8–3 and 8–4).

Theory of Writing Development

In the broadest sense, children's language development can be viewed as part of their process of learning to participate in sharing

FIGURE 8–3 · *Jennifer, age three and a half, practices writing through the repetition of similar letter patterns from left to right across the page.*

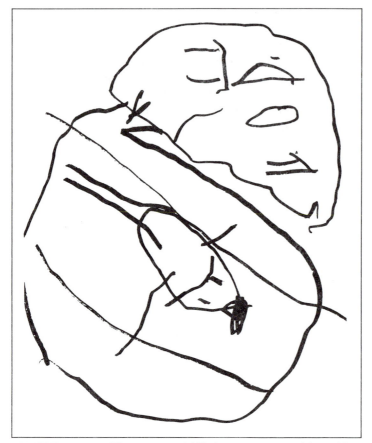

FIGURE 8–4 • *Three-year-old Robert separates his writing from his drawing by enclosing each in a circle during self-initiated practice.*

and making social meanings (Halliday, 1975). To achieve this participation, they learn to understand, use, and make various symbols. Though language is just one of the symbol systems used, it is the most important and pervasive one. Thus, as part of their broad process of symbol development, children learn to listen, talk, write, and read—that is, they develop language in all four of its uses. Their language learning begins in the prespeech communication that parents and infants construct, and it builds through listening to talking, to gesturing, to playing symbolically, to drawing, and from there to writing and reading (Vygotsky, 1978). Children's main resource for literacy learning is their knowledge of ways to symbolize experience and to communicate through those symbols in pre- and postspeech interactions.

This overall theoretical framework can be summarized as follows:

1. Literacy development is part of language development.
2. Language development is part of symbol development.
3. Symbol development is part of the development of social and cultural meanings.

For most children, the process occurs as a continuum. There are no sharp gaps or transitions from one aspect to another. Under normal circumstances, children's literacy development begins with the continual process of learning to communicate—first non-verbally, then by talking, next with symbolic play, and finally by drawing. Each new phase is rooted in earlier phases and forms a new network of communication resources and potential.

Further, this literacy learning occurs naturally in the inter-actions of family and community life. In the process, children move from playing with written language to using it to communicate. They invent and reinvent forms. When children first begin making marks on paper, most do so with no knowledge of the alphabetic nature of the written language's symbol system. Initially, they do not conceive of writing as a means of encoding speech (Dyson, 1985; Ferreiro, 1978; Ferreiro and Teberosky, 1982). Shortly thereafter, they view letters as referring to actual people or things, though they still believe that writing, like drawing, only encodes or reflects specific objects, not "filler" words such as articles or adjectives. Only later do they realize that writing represents language (Figure 8–5.)

The Development of Writing Ability

Researchers have arrived at various descriptions of what can be viewed as developmental stages of writing in early childhood (Clay, 1975; Dyson, 1985; Sulzby, 1986b; Teale, 1986; Vukelich & Golden, 1984). Most agree, though, that if there are indeed stages, they are not rigorously defined or necessarily sequential. Dyson

FIGURE 8–5 • *Scribble writing by Justin (age four)
that goes from left to right across the page. An
illustration accompanies the writing, and the child
explained to the teacher what the writing said about the
picture. The child understands that writing represents
language.*

(1986) describes children's writing development as having two
broad phases. From birth to about age three, children begin to
explore the form of writing by scribbling. Then, as children progress from three to six, their "controlled scribbling gradually develops into recognizable objects which they name, and similarly,
the scribbling gradually acquires the characteristics of print, including linearity, horizontal orientation, and the arrangement of
letter-like forms . . ." (p. 118). In fact, as we have noted, children
may initially attempt to encode objects directly, as in drawing, and
only later attempt to encode language.

Sulzby (1985) identified six broad categories of writing in a
sample of twenty-four kindergarten children, cautioning that

these should not be considered a reflection of developmental ordering. They do describe, however, children's early attempts at writing.

1. **Writing via drawing.** The child will use drawing to stand for writing. The child is working out the relationship between drawing and writing, not confusing the two. The child sees drawing/writing as communication of a specific and purposeful message. Children who participate in writing via drawing will read their drawings as if there is writing on them (Figure 8–6).
2. **Writing via scribbling.** The child scribbles but intends it as writing. Often the child appears to be writing and scribbles from left to right. The child moves the pencil as an adult does, and the pencil makes writing-like sounds. The scribble resembles writing (Figure 8–7).
3. **Writing via making letter-like forms.** At a quick glance, shapes in the child's writing resemble letters. However, close observation reveals that they only look like letters. They are not just poorly formed letters though, they are creations (Figure 8–8).
4. **Writing via reproducing well-learned units or letter strings.** The child uses letter sequences learned from such sources as his or her own name. The child sometimes changes the order of the letters, writing the same ones many different ways, or reproduces letters in long strings or in random order (Figure 8–9).
5. **Writing via invented spelling.** Many varieties and levels of invented spelling are demonstrated by children. Basically, children create their own spelling for words when they do not know the conventional spellings. In invented spelling, one letter may represent an entire syllable and words sometimes overlap and are not properly spaced. As the child's writing matures, the words look more like conventional writing, with perhaps only one letter invented or left out (Figure 8–10).
6. **Writing via conventional spelling.** The child's writing resembles adult writing (Figure 8–11).

Sulzby's general description of early writing is most helpful for parents and teachers when they are observing and describing children's writing. As we have noted, however, Sulzby emphasizes that these categories are not necessarily developmental or sequentially invariant.

FIGURE 8–6 • *Writing via drawing: When asked to write something, Brad (age four) drew a picture. The same request over time yielded the same response, a drawing for writing.*

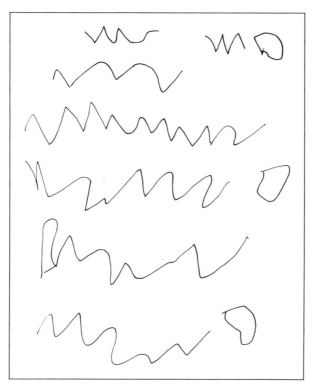

FIGURE 8–7 • *Writing via scribbling: When asked to write, Katie (age three) began by scribbling randomly on the page. She eventually progressed to a left-to-right scribble and then purposeful marks that began to look like letter forms.*

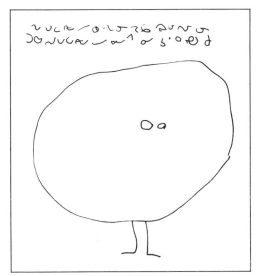

FIGURE 8–8 • *Writing via making letter-like forms. Very carefully written by Olivia (age four), these letter-like forms go from left to right across the page.*

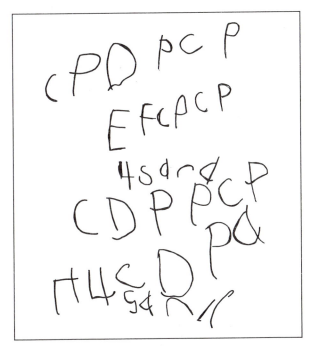

FIGURE 8–9 • *Writing via reproducing well-learned units or letter strings. These random letters written by Brian (age four) go from left to right across the page.*

243

I Love cat's Bcuz Thea are So Prety To. and I lik uTher anmlz I Love mi famle and Thea Love me bac.

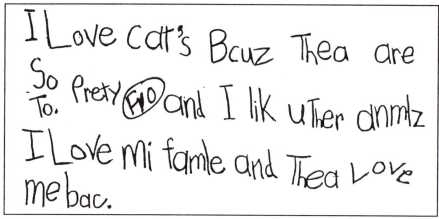

FIGURE 8–10 • ***Writing via invented spelling: "I love cats because they are so pretty and I like other animals too. I love my family and they love me back." This was written by Jenny C. Wilkinson in the spring of her kindergarten year.***

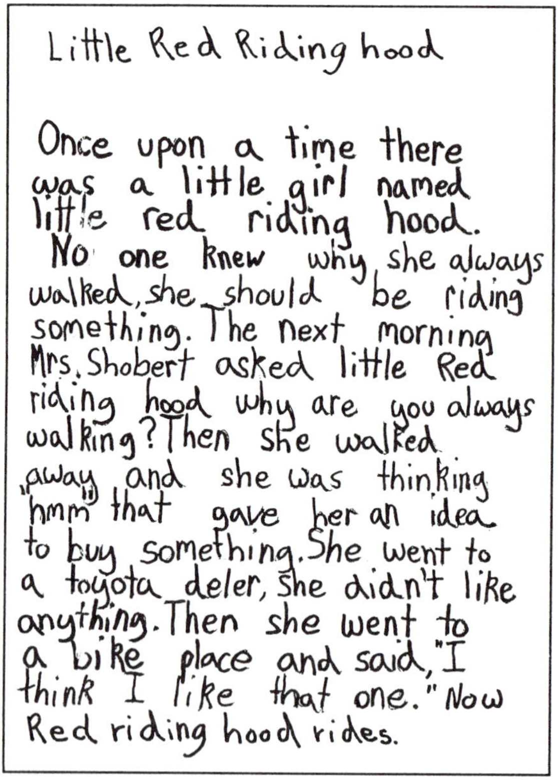

Little Red Riding hood

Once upon a time there was a little girl named little red riding hood. No one knew why she always walked, she should be riding something. The next morning Mrs. Shobert asked little Red riding hood why are you always walking? Then she walked away and she was thinking "hmm" that gave her an idea to buy something. She went to a toyota deler, she didn't like anything. Then she went to a bike place and said, "I think I like that one." Now Red riding hood rides.

FIGURE 8–11 • ***Conventional spelling. This story was written by Kevin, who was in second grade.***

Strategies and Objectives for Promoting Writing Development

Parents and teachers can use various strategies to encourage and respond to children's self-initiated writing efforts. They can create situations that will engage children in producing and learning about written language. These situations reflect our growing understanding that children's literacy develops within the context of family and community events that involve writing and reading, but for which literacy instruction is only infrequently an immediate goal.

Of all the new ideas, theories, and strategies concerning emergent literacy, the way in which we think about writing represents the most obvious break with tradition. We have allowed children to use crayons and paper to encourage development of motor coordination in preparation for writing, but we never thought of writing to convey meaning as being an integral part of an early literacy program for children as young as two. From now on, we will be suggesting the integration of strategies for writing into the daily routines of babies, toddlers, preschoolers, kindergartners, and first graders. We will consider even the youngest child's marks on paper as early attempts at writing, rather than as random marks. This perception is indeed a new element in programs for early literacy development.

The following objectives are posed from the perspective that children learn language, including writing and reading, by using it purposefully in social situations (for example, in playing or communicating), not by practicing isolated or abstracted skills. Generally, the best way to assist children in language and literacy development is to create situations for meaningful use rather than offering direct parceled language instruction. This principle applies equally in the home, day-care center, nursery, kindergarten, or first or second grade.

1. Children will be provided with an environment in which they are regularly exposed to many kinds of print.
2. Children will experience print as a source of pleasure and enjoyment.
3. Children will regularly observe adults writing, both for work and for leisure.
4. Children will be given opportunities and materials for writing themselves.

5. Children will be assisted in deciding what to write about, but left alone to make such decisions.
6. Children will be supported in constructing invented forms of letters, words, and messages.
7. Children's efforts at writing, whatever the form, will be responded to as meaningful communication (e.g., scribble writing, letter-like forms, random letters, invented spelling).
8. Children will be encouraged to use writing for a wide range of individual and social purposes, such as making lists, cards, letters, signs, announcements, stories, expository pieces, and books.
9. Children will be read stories in a variety of styles, which may serve as eventual models for their writing.
10. The use of writing will be integrated throughout the curriculum.
11. Teachers will take the opportunity through children's writing to point out sound-symbol correspondences as the spoken word is transformed into the written.
12. Children will be exposed to the appropriate way to write letters in manuscript.
13. Children will be exposed to the use of some aspects of punctuation: periods, commas, and quotation marks.

Strategies for Writing Development from Birth to Two

Earlier chapters have described strategies that parents can use in helping children with oral language development and early reading. Some of those strategies can be applied directly to children's early writing development; others can be adapted. Some strategies are helpful specifically with writing development. It is crucial to remember, though, that speaking, reading, and writing are dynamically linked in children's development. When we help children with oral language, we also contribute indirectly to their literacy development by increasing their language experience. Similarly, reading development contributes to speaking and writing, and writing to speaking and reading. This understanding forms the basis for the *whole language* approaches used in some elementary schools (Newman, 1985).

In a detailed case study, Baghban (1984) describes observations of her daughter Giti's writing development from eighteen months, when Giti first began marking on paper, to twenty-four months. When Giti began scribbling, her productions sprawled all over the page. By nineteen months she had begun to make dots and her sprawl was noticeably less extreme. By twenty months she had added circles and wavy lines to her repertoire. When she wrote after watching one of her parents write, her productions "more closely resembled English script" (p. 48). At twenty-three months she averaged ten minutes per writing session, and at twenty-four months she began babbling over her own writing. She also attempted to write her first letter, *M* for *McDonald's* and for *Marcia*, her mother's first name. Throughout the period, and later as well, Giti's parents followed her literacy experiences and efforts attentively. Such attentiveness is something we urge all parents and primary care givers to adopt.

As suggested in earlier chapters, another important way that we can support children's writing development is to become more aware of their experiences with environmental print, including print they see on television, in religious environments, on food cans and boxes, on signs, and in stores. Not only can we become more aware of the variety and frequency of children's experiences with environmental print, we can talk with them about these experiences, commenting, asking questions, and encouraging them to identify and remember signs, letters, and bits of print out of their normal contexts (for instance, an *M* used somewhere other than in a *McDonald's* sign). If we so interact with children, especially from their second year on, we are ready to support them when, as a part of their scribble writing, they try to write one or more of these environmentally learned letters. In fact, some children may make their first attempts to do this between eighteen and twenty-four months, though most children will not begin until twenty-four to thirty-six months.

We can also assist children in their first attempts to make marks on paper. Often, when children begin scribbling (some at eighteen months), they bang on the paper with their writing implements. Only a bit later do they begin using smoother, more deliberate, more coordinated movements to make their marks. When children are in their first, primitive stages of scribbling, we can show them how to hold markers or crayons. We can guide their hands to paper, not making marks for them but helping them understand that the paper is the place for writing.

Our responses to children's early scribbling are important. It is better not to urge children to write particular things. They should make marks spontaneously and decide for themselves when these marks are intended to represent something. It is important not to press them to tell us what their marks mean or represent. It is better to say, "I like that," than to ask, "What is it?". "Can you write some more?" is also a helpful response, but do not insist if the child says no. Expressing genuine pleasure in children's early markings, whether they resemble writing or not, and seeing them as an important step in a long developmental process are positive responses that will encourage children to continue. By continuing their "writing," they will incorporate in it what they are learning about print from the literacy events that fill their lives.

Beyond responding supportively to children, we can model writing for them by writing in their presence. As we have seen, we can let them see us writing letters, lists, and notes and filling out forms and bills, and we can interact with them about what we are doing. For example: "I'm writing a letter to Grandma and Grandpa. I'm telling them that we miss them. Do you want to tell them something? Do you want to write something on the paper to them?" When writing, invite the youngsters to sit with you, watch you, ask questions, and try their own hand at writing. This gives children opportunities to see how we go about writing and to begin to understand that the marks we make convey meaning.

Junk mail is a form of environmental print that can arouse interest in writing. Children enjoy writing or making marks on flyers, brochures, ads, announcements, and forms. They will write over the print and in the blank spaces. Apparently, the look and arrangement of the print gives them the model and inspiration to make their own marks.

Repeating rhymes and singing songs can also contribute to children's early writing. So can using hand puppets and playing with toys and games, such as puzzles that can be taken apart and put back together. Manipulative toys that require dexterity help with the motor development needed to shape letters. Playing with clay or play dough, finger painting, using chalkboards, and painting on easels help build motor coordination as well. Birnbaum (1981) found that involvement in such activities was associated with learning to write and read easily and naturally. Of course, reading to children not only develops oral language and promotes early reading attempts, as discussed earlier, it can also motivate children to emulate the writing or to make their own books, no matter how crude the first attempts. Parents and care givers in day-care centers can display children's early writings on walls, doors, and appliances, to be enjoyed and not judged or corrected.

Homes as well as day-care centers should provide environments for writing—comfortable spots with rugs and child-size tables and chairs—and storage for writing materials. The latter should include felt-tip markers, pencils, crayons, and chalk. There should be ample supplies and varied sizes of large unlined paper (newsprint works well) and a chalkboard. Materials should be stored consistently in the place provided for writing so that the child can learn how to select materials and put them away independently (Glazer, 1980).

Strategies for Writing Development in Early Childhood Classrooms

Parents and teachers can expect to see rapid development in writing in children from two to eight years of age. As we have seen, it is during this period that most children move from scribbling to producing random letters, to writing letters, to writing words with invented spellings, to beginning to use conventional writing. They will begin to space properly between words and use some marks of punctuation. They tend to write longer pieces, and their productions often represent wider ranges of functions and forms. In short, this is a time when children show intense bursts of writing activity, perhaps alternating these with intense bursts of reading activity (Bissex, 1980). It is important, therefore, that teachers have a sense of children's writing needs and interests at this time and know how to interact with them in order to support their efforts, learning, and growth.

Like younger children, preschoolers and kindergarteners for the most part take more pleasure in the *process* of writing than in its *products.* The act of writing is their center of interest. Gradually they do develop concern for the products. When they play waiter or waitress, for example, and take an "order," they may be concerned that others can "read" it. The same thing might happen with notes or greeting cards sent to relatives or friends. Children begin to evidence concern that recipients are able to read their messages—perhaps so they can write back. Children who have had little experience pretending to write might be reluctant to make marks on paper even by kindergarten age, possibly because they have become aware that their marks are not conventional writing and thus might not be accepted. It is important to let them know that writing that is not conventional will be accepted. Some children may request conventional spellings and will not write unless they know it is correct. They should be given the help they request.

Children in societies such as ours have experienced literacy through preschool and kindergarten, and they have constructed useful though usually asystematic knowledge about writing and reading. Some may also have begun to write and read on their own, though in unconventional and invented forms. Therefore, it is inappropriate to think of these youngsters as preliterate. The challenge for schools is to provide experiences that complement children's prior experiences and to recognize individual differences in development among youngsters (Clark, 1984). It is important that adults observe the signs and pace of the growth of children's understanding of writing, of their use of writing for a widening range of purposes, and of their ability to control various writing conventions in less primitive, more adult-like ways. Observing children's early writing development creates a context for the planned learning events and spontaneous interactions through which adults can contribute so fundamentally to children's emergent literacy.

Adults should take children's early writing seriously as interesting evidence of the kinds of experiments with writing that contribute centrally to their literacy development. Children's early writings are to be enjoyed, valued, and understood. At the same time, they should usually not be made the occasion for the hunting and correction of errors or for excessive direct teaching. The latter should follow only from children's questions and expressed needs and should thus be individualized. Direct teaching should also be given in proportion to the magnitude of the request. Often, adults respond to children's requests with information and explanations that are appropriate and helpful but too long or detailed.

We must realize that what young children write about and how they approach writing is more important than their mechanics of writing (spelling, handwriting, punctuation, and spacing). Mechanical skills *are* related to writing, but not writing as we are concerned with it in early childhood literacy development. Learning to write involves learning to compose texts that convey meaning. As children gain experience with writing, they will learn the peripheral skills and mechanics of writing through practice and instruction when the need arises and by asking for the information.

When children are free to write in unconventional ways, such as using invented spellings as illustrated in Figure 8–10, p. 244,

they are enhancing phonemic awareness and eventually knowledge of phonics. When children write they have to transform the
spoken word into written language. This fosters understanding of
the structure of spoken language and how it is related to written
language. The more children write, the better they become at
segmenting sounds into words, which not only develops their
ability to write, but their ability to read independently as well.

No distinctions should be made among the kinds of writing
young children undertake. A list of words is as important as a
creative story. For young children, the functions of writing are
more important than the form or content. They choose to write if
a situation has meaning for them. If we impose upon them our
selection of what they should write about, we are not likely to see
positive results. With these basic ideas in mind, we can create
strategies and appropriate environments for helping children write
naturally.

The Writing Center

The literacy area in the classroom should include a place
designated for writing. It should be easily accessible, attractive,
and inviting. This area can be a part of the library corner. It should

*The computer allows very young children to
communicate thoughts they do not yet have
the manual dexterity to write on paper. Early
introduction to the computer will make it part
of the child's everyday life.*

be furnished with a table and chairs, plus a rug for youngsters who want to stretch out and write on the floor. Writing implements should include plenty of colored felt-tip marking pens, large and small crayons, large and small pencils (both regular and colored), and chalk and a chalkboard. Various types of paper should be available, lined and unlined, plain white or newsprint, ranging from 8 1/2 × 11 inches to 24 × 36 inches. Do not, however, use manuscript practice paper that is lined with different colored and dotted lines specifically to encourage proper size of letters and spacing between lines. Most preschoolers and kindergartners are not ready for such discipline of form.

Index cards for recording Very Own Words should be stored in the writing area, as should the children's collections of Very Own Words. Each child should have a writing folder in which to collect written samples of his or her work over the course of the school year. If available, a typewriter is useful, as is a computer for word processing. Materials for making books should also be available, including colored construction paper for covers, plain white paper for inside pages, a stapler, and scissors. Teachers can prepare blank books, keyed to special occasions, for children to use. For example, a blank Valentine's Day book shaped like a heart and made of red construction paper with five or six sheets of plain white paper stapled inside provides inviting space that children can fill with their written greetings. (See Figures 8–12, 8–13, and 8–14 on preparing blank books.) Stock *bare books* (books with hard covers but no print inside) for special projects, and blue books used for examinations are perfect for young children's writing. They can be purchased from school supply companies and are very inexpensive. They come with twelve or sixteen pages, which is usually just right for an original story by young children. Keep a supply of interesting pictures, posters, magazines, and newspapers; these can stimulate, decorate, or illustrate children's writing.

An alphabet chart in easy view helps children identify and shape letters they may need while writing. Tactile plastic, magnetic, wooden, and felt letters should be among the language arts manipulatives. These help develop motor dexterity for the act of writing and aid in letter recognition and formation. A bulletin board should be available for children to display their own writing with a space for posting notices or sending and receiving messages. "Mailboxes" for youngsters' incoming and outgoing "mail" can be placed in the writing center. The mailboxes for a pen pal program are discussed later in the functional writing section. The

Allison adds her page to the class book at the writing table in the writing center.

writing center should be labeled with a sign that could say "Author's Spot" or whatever name is selected by the children.

Basic implements and supplies for writing should be stocked in every other learning center in the room as well. The accessibility of these materials will encourage writing (Morrow, 1990). A child might want to copy the dramatic play, record the outside temperature on a chart in the science center, protect a construction of blocks with a "Do Not Touch" sign, or copy a Very Own Word in the social studies or science area. A group might decide to turn

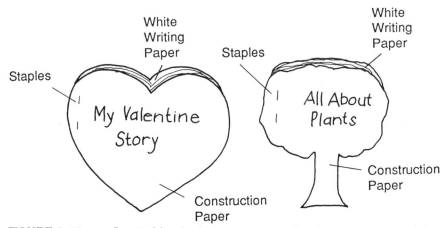

FIGURE 8–12 • *Stapled book. Cut colored construction paper and white writing paper into a desired shape. Staple at the side.*

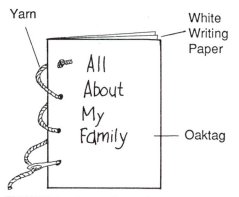

FIGURE 8–13 • *Sewn book. Punch holes into oaktag and white writing paper. Sew together with yarn.*

the dramatic-play corner into a dentist's office, including in it an appointment book for recording dates, times, and patients' names; appointment cards; patients' records; and a prescription pad for medication.

In all such situations, children should write independently according to function and interest. The teacher has prepared the environment in which such writing can occur and has introduced the materials and made suggestions to the children. With this

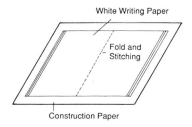

a. Sew a running stitch down the center of eight to ten sheets of eight-and-a-half-by-eleven plain white writing paper backed with a piece of nine-by-twelve colored construction paper.

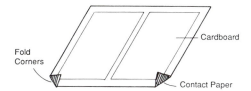

b. Place an eleven-by-fourteen piece of contact paper or wallpaper face down. Paste two pieces of six-by-nine oaktag or cardboard on the peeled contact paper a quarter inch apart, leaving about a one-inch border. Fold each corner of the contact paper onto the oaktag to form a triangle (glue if using wallpaper).

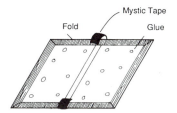

c. Fold the edges of the contact paper onto the oaktag (paste down if using wallpaper). Place a twelve-inch piece of Mystic Tape down the center of the contact paper and over its edges. Put glue on the two exposed pieces of oaktag and on the quarter-inch space between them.

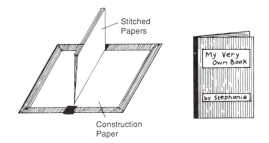

d. Place the folded and stitched edge of the construction paper and plain white paper in the quarter-inch glued space. Paste the construction paper onto the oaktag and over the contact-paper border to make the inside covers.

FIGURE 8–14 • *Folded, stitched, and glued book.*

preparation, children look naturally to writing as a means of communication.

Independent Writing

In Chapter 5, the independent reading and writing period, which gives children the opportunity to participate in literacy activities, was discussed. Children could choose what to do based on several options, and they could choose to work alone or collaboratively with others. Chapter 5 emphasized pleasurable experiences with reading, and collecting anecdotes concerning reading behaviors during this time. It is difficult to separate reading and writing, especially during this independent time when children direct their own behavior. It is interesting to note when observing children during independent reading and writing periods that equal time is spent at reading and writing. When children decided to engage in writing, it often was a cooperative effort. During this period, children had the opportunity to select from a list of literacy activities, such as:

Read a book, magazine, or newspaper alone or with a friend.

Listen to a story on the headsets at the listening station.

Read or tell a story using a felt-board and story characters.

Read or tell a story using a roll movie.

Read or tell a story using the chalk talk technique.

Read or tell a story using puppets.

Prepare a tape story by recording your reading of a book.

Write a story alone or with a friend.

Write a story and make it into a felt story.

Write a story and record it for the listening station.

Write a story and perform it as a puppet show.

Write a story and make it into a roll movie.

Write a story and present it as a chalk talk.

Present a play based on a story you wrote or read.

Bind a story you've written into a book and place it in the library corner for others to read.

Participate in content-area activities that involve reading and writing.

The following anecdotes relate to the writing that took place during observations of independent reading and writing periods. It is evident how closely reading and writing are linked. So many of the things children chose to do were motivated by what they had read or what was read to them. When writing, they often looked for additional information by going to sources to read more.

After listening to the teacher read *The Magic School Bus Inside the Earth*, Stephanie, Jason, Kevin, and Nicky decided to make a poster about the book that showed key pictures with captions for each picture. The children delegated responsibilities. They made up a title for the poster and called it, *Scenes from The Magic School Bus Inside the Earth*. They drew episodes from the story and wrote their own captions for the pictures. The poster took several days to complete. (One of the characteristics of independent reading and writing is that projects can be worked on over a long period of time.) When the poster was complete, the children presented their work to the class. Stephanie and Jason held the poster and Kevin and Nicky were the spokespersons. Kevin explained how the group wanted to illustrate the story in an unusual way and decided on a poster. Kevin and Nicky took turns pointing to the pictures they had all drawn and reading the captions they had written for each.

Heather, Kim, and Tina read a biography about *Willie Mays, the Baseball Star*. They decided to make a roll movie about the book. They wrote dialogue for the pictures they drew. Their information came from the book they had read. Heather was concerned that they might need more information about Willie Mays and suggested they look in the dictionary. Kim told Heather that dictionaries are for finding out how to spell words and getting their definitions and encyclopedias were for finding out information. The girls did find additional information about Willie Mays in the encyclopedia. They copied it down and continued with their work.

Motivated by a movie entitled *A Fish Called Wanda*, Zarah and Shakiera decided to write their own story about Wanda. Shakiera asked Zarah to write and Shakiera suggested that she would do the pictures for the story. Shakiera also offered her help in thinking of the words to write. Zarah began to write the first line: "A fish called Wanda was a talking fish." Shakiera told Zarah to add to the sentence, "and she had magic."

Zarah said, "Magic, I don't know if that's the right word. I think she had powers." Shakiera said, "I think that magic and power are the same thing." The girls agreed and went on to write the rest of the story.

Television shows, rock stars, and current events motivated writing during independent reading and writing. Three girls created a roll movie that included biographies of each member of the singing group "The New Kids on the Block." Another group made a felt story for an original episode they created for the television program "In Living Color." One boy created an episode in book form for the TV show "The Simpsons."

Current events along with books children read motivated writing. Joey was reading a book about the Civil War. He asked the teacher to read it to the class, which she did. Joey decided to write his own book about the Civil War, and Christopher joined him. Christopher called the book "U.S. Saratoga." As they were drawing pictures, they made bombing sounds. Suddenly Joey said, "Wait a minute, this is weird. We're making airplane carriers fighting in the Civil War." The two boys changed their minds and decided to do a book on the Persian Gulf War, which was happening at that time. They included "Stormin' Norman" and Saddam Hussein in the story. It was an intense piece.

These episodes during independent reading and writing reveal a wide variety of topics that were written about. Many of them we would never think to ask children to write about. If we did, they probably would never have the enthusiasm they demonstrated because they didn't select them themselves. We also don't know what all of their interests are. Children have original ideas that

Second-grade boys engage in a cooperative writing experience.

they can draw from their varied and rich life experiences. The topics they select have meaning and function for them, and therefore they write freely and enthusiastically about them. As in Chapter 5, these activities can be adapted for children with special needs. Children can write to other youngsters who may share their problems. As teachers have said, "There was something for everyone during independent reading and writing, the gifted, the child who attended basic skills classes, and youngsters from bilingual backgrounds."

Functional Writing

Children need to see purpose before they write. Class writing projects that are particularly purposeful include **greeting cards** for all occasions to parents, grandparents, sisters, brothers, friends, and relatives. Don't forget birthdays and holidays. Write **thank-you notes** to guest speakers who come to class, to mothers or other adults who help on class trips, to the director of the zoo you visited, or to the librarian who spent time with the class at the public library. Prepare **lists** of things to remember to do in preparing a party, a special program, or a class trip. Make **address and telephone books** with entries from class members. Write notes to parents about activities in school. Encourage individual children to write to their parents about specific things they are doing in school.

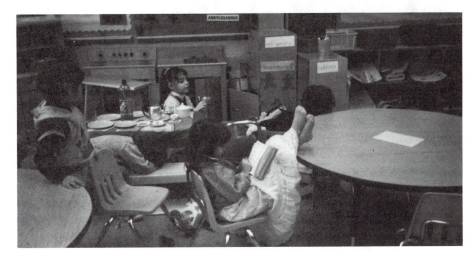

While participating in dramatic play, Melissa writes her phone number in the class address book, found in the dramatic-play center.

Collecting and using Very Own Words offer opportunities for writing and copying and so does using classroom environmental print in one's own writing. Some preschools and kindergartens, as well as elementary classrooms, have established **mail service** and **pen pal** programs (Green, 1985; Martinez & Teale, 1987; Mason, 1986). Children are offered pen pals to write to regularly (once a week is reasonable). Teachers or aides may have to help children write their letters or take dictation. Encourage children to use what writing capabilities they have, even if they cannot produce conventional writing. Teachers may have to read the incoming letters to students who cannot yet read conventionally.

A **notice board** for exchanging messages also motivates functional writing (Newman, 1984). Children can tack up pictures for each other as beginning messages. The teacher needs to provide a model by leaving messages for individuals and for the entire class. Notices about school or class events are appropriate. It is important to draw attention to the board when posting a class message or when leaving messages for individuals, so that children get into the habit of looking for messages and leaving them themselves.

Teachers may need to take dictation for journal writing and for writing to pen pals. Eventually children should be encouraged to do their own writing.

Journal writing can be carried out successfully in early childhood rooms, with entries made daily or at least several times a week. Children are encouraged to write anything they want in their journals and to write at their own developmental levels. Thus, some children's journals might include only pictures, scribble writing, random letters, or invented spelling. The teacher models journal writing, perhaps with a personal message such as, "I'm very excited today. My daughter is going to be in a play tonight, and I'm going to watch her." By example the child is given an idea about the kinds of entries that are appropriate. Some children draw or write stories in their journals as well as personal experiences (Hipple, 1985). From time to time the journal can also take on dialogue form, the teacher responding to a child's journal entry with a comment. If the child writes, "I had a picnic," the teacher might respond, "That sounds like fun. What did you eat?" The length and fluency of children's journal entries show great gains when the activity is continued regularly throughout a school year (Newman, 1984). Journals can be written about a child's personal life. They can be related to topics studied such as recording the growth of a seed that was planted, charting daily temperature, or reacting to a story that was read. Journals can be written in notebooks or pages stapled together to create a book.

Print in the classroom provides an opportunity for children to copy writing. This is a task enjoyed by four-, five-, and six-year-olds and encourages independent writing.

Children's Literature and Writing

Children's literature and writing is as natural a medium for encouraging writing as it is for encouraging oral language and reading (Routman, 1991). Reading several books by the same author or illustrator can prompt a class letter asking the author how he or she gets ideas to write or asking the illustrator what kind of art materials he or she uses. It is best to identify authors or illustrators who are likely to respond, for it is important to receive a response, even if it comes from a publisher's representative. Series books—those that use the same character in several different books, such as *Madeline* (Bemelmans, 1939), *Curious George* (Rey, 1941), and *Harold and the Purple Crayon* (Johnson, 1955)—can motivate children to write their own books or a class book about the character. Books such as *Swimmy* (Lionni, 1963) and *Alexander and the Terrible, Horrible, No Good, Very Bad Day* (Viorst, 1972) involve the main character in a series of adventures or incidents as the story proceeds. Children can be asked to write still another episode or adventure for the character. Some stories, such as *Alexander and the Terrible, Horrible, No Good, Very Bad Day*, lend themselves to writing about personal experiences. (Fig-

FIGURE 8–15

ure 8–15 illustrates one child's response to this task.) Shared book experiences, directed listening/reading–thinking activities, one-to-one and small-group story readings (described in Chapter 6) can all lead to writing experiences. Predictable books provide patterns that children can imitate in their own writing through: cumulative patterns, as in *I Know an Old Lady* (Westcott, 1980); repetitive language, as in *Are You My Mother?* (Eastman, 1960); familiar sequences, as in *The Very Hungry Caterpillar* (Carle, 1970); or catch-phrases, as in *Horton Hatches the Egg* (Seuss, 1940). (See Appendix A for a list of such books.)

Children need to share their writing with some audience. When they know they will be sharing their work, they will write for that audience and have a greater purpose for writing. At a designated time during the day, usually at the end when the class gets together to review the day's happenings, a child can be selected as Author of the Day to share something that he or she has written (Graves & Hansen, 1983). More than one piece can be read and more than one child can be Author of the Day. Those authors who read their writings in a particular week should display them on a bulletin board in the writing center along with photographs of themselves. When sharing work, the child can sit in a chair marked "Author's Chair." This is a permanent fixture in the room for all to use at some particular time. Children in the audience should be encouraged to comment about their friends' work with

John reads one of the books published by his kindergarten class. They tend to be very popular among the children.

such statements as "I like what you wrote" or "I fell and cut my knee once, too." Because at first the children may not comment readily, the teacher needs to model comments for the audience, whose young members will soon emulate the behavior.

It was Steven's turn in the Author's Chair. He sat down, and organized his materials, and said,

> *I've been working on a series of stories. They are all about the same character and in each one he had another adventure. It is sort of like the books about* Clifford the Big Red Dog. *My stories are about a cat and the first one is called* The Cat Named Buster. *I call that Part I; I already have Part II and Part III. Part II is called* Buster Meets Pretzel. *Pretzel is a dog. Part III is called* Buster Gets Lost. *I'll read Part I to you.*

After reading Part I of his stories, Philip said, "Can I read one?" Steven replied, "Sure but you should read all of them. They go together." Philip continued, "I just want to read the first one now." Steven said, "O.K., but you don't know what you're missing."

Children's work should be published. "Why publish?" almost answers the question "Why write?" "Writing is a public act, meant to be shared with many audiences" (Graves, 1983, p. 54). When children know their work will be published, they write for a defined purpose. When work is to be published it becomes special; it needs to be done carefully and refined. Children can publish their work in many ways. The most popular is to bind writings into books, which are placed in the literacy center and featured on open bookshelves for others to read. Other means of publishing include creating felt-board stories or roll movies, telling stories to classmates, role-playing what has been written, or presenting the story in a puppet show. A computer can be used to type, save, and print original material.

The Process Approach to Writing in Early Childhood

For rather experienced early writers, publishing can be the motivation for beginning the **process approach** to writing. The process approach makes children realize that writing involves thinking, organizing, and rewriting before a piece is complete. They become aware that a first writing rarely constitutes a finished product. Typical steps in this approach include prewriting, drafting, conferencing, revising, and editing (Calkins, 1986). **Pre-**

These two children are publishing a story they have written by creating a roll movie that they will tell to the class or a friend.

Stephanie puts the finishing touches on the cover of a book she has written.

writing involves some brainstorming related to the topic. Brainstorming can take place with the entire class, a friend, the teacher, or alone. If the topic is the writer's favorite food, brainstorming might include listing the characteristics of the food, the different ways the writer likes it prepared, and what in particular he or she likes about it. The prewriting activity helps generate ideas and organizes thoughts prior to writing. The prewriting ideas made into an outline help determine what to write about first, second, and so on. **Drafting** is the second part in the process. The author makes his or her first attempt at writing the piece by getting the words down on paper. The lists prepared in the prewriting phase are used as a guide. The **conference,** which is next, can be done with a teacher or a friend. This is a time to reflect upon what has been written to see if changes need to be made and, if so, just what they ought to be. It is preferable to reflect with someone else but a child can also do it alone. The fourth part is **revising.** During the conference, suggestions arise that may demonstrate the need for change, and this is the time to make those changes. When the revision is made, the author goes on to the fifth step, which is called **editing.** Editing requires minor changes to the piece, mostly attending to such things as punctuation, grammatical corrections, and spelling.

The process approach should be used cautiously with pre-schoolers and kindergarteners. The prewriting phase may be accomplished through discussion and word lists. The drafting or initial writing can be carried out, but the teacher must be sensitive to the child's attempted writing behavior. The teacher then asks the child if he or she can think of any changes to be made or other ideas to be added. This is the revision stage. The final task is editing, and with young children this means copying the work over. If the child is publishing a book, it might mean copying it into a bound book. (Three ways of making a book are illustrated earlier in this chapter in Figures 8–12 to 8–14).

Some children may be frustrated by revisions and editing, particularly by having to copy their work over. Be selective in choosing the youngster with whom to use the process approach. Involve only those who seem capable of handling it.

Writing conferences between a teacher and a child are times to discuss what the child has written, to encourage the child in writing, and to assess progress by observing and reviewing the writing products gathered in the child's folder. During the conference the teacher can take dictation or help the child with a word, a caption, a picture, or a publishing activity. This is an especially good time to work with those students capable of dealing with any of the steps in process writing and to encourage reluctant writers. The process approach is used only occasionally with young children. As they increase their skills, more of the steps can be utilized. Only use the approach with children who seem ready to deal with it.

Writing programs in early childhood should be initiated at the beginning of the school year. Teachers should refer to children as authors and writers so that they perceive themselves as such. Teachers need to model writing through messages on the message board, notes to parents, thank you notes to children, and experience charts dictated by the class. They must be supportive when working with young writers. Reluctant writers need to be encouraged to write in "their very own way" (Martinez & Teale, 1987; Sulzby, 1986b). Youngsters need to know that their work does not have to look like adult writing. Showing them samples of other children's writing, including drawings, scribble writing, and random letters, helps them see that they can do the same thing. Adults need to facilitate young writers' attempts by taking dictation if children cannot or will not write themselves, spelling words, showing children how to form letters when asked, and answering questions that arise during writing. Like other areas of literacy, writing requires social interaction if it is to promote development. Therefore, teachers need to offer young writers feedback, encouragement, and positive reinforcement.

The Mechanics of Writing

Thus far this chapter has emphasized the importance of promoting children's interest in writing and giving them opportunities to write that will prove to be enjoyable. The mechanics of writing have not been dealt with.

Writing requires dexterity. Although it is unnecessary and often unwise to bog down preschoolers and kindergarteners with the particulars of proper letter formation, they can be encouraged to use manipulatives such as puzzles and sewing cards that strengthen their fine motor coordination. In our earlier discussion of the literacy center, other materials that will help with writing and identifying letters were mentioned, including magnetic letters and letter forms to trace and copy. The letters of the alphabet should be displayed at eye level for children, and the teacher can model the correct formation of upper- and lowercase manuscript

(Figure 8–16). We are all individuals; therefore, we need not all write in the same style. Legibility needs to be the main goal for handwriting. Learning about spaces between words is important so that words will not run into each other.

Punctuation and capitalization are best taught when the need arises. Opportunities for dealing with commas, question marks, periods, and capital letters occur when reading a Morning Message, for example, and the mechanics of writing are discussed in a natural setting. Knowing sound–symbol correspondences helps with spelling. There will need to be some direct instruction when dealing with these skills, but whenever possible, they should

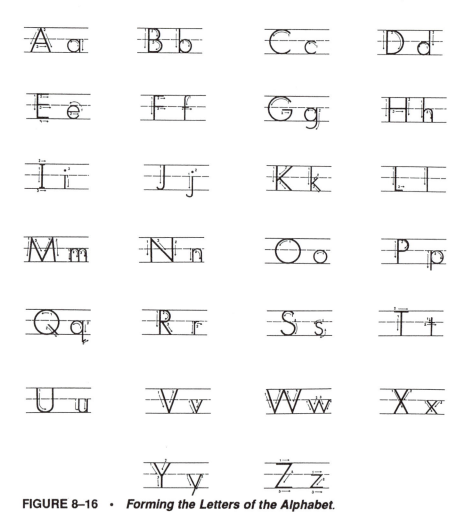

FIGURE 8–16 · *Forming the Letters of the Alphabet.*

be handled when opportunities arise to discuss them in the print used in your classroom such as that appearing in experience charts.

Transitions

Throughout this chapter theories and strategies for helping children develop the desire to write have been discussed. It is the opinion of the author that all are appropriate for preschool through second grade, with adaptations based on the particular age group. Teachers often want to know how children move from one level of writing ability to another or from unconventional writing to conventional. It is somewhat individual for every child, but trends do emerge. First and foremost we want to provide an atmosphere in which children will write. Therefore, acceptance of what they can do at a given time is acknowledged. Children who are reluctant to write because they think they can't can be shown work done by others of their own age so that they see that unconventional writing is acceptable. We foster acceptance so that children will attempt writing. As youngsters learn more about phoneme–grapheme correspondence, they begin to realize that their invented spelling is not conventional spelling. At this point they begin to ask for correct spelling as they move into the conventional stage of writing. It may seem as if they are taking a step backward because suddenly they will not be writing as much or spontaneously as they did in the past. Their concern for writing correctly has that effect on their performance. This will last for a short period of time as their spelling vocabulary increases, they learn to use the dictionary, and they seek help from friends and the teacher. Conventional writing does not just occur one day. It is a gradual process in which a child often goes back and forth from conventional to unconventional writing until sufficient proficiency is gained for the writing to be considered completely conventional.

Portfolio Assessment of Children's Writing Development

As in other areas of literacy, assessment of a child's writing should take place from the beginning to the end of the school year. That way the teacher can determine a child's level of development,

Checklist for Assessing Writing Development

	Always	*Sometimes*	*Never*
Explores with writing materials			
Dictates stories, sentences, or words he or she wants written down			
Copies letters and words			
Independently attempts writing to convey meaning, regardless of writing level			
Can write his or her name			
Collaborates with others in writing experience			
Writes in varied genres: narrative (stories), expository (personal and informational reports)			
Writes for functional purposes			
Check (✓) the level or levels at which the child is writing			

_____ uses drawing for writing and drawing

_____ differentiates between writing and drawing

_____ uses scribble writing for writing

_____ uses letter-like forms for writing

_____ uses learned letters in random fashion for writing

_____ uses invented spelling
for writing

_____ writes conventionally
with conventional spelling

Mechanics for Writing	*Always*	*Sometimes*	*Never*
Forms uppercase letters legibly			
Forms lowercase letters legibly (see Figure 8–16)			
Writes from left to right			
Leaves spaces between words			
Uses capital letters when necessary			
Uses periods in appropriate places			
Uses commas in appropriate places			

monitor progress, and plan programs accordingly. Using a check-list is one means of assessment, such as the one beginning on p. 270.

The assessment checklist is used, of course, to analyze individual writing samples collected through the year. In addition to a child's own writing folder, the teacher should maintain a folder for each child that includes notes on observations, samples of their writing, notes from conferences with the child or his or her parents, and completed checklists. The folder can be used during parent conferences and can accompany a child to his or her next teacher. Assessment should be kept as informal as possible and be based on children's self-initiated activities and on teachers' observations of and interactions with them. There should be no formal evaluation of individual writing, no marking or correcting on children's work. The purpose of assessment is to enhance the teacher's understanding of children's writing ability and aid in program planning.

AN IDEA FOR THE CLASSROOM

The following experience was *created by second-grade children.*
You may find it useful for your teaching.

*During independent reading and writing, children did a great
deal of writing. They wrote stories based on children's literature
they had read; they wrote informational pieces based on things
they were studying, current events, and popular television programs. Their writing was sometimes done in books, made into felt
stories, or done on roll paper for a roll movie. Three boys, Raymond,
Wayne, and Richard, created an unusual book that provided a
model for other children to follow.*

*These children were very interested in computer games that
they played a great deal. Nintendo was quite popular at the time
that this book was being written. Raymond, Wayne, and Richard
decided to create their own computer game based on a Nintendo
game entitled Mario Brothers. They used the characters in the
game and the basic game format; however, they made up how the
game progressed. On the left side of the page, they drew the video
illustration of what was happening in the game; on the right side
of the page, they created dialogue to go along with the illustration.
The book was several pages long, and at the end the boys wrote,
GAME OVER, YOU WIN. When the boys presented their book to the
class, it triggered the creation of a large number of original games
based on different characters that already existed in computer
games and on new characters thought up by the children. The
games that were created were very original and intricate.*

*It is apparent that in a program that allows children to make
decisions about what activities to participate in, they will develop
interesting ideas not only for themselves but for their teachers and
peers.*

Mrs. Shenkman's Second-Grade Class
Franklin Township Public Schools

ACTIVITIES

1. Answer the focus questions at the beginning of the chapter.

2. Ask three children of different ages, for example, three, five,
   and seven, to write about their favorite food, television show,
   storybook, or game. Take notes on their behavior during

writing and analyze the sample of their writing to determine the child's writing developmental level.

3. Many functional and meaningful writing experiences are related in this chapter. Try and think of writing experiences not dealt with in the chapter that you could suggest for children to participate in.

4. Think of several dramatic-play themes that you could create in an early childhood classroom, such as a restaurant. For each theme, think of the writing materials you could provide for that play area for children to use.

5. Continue the portfolio assessment for the child you selected to assess for language development in Chapter 3. Observe the child using the assessment checklist provided in this chapter concerning the evaluation of writing development. Collect writing samples from the child over the course of several months. Evaluate them to determine the child's development in writing over time.

6. Continue the thematic unit that you began in Chapter 3. Select three objectives in the area of writing development and describe three activities that will satisfy each of the objectives using your theme. Be sure that your activities reflect functional and meaningful writing tasks.

Case Study Activity

This year unlike other years you have many children with special needs. There are several children with limited facility with English because it is their second language. There is a large group identified as "at risk" due to poor scores on tests that are used in the district, and finally you have a group of youngsters classified as gifted. You are aware of the importance of writing for literacy development with young children. How will you handle the needs of these different children within your writing program? Describe strategies appropriate for the groups mentioned and include parent involvement, because in many cases without the support of the home or instruction for the parents the child cannot be successful at school.

CHAPTER NINE

Organizing and Managing the Learning Environment for Literacy Development at School

QUESTIONS TO FOCUS ON AS YOU READ THE CHAPTER

- Describe environments for classrooms that are rich in literacy materials and support optimal literacy instruction.
- What is meant by integrating literacy learning into content areas through the use of themed units?
- How can literacy development be integrated into the following content areas: art, music, math, science, social studies, and play?
- Identify different grouping methods, or organizational arrangements, for working with children to meet their individual needs.
- How can literacy learning be integrated into activities throughout an entire school day?

"What is honored in a country will be cultivated there." In classrooms in which teachers honor literacy development, it will be cultivated as an integral part of the school curriculum.
—PLATO

Mrs. Schenkman wanted to integrate literacy activities in content-area subjects. The children often found science boring with only the textbook, because it didn't feature real-life situations. She decided to use selections of children's literature that related to different topics in science to make them more relevant.

The children were learning about "The Changes in our Earth," a unit that focused on topics such as hurricanes, glaciers, and the composition of the earth. Mrs. Schenkman found several excellent selections of children's literature for this unit. Two of them were *How to Dig a Hole to the Other Side of the World* and *The Magic School Bus inside the Earth.* Both books combined good children's literature with factual information about the topic. These books motivated a great deal of enthusiasm and discussion in class. Mrs. Schenkman asked the children to write a science story—one that told a story, but included many science facts they had learned. This proved to be a difficult task for the children. Most of them wrote informational pieces that gave facts about the composition of the inside of the earth and what a volcano is and does. Those who wrote stories did not include very many science facts. Mrs. Schenkman decided to have the children write a whole-class science story by having the students generate science vocabulary and concepts they learned and using those ideas to write the story together. The story they wrote follows.

Our Class Adventure

One sunny day in Sacramento, California, our class went on a camping trip to a mountain. We put down all our bags and set up the tents. Kevin, Alex, Jason, and Keri went to the stream to catch fish for lunch. Antoinette and Emily went to get wood for a fire since it was cold on the top of the mountain. While the other kids were setting up their tents, a bear came out. The bear saw the fish, ate them and went away. Two hours later, our class decided to go for a hike. Along the way we saw a river and rocks that were weathered. We also saw two glaciers which were blocking a river. Suddenly, everything started to rumble and shake and everyone fell to the ground. Little and big rocks tumbled down the mountain. Smoke started coming

*out of the mountain and everyone started to yell. Amber
started running around in circles. Then what we thought was
just a mountain blew its top. Lava started coming down out of
the volcano and an earthquake started. It was a good thing we
brought our earthquake survival kits. We all ran to our camp
for cover, but the camp was destroyed. The survival kits were
fireproof and lava proof, so they were okay. Inside there were
tools which we used to fix up the camp. We fixed it up so well
that it looked like new.*

This anecdote describes the integration of literacy into a
content area, specifically science. The concept of integration is one
topic discussed in this chapter. The success of any program depends to a large extent on how it is organized, designed, and
managed. Even creative and knowledgeable teachers fail without
careful planning, preparation of the environment, organization of
lessons, and management of daily routines. This chapter ties
together all the prerequisites for successful implementation of all
the ideas described earlier in this book. Specifically, it focuses on
(1) preparation of the physical environment, including selection of
materials and their placement in the classroom, (2) integration of
literacy activities throughout the school day in all content areas,
(3) grouping practices to meet individual needs, and (4) a suggested outline for a school day that provides literacy experiences
throughout.

This chapter is concerned with the teaching of youngsters
from two-and-a-half to eight—preschoolers, kindergarteners, and
first and second graders. (Chapter 2 addressed home literacy
environments and daily routines appropriate for infants and toddlers. Day-care centers for children of that age need to organize
rich literacy environments, routines, programs, and activities similar to those described for homes.)

Preparation of the Physical Environment

The physical design of a classroom has been found to affect the
choices children make among activities (Bumsted, 1981; Morrow
& Weinstein, 1982, 1986; Phyfe-Perkins, 1979; Sutfin, 1980;
Weinstein, 1977). The design of the room should accommodate the
organization and strategies of the teaching that goes on there.
Programs that nourish early literacy require a literacy-rich environment, an interdisciplinary approach to the development of

literacy, and recognition of individual differences and levels of development.

Classrooms that accommodate those characteristics are arranged in centers designed for particular content areas. Centers contain both materials specific to topics currently under study and general supplies, materials, and resources. The materials are usually manipulative and activity-oriented. They are also designed so that children can use them independently or in small groups. Centers are partially separated from each other by furniture that houses their materials. Center materials can be stored on tables, on shelves, or in boxes. Centers often include bulletin boards. Areas are accessible and labeled. Each piece of equipment in a center should have its own designated spot so that teachers can direct children to it and children can find and return it easily. Early in a school year, a center need hold only a small number of items; new materials are gradually added as the year progresses. The teacher should introduce the purpose, use, and placement of each item added.

The literacy center, which includes the library corner, writing area, oral language area, and additional language arts materials, is the focal point of the room (Stauffer, 1970). It is situated so that it is immediately visible when one enters the classroom. It is visually attractive and physically accessible (Morrow, 1982, 1983). Placement and size of materials, shelves, chairs, and tables are appropriate for young children, and all posters are at the child's eye level. According to Coody (1973) and Huck (1976), the effort of creating an inviting atmosphere for a classroom library corner is rewarded by the increased interest of children in participating in the activities offered there. The specific design of a library corner is described in Chapter 5, an oral language area in Chapter 3, a writing center in Chapter 8, and materials for developing concepts about print in Chapter 7. Although they have been described separately in this book, these areas should be placed together, forming one center for literacy development.

The literacy center can occupy at least one-quarter of the wall space in a classroom. This says to the child that the use of reading, writing, and oral language is a valued and important part of the classroom. The materials range in difficulty so that they can meet individual needs and the different developmental levels of the children. Each set of materials has its own place, is to be respected, and is designed for independent use (Morrison, 1984).

Because the environment, organization, and strategies incorporate an interdisciplinary approach to literacy development, the rest of the room is set up in additional centers, including those for content areas, as shown in the accompanying floor plan (Figure 9–1). The art center is placed by the sink for easy access to water. In this same area are children's cubbies for storage of individual work. Because the working needs of early childhood classrooms are better met by table surfaces than by desks, children need to be provided with these storage areas. The contents of the various centers diagramed in the figure have been described in Chapter 3. In addition to all the materials available in them, it is important that each has books and writing materials. The music center, for example, can include picture storybooks adapted from songs, such as Ezra Jack Keats's *Over in the Meadow* (1971). In addition

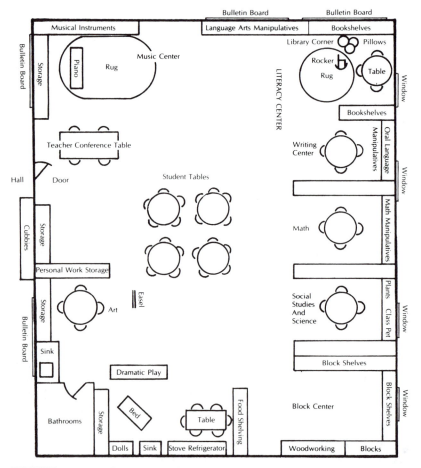

FIGURE 9–1 · *Classroom Floor Plan.*

to looking at the book, children may choose to copy words from the story. Certainly social studies and science centers should hold informational books and children's literature that relate to the topic at hand. The art center might have books with craft ideas, including directions and diagrams. Books are appropriate as well in the dramatic-play area. If the class is discussing space, the area should have books about space and space stories for pretend mothers and fathers to read to their "children." The block center can contain books that help develop ideas for building. Books that contain maps or plans of communities might motivate children to create such communities in their block play.

Each content-area center is a source for literacy development: each contains things to listen to and read, write, and talk about. These materials create excitement and interest, a wealth of new vocabulary and concepts, and a reason for participating in literacy activities. With each new unit topic of instruction, additional books, posters, artifacts, music, art projects, dramatic-play materials, and scientific objects can be added to create new interest.

In addition to generating a rich literacy atmosphere and an interdisciplinary approach, the room is designed to cater to different teaching methods, organizational strategies, and grouping procedures so that the differences among the children can be accommodated. The centers provide space for independent or social learning, exploration, and self-direction. The tables illustrated in the classroom floorplan (Figure 9–1) provide a place for whole-class instruction, as does the open area in the music center with the rug on which children can sit. The teacher's conference table is a place for individual learning or small-group lessons. All furniture is, of course, movable so that any other needed teaching arrangement may be accommodated. The centers are located so as to create both quiet, relatively academic areas and places for more active play. The literacy center, for example, which houses the library corner, writing and oral language areas, and language arts manipulatives, is next to the math center. These areas generally house activities that require relative quiet and are therefore in close proximity. On the other hand, dramatic play, woodworking, and block play tend to be noisier activities and so are placed at the opposite end of the room from the quiet areas. The art center can also be a noisy area and is set aside from the quieter sections of the room. The teacher's conference table is situated in a quiet area yet allows the teacher a view of the rest of the classroom. While the teacher is involved, as he or she usually is, in small-group or individualized instruction at the conference table, the rest of the class is working independently. The table's location allows the teacher to see all the children even while working with just a few.

The classroom should be filled with functional print—labels on classroom items and areas; signs communicating functional information and directions, such as <u>Please Clean Up Now</u> and <u>Quiet, Please;</u> and charts labeled *Helpers, Daily Routines,* and *Attendance* (Schickedanz, 1986). The outdoor environment should also accommodate literacy development. In addition to the usual playground equipment, new materials that reflect unit instruction add to the interest of outdoor play. Where climates are seasonal, for example, flowers should be planted in the spring; rakes provided in the fall for leaf gathering; and pails, shovels, and other digging and building equipment provided in winter for snow play. Creative materials such as crates, boxes, plastic containers, boards, ropes, and balls give children incentives to play creatively. The materials generate language during play, discussions in class, and information for writing experience charts and class books

The plan for the physical environment is utilized in many nursery schools and kindergartens, and some first and second grades. The assumption is that it is for younger children. Teachers in first and second grade should consider these designs because they encourage literacy learning. Evaluate the richness of your literacy environment, using the following checklist.

A Checklist to Evaluate the Rich Literacy Environment

The classroom includes a literacy center for reading and writing that is in a quiet section of the room, is visually and physically accessible, and is somewhat partitioned off from the rest of the room for privacy. It is designed to be attractive by choice of color and decorations and comfortable and inviting to visit.

The Library Corner Portion of the Literacy Center Includes:

Yes No

1. Open-faced bookshelves for displaying books about unit themes being studied
2. Bookshelves for the rest of your selections placed with spines showing and color-coded for categories (e.g., yellow stickers for poetry books, etc.)

Yes No

3. Multiple copies of several titles

4. Felt-board and story characters with accompanying books; materials for child-made felt stories

5. Roll movie and roll stories with accompanying books; materials for child-made roll stories

6. Puppets for storytelling and creating stories

7. Headsets and taped stories that accompany books

8. A rocking chair, pillows, rug, and stuffed animals; private spots for reading, under tables or in boxes

9. Read posters and an attractive read bulletin board

10. A checkout system for taking books home from the classroom

11. A system for recording books read

12. Five to eight books per child representing three to four grade levels

13. The following genres of children's literature: magazines, big books, concept books, picture storybooks, novels, folktales, fairy tales, fables, informational books, wordless books, biographies, newspapers, realistic literature, easy-to-read books, song books, craft books, cook books, books featured on television, books related to unit themes, series books, joke books, books written by children and teachers, books representing different multicultural groups

14. Circulation of new books into shelves every few weeks

The Writing Center Portion of the Literacy Center Includes:

Yes No

1. Table and chairs

2. Writing posters and bulletin board for children to display their writing themselves

3. Writing utensils (pens, pencils, crayons, magic markers, colored pencils, etc.)

4. Typewriter and/or a computer

Continued

Yes   No

5. Writing materials (many varieties of paper in all sizes, booklets, pads)

6. A message board for children to post messages for the teacher and other members of the class

7. A place to store Very Own Words

8. Folders for children to place samples of their writing

Literacy Rich Environment for the Rest of the Classroom

The classroom should include literacy materials in all centers. Materials should be changed often to reflect the unit being studied—for example, in the science center there should be books on the unit topic, and in the music area posters of songs related to themes. Play areas should reflect units with themed play and literacy materials. All centers should contain

Yes   No

1. Environmental print, such as signs related to themes studied, directions, rules, functional messages

2. A calendar

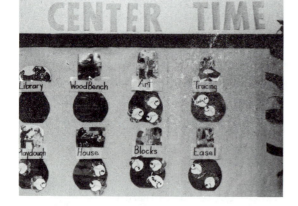

Functional print as a part of the classroom physical environment, such as helper charts and charts designating activities for Center Time, encourage reading for a purpose.

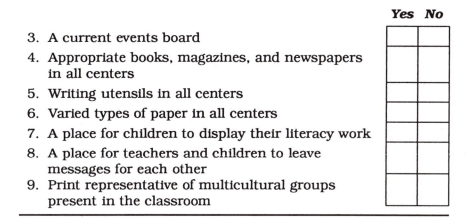

	Yes	No
3. A current events board		
4. Appropriate books, magazines, and newspapers in all centers		
5. Writing utensils in all centers		
6. Varied types of paper in all centers		
7. A place for children to display their literacy work		
8. A place for teachers and children to leave messages for each other		
9. Print representative of multicultural groups present in the classroom		

Thematic Units: The Integration of Literacy Learning into Content Areas

Dewey (1966) was largely responsible for bringing the concept of an interdisciplinary approach to teaching to the attention of educators. This interdisciplinary approach, or the integrated school day, teaches skills from all content areas, within the context of a topic or theme being studied. The themes that are studied at school are derived from children's real life experiences and topics that they demonstrate having an interest in. Learning experiences are socially interactive and process oriented, giving children time to explore and experiment with varied materials. If, for example, a class is studying dinosaurs, they talk about them, read about them, write about them, do art projects related to dinosaurs, and sing songs related to the theme. In doing so they learn about dinosaurs and also develop skills in other content areas.

Literacy activities can be integrated into the study of themes and in all content areas throughout the school day. Several are described here to demonstrate how some of the strategies to develop literacy that are discussed in previous chapters, can be used in other areas of the curriculum.

Experiences with *art* in early childhood offer children the opportunity to:

1. Be exposed to varied art materials
2. Explore and experiment with these materials
3. Express feelings through art
4. Represent experience through visual art forms

5. Gain an appreciation for varied art forms
6. Name and discuss content of art: line, color, texture, form, and shape
7. Experience literacy learning in art activities

Art experiences allow children to explore and experiment with such interesting materials as finger paints, watercolors, printing, string painting, sponge painting, colored pencils, felt-tip markers, crayons, colored construction paper, tissue paper, foil, transparent wrap, paste, scissors, yarn, fabric scraps, pipe cleaners, clay, and play dough. If children are encouraged to discuss such materials as they use them, language development flourishes. Children immersed in finger painting, for instance, use such words as *mushy, smushy, gushy,* and *squiggle.* Playing with dough or clay elicits *pound, squeeze, roll, press,* and *fold.* Watercolors stimulate such comments as "Oooh, it's drippy," "The paint is running down the page like a stream of water," "Look how the colors all run together. The red is making the blue turn purple," and "My picture looks like a rainbow of colors across the sky." The teacher can take the opportunity to make word lists from the language generated in art activities and to encourage the children to share and talk about what they are doing. The words that individual children generate are a source of Very Own Words.

Children are often eager to exhibit their creations. This practice is likely to result in children's asking each other how they made their projects. The resulting description provides an excellent opportunity for literacy development. Children sometimes ask to dictate or write sentences and stories about their artwork, or write about it themselves. Individual works of art on similar subjects can be bound together in books that include captions, titles, or stories. Art activities can appropriately highlight concepts such as the letter *p,* for example, through the use of purple and pink paint, paper, and play dough.

Objectives for *music* experiences in early childhood include:

1. Having intense involvement in and responding to music
2. Exposure to different forms of music (instruments, singing, types of music) to be able to discriminate between them and develop an appreciation for varied forms
3. Music experiences that involve listening, singing, moving, playing, and creating
4. Expressing feelings through musical experiences
5. Experiencing literacy learning in music activities

Music provides ample means for literacy development. Children find new words in songs, thus increasing vocabulary. Songs emphasize syllabic patterns in words, which should be brought to the attention of the children. Songs can be written on charts and sung, the teacher pointing to the individual words. Picture storybooks adapted from songs, such as *Old MacDonald Had a Farm* (Quackenbush, 1972), provide predictable reading material for young children. Listening to classical music often creates images and is a rich source for descriptive language. Children can create stories about the music, describe their feelings, or describe the sounds of various instruments.

Objectives for *play* experiences in early childhood include providing opportunities for children to:

1. Problem solve
2. Acquire new understandings
3. Role-play real-life experiences
4. Cope with situations that require sharing and cooperating
5. Develop language and literacy through play

Dramatic play provides endless possibilities for development of literacy through the use of oral and written language and reading. The materials and activities typical of dramatic-play areas stimulate considerable language, and the addition of new props and materials provides the opportunity for continued growth. Dramatic play provides realistic settings and functional reasons for using print. New units in social studies and science trigger opportunities to add print materials that stimulate reading, writing, and oral as well as speech. A unit on community helpers—a topic familiar to early childhood teachers—invariably leads to a discussion of fire fighters, police officers, supermarket clerks, doctors, nurses, mail carriers, and office workers. The mention of any of these community helpers is an opportunity to add literacy materials to the dramatic-play area.

Role-playing supermarket, for instance, is aided by the addition of food and detergent containers, a toy cash register, play money, note pads, a telephone and directory, store signs, a schedule of hours, advertisements, and posters for food and other products. Teachers or aides might visit a nearby supermarket to note for the classroom the print that is there, and to pick up outdated signs and posters. Store managers readily give away such materials when they no longer need them. Definitely include, among materials for dramatic play about supermarkets, a bookshelf full of magazines and books "for sale." All these materials help children engage in conversation as they role-play a store manager, clerk, or shopper. They read posters, books, signs, and magazines and write shopping lists, orders, and new signs when they are needed.

Many topics lend themselves to dramatic play and incorporating literacy materials. A study of health-care personnel can lead to the creation of a doctor's office. A waiting room can be set up with magazines for the patients to read and pamphlets about good health. There can be a <u>No Smoking</u> sign, a notice containing the doctor's hours, and posters on the wall concerning good health habits. There should be an appointment book for the nurse and a pad for writing down appointment reminders for patients to take with them, a pad for writing prescriptions, patient folders containing forms to be filled out, and a patient address and phone book.

When studying transportation, the class can create a travel agency. Here there would be maps, travel posters, pamphlets about places to visit, and tickets to be issued for planes and trains.

The possibilities are numerous. The materials are easy to obtain, and they encourage functional reading and writing. Dramatic play involves children in literacy that relates to real life. The children enjoy role playing in these situations because the activity includes meaningful experiences. In dramatic play, children are voluntarily participating in reading and writing.

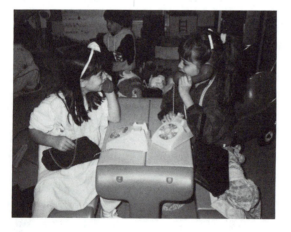

Creative play in the dramatic-play center encourages social interaction, vibrant discussion, and language development.

Dramatic play has been considered appropriate in preschools and kindergartens; however, we seldom leave time for it in first and second grades or think of it as an area in which learning can take place. In classrooms that integrate content themes into dramatic play with six- to eight-year-olds, extremely sophisticated productions of reading, writing, and oral language result. It is suggested that first- and second-grade teachers incorporate play into their curriculum.

Social studies and science themes for the most part provide the meaning and function for learning, particularly for literacy learning. Themes provide a reason to read and write about topics of interest. Skills are learned within a context rather than in isolated lessons for skill development.

Objectives for *social studies* experiences in early childhood include:

1. Fostering self-esteem
2. Learning social skills for functioning, such as sharing, cooperating, and communicating with others
3. Recognizing and respecting similarities and differences in others
4. Increasing knowledge of other cultures and ethnic and racial groups
5. Increasing understanding of the nature of our social world through the study of history, geography, and economics
6. Using the content of social studies to promote literacy development

Objectives for *science* experiences in early childhood include activities that involve:

1. Observing, hypothesizing, recording data, summarizing, analyzing, and drawing conclusions
2. Increasing understanding in
   a. Biological science, the study of living things
   b. Physical science, including the study of
      (1) astronomy—heavenly bodies and their movements
      (2) chemistry—materials found on the earth and the changes that occur in them
      (3) meteorology—weather and air
      (4) physics—the nature of matter and energy
3. Using the content of science to promote literacy development

Science and social studies are the two content areas that probably provide the greatest opportunities for literacy development. Their contents typically generate enthusiasm, meaning, and a purpose for using literacy strategies. A unit on the farm can lead to oral language development through discussions about farm work, different types of farms, and farm animals. Word lists of farm animals, crops, and jobs on the farm can be made. Pictures of farm scenes, a trip to a farm, or a visit by a farmer generates discussion, reading, and writing. To encourage positive attitudes toward books, the teacher can carefully select good pieces of children's literature about farms to read to the class. The *Petunia* series (Duvoisin, 1950) deals with a delightful goose who lives on a farm. *The Little Red Hen* (Galdone, 1973), *The Tale of Peter Rabbit* (Potter, 1902), *The Little Farm* (Lenski, 1965), and *Charlie Needs a Clock* (DePaola, 1973) are just a few examples of good children's literature that relate to the farm. These stories will motivate youngsters to pick up the books on their own, retell them, role-play them, and share them with each other. A farm visit can be retold in stories or drawings bound into class books, recaptured in a language experience chart, or reflected in Very Own Words. The teacher can associate letters and sounds in farm words with those in children's names or in environmental print.

Science experiments and food preparation offer opportunities for more discussion, generation of interesting word lists, and reading and writing of recipes. The block center, too, can stimulate literacy activities. For instance, when introducing a unit on transportation, the teacher can add toy trucks, trains, cars, boats, and airplanes to the block corner, along with travel tickets, luggage and freight tags, maps, travel guides, tour brochures, travel posters, and signs common to airports, train stations, and bus depots, such as gate numbers, names of carriers, and arrival and departure signs.

The integrated language arts curriculum, includes mathematics within the themed units and literacy learning in math as well.

Objectives for *mathematics* experiences in early childhood include activities that involve:

1. Many opportunities to handle and deal with mathematical materials and ideas
2. Movement from dependence on the concrete to abstract ideas

3. Opportunities to classify, compare, seriate, measure, graph, count, identify, and write numbers and perform operations on numbers
4. Using mathematical vocabulary
5. Using mathematics to promote literacy development

In all of the other content areas, a teacher can feel quite confident that he or she is providing a fairly adequate program of study through the themed units used in social studies and science that incorporate music, art, play, and literacy development. Math, however, is a specialized area that needs more attention than can be dealt with in a content-area unit. There are many activities, however, that bring meaning to mathematics through unit topics and include literacy as well. Stories related to numbers can be read; children can count out cookies for snack to make sure there are enough for the class; and children can be in charge of collecting and counting milk money. When studying weather, a chart of daily temperatures can be graphed to observe the variability from day to day.

When literacy skills are developed in an integrated fashion, as in practices and approaches described here, children see purposes and reasons for becoming literate. When we teach literacy skills that do not reflect real-life experience and lack content, children are not likely to perceive the usefulness in those skills. When taught in an integrated, interdisciplinary fashion, children ask for the skills they find they need in order to participate fully in experiences that interest them during their work and play at school and at home. During a unit on transportation in a kindergarten class of my own, children asked for even more materials than I had already made available in the several centers. Books on transportation led to requests for books on space travel and various maps of places not already represented in the center. Many children added to their Very Own Words. Children asked for help in preparing signs representing places they wanted to visit and highway signs indicating mileage to various destinations. Some dictated travel directions. The need for literacy information was created by the preparation of an environment that reflected interesting, real-life experiences. In such an environment, learning is to a great extent self-generated. In the section entitled "An Idea for the Classroom," at the end of the chapter, I have included a science unit dealing with nutrition that integrates literacy learning throughout all the content areas in the early childhood curriculum. This type of unit is often referred to as a whole language unit.

Strategies for Meeting Individual Special Needs

There are, of course, a variety of strategies for organizing instruction. Children can be taught as a whole class, in small groups, and individually. Children can be grouped homogeneously or heterogeneously by ability, interests, or skills, or they can be divided into peer groups for cooperative learning. The use of a variety of organizational strategies is important, because some children benefit more in one setting than in another. The use of several different grouping schemes within the same classroom also tends to eliminate the stigmas attached to a single grouping system. Variable grouping makes it likely that children will interact with all others in one group or another. Finally, using varied organizational strategies provides children with a more interesting and broader educational experience.

Whole-group lessons are inappropriate until the children are almost three. Children younger than three lack the ability to concentrate or to sit and listen. Whole-group lessons are appropriate when the subject needs to be introduced to all the children and the presentation can be understood by all the children. In early childhood literacy development, story readings by an adult, group singing, class discussions, and brainstorming sessions are appropriate whole-group activities.

Small groups are effective for instruction in specific skills and other more intricate lessons that require careful supervision or close interaction with children. Appropriate literacy activities in small groups include directed listening/reading–thinking activities that involve interpretive or critical thinking, cooperative projects such as creating pictures for a class book on a particular topic, storybook reading, and assignments in a specific center or area (because whole groups cannot fit into these areas at the same time). Teachers often prefer a small, homogeneous group for skill development, because this organizational arrangement allows the teacher the opportunity to work closely with a few children who seem to be at a similar literacy level and have similar needs at the same time. Grouping should be flexible; for example, when members of a small group have mastered a particular skill, the group can be disbanded and new groups formed when necessary.

This flexible arrangement for grouping allows children to work with many others and eliminates the stigmas often attached to fixed homogeneous grouping that assigns general ability labels to groups. When children as young as four are organized for instruction into fixed high, middle, and low groupings, they become as aware of their group placement as children in third or fourth grade.

In addition to teacher-organized groups, children should be given opportunities to select groups they might like to be in because of interest and friendships.

Working with children on a one-to-one basis and allowing them to work independently are both forms of individualized instruction. Although children need to work cooperatively with peers and interact socially with both peers and adults, one-to-one instruction offers personal attention and an opportunity for the teacher to learn a great deal about the child. Literacy activities particularly appropriate for one-to-one instruction include (1) story retellings, (2) attempted readings of favorite storybooks, (3) helping children with specific skill needs, such as letters of the alphabet or color identification, (4) assessing a child's ability or knowledge in a particular literacy area, (5) reading stories, with

Children need to experience literacy learning in many contexts. The teacher should arrange for whole-class experiences, small-group learning (pictured here), one-to-one conferences, and activities in which children learn from other children.

prompts for questions and comments, and (6) taking dictation of original stories or helping children to write themselves.

Regular one-to-one sessions can be extremely productive. A teacher can establish twenty minutes of conference time each day, thus allowing a one-to-one session with each child for at least a few minutes each week. During conferences, teachers can assess a child's special needs, record accomplishments, offer instruction, and assign tasks or suggest goals. Conference time lets the teacher accommodate both the child who is already reading and the child who cannot yet differentiate print from pictures. Conference time with one child might best be used for reading a story and encouraging responses, with another child helping record Very Own Words.

At the end of each conference period, the teacher announces which children will be seen the next day, writing their names on the board. The agenda for each conference with each child is determined by the needs, interests, and abilities of that child at that time. Although children can participate in conferences from age three, their maturity determines exactly how a conference is carried out. The typical conference lasts about five minutes, but it can be as short as two minutes or as long as fifteen. The atmosphere is informal and the session is usually a very special time for both teacher and child.

The value of meeting children one-to-one was made quite apparent to me early in my teaching career. A mother told me that her child liked to be absent from school. I was quite upset by this comment, assuming immediately that he liked being absent because he was unhappy in my class. The mother went on to say that her son liked being absent because when he returned to school he was given "private time with the teacher." I had made a practice of meeting "privately" with absentees on their return to school to share work we had accomplished during their absence.

On another occasion, I noticed several children reading on their own during free-choice time—an ability I was unable to recognize in them during my whole-class instruction in reading readiness skills. I began to work with children one-to-one, discovering what they knew, wanted to know, and needed to know. One-to-one instruction can be more easily and accurately designed to meet children's individual interests and needs. Assignments or suggestions can involve specific materials at a particular center or area of the room. Such targeted instruction not only gives children practice they specifically need, but instills in them a sense of responsibility in accomplishing assigned tasks. Conferencing not only meets the usual needs of children in a given classroom but is also particularly suited to meeting the needs of children with special problems.

To make an assignment "official" and to help the child remember it, the teacher can draw up a contract or assignment sheet. For preschoolers and kindergartners who cannot read conventional print, their contracts are composed of both pictures and words. The teacher and child check off the areas in which the child is to work. At the next conference they read over the contract together to check what the child has done. A typical assignment might be to read a book in the library corner, to read over one's Very Own Words, to copy words from a new word list, or to make a book of pictures about a particular topic. Assignments are based on the needs, interests, and ability levels of individual learners. A sample contract is illustrated in Figure 9–2.

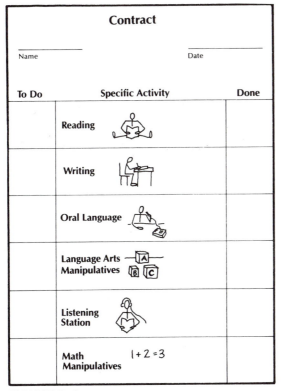

FIGURE 9–2

During a one-to-one conference, the teacher takes notes and records anecdotes of the child's behavior. These notes, collected in one folder for each child, become part of the running records on the child's progress and prescriptions for future work. The folder also holds periodic samples of the child's drawings, writing, and dictated stories. It is helpful for the teacher to include in each folder copies of the various checklists and sets of objectives described throughout this book as an aid in observing and nurturing a child's development. The checklist on p. 295 is a guide to the assessment of early literacy development. The list is a compilation of the objectives and assessment information that appears in chapters throughout the book. Assessment during conferences adds to the child's total assessment portfolio, which contains material collected throughout the school year.

Working individually or with a friend can also mean working independently. Children sometimes read alone during independent reading and writing periods. They enjoy working alone or in small groups with their Very Own Words. They listen to books on headsets and create books. They need practice in working independently, especially while the teacher is holding individual conferences. Montessori schools tend to be very effective in helping young children to be independent, self-directive, and capable of working individually or in small groups without the need for teacher supervision.

Children working individually or in small groups use manipulative learning materials placed in centers on accessible shelves. Teachers illustrate the use of all such materials before placing them on the shelves, each item in its own place. Children select new items only after they replace those they have been using. During conference periods, only relatively quiet materials may be used independently, perhaps assigned during a student's own conference time.

It is important that the teacher use a variety of organizational strategies to meet the individual learning styles and to make the school day more interesting. Teaching children in groups and on a one-to-one basis may not seem as if one is creating a literacy environment in which literacy can emerge naturally; rather, it seems somewhat structured. Yet, it is not realistic to rely totally on a child's initiative and expect learning to take place. The teacher must create the climate and conditions and plan the learning opportunities within which the reading process can be nurtured and developed.

Checklist for Assessing Early Literacy Development

Child's Name_____

Date_____

Language Development	*Always*	*Sometimes*	*Never*
Makes phoneme sounds			
Speaks in one-word sentences			
Speaks in two-word sentences			
Identifies familiar sounds			
Differentiates similar sounds			
Understands the language of others when spoken to			
Follows verbal directions			
Speaks to others freely			
Pronounces words correctly			
Has appropriate vocabulary for level of maturity			
Speaks in complete sentences			
Uses varied syntactic structures			
Can be understood by others			

Attitudes Toward Reading and Voluntary Reading Behavior	*Always*	*Sometimes*	*Never*
Voluntarily looks at or reads books			
Asks to be read to			

Continued

	Always	Sometimes	Never
Listens attentively while being read to			
Responds with questions and comments to stories read to him or her			
Takes books home to read			
Reads voluntarily at home			

Concepts about Books

	Always	Sometimes	Never
Knows that a book is for reading			
Can identify the front, back, top, and bottom of a book			
Can turn the pages properly			
Knows the difference between the print and the pictures			
Knows that pictures on a page are related to what the print says			
Knows where to begin reading			
Knows what a title is			
Knows what an author is			
Knows what an illustrator is			

Comprehension of Text

	Always	Sometimes	Never
Attempts to read storybooks resulting in well-formed stories			
Participates in story reading by narrating as the teacher reads			

	Always	*Sometimes*	*Never*
Retells stories			
Includes story structure elements in story retellings:			
Setting			
Theme			
Plot Episodes			
Resolution			
Responds to text after reading or listening with literal comments or questions			
Responds to text after reading or listening with interpretive comments or questions			
Responds to text after reading or listening with critical comments or questions			

Concepts about Print	*Always*	*Sometimes*	*Never*
Knows print is read from left to right			
Knows that oral language can be written down and then read			
Knows what a letter is and can point one out on a page			
Knows what a word is and can point one out on a printed page			
Knows that there are spaces between words			
Reads environmental print			

Continued

	Always	Sometimes	Never
Recognizes some words by sight			
Can name and identify rhyming words			
Can identify and name upper- and lowercase letters of the alphabet			
Associates consonants and their initial and final sounds (including hard and soft *c* and *g*)			
Associates consonant blends with the sounds (*bl, cr, dr, fl, gl, pr, st*)			
Associates vowels with their corresponding long and short sounds (*a*—acorn, apple; *e*—eagle, egg; *i*—ice, igloo; *o*—oats, octopus; *u*—unicorn, umbrella)			
Knows the consonant digraph sounds (*ch, ph, sh, th, wh*)			
Can blend and segment phonemes in words			
Uses context, syntax, and semantics to identify words			
Can count syllables in words			
Attempts reading by attending to picture clues and print			
Guesses and predicts words based on knowledge of sound–symbol correspondence			
Can identify suffixes and prefixes			

	Always	Sometimes	Never
Demonstrates knowledge of the following phonic generalizations:			
a. In a consonant-vowel-consonant pattern, the vowel sound is usually short			
b. In a vowel-consonant-e pattern, the vowel is usually long			
c. When two vowels come together in a word, the first is usually long and the second is silent (train, receive, bean)			

Writing Development

	Always	Sometimes	Never
Explores with writing materials			
Dictates stories, sentences, or words he or she wants written down			
Copies letters and words			
Independently attempts writing to convey meaning, regardless of writing level			
Can write his or her name			
Collaborates with others in writing experience			
Writes in varied genres: narrative (stories), expository (personal and informational reports)			
Writes for functional purposes			

Continued

Check (✓) the level or levels
  at which the child is
  writing

_____ uses drawing for writing
and drawing

_____ differentiates between
writing and drawing

_____ uses scribble writing for
writing

_____ uses letter-like forms for
writing

_____ uses learned letters
in random fashion for
writing

_____ uses invented spelling
for writing

_____ writes conventionally
with conventional spelling

Mechanics for Writing	*Always*	*Sometimes*	*Never*
Forms uppercase letters legibly			
Forms lowercase letters legibly (See Figure 8–16)			
Writes from left to right			
Leaves spaces between words			
Uses capital letters when necessary			
Uses periods in appropriate places			
Uses commas in appropriate places			

Meeting individual needs is a major concern in our country. There are children with language differences and children who are considered "at risk" or are experiencing difficulty based on performance in kindergarten or first grade or on a test given by their school. There are many programs that have been used throughout the years to help these youngsters, and it has become apparent that meeting individual needs requires time with a teacher and child working together on a one-to-one basis. In this chapter, I have discussed a plan for meeting individual differences through the use of one-to-one conferences held in the classroom between teacher and child. This particular approach is meant for all children within their regular classroom. But with only one teacher for approximately twenty-five children, a limited amount of time can be spent per child.

Other programs are geared more to meeting the needs of children who are experiencing difficulties. One such program is *Reading Recovery*, developed in New Zealand (Clay, 1987) and studied extensively at Ohio State University (Pinnell, Freid, & Estice, 1990). Reading Recovery is an early intervention program for young readers who are having problems in their first year of reading instruction. Children receive daily thirty-minute one-to-one instructional sessions in addition to their regular classroom reading instruction. Reading Recovery lessons are tailored to the special needs of children and contain authentic literacy experiences that are collaborative and active between teacher and child. A typical Reading Recovery lesson includes (1) the reading of a familiar story, (2) the teacher's taking records of the text reading and analyzing the strengths and weaknesses of the child, (3) work with letters and features about print that is often worked into and from the book reading and writing that occurs in the lesson, (4) writing a message or story, and (5) reading a new book. Teachers who participate in Reading Recovery receive special training that emphasizes the development of their ability to observe and describe the behavior of children when they are engaged in literacy acts. Reading Recovery teacher training emphasizes how to respond to children with appropriate modeling and scaffolding to help them progress. Another feature of the program is the use of authentic literacy experiences such as using children's literature as the source for reading instruction and writing stories, instead of a skill–drill approach. This is just one program; there are many others and there will be more in the future. We must be aware of the need to find the best ways to deal with special needs effectively.

The Daily Schedule

Scheduling the daily routine in nursery school, kindergarten, and first and second grade must take into account the social, emotional, physical, and intellectual level of the children. It must also reflect the best from theorists' models of early childhood education, including those of Piaget, Froebel, Dewey, Montessori, the behaviorists, and Vygotsky. The environment should be prepared so that learning can take place naturally, but with the guidance and instruction that will help children achieve their fullest potential.

Young children cannot sit for long periods; their schedule must vary. Whole-class lessons that require sitting and listening must be few and short. Children need large blocks of time for exploring environments. They need play situations, manipulative materials, learning centers, and outdoor areas. Children need small-group and one-to-one instruction. Activities that require sitting and listening need to be followed by ones that allow movement. Quiet times must be followed by noisier times. To nurture literacy, the teacher must allow for rich literacy experiences throughout the day, experiences in using and enjoying language in all its forms and functions.

The sample schedules that follow illustrate where and when specific opportunities to promote literacy can occur. The schedule provides a routine or structure for the day that seems to make children comfortable.

Several examples of early childhood programs are provided. They include:

1. Day-care for infants and toddlers
2. Half-day preschool and kindergarten
3. Full-day preschool and kindergarten
4. A program appropriate for kindergarten, first, or second grade

Day-Care Centers

Full-Day Program for Infants and Toddlers

8:00–9:45
Arrival, caring for infants' needs (diapering, feeding). When involved in these routine activities, care-givers talk to babies, sing nursery rhymes, recite poems, reinforce babies' responses.

Activity period consisting of play (in small groups or one-to-one) with blocks, manipulative toys, books, or paper and crayons. Teacher and aides provide language models by identifying materials and talking about their use and provide positive reinforcement for such literacy activity as attempting oral language, looking at books, and using crayons on sheets of paper.

9:45–10:00
Snack for toddlers, accompanied by song or poetry. (Infants are fed whenever necessary.)

10:00–10:45
Rest or nap. Adults sing a napping song before children lie down.

10:45–11:15
Washing, diapering, caring for babies' needs in preparation for lunch. Adults interact with children verbally through conversation, song, or rhymes.
Activity time focuses on reading stories and looking at pictures, using taped stories, paper, and crayons.

11:15–12:00
Lunch. Conversation involves the taste, smell, and texture of the food. After lunch, babies are readied for nap time with washing, diapering, and caring for infant needs.

12:00–1:45
Naps, begun with a song and carried through with quiet background music.

1:45–2:00
As children wake, their needs are taken care of again and a small snack is provided.

2:00–3:30
Indoor and outdoor play. In either setting, adults work with small groups, reading stories, encouraging responses from children, pointing out print.

3:30–4:00
Teacher attempts a group session involving singing a song or reading a book aloud. The last ten minutes of the day are spent in preparing the children to leave—toileting, diapering, and general care.

As noted in the introduction to this chapter, the day-care center needs to emulate as much as possible homes with rich literacy environments if they are to ensure the natural development of literacy in infants and toddlers.

Preschools and Kindergartens

There is no one daily routine that has been established as the model for all preschool and kindergarten programs. There are, however, basic categories of activities that ought to be included. The daily routines for preschool and kindergarten do not vary much in the blocks of time allocated to specific activities. The tone, content, and means of what actually occurs in those time periods are far more important. Time allotments for activities should be flexible to accommodate spontaneous educational experiences. When activities are particularly productive, they should be continued beyond allotted time schedules.

Two sample schedules follow, one for a half-day program and one for a full day.

Half-Day Program for Preschool and Kindergarten

8:30–8:50
Arrival at school, storage of outdoor clothing. Quiet activities.

8:50–9:20
Morning get-together, opening exercises, morning message, discussion of unit topic, songs or musical movement activities related to unit topic, daily news, planning for the school day.

9:20–9:40
Whole-class lesson in language arts, mathematics, social studies, or science, varying from day to day, with an assignment to complete that flows into the next period.

9:40–10:00
Conference period or small-group work. The rest of the class completes work from the whole-class lesson; children work on individual contracts in small groups or at designated centers (literacy, social studies, science, or mathematics).

10:00–10:35
Center time. All centers open, including art, music, blocks, dramatic play, literacy, science, and social studies. Special projects may be set up at different centers, such as art or science.

10:35–10:50
Clean-up and snack.

10:50–11:10
Independent reading and writing. Children use materials from the literacy center (library corner, oral language area, writing area).

11:10–11:30
Outdoor play, if weather permits, or large-motor games in the gymnasium.

11:30–12:00
Storybook reading with varied strategies, including shared book experiences, role playing, creative storytelling. Summary of the school day. Dismissal.

Full-Day Program for Nursery School or Kindergarten

(It should be noted that full-day schedules allow for larger blocks of time and more time for learning through exploration and manipulation of materials.)

8:30–9:00
Arrival at school, storage of outdoor clothing. Quiet activities.

9:00–9:30
Morning get-together, opening exercises, morning message, discussion of unit topic, songs and musical movement activity related to the unit topic, daily news, planning for the school day.

9:30–9:50
Whole-class lesson, either in language arts or mathematics, varying from day to day, with an assignment to complete that flows into the next period.

9:50–10:15
Conference period or small-group work with emphasis on literacy development and math skills. The rest of the class completes work from the whole-class lesson or works on individual contracts from small groups or at centers designated for use during this quiet period (literacy center, math, social studies, science).

10:15–10:45
Free play. All centers open, including dramatic play, blocks, and woodworking. Special art or food-preparation projects are set up in the art center once each week for small groups.

10:45–11:00
Clean-up and snack.

11:00–11:30
Storybook reading, creative storytelling, repeated story readings, role playing, shared book readings, use of Big Books.

11:30–12:15
Independent reading and writing. Children use materials in the literacy center (library corner, writing area, oral language area, language arts manipulatives), including Very Own Words.

12:15–1:15
Lunch and outdoor play, if time and weather permit. Otherwise, large-motor activities in the gymnasium.

Afternoon Schedule for Kindergarten

1:15–1:45
Whole-group lesson in science or social studies incorporating language arts, music, or art.

1:45–2:15
Center time (literacy, mathematics, science, social studies). Special projects can be set up in any of these for small groups to rotate through in a given week. The teacher meets with small groups for instruction in math or literacy skills.

2:15–2:50
Circle time. Summary of the day's activities, planning for the next day, sharing of items brought from home that are related to

study units, sharing work created by children, songs, and adult story reading.

2:50–3:00
Preparation for dismissal. Dismissal.

Afternoon Schedule for Preschool

The morning schedule would be the same for preschool and kindergarten. In preschool, however, the afternoon would differ somewhat and look more like this:

1:00–1:45
Rest period.

1:45–2:10
Center time. All centers open and a special project is in one of the areas.

2:10–2:35
Outdoor play, large-motor play in gymnasium, or large-motor musical movement activities.

2:35–2:50
Circle time. Summary of the day's activities, planning for the next day, sharing items brought from home that are related to the unit, sharing work created by children, songs, story reading.

2:50–3:00
Preparation for dismissal. Dismissal.

A Program for Kindergarten, First, and Second Grade

The detailed outline that follows illustrates how literacy development and content-area instruction can be integrated throughout a school day. Let us assume that the topic under study is animals.

8:30–9:00 Arrival and quiet activities: Books about animals are featured on the open-faced bookshelves in the library corner. The science and social studies table holds collections of pictures and figures of four different types of animals: farm, zoo, pet, woodland. Farm and woodland animals are particularly featured here, zoo and pet animals are featured in the block and dramatic-play areas. Also in the classroom are one or more live animals, such as fish in an aquarium, gerbils, hamsters, guinea pigs, newts, hermit crabs, or rabbits. They are located near the dramatic-play area, which is designed as a veterinarian's office. Children are encouraged to look at the books, work on written stories or reports that are in progress, explore with the model animals, or play with the pet animals during this quiet activity period. Background pictures of barns, a silo, farm equipment, mountains, trees, and zoo scenes encourage interesting play and language use. Index cards are readily available for labeling animals or making signs such as Deer Crossing, No Hunting, or Endangered Species. A Morning Message on the chalkboard says, "We will be going on a trip to a farm."

9:00–9:30 Morning get-together: A child leads the opening exercises. Children are encouraged to tell news for the day, including things that have happened outside of school that they would like to share. The teacher writes on an experience chart what the children have to say—for example, "I got new red sneakers after school yesterday," or "My dad got a flat tire while we were driving home. We had to use the little tire from the trunk until we got to the gas station to buy a new one."

The teacher asks if anyone can read the Morning Message: "We will be going on a trip to a farm." After children attempt to do so, she reads it with them, asking them to join in unison. To generate discussion and build anticipation she asks, "What do we need to think about before going to the farm?" She generates further discussion about the unit topic, asking the children to name all the farm animals they can think of and listing them as they are named. She then asks the function or purpose of each animal—for example, "Cows give milk for the farmer to sell." The group sings "Old MacDonald Had a Farm" and "The Farmer in the Dell."

The teacher and children discuss plans for the rest of the day and the work children will choose during their independent work period. The teacher reminds the children to look for messages on the notice board and to leave messages there for friends.

9:30–9:50 Whole-group language arts lesson: The class makes its fourth book about animals. Thus far they have completed one each for pet, zoo, and woodland animals; this one deals with farm animals. The teacher asks each child which animal he or she will draw and tries to include as many animals as possible from the list just completed. The teacher asks the children to write sentences, stories, or simply names connected with their animals. Children who finish early can choose to write to pen pals, write messages for the notice board, copy from charts, or ask the teacher for help with their writing. Children who are hesitant to write are encouraged to dictate to the teacher, who provides a writing model for them.

9:50–10:45 Conference period or small-group work: The teacher reminds the children that most of them will work independently, alone or with friends, during conference time. Each child's individual folder holds a contract suggesting individual activities to complete. Children use the literacy, math, and science centers. They complete their page for the farm animal class book if they have not already done so.

The teacher meets with three or four children individually, tailoring work to their individual needs, interests, and abilities. For example:

Christopher is functioning below grade level. The teacher tries to provide him with experiences that many of the children have already mastered. She continues a discussion begun at his last conference, encouraging him to differentiate print and pictures. She uses a book that is familiar to him, one she has read to him before. They talk about the book, pointing out its front and back. The teacher reads the story to Christopher, occasionally asking him to point out the print or the picture on a page, or where she should start to read on a new page. For his contract assignment, she asks Christopher to look at books and find their beginning and end, their print and pictures. Before Christopher leaves, she asks him if he would like a new word for his Very Own Word collection. If he does, she writes it for him on an index card.

Jim is beginning to merge narrational reading and conventional reading. Jim has shown an interest in words and asks to have them identified. He likes to associate letters and sounds because it helps him become more independent in his reading. The teacher selects a familiar story, *Are You My Mother?* (Eastman, 1960) and asks Jim to read it. He uses the intonation of conventional reading and looks at the print as he narrates the story. In particularly predictable parts, he attends to the print, a behavior the teacher encourages. She asks him to point out the words *Are you my mother?* wherever the main characters say them in the story. When Jim is finished reading the story, the teacher asks, "If you were the baby bird, would you have looked for your mother or just waited for her?" and follows his response with "Why?" For his contract assignment, she asks Jim to read three familiar storybooks and write down all the words he recognizes in print. Before he leaves, she asks if he would like a new word for his Very Own Word collection. He selects two words from the story he just read.

Jennifer is reluctant to try to write. The teacher initiates a discussion of the child's family. She knows a new baby has just arrived. The baby's name is Joseph. The teacher asks Jennifer if she would like to write something about her new brother. Jennifer responds that she can't write. The teacher explains that she doesn't have to write like a grownup but that children can write in their own ways. The teacher shows Jennifer samples of other children's writing, which include invented spelling, random letters, scribble writing, and conventional writing. Jennifer responds that she would like to write Joseph's name but she can't do it. Because of Jennifer's reluctance, the teacher writes the name *Joseph* on an index card and asks Jennifer if she can copy some of it. Jennifer copies the *J* and comments that it is the first letter of her name, too. As a contract activity, the teacher asks Jennifer to draw a picture of her new brother and to think of things she would like to say about him and try to write them in her own way. The word *Joseph* becomes Jennifer's new Very Own Word.

(These conferences were samples of work with kindergarten or early first-grade children. They would be different in content with children at the end of first grade or second grade.)

10:15–10:45 Themed play: Children may select activities in any area in the room. This is the only time during the day that blocks, art, workbench, and dramatic-play areas are open. Items that incorporate the animal theme have been added to the areas. The dramatic-play area is set up as a veterinarian's office, with typical signs such as *No Smoking* and *Doctor Is In [or Out]*. There are pictures of pets with their names, waiting room magazines, pamphlets on animal health, appointment pads, a telephone and directory, prescription pads, and health charts. The classroom pets and stuffed animals serve as patients; students role-play the doctor, nurse, secretary, and pet owner.

The block corner is set up as a zoo. It includes tickets for admission, posters of zoo animals with their names, pamphlets and brochures about a real zoo, and pamphlets on zoo animals.

Children use figures of zoo animals as they construct a zoo from the blocks. Typical signs include the name of the zoo, *Don't Feed the Animals, I Bite, Petting Zoo, Pony Rides,* and signs identifying various animals.

The art center offers on a large chart a simple recipe for play dough, to be used for making animals. The ingredients and equipment are laid out. The teacher is there to offer assistance.

How to Make Play Dough

Put 2 cups of flour into a bowl.
Add 1 cup of water.
Add 1 tablespoon of salt.
Add 1 teaspoon of food coloring of your choice.
Mix together with your hands till it feels like play dough.
If it is too sticky, add more salt.
If it is too dry, add 1 tablespoon of water.
If it is too wet, add 1 tablespoon of flour.

Each child in the art center who makes a piece of play dough then shapes it into an animal of his or her choice. Conversation is encouraged as the children follow the recipe, discuss textures, and create their animals. It is advisable that an adult be available for supervision.

The social studies center is set up with materials that focus on farm and woodland animals. It includes a store for selling farm products such as eggs, milk, vegetables, and wool. Also included are signs (*Fresh Farm Products, Open, Closed*), a cash register, order pads, shopping lists, name and price tags for various products, food posters, bags for groceries, play money, and markers for pricing food.

10:45–11:00 Clean-up and snack: Children receive animal crackers with juice, and conversation is encouraged.

11:00–11:30 Storybook reading: The teacher has selected *The Little Red Hen* for a shared book reading. She tells the story, using felt figures on a felt-board and asks the children to participate every time the animal characters say, "Not I." After telling the story she uses a Big Book to review the pages and points out the words *Not I.* She asks the children if they think the little red hen is right in not sharing her bread with the other animals, and why. She asks if there are other ideas for ending the story. She then leads the children into an independent reading and writing period and says that the Big Book and the felt figures for the story will be in the library corner for those who want to use them.

11:30–12:15 Independent reading and writing: Featured on the open-faced bookshelves are books dealing with farm, zoo, pet, and woodland animals. Animal puppets are available, as are taped stories about animals. The writing area includes animal pictures and word lists, plus all the usual materials needed for drawing and writing. The language arts manipulatives include animal puzzles, labeled pictures of animals that can be alphabetized, animal Lotto, animal dominoes, a concentration card game on animals, and animal sewing cards. Although children may participate in any activities in the literacy center during this period, they are encouraged to use books during the period and to write a few times a week. The special writing project this week is making a book about animals, either a book about one of the four types under study or a book about all four. Children are encouraged to use their Very Own Words during this period and to ask for new ones.

12:15–1:15 Lunch and outdoor play: Part of the outside play area has been turned into a farm where seeds can be planted and vegetables grown. Markers identify plantings, and other signs say *Careful* and *Don't Step on the Plants.*

1:15–1:45 Whole-group lesson in science or social studies: The class discusses its upcoming trip to a farm. With the teacher using an experience chart, the class lists things to remember for the trip: behavior reminders, safety rules, spending money and lunch, animals of particular interest, things they would like to see or do at the farm, questions to ask the farmer. Each child is encouraged to think of a question accompanied by a picture that will be sent to the farmer in advance so he will know what to discuss when the class visits.

1:45–2:15 Center time: The literacy, science, social studies, and math centers are open. At the science center a special project has been set up for churning butter. If possible, have cream and a churn available. If not, five or six children with an adult supervisor can make butter by following a simple recipe posted on a large chart; materials and ingredients should be at hand. Each day, five or six other children can be assigned to the center for this activity.

Recipe for Making Butter

Two children work together.
Take one baby food jar.
Fill it halfway with whipping cream.
Place the lid on the jar tightly.
Take turns shaking the jar briskly for a total of five minutes.
Let it stand for a few minutes and pour off the liquid.
Run cold water over the butter and pour off the water.
Add a little salt, spread on a cracker, and eat.

The teacher may meet with small groups or individuals to help with particular needs or projects, or read to small groups during this time.

2:15–2:50   Circle time and review of the day: Several children share items from home that are related to farm, pet, zoo, or woodland animals. They are encouraged to speak in sentences. Other children share on other days. The teacher displays work that students have prepared earlier in the day for the class book on animals. With an alphabet chart visible, she suggests that the book be assembled in alphabetical order and leads the children as they do so in a whole-group activity. Student Authors of the Day are asked to share their part of the letter that will go to the farmer before the class visit to the farm. With a few children sharing each day, over the course of a week each child will have shared some writing. Children also take turns telling about good books they have read. The day's activities are reviewed, with children commenting on things they liked or did not like and things they accomplished or still have to do. As a large-motor musical activity, children listen to music, decide which animals the music brings to mind, then act out how those animals might move, walking like elephants, jumping like kangaroos, waddling like ducks, and so forth. The class sings "Go Tell Aunt Rhody." The words to the song have been posted on a chart, and the teacher points to each word as it is sung. She then reads and displays a book version of the song to end the day.

2:50–3:00   Preparation for dismissal: Dismissal.

AN IDEA FOR THE CLASSROOM

On the following pages you will find a thematic unit dealing with nutrition written for children in preschool through second grade. The unit includes all content areas and weaves literacy instruction throughout. It can be considered a whole language unit that integrates the language arts throughout the school day. When using the unit, adapt the ideas for the children you teach. Try your hand at creating another thematic unit for the youngsters in your classroom.

Good Nutrition
A Whole Language Unit for Early Childhood

Lesley Morrow
Kathleen Cunningham
Donna Fino
Melody Olsen

Nutrition Facts

Why Is Food Important?

All people need food to eat and water to drink in order to live. Food and water are also necessary for animals and most plants to live. Food is important because it gives us the energy, strength, and nutrients we need to grow, work, and play.

What Are the Four Food Groups?

There are many types of food. Eating properly, along with plenty of sleep and exercise, will keep a person's body healthy and strong. Foods are separated into four major groups, and eating a proper amount of each daily will help ensure good health. Foods are categorized in the following manner:

1. Vegetable–Fruit Group: *It is recommended that four servings are eaten daily from this group. Most vitamins and roughage are obtained from fruits and vegetables. A good diet should contain dark green and yellow vegetables and citrus fruits.*
2. Bread–Cereal Group: *This group includes breads, rolls, bagels, crackers, cereals such as oats and rice, and pastas. Carbohydrates, necessary for the energy to work and play, and fiber are the primary benefits of this group. Four daily servings are suggested.*

3. Meat–Poultry Group: *Also included in this group are fish, beans, nuts, and eggs. This group provides minerals and much of the protein in one's diet. Protein is essential for building and maintaining muscles. It is also important for overall growth. Two servings are suggested daily.*

4. Milk–Cheese Group: *This group includes all dairy products, such as milk, cheese, yogurt, and cottage cheese. These products are also high in protein and contain nutrients that build strong bones and teeth. Many products in this group tend to have a high fat content. Three servings are the recommended daily intake.*

A proper diet, including ample portions from the food groups are essential for a healthy, growing child. However, there are also foods known as "empty calorie foods" or "junk foods." These items provide no vitamins, minerals, or protein and are not necessary for good health. Foods in this group include soda, candies, potato chips, and some seasonings and spices. On occasion these foods are fine in moderate doses, but a well-rounded diet containing items from the four major food groups is best.

What Are the Sources of Food?

Most of our food is grown on farms (plants, for fruits and vegetables, and animals for meats and poultry). Other foods we eat, such as fish and shell food, come from rivers, lakes, and oceans. Many people are involved in the food process and work hard on farms to grow the food we eat or on boats to catch fish.

Most people purchase their food in supermarkets. Food can be bought either fresh, frozen, dried, canned, packaged, or processed. Some people also have small vegetable gardens in their backyards or flower boxes and grow foods such as tomatoes, string beans, cucumbers, and zucchini.

How Do People Prepare and Eat Food?

Different foods have different colors, tastes, textures, and odors. Our senses of taste and smell play a large part in what we like to eat. Foods can be eaten raw, cooked, or dried. Also, not all parts of all foods can be eaten. The flesh of fruit is eaten, but not the seed, while the skin of some fruits, such as apples and grapes, is eaten, but the skin of others, such as bananas and oranges, is not. The leaves, stems, roots, or flowers of vegetables are eaten, but rarely is more than one part of the same vegetable used.

Likewise, the meaty part of some animals is eaten, while the bones and fat sections are not.

Much of the food we eat is prepared in a kitchen environment. Some foods are specially prepared for people with diet restrictions, such as babies or those with allergies or physical handicaps. Special preparation can include strained or pureed foods or mildly seasoned foods.

Food can be eaten in many ways, such as drinking or using forks, spoons, chopsticks, or fingers. Foods we drink are called beverages.

People from different cultures eat different food. It is important to learn about and appreciate foods from different multicultural backgrounds.

Source: B. Flemming, D. Hamilton, J. Hicks. (1977). Resources for creative teaching in early childhood education. New York: Harcourt Brace Jovanovich.

Newsletter to Parents about Nutrition

Dear Parents:

Your child will be participating in a unit about nutrition. This unit will include the study of why food is important, the four food groups, sources of food, and how people of many cultures prepare food.

The nutrition unit will cover all subject areas—play, art, music, social studies, science, math, and literacy (reading, writing, listening, and oral language) that will be incorporated within the theme. Some of the exciting activities we do here at school may be carried out at home with your child.

At School and at Home

Art: Art can be a wonderful learning experience for your child. Your child will refine eye–hand coordination and visual discrimination skills and explore and experiment with different art materials as he or she engages in many different art activities. At school we will be creating macaroni collages and abstract designs with egg shells. At home you can encourage your child to use his or her imagination by providing these and other food-related materials for art activities. Remember art is for exploring what can be done with different materials rather than copying an adult model.

Science: *Science explorations will be related to meaningful aspects of your child's life. We will be making a fruit salad, and the children will have the opportunity to listen, follow directions, and learn where the fruit comes from and how it is grown. Making something simple at home such as fruit or lettuce salad, or peanut butter, and involving your child in the preparation of foods using simple recipes, will help to extend listening skills at home. During cooking experiences, children observe the changing forms of food.*

Literacy: *The letters B, D, M, and F, associated with the words Bread, Dairy, Meat, and Fish are being highlighted throughout this unit. Please assist at home by labeling food items with appropriate letters or words that have these and other beginning sounds. Items such as coupons, supermarket sale signs, and other print may be pointed out when you are outside the home.*

Please read stories, informational books, cookbooks, poems, and so on related to nutrition to your child. Discuss magazine and newspaper ad pictures of food. Reading to your child, having him or her read to you using illustrations, and retelling a story are all fine literacy activities that are valuable and enjoyable. Some books with food themes that can be found in the library are:

The Magic School Bus Inside the Human Body, *Cole, 1988.*

Poem Stew, *Cole, 1981.*

Pancakes, Crackers and Pizza, *Eberts, 1984.*

The Lip-Smackin', Joke-Crackin' Cookbook for Kids, *Chambers, 1974.*

We Need Your Help

We would like your assistance with our multicultural food of the week or your favorite food at home. If you are able to help prepare a snack one day and discuss it, please sign your name and type of snack you would like to prepare on the attached sheet.

If you have any other materials at home related to our nutrition unit, such as empty food containers, boxes, plastic food, seeds, nuts, beans, and magazine pictures that we may use in our dramatic-play area, please send them in with your child.

Other Activities to Do with Your Child

Go to the supermarket together. Prepare a list beforehand of the food you need to purchase. Try to purchase foods from each food group.

Plant watermelon, avocado, or carrot seeds at home. Keep a diary or record of their growth.

Make simple nutritious recipes at home, such as fruit salad, lettuce salad, butter, or peanut butter, to help our lessons in school carry over.

Child's Corner

Ask your child to write or draw about something he or she did in school or with you about nutrition.

Help your child keep a journal of food he or she eats each day. The journal can be written in a notebook, on a pad, or on pieces of paper stapled together like a book.

If you have questions about the unit, please contact me. If you have additional ideas for the unit, please share them with us.

Sincerely,

I would like to prepare the following snack during your nutrition

unit _____ *Parent's Name*_____

Preparing Classroom Environment for the Nutrition Unit

To begin the unit on nutrition, prepare the room so that the theme is evident to those who enter. Begin with some of the following suggestions and continue to add as the unit progresses. Display environmental signs and labels about nutrition wherever possible. Feature colors that represent the nutrition unit, such as white for dairy products, green for vegetables, and red and yellow for fruit.

1. **Dramatic Play.** *Turn this center into various restaurants and add the following items: menus, receipts, order-taking slips, recipe cards, 3 × 5 blank cards, charts, cookbooks, baking utensils, prop foods, signs commonly seen in restaurants, a cash register, play money, food posters, cooking magazines, and waiter and waitress clothing.*

2. **Block Area.** *In order to create places that food comes from, such as farms and supermarkets, the following items can be added: farm props (animals and plants), supermarket props (play foods, receipts, money, and bags), environmental print signs and posters displaying food information, and cards for making signs.*

3. Outdoor Play. *In order to play lemonade stand or any other food stand outside, the following items can be added: tables for stands, signs to represent stand information, play money, a cash register, receipts, recipe charts for directions, and paper and pencils.*

4. Music. *Various songs on nutritional topics can be added to this center, such as "Chicken Soup with Rice." All tapes should be accompanied by the written lyrics posted on the wall. Props to act out the songs may also be motivating.*

5. Art. *Include play dough and a poster with play dough recipe to make play foods; include cooking and health magazines, dry foods to make collages (macaroni, peas, seeds), fruits and vegetables for printing with paint, and paints and scraps that represent the nutrition colors—green, red, yellow, and white.*

6. Science. *Materials for various nutrition projects may be added: planting equipment, recipes and the ingredients needed, foods to be classified into the four food groups, seed packages, and goods to be tasted. All of these should be accompanied with charts and journals to record ongoing progress. Informational books about food and nutrition should also be added.*

7. Social Studies. *Pictures of foods and the four food groups and maps that depict where certain foods are produced may be added to this center. Recipe books representing different cultures may also be added.*

8. Math. *Various foods can be used as counters, such as macaroni or hard candies. Counting books that contain foods and blank books for children to create their own number books are also needed.*

9. Literacy Center

   a. **Writing Center.** *Materials needed include a recipe box to share favorite recipes, food-shaped blank books, and a message board on which to share nutrition unit events for the day.*

   b. **Library Corner.** *Include cooking magazines, such as Good Housekeeping, pamphlets about good nutrition, and a collection of nutrition books from all literature genres. (See the following list.)*

Library Corner Book List with Suggested Activities

CHAMBERS, W. (1974). *The lip-smackin', joke-crackin' cookbook for kids.* New York: Golden Press. (cookbook)
Have students select a recipe from the book and make it in class.

Cole, J. (1988). *The magic school bus inside the human body.* New York: Scholastic. (informational)
Students can create a Big Book of how food travels through the body.

DePaola, T. (1978). *The popcorn book.* New York: Holiday House. (picture book)
Children can make a chart of the popcorn recipe and then follow the directions in order to make the popcorn.

Hoban, R. (1976). *Bread and jam for Frances.* New York: Harper & Row, Publishers. (picture book)
Have children make and eat bread and jam. Afterwards create an experience chart by asking the students to list words they would use to describe how it tasted.

Hopkins, L. B. (1985). *Munching: Poems about eating.* Boston: Little, Brown (poetry)
Each child can write a poem that describes a food and it can be written on paper that is shaped like the food they are describing.

Hutchins, P. (1986). *The doorbell rang.* New York: Mulberry Books. (predictable book)
Children can make their own small predictable books based on this story.

Krauss, R. (1945). *The carrot seed.* New York: Scholastic. (picture book)
Children can make a felt-board story of the carrot seed. They can also have a carrot for a healthy treat.

McCloskey, R. (1948). *Blueberries for Sal.* New York: Penguin. (picture book)
Children can make and eat a fruit salad that contains blueberries. Then they can make a class book that describes the steps in making fruit salad.

Sharmat, M. (1980). *Gregory the terrible eater.* New York: Scholastic. (picture book)
Collect props of empty food containers that have environmental print on them to use to tell the story.

Introductory Lesson: Morning Message

Objective

Children will understand that print is functional because it relays a message. This written message provides for vocabulary development and sound–symbol association.

Activity

Introduce the students to the nutrition unit by writing a message on the board to them about some of the interesting facts they will be learning during the unit. The message could be based on the four food groups and look something like this: *"Today we are going to begin learning about nutrition and how to care for ourselves. One way to take care of ourselves is to eat healthy foods. There are four major food groups: Meat, Dairy, Breads/Cereals, and Fruits/Vegetables."* Several examples of each should also be listed.

Read the message with the class using a pointer to track the print. Afterwards discuss the content of the message as well as special words, letters, and sounds. Identify M, D, B, and F as the letters we will learn in the unit and associate it with the words Meat, Dairy, Bread, and Fish. Allow children to add to the message. Do a Morning Message daily to inform students of new nutrition facts as well as any special events or questions that are related to the unit.

Concepts about Print

Objective

1. Children will recognize that spoken words may be written down and read. Oral vocabulary and sight vocabulary will be increased as they discuss, see, and write their Very Own Words.

2. Students will read a chart with functional environmental print. They will increase sight vocabulary and will follow the directions on the chart.

3. Students will be able to identify the featured letter in a word, story, or song. They will associate the sound–symbol relationship of the letter and will copy the letter from a story chart.

Activity

1. **Very own words:** Before reading *The Old Lady Who Swallowed A Fly*, discuss with the children why it is dangerous to eat inappropriate food. After reading the story, the children will discuss food they shouldn't eat. Then ask them to name foods they like that are also good for them and *The Old Lady*. Write each child's favorite food on a 3 × 5 index card to be stored in their Very Own Word container.

2. **Environmental print:** A helper chart will be made that lists jobs for students to perform. The chart should be located in a visible area and will relate directly to the unit. Jobs may include cafeteria monitor, reading the lunch menu, and helping with the daily snack.

3. **Featured letters:** Display pictures of foods associated with the featured letters: B–Bread, D–Dairy, F–Fish, M–Meat. Simple stories and songs with words beginning with the featured letters may also be used. For example: **Fanny Fish has flippers that she flaps as she floats on the waves.** Emphasize the sound the letter makes in each word and have the children write the letter. Students may be encouraged to bring in items from home that begin with the featured letter. Pictures of items that begin with

4. By creating an alphabet book, the children will review many of the nutrition words they have learned in the unit. Children will demonstrate knowledge of letters, both vowels and consonants, and words that are identified with specific letters and sounds.

the letter may also be made and added to a class book. Do one letter at a time and repeat the activities suggested.

4. **Nutrition Alphabet Book:** An alphabet book will be made and photocopied for each child in the class. Each letter will relate to nutrition (i.e., A–apple, B–bread, C–carrot, D–donuts, E–eggs, F–fish, etc.) and a complete sentence will be written with each letter (i.e., I like ____). The students will read the letters, words, and sentences with the teacher and with each other.

Oral Language

Objective

1. Children will be given the opportunity to speak in complete sentences and improve their listening skills.

2. Children will understand the language of others when spoken to as well as be understood by others when they speak.

Activity

1. **Show and tell:** Have students bring in their favorite foods from home representing different cultural backgrounds. Display and discuss with the class.

2. **Describing game:** The class is divided into the four food groups. Each child brings in foods from his or her food group. Have students describe their food to the class without them seeing it. The class must then guess what the food is.

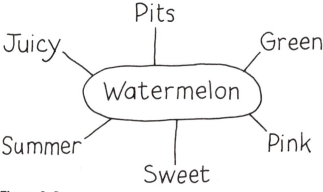

Figure 9–3

3. Children will use appropriate vocabulary for their level of maturity when retelling a story.

3. **Story retelling:** Read a story related to nutrition, such as *The Very Hungry Caterpillar*, and allow the class to retell the story using food props that are in the book.

4. Children will have the opportunity to increase their language complexity through the use of adjectives.

4. **Food group webs:** List the four food groups on a chart. List food that goes into each group. Select one food from time to time, brainstorm words that describe it, and illustrate it graphically with a web.

Developing Positive Attitudes

Objective

Activity

1. Children will develop positive attitudes toward reading through interaction in a well-designed literacy center.

1. **The library corner:** Provide books in the classroom library relating to nutrition, the four food groups, and multicultural foods. Provide hand/stick puppets, taped stories, felt stories, roll movies, and so on. Include different genres of literature related to the theme of nutrition (realistic literature, fairy tales, poetry, informational books, magazines, and newspapers). (See list in previous section.)

2. Children will be provided with an independent reading and writing period to engage in different forms of literacy to develop an appreciation for literature.

2. **Independent reading/writing period:** Introduce any new materials added to the literacy center related to nutrition. Review with the children the activities that may be selected during this time, as well as the rules to follow. When children are engaged in reading and writing, circulate among them and work along with them.

3. Children will experience enjoyable literature while predicting outcomes and using the context of a story.

3. ***Goldilocks and the Three Bears* prop story:** Read "*Goldilocks and the Three Bears*" storybook to the children. Use props such as a girl doll, three stuffed bears, cereal bowls, and so on to tell the story again to the class. Encourage participation by having children use their knowledge of rhyme and context. Place the props in the library corner for the children to use.

4. Children will tell a story through the use of a storytelling technique (chalk talk).

4. *Mr. Rabbit & the Lovely Present*—Chalk Talk: Read *Mr. Rabbit & the Lovely Present* and discuss the food in the story. Now retell the story and draw the fruit in the story as you come to each part. Use colored chalk or the chalk board. Encourage children to retell the story themselves.

Concepts about Books

Objective

1. Children will differentiate print from pictures and know what books are for.

2. Children will know that an author writes the words to a story.

3. Children will know that an illustrator draws the pictures in a book.

4. Children will understand that print is read from left to right

Activity

1. **Big Book:** Create a class Big Book that contains pictures and sentences about each child's favorite food. After the class completes the book, read it together.

2. **Authors:** Read *The Gingerbread Boy* to the class. Discuss the author of the story and explain that the author is the person who writes the words in a story. Allow the students to become authors by writing their own gingerbread boy adventures.

3. **Illustrators:** Read *It Looked Like Spilt Milk* to the class. Discuss the illustrator of the story and allow the students to become illustrators by drawing their own picture of what they see when they look at a cloud. Create a class Big Book of all the pictures.

4. **Poetry reading:** Display a poem (such as "Peas Porridge Hot") about foods on a large chart and read with the class. Use a pointer to show them how print is read from left to right. Create a class poem and read it in the same manner. (_____)
Name the poem

Comprehension

Objective

1. Children will learn about story structure by identifying story elements (setting, theme, plot episodes, resolution).

Activity

1. **Story structure:** The story of *The Carrot Seed* by Crockett Johnson has been read to the children in the past to discuss the food included. Before reading the story this second time, ask the children to try and remember the *time* that the story takes place, *where* the story takes place, and who the

characters are. After reading have the children identify the three setting elements: *time, place* and *characters*. Do the same thing on other days with other story elements such as the *theme, plot episodes,* and *resolution.* Have the children prepare a roll movie with four headings: Setting, Theme, Plot Episodes, and Resolution. Encourage them to draw pictures and include narrative for each of the four sections of the roll movie. Do one section of the movie at a time. Repeat with other stories.

2. Children will identify details in a story through literal questions asked by the teacher and demonstrate literal knowledge by acting out a story using stick puppets.

2. **Literal activity:** Before reading *The Little Red Hen,* tell the children to remember the things the hen wanted help with when baking the bread. After reading the story, have the children dramatize the episodes with stick puppets of the animals and the hen.

3. Children will express feelings, predict, generalize, and problem solve.

3. **Critical activities:** The story of *The Little Red Hen* is repeated. Role-play the "Donahue Show" and have a child take the part of Donahue interviewing the animals in *The Little Red Hen* story, asking why they didn't help the hen and what they think about the fact that she didn't share the bread with them. Then interview the hen as well. With another story such as *Gregory the Terrible Eater,* interview his parents to try and find out why his eating problem exists. With *Goldilocks and the Three Bears,* interview the bears to find out how they felt about what Goldilocks did in their house.

4. Children will be exposed to poetry and create a poem.

4. **Webbing and creating poetry:** Brainstorm characteristics of food such as an apple and provide a graphic presentation with a web (Fig. 9–4). List the characteristics of the food by writing adjectives to describe it. Create a web on the chalkboard. Encourage children to assist in putting together a poem by using the information on the web. Write the poem on the chalkboard. Encourage children to read it with you, tracking print from left to right as you read. Rewrite the poem on chart paper to display.

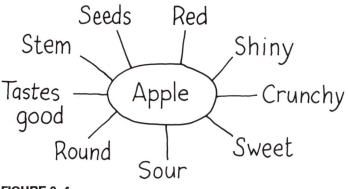

FIGURE 9–4

Our Poem about App es
Apples can be shiny, Apples can be crunchy,
Apples taste good, Apples can be sour or sweet,
Apples can be red

Writing

Objective

1. Students will communicate with each other through writing about nutrition. They will see and use functional writing.

2. Children will be introduced to journal writing as a form of written expression. They will have the opportunity to use writing to convey meaning about things they have learned in the unit. The students will become authors and illustrators.

Activity

1. **Notice bulletin board:** A Notice Bulletin Board with student and teacher sections will be prepared in the classroom. Children may display their work on the board, as well as leave and receive messages in their space. Students can share messages, such as what they had for lunch and what food group each item belonged to. They may also decorate their personal space by drawing pictures related to nutrition.

2. **Journal writing:** *Green Eggs and Ham* (Dr. Seuss) will be read to the class. The children will be told about journal writing, with an emphasis placed on their becoming authors and illustrators. As in the story, the children will be encouraged to write about a food they do or do not like. They will also write periodically about their experiences with the nutrition unit. Conventional or invented spelling, scribbling, and pictures are acceptable entries.

3. Students will participate in brainstorming, drafting, conferencing, editing, and revising. They will engage in brainstorming and use an experience chart as a prewriting activity. The students will learn that books are written by authors and that they, too, are authors.

4. Students will be introduced to letter writing. They will learn that writing is a form of meaningful communication and will be participating in this important type of communication.

3. **Nutrition shaped books:** Story webs can be made on experience chart paper as students talk about different characteristics of nutritional items. Each child will be writing stories about nutrition and teacher conferencing will take place. Finished products will be placed in books shaped like the food they are written about. Pictures, scribbling, invented spelling, and conventional writing will be accepted. Books can be in the shape of apples, strawberries, meat, fish, slices of bread, and so on.

4. **Nutritional mail service:** The students will write letters to each other about nutrition through an in-class mail service. The class as a whole will write the U.S. Department of Agriculture or any type of food-related organization to request pamphlets about good nutrition.

Play

Objective

1. Children will engage in problem solving in dramatic play related to the nutrition theme and use environmental print.

2. Block play will be enhanced with theme-related play to acquire new concepts and participate in reading and writing.

3. Children will follow written directions and use print in a functional manner in their outdoor play, which provides a real-life experience.

4. Children will expand their vocabulary that is related to nutrition and read environmental print during theme-related dramatic play.

Activity

1. **Dramatic play: Health Food Restaurant.** Turn the dramatic-play area into a health food restaurant by adding menus, cookbooks, recipe charts, receipts, and other signs that would appear in a restaurant.

2. **Block play: Where We Get Food.** Have children create block constructions of the places that our food comes from, such as farms and supermarkets. Provide labels and appropriate props for their construction.

3. **Outdoor play: Lemonade Stand.** Create a lemonade stand outside. Post signs about how to make lemonade and how much it costs. Allow children to write receipts and keep lists of who has bought lemonade.

4. **Dramatic play: World Dining.** Create restaurants based on the ethnic make-up of your class. Provide menus and food props to go along with each new restaurant, such as all the things needed for a Chinese or Italian restaurant, and so on.

Art

Objective

1. Children will have the opportunity to be creative using unusual materials. They will develop eye–hand coordination, fine motor skills, and listening skills.

2. The children will learn that parts of most vegetables can be used for print painting as they explore and experiment with these materials.

3. Children will gain an appreciation for creativity and ingenuity by designing pictures and jewelry based on different cultures. They will also increase visual discrimination and enrich vocabulary through observation and discussion.

4. Children will develop fine motor skills and increase visual discrimination through creating a collage. Oral communication will also be enhanced through discussion of the shape, color, form, line, and texture of the pictures they use in their collage.

Activity

1. **Egg art:** The poem "Humpty Dumpty" will be read to the class. The teacher will provide egg shells broken into small pieces to create a collage representing Humpty Dumpty's broken shell.

2. **Vegetable print painting:** Vegetable printing with ink or tempera paint will be carried out. The ends of discarded vegetables and fruits will be used for print painting. Children will discuss their pictures and describe how they made them. A discussion of conversation and recycling may be conducted.

3. **Macaroni art:** Pictures using macaroni, beans, dried fruits, seeds, and so on can be made. Jewelry can also be made by using macaroni and string. Macaroni can be dyed by placing it in food coloring and water for three minutes. A multicultural theme may be introduced by stressing the use and design of different objects (Mexican or Native American necklaces). Students will observe each other's work and describe their own to the class.

4. **Food collage:** Each student will make a collage using magazine or book pictures of different cultures. Pictures of food can be placed in groups representing different cultural backgrounds. Children can describe and display their collages in the classroom and to visiting parents and guests.

Music

Objective

1. Children will sing about food, increase listening skills, and track print from left to right while reading a familiar book/lyric and singing a song about food.

Activity

1. **Chicken soup:** Present the book *Chicken Soup with Rice* by Maurice Sendak along with the cassette tape sung by Carol King. As you sing the song, encourage children to read highlighted or repeated words such as

eating, chicken, soup, and so on . . . as well as emphasizing the months of the year for sight vocabulary reinforcement. Discuss with the children if they recall how chicken soup was eaten during each month. Encourage children to include their favorite words in their Very Own Words container.

2. Children will create lyrics for a song, increase listening skills, and recognize rhyming words by singing a song about food.

2. **Singing rhymes:** Sing the song "On Top of Spaghetti" (sung to the tune of "Old Smokey") with the class. Have the words written on an experience chart, and track print from left to right. Highlight the rhyming words in a different color to assist recognition of the rhymes.

3. Children will increase listening skills and refine large motor skills as they sing and act out a song about food.

3. **Oats, Peas, Beans song and dance:** Have words printed on experience chart paper. Sing the song "Oats, Peas, Beans," demonstrating actions to be used and referring to a chart where the action may be written and drawn. Encourage children to join in the second time, modeling movements as they sing. Props may be used (such as a hoe) to further encourage the actions to the song.

Social Studies

Objective

1. The students will be shown the importance of working together and sharing. They will also be exposed to different cultures. Children will improve oral and written communication through discussion of the story and sharing of home soup recipes.

Activity

1. **Stone Soup:** The story *Stone Soup* will be read to the class. After reading, children may discuss the story, highlighting the parts where the community members add what they have to the soup. Cultural variation could be included, such as Chinese–eggdrop soup; Mexican–gazpacho soup; Jewish–chicken noodle soup, American–vegetable soup. Children will write and talk about soups from their family/culture. Favorite recipes can be added to a class Big Book.

2. Children will focus on the importance of helping and caring for others when in need. Being careful of

2. **Hansel and Gretel:** The fairy tale *Hansel and Gretel* will be read to the class. After reading, the students can discuss how Hansel and Gretel help

strangers will be addressed. Children will increase oral communication skills and will practice sharing through family photographs.

each other in the story. Note how food is used throughout the story. A discussion of families can also be held. The focus will be on the positive aspects that each unique person adds to the family unit. Students may bring in photographs of their families and a class photo album can be made.

3. Children will be exposed to aspects of conflict and resolution. They will see how cooperation and communication are important in developing and maintaining friendships. Cooperation and friendship skills will be increased through role playing. It will be noted how food is the source of conflict.

3. ***The Three Billy Goats Gruff:*** Before reading, the children will be asked to listen for the problems and resolution in the story, *The Three Billy Goats Gruff*. Point out how food is the source of conflict. After the story is read, the students will discuss the problems (i.e., the goats needing grass to eat, how to get across the troll's bridge) and the resolution (i.e., they became friends). The students can then take turns role playing the story.

4. Children will be exposed to the foods and customs of different countries. They will develop an appreciation for the differences and contributions of other people and cultures. Oral and written communication skills will be further developed.

4. **Country of the Week:** A "Country of the Week" will be focused upon. Customs, foods, and major contributions of each will be highlighted. Children will discuss the differences and similarities among the countries, with an emphasis on foods and the healthfulness of each. The students may also write about their favorite food from each country. Different food will be featured at snack time.

Science

Objective

1. Children will observe changes that occur in the form of food as they follow directions in preparing a recipe.

Activity

1. **Making applesauce:** Read *Johnny Appleseed* to the class. Discuss the nutritional value of apple products. Make applesauce with the class. Post the recipe and use it as a reference to point out all the steps involved in making applesauce.

2. Children will hypothesize what will happen during the growth of a seed they plant. They will record their observations of the growth as it occurs.

2. **Planting:** Allow each student to plant a lima bean seed and keep the plants in the classroom. Have the students write entries in journals each day to record the progress of their plant's growth.

3. Children will understand the connection of oral and written language as they observe and record the growth of a plant. They will summarize the growth process when it is complete.

4. Seeds and plants will be classified and labels read from seed packages and matched to each other.

3. **Potato growth:** Have students place potatoes in clear plastic cups filled with water. Watch their growth daily and discuss as well as graph the progress of each student's project.

4. **Seed exploring:** Display many types of vegetable seed packets and their corresponding products. Allow students to attempt reading the packages and matching them with their correct products.

Math

Objective

1. Children will follow oral directions as they compose a nutrition counting book. Children will count and write numbers to ten.

2. Children will relate pictures to text and see that pictures and print go together. Children will classify objects according to shape (triangles, circles, squares).

3. Children will practice counting to twelve and match the correct number of items to number words.

Activity

1. **My Nutrition Counting Book:** Explain to the children that they will be authors and artists of their own nutrition counting book. Pass out copies of premade number books and review directions. Children will need to color illustrations and trace the number on each page. Each page will feature a number and a food. For example, 3 with 3 carrots.

2. **Sort a Food:** Read *Pancakes, Crackers and Pizza* (Eberts, 1984) to the class. Emphasize the different shapes of food as you read: round pancakes, square crackers, and triangular shaped pieces of pizza. Create a chart with three columns (triangles, circles, squares). Encourage children to classify cut-out pictures of food from magazines or newspapers) in the appropriate columns on the chart. Provide three shoe boxes labeled with each shape so that children may continue to classify different foods on their own.

3. **Counting "Eggsactly":** Display an egg carton with number words printed on the bottom of each hole. Provide a variety of seeds, nuts, and beans for children to match to the correct number by placing them in the egg holes of the carton.

Culminating Activity

Objective	Activity
1. Share the products of the unit with parents and/or other classes in the school.	1. Prepare a nutritious food for a snack to share with guests, such as fruit salad.
	2. Sing a song related to food from the unit, such as *Chicken Soup with Rice.*
	3. Role-play a story such as *The Little Red Hen,* related to the theme of nutrition.
	4. Show plants in science portion of the unit and discuss how they grew.
	5. Display art projects related to the unit and describe how they were made.

ACTIVITIES AND QUESTIONS

1. Answer the focus questions at the beginning of the chapter.

2. During the course of reading and working on the activities in this book, you have been preparing a whole language thematic unit based on a topic in social studies or science. To complete this unit, do the following:

a. Prepare a classroom environment with materials based on your topic that promote literacy in different content-area centers. Be sure to add materials to the following centers: art; music; math; science; social studies; the literacy center (reading and writing); and block, dramatic, and outdoor play areas. (Refer to the environment portion of the Nutrition Unit provided in the "An Idea for the Classroom" section.)

b. Prepare a newsletter to send home to parents concerning the activities you have designed for this unit and the things they can do at home with their child to enhance learning. (Refer to the newsletter in the Nutrition Unit provided in the "An Idea for the Classroom" section.)

c. Provide a few pages of factual information for the teacher about your unit. (Refer to the factual information portion of the Nutrition Unit provided in the "An Idea for the Classroom" section.)

d. Add activity sections to your unit in these content areas: science; social studies; art; music; and block, dramatic, and outdoor play. Be sure to include activities that reflect the objectives for the content area and literacy development as well. (Refer to the content area sections in the Nutrition Unit provided in the "An Idea for the Classroom" section.)

e. Plan an entire school day for an early childhood classroom of your choice (preschool, kindergarten, first or second grade) and incorporate some of the themed activities and literacy activities prepared in your unit.

f. In your plan for the day, include three conferences to meet individual needs. One of the children you will be working with is gifted, one is a child who attends a basic skills class, and one is from a bilingual background.

3. Observe in an early childhood classroom to evaluate how rich the literacy environment is. Use the "Checklist to Evaluate the Rich Literacy Environment" provided in this chapter.

4. Review the sample materials you have collected in the assessment portfolio you began for a child at the beginning of the book. Write a summary concerning the child's literacy development at this time and the progress he or she has made in the months you've been collecting the materials; include suggestions you have for his or her program of instruction.

Case Study Activity

As a recognized professor in the field of early literacy, you have been asked by the editors of *The Reading Teacher* journal to write a review for this book, *Literacy Development in the Early Years: Helping Children Read and Write*. In your review you are to discuss the content of the text, the organization and writing style, and the special features (such as photographs, illustrations, checklists, activities, ideas for the classroom, case studies, bibliographies, and so on). You are reviewing the book for college professors who might adopt it as a text for a course in early literacy development or for practicing teachers who wish to broaden their knowledge of early literacy development. Let these individuals know why they should or should not adopt or read this text. Is the book appropriate for undergraduates, graduate students, or both? Is this book appropriate for teachers new to the field or those who have been teaching for some time? Because the book is going into a new edition soon, provide suggestions in your review about how the book might be improved.

AFTERWORD

We must reignite our romance with the written word.
— STEPHEN SPIELBERG, 1987

This volume has presented a theory- and research-based program for developing literacy in early childhood. It has emphasized the importance of literacy-rich environments; social interaction; peer collaboration; and whole-class, small-group, and individual learning with adult guidance. The activities suggested underscore the concurrent, integrated nature of learning how to use oral language, reading, and writing. The volume has outlined education that is functional and related to real-life experiences and is thus meaningful and interesting to the child. It has provided for the integration of literacy activities into content areas through units of study that are based on themes that add enthusiasm, motivation, and meaning. It has suggested careful monitoring of individual growth through direct instruction and frequent assessment using multiple measures and allowing ample space for children to learn through play, manipulation, and exploration. Attending to children with special needs has been a concern throughout the volume.

New information about learning is constantly being generated and subsequently changes the strategies we use to help children learn. Teachers must stay abreast of the constant stream of literature that is available after they complete their formal education. Teachers need to be researchers and reflect upon their own teaching to discover their strengths and weaknesses. When teachers are researchers, they will increase their knowledge and skill. To be a teacher–researcher means to formulate questions about teaching strategies, child development, classroom environment, curriculum development, or other relevant topics that will clarify issues or help generate new information. Questions should generate from your daily experiences in the classroom and be of interest to you personally.

When an area of inquiry is decided upon, the teacher should focus on collecting data that will help to answer questions posed or clarify issues. Data can be collected in the following ways: observe and record anecdotes of classroom experiences that are relevant to the question being asked; videotape classroom segments; collect samples of children's daily work over a period of time; interview children, teachers, and parents; administer formal and informal tests; and try new techniques.

As a teacher–researcher, you will always be on the cutting edge of what is current and appropriate. You will always find your teaching interesting because you will be learning about new things on a daily basis. You will enjoy your work more because you have extended your role to include additional professional activity. As a teacher–researcher, you are practicing both the art and science of teaching. The science involves inquiry, reading, observing, and collecting data. The art involves reflecting on findings and making appropriate changes. Teacher–researchers empower themselves to be decision makers and catalysts for making change in their schools. As they study questions for which they have tangible data, they are more likely to be heard when they propose new ideas and change. Rather than having change mandated based on the research by individuals outside your school district or by administrative personnel, take the responsibility for what change will occur by researching issues yourself. Each year that you teach, select another area of inquiry to study. When appropriate, collaborate with colleagues on research projects. Collaboration with adults, as with children, results in projects that you might not have been able to do alone (Pinnell & Matlin, 1989; Routman, 1988).

The program described in this volume is meant to be enjoyable for both teachers and children. Enjoyment allows the teacher to work with vigor and enthusiasm. Enjoyment allows the child to associate literacy with a school environment that is pleasurable, positive, and designed to help children succeed. The single most important element in learning to read and write is having a desire to read and write. This desire motivates an interest in learning the skills necessary to become proficient in literary activities. Such an environment ensures a lifelong interest to refine and use literacy skills. The program is designed to help us "reignite our romance with the written word" (Spielberg, 1987).

APPENDIX A

Children's Literature

I am indebted to Mary Joyce Santoloci and Tricia Lyons for preparing a major portion of the appendixes.

1. Books for Babies

a. Cardboard Concept Books

BOONE, E. (1986). *It's spring*. Peterkin, NY: Random House.
DURRELL, J. (illus.). (1986). *The pudgy book of farm animals*. New York: Grosset & Dunlap.
DYER, J. (1986). *Moo, moo, peek-a-boo*. New York: Random House.
HANDS, H. (1985). *First-look nature books*. New York: Grosset & Dunlap.
HAUS, F. (1986). *Beep! Beep! I'm a jeep*. New York: Random House.
HAYES, G. (1986). *Patrick and his grandpa*. New York: Random House.
HILL, E. (1985). *Spot at play*. New York: Putnam's. (Other titles: *Spot at the fair* and *Spot on the farm*.)
LILLY, K. (1982). *Baby animal board books*. New York: Simon & Schuster.
OXENBURY, H. (1986). *I can*. New York: Random House. (Other titles: *I hear; I see; I touch*.)
SCARRY, R. (1963). *I am a bunny*. Racine, WI: Western Publishing Co., Inc.

b. Cloth Books

ANGLUND, J. W. (1985). *Baby's first book*. New York: Random House.
ATTINELLO, L. (illus.). (1986). *Baby piggy's purse*. New York: Random House.
BEASLEY, R. (illus.). (1986). *Baby's cradle songs*. New York: Random House.
BRACKEN, C. (illus.). (1984). *Baby Strawberry Shortcake's playtime words*. New York: Random House.
COOK, T. (illus.). (1986). *In a popple's pocket*. New York: Random House.
GORBATY, N. (illus.). (1986). *Baby animals say hello*. New York: Random House.
MARKSBURY, T. (1986). *Nighty-night Teddy beddy bear*. New York: Random House.
PARR, J. (1979). *Baby's animal book*. New York: Random House.

SCARRY, R. (1979). *Richard Scarry's huckle's book.* New York: Random House.
SHORTALL, L. (1980). *Zoo animals.* New York: Random House.

c. Plastic Books

ANGLUND, J. (1986). *Tubtime for Thaddeus.* New York: Random House.
BERENSTAIN, S. and J. (1985). *The Berenstain bears bath book.* New York: Random House.
CHAUHAN, M. (1986). *Muppet babies take a bath.* New York: Random House.
DAVIS, J. (illus.). (1985). *Garfield's water fun.* New York: Random House.
HILL, E. (1984). *Spot goes splash.* New York: Putnam's.
MILLER, J. (1984). *The duck says quack book.* New York: Random House.
SCARRY, R. (1984). *Richard Scarry's lowly worm bath book.* New York: Random House.
SESAME STREET. (illus.). (1982). *Ernie's bath book.* New York: Random House.
SUSTENDAL, P. (illus.). (1986). *The Care Bear bath book.* New York: Random House.
WALT DISNEY PRODUCTIONS. (illus.). (1985). *How do you do, I'm Winnie the Pooh.* New York: Random House.

d. Touch-and-Feel Books

CARLE, E. (1972). *The secret birthday message.* New York: Thomas Y. Crowell.
GEORGE, G. (1986). *If you rub a wrinkle.* New York: Random House.
KUNHARDT, D. (1984). *Pat the cat.* Racine, WI: Western Publishing Co., Inc.
KUNHARDT, D. (1984). *Pat the bunny.* Racine, WI: Western Publishing Co., Inc.
LEWIS, S. (1976). *Zoo city.* New York: Greenwillow.
MUNARI, B. (1975). *The circus in the mist.* New York: Collins Publishers.
PENICK, E. and I. (1983). *The good morning book.* New York: Western Publishing Co., Inc.
PERRYMAN, J. (1984). *Where are all the kittens?* New York: Random House.
WHITE, E. and P. (1984). *The touch me book.* New York: Western Publishing Co., Inc.
WHITE, E. and P. (1976). *Who lives here?* New York: Greenwillow.

2. Concept Books

BERENSTAIN, S. and J. (1968). *Inside, outside, upside down.* New York: Random House.
BYRON, B. (1981). *Wheels.* New York: Thomas Y. Crowell.
CARTWRIGHT, S. (1973). *Water is wet.* New York: Coward, McCann & Geoghegan.
HOBAN, T. (1972). *Push, pull, empty, full.* New York: Macmillan.
HOBAN, T. (1976). *Big ones, little ones.* New York: Greenwillow.

KESSLER, E. and L. (1966). *Are you square?* New York: Doubleday.
PIENKOWSKI, J. (1975). *Shapes.* New York: Harvey House.
PROVENSEN, A. and M. (1967). *What is color?* New York: Golden Press.
ROBBINS, K. (1983). *Tools.* New York: Four Winds Press.
ROUND, G. (illus.). (1976). *Top and bottom.* New York: Grosset & Dunlap.

3. Alphabet Books

ANNO, M. (1975). *Anno's alphabet: Adventure in imagination.* New York: Thomas Y. Crowell.
BASKIN, L. (1972). *Hosie's alphabet.* New York: Viking.
BOYNTON, S. (1983). *A is for angry: An animal and adjective alphabet.* New York: Workman Publishers.
FEELINGS, M. (1974). *Jambo means hello: A Swahili alphabet book.* New York: Dial Press.
FUJIKAWA, G. (1974). *A to Z picture book.* New York: Grosset & Dunlap.
GAG, W. (1971). *The ABC bunny.* New York: Coward, McCann & Geoghegan.
HAGUE, K. (1983). *Alphabears.* New York: Holt, Rinehart & Winston.
KRAUS, R. (1972). *Good night little ABC.* New York: Scholastic.
LARRICK, N. (1965). *First ABC.* New York: Platt & Munk.
LEAR, E. (1983). *An Edward Lear alphabet.* Glenview, IL: Scott, Foresman.
NOLAN, D. (1977). *Alphabrites.* Englewood Cliffs, NJ: Prentice Hall.
SCARRY, R. (1963). *Best word book ever.* New York: Random House.
SEUSS, DR. (1963). *Dr. Seuss's ABC.* New York: Random House.
WILDSMITH, B. (1963). *Brian Wildsmith's ABC.* New York: Franklin Watts, Inc.

4. Number Books

ANNO, M. (1977). *Anno's counting book.* New York: Thomas Y. Crowell.
BAUM, A. and J. (1962). *One bright Monday morning.* New York: Random House.
CARLE, E. (1968). *1,2,3 to the zoo.* New York: William Collins.
EHRLICH, A. (1977). *The everyday train.* New York: Dial Press.
FEELINGS, M. (1971). *Moja means one: A Swahili counting book.* New York: Dial Press.
FUJIKAWA, G. (1977). *Can you count?* New York: Grosset & Dunlap.
HOBAN, T. (1972). *Count and see.* New York: Macmillan.
KEATS, E. J. (1972). *Over in the meadow.* New York: Four Winds Press.
LIVERMORE, E. (1973). *One to ten, count again.* Boston: Houghton Mifflin.
MACK, S. (1974). *10 bears in my bed.* New York: Pantheon.
MOORE, L. (1956). *My first counting book.* New York: Simon & Schuster.
OXENBURY, H. (1968). *Numbers of things.* New York: Franklin Watts, Inc.
WILDSMITH, B. (1965). *Brian Wildsmith's 1, 2, 3.* New York: Franklin Watts, Inc.

YEOMAN, J. (1971). *Sixes and sevens.* New York: Macmillan.
ZINER, F. (1962). *Counting carnival.* New York: Coward, McCann & Geoghegan.

5. Nursery Rhymes

BATTAGLIA, A. (1973). *Mother Goose.* New York: Random House.
DeANGELI, M. (1954). *The book of nursery and Mother Goose rhymes.* New York: Doubleday.
dePAOLA, T. (1985). *Tomie dePaola's Mother Goose.* New York: Putnam's.
GALDONE, P. (1961). *Old Mother Hubbard and her dog.* New York: McGraw-Hill.
GALDONE, P. (1966). *The history of Simple Simon.* New York: McGraw-Hill.
JEFFERS, S. (1973). *Three jovial huntsmen: A Mother Goose rhyme.* New York: Bradbury Press.
LOBEL, A. (1986). *The Random House book of Mother Goose.* New York: Random House.
PIPER, W. (1972). *Mother Goose: A treasury of best loved rhymes.* New York: Platt & Munk.
TUDOR, T. (1944). *Mother Goose.* New York: D. McKay.
WATSON, C. (1971). *Father Fox's penny rhymes.* New York: Thomas Y. Crowell.
WILDSMITH, B. (1964). *Brian Wildsmith's Mother Goose.* New York: Franklin Watts, Inc.

6. Picture Storybooks

The following books represent a careful selection of some distinguished authors and excellent children's literature not to be missed.

BARRETT, J. (1970). *Animals should definitely not wear clothing.* New York: Atheneum.
BEMELMANS, L. (1939). *Madeline.* New York: Viking.
BERENSTAIN, S. and J. (1966). *The bear's picnic.* New York: Random House.
BROWN, M. W. (1957). *Goodnight moon.* New York: Harper & Row, Publishers.
CARLE, E. (1969). *The very hungry caterpillar.* New York: Philomel.
dePAOLA, T. (1975). *Strega nona: An old tale.* Englewood Cliffs, NJ: Prentice Hall.
EASTMAN, P. D. (1960). *Are you my mother?* New York: Random House.
FLACK, M. (1932). *Ask Mr. Bear.* New York: Macmillan.
GALDONE, P. (1975). *The little red hen.* New York: Scholastic.
HOBAN, R. (1969). *Best friends for Frances.* New York: Harper & Row, Publishers.
HUTCHINS, P. (1978). *Don't forget the bacon.* New York: Puffin Books.
JOHNSON, C. (1955). *Harold and the purple crayon.* New York: Harper Books.

KEATS, E. J. (1962). *The snowy day.* New York: Viking.

KEATS, E. J. (1967). *Peter's chair.* New York: Harper & Row, Publishers.

KELLOGG, S. (1971). *Can I keep him?* New York: Dial Press.

KRAUS, R. (1971). *Leo the late bloomer.* New York: Windmill.

LIONNI, L. (1966). *Frederick.* New York: Pantheon.

LIONNI, L. (1973). *Swimmy.* New York: Random House.

LOBEL, A. (1972). *Frog and toad together.* New York: Harper & Row, Publishers.

MAYER, M. (1974). *One monster after another.* Racine, WI: Western Publishing Co., Inc.

McCLOSKEY, R. (1941). *Make way for ducklings.* New York: Viking.

McCLOSKEY, R. (1948). *Blueberries for Sal.* New York: Penguin.

PIPER, W. (1954). *The little engine that could.* New York: Platt & Munk.

POLUSHKIN, M. (1986). *Mother, mother I want another.* New York: Crown.

POTTER, B. (1902). *The tale of Peter Rabbit.* New York: Scholastic.

REY, H. A. (1952). *Curious George rides a bike.* Boston: Houghton Mifflin.

SENDAK, M. (1963). *Where the wild things are.* New York: Harper & Row, Publishers.

SEUSS, DR. (1940). *Horton hatches the egg.* New York: Random House.

SEUSS, DR. (1957). *The cat in the hat.* New York: Random House.

SHAW, C. (1947). *It looked like spilt milk.* New York: Harper.

SLOBODKINA, E. (1947). *Caps for sale.* Reading, MA: Addison-Wesley.

STEIG, W. (1969). *Sylvester and the magic pebble.* New York: Simon & Schuster.

VIORST, J. (1972). *Alexander and the terrible, horrible, no good, very bad day.* New York: Atheneum.

WABER, B. (1975). *Ira sleeps over.* Boston: Houghton Mifflin.

ZOLOTOW, C. (1962). *Mr. Rabbit and the lovely present.* New York: Harper & Row, Publishers.

7. Traditional Literature (Fairy Tales, Fables, Myths, and Folktales)

ADAMS, A. (illus.). (1975). *Hansel and Gretel.* New York: Scribner's.

ASBOJORNSEN, P. C., and JORGEN, E. M. (1957). *The three Billy Goats Gruff.* New York: Harcourt Brace Jovanovich, Inc.

GALDONE, P. (1972). *The three bears.* New York: Scholastic.

GALDONE, P. (1975). *The gingerbread boy.* New York: Seabury Press.

GRIMM BROTHERS. (1968). *Grimm's fairy tales.* Chicago: Follett.

GRIMM BROTHERS. (1968). *Little red riding hood.* New York: Harcourt Brace Jovanovich, Inc.

HAVGAARD, E. (trans.). (1978). *Hans Christian Andersen: His classic fairy tales.* New York: Doubleday.

HAVILAND, V. (1980). *The fairy tale treasury.* New York: Dell Pub. Co. Inc.

KENT, J. (1974). *Fables and Aesop.* New York: Parents Magazine Press.

McDERMOTT, J. (1972). *Anansi the spider.* New York: Puffin Books.

PERRAULT, C. (1954). *Cinderella.* New York: Scribner's.

ROCKWELL, A. (1984). *The three bears and fifteen other stories.* New York: Harper & Row, Publishers.

STEVENS, J. (1971). *The tortoise and the hare.* New York: Holiday House.
STOBBS, W. (1970). *Rumplestiltskin.* New York: Walck.

8. Easy-to-Read Books with Limited Vocabulary

EASTMAN, P. D. (1960). *Are you my mother?* New York: Random House.
LESIEG, T. (1961). *Ten apples up on top.* New York: Random House.
LOBEL, A. (1972). *Frog and toad together.* New York: Harper & Row, Publishers.
MARTIN, B. (1967). *Brown bear, brown bear, what do you see?* New York: Holt, Rinehart & Winston.
PERKINS, A. (1968). *The ear book.* New York: Random House.
SEUSS, DR. (1957). *The cat in the hat.* New York: Random House.
SEUSS, DR. (1960). *Green eggs and ham.* New York: Random House.
SEUSS, DR. (1963). *Dr. Seuss's ABC.* New York: Random House.

9. Books about Realistic Issues

ALEXANDER, M. (1971). *Nobody asked me if I wanted a baby sister.* New York: Dial Press.
ARDIZZONE, E. (1970). *The wrong side of the bed.* New York: Doubleday.
HOBAN, R. (1960). *Bedtime for Frances.* New York: Harper & Row, Publishers.
LAPSLEY, S. (1975). *I am adopted.* New York: Bradbury Press.
MAY, J. (1971). *Why people are different colors.* New York: Holiday House.
PRESTON, E. (1969). *The temper tantrum book.* New York: Viking.
SHERMAN, I. (1973). *I do not like it when my friend comes to visit.* New York: Harcourt Brace Jovanovich, Inc.
SONNEBORN, R. (1970). *Friday night is papa night.* New York: Viking.
SONNEBORN, R. (1971). *I love Gram.* New York: Viking.
VIORST, J. (1971). *The tenth good thing about Barney.* New Atheneum Press.
WEBER, A. (1969). *Elizabeth gets well.* New York: Thomas Y. Crowell.
ZOLOTOW, C. (1963). *The quarreling book.* New York: Harper & Row, Publishers.

10. Wordless Storybooks

ALEXANDER, M. (1968). *Out! Out! Out!* New York: Dial Press.
ALEXANDER, M. (1970). *Bobo's dream.* New York: Dial Press.
ARUEGO, J. (1971). *Look what I can do.* New York: Scribner's.
HUTCHINS, P. (1968). *Rosie's walk.* New York: Macmillan.
HUTCHINS, P. (1971). *Changes, changes.* New York: Macmillan.
KEATS, E. J. (1973). *Skates.* New York: Franklin Watts, Inc.
MAYER, M. (1967). *A boy, a dog, and a frog.* New York: Dial Press.

OXENBURY, H. (1982). *Good night, good morning.* New York: Dial Press.
WARD, L. (1973). *The silver pony.* Boston: Houghton Mifflin.
WEZEL, P. (1964). *The good bird.* New York: Harper & Row, Publishers.

11. Poetry Books

ADOFF, A. (1973). *Black is brown is tan.* New York: Harper & Row, Publishers.
ADOFF, A. (1975). *Make a circle to keep us in.* New York: Delacorte.
BENNETT, J. (1981). *Roger was a razor fish and other poems.* New York: Lothrop.
COATSWORTH, E. (1966). *The sparrow bush.* New York: W. W. Norton & Co., Inc.
COLE, W. (1981). *Poem stew.* New York: Lippincott.
FISHER, A. (1963). *Cricket in a thicket.* New York: Scribner's.
GEISMER, B., and SITER, A. (1975). *Very young verses.* Boston: Houghton Mifflin.
GOLDSTEIN, S. BOBBYE (1989). *Bear in mind: A book of bear poems.* New York: Viking.
HOPKINS, L. B. (1979). *Go to bed: A book of bedtime poems.* New York: Knopf.
KNIGHT, H. (1983). *The owl and the pussy-cat.* New York: Macmillan.
KUSKIN, K. (1980). *Dogs and dragons, trees and dreams.* New York: Harper & Row, Publishers.
LARRICK, N. (1968). *On city streets.* New York: M. Evans.
McCORD, D. (1977). *One at a time: Collected poems for the young.* Boston: Little, Brown.
MERRIAM, E. (1966). *Catch a little rhyme.* New York: Atheneum.
MILNE, A. A. (1958). *The world of Christopher Robin.* New York: Dutton.
NICHOLLS, J. (1985). *Magic mirror and other poems for children.* Winchester, MA: Faber & Faber.
O'NEIL, M. (1961). *Hailstones and halibut bones.* New York: Doubleday.
PRELUTSKY, J. (1983). *Random House book of poetry for children.* New York: Random House.
SENDAK, M. (1962). *Alligators all around us.* New York: Harper & Row, Publishers.
SILVERSTEIN, S. (1974). *Where the sidewalk ends.* New York: Harper & Row, Publishers.
SILVERSTEIN, S. (1981). *A light in the attic.* New York: Harper & Row, Publishers.
STEVENSON, R. L. (1977). *A child's garden of verses.* New York: Platt & Munk.

12. Informational Books

BESSAR, M. (1967). *The cat book.* New York: Holiday House.
COLE, J. (1983). *Cars and how they go.* New York: Thomas Y. Crowell.

M<small>AY</small>, J. (1969). *Living things and their young.* New York: Follett.
M<small>ITZUMURA</small>, K. (1971). *If I built a village.* New York: Thomas Y. Crowell.
R<small>OCKWELL</small>, A. (1971). *The toolbox.* New York: Macmillan.
R<small>OCKWELL</small>, A. (1972). *Machines.* New York: Macmillan.
S<small>ELSAM</small>, M. (1973). *How kittens grow.* New York: Four Winds Press.
S<small>KAAR</small>, G. (1966). *All about dogs.* New York: Young Scott Books.
S<small>WALLOW</small>, S. (1973). *Cars, trucks, and trains.* New York: Grosset & Dunlap.
W<small>HILE</small>, R. (1972). *All kinds of trains.* New York: Grosset & Dunlap.
Y<small>EPSEN</small>, R. (1983). *Train talk.* New York: Pantheon.

13. Biography

A<small>LIKI</small>. (1977). *The many lives of Benjamin Franklin.* Englewood Cliffs, NJ.: Prentice Hall.
A<small>USTIN</small>, M. C. (ed.). (1960). Easy to Read Discovery Books (titles follow). Champaign, IL: Garrard Publishing Co.
  Daniel Boone; Lafayette; Theodore Roosevelt; Abraham Lincoln; George Washington Carver; Clara Barton; Paul Revere; The Wright Brothers.
B<small>URCHARD</small>, M., and B<small>URCHARD</small>, S. H. (1976). *Sports star: Tom Seaver.* New York: Harcourt Brace Jovanovich, Inc.
B<small>URCHARD</small>, M., and B<small>URCHARD</small>, S. H. (1979). *Sports star: Tony Dorsett.* New York: Harcourt Brace Jovanovich, Inc.
G<small>RAVES</small>, C. P. (1966). *John F. Kennedy.* New York: Dell Pub. Co., Inc.
H<small>ALLIBURTON</small>, W. J. (1984). *The picture life of Jesse Jackson.* New York: Franklin Watts, Inc.
M<small>ONTGOMERY</small>, E. (1971). *Walt Disney: Master of make believe.* Champaign, IL: Garrard Publishing Co.
Q<small>UACKENBUSH</small>, R. (1985). (titles follow). Englewood Cliffs, NJ: Prentice Hall.
  Ahoy! Ahoy! Are you there? A story of Alexander Graham Bell; Don't you dare shoot that bear! A story of Theodore Roosevelt; Here a plant, there a plant, everywhere a plant, plant! A story of Luther Burbank; Mark Twain? What kind of name is that? A story of Samuel Langhorne Clemens; Quick, Annie, give me a catchy line! A story of Samuel F. B. Morse; The Beagle and Mr. Flycatcher: A story of Charles Darwin; What got you started, Mr. Fulton? A story of James Watt and Robert Fulton; What has wild Tom done now!!!? A story of Thomas Alva Edison.
S<small>UTTON</small>, F. (1968). *Master of ballyhoo: The story of P. T. Barnum.* New York: Putnam's.

14. Magazines for Children

Chickadee. Young Naturalist Foundation, 17th and M Streets NW, Washington, DC 20036. (ages 4–8)
Cricket. Open Court Publishing Co., Box 100, La Salle, IL 61301. (ages 6–12)

Ebony, Jr. Johnson Publishing Co., 820 South Michigan Avenue, Chicago, IL 60605. (ages 6–12)

Highlights for Children. 803 Church Street, Honesdale, PA 18431. (ages 2–12)

Humpty Dumpty's Magazine. Parent's Institute, 80 Newbridge Road, Bergenfield, NJ 07621. (ages 3–7)

Jack And Jill. Curtis Publishing Co., Independence Square, Philadelphia, PA 19106. (ages 5–12)

Ranger Rick. National Wildlife Federation, 1412 16th Street NW, Washington, DC 20036. (ages 5–12)

Sesame Street. Children's Television Workshop, One Lincoln Plaza, New York, NY 10023. (ages 3–6)

Stone Soup. Children's Art Foundation, P.O. Box 83, Santa Cruz, CA 95063 (ages 6–12)

Your Big Backyard. National Wildlife Federation, 1412 16th Street NW, Washington, DC 20036. (ages 1–4)

15. Predictable Books

a. Repetitive Phrases

Arno, E. (1970). *The gingerbread man.* New York: Scholastic.

Brown, M. (1957). *The three Billy Goats Gruff.* New York: Harcourt, Brace, Jovanovich.

dePaola, T. (1975). *Strega nona: An old tale.* Englewood Cliffs, NJ.: Prentice Hall.

Galdone, P. (1970). *The three little pigs.* New York: Seabury Press.

Galdone, P. (1975). *The little red hen.* New York: Scholastic.

Langstaff, J. (1984). *Oh, a-hunting we will go.* New York: Atheneum.

Lobel, A. (1979). *A treeful of pigs.* New York: Greenwillow.

Martin, B. (1967). *Brown bear, brown bear, what do you see?* New York: Holt, Rinehart & Winston.

Piper, W. (1954). *The little engine that could.* New York: Platt & Munk.

Polushkin, M. (1978). *Mother, mother I want another.* New York: Crown.

Sendak, M. (1962). *Chicken soup with rice.* New York: Harper & Row, Publishers.

Seuling, B. (1976). *Teeny-tiny woman.* New York: Viking.

b. Rhyme

Ahlberg, J. A. (1978). *Each peach pear plum.* New York: Viking.

Bonnie, R. (1961). *I know an old lady.* New York: Scholastic.

Brooke, L. (1967). *Johnny Crow's garden.* New York: Frederick Warne.

Cameron, P. (1961). *I can't said the ant.* New York: Coward, McCann & Geoghegan.

deRegniers, B. S. (1968). *Willy O'Dwyer jumped in the fire.* New York: Atheneum.

Dodd, L. (1976). *The nickle nackle tree.* New York: Macmillan.
Emberley, B. (1967). *Drummer Hoff.* Englewood Cliffs, NJ: Prentice Hall.
Hoberman, M. A. (1978). *A house is a house for me.* New York: Viking.
Kraus, R. (1970). *Whose mouse are you?* New York: Macmillan.
Lodge, B. (1979). *Rhyming Nell.* New York: Morrow.
Seuss, Dr. (1965). *Fox in socks.* New York: Random House.

c. Familiar Sequences (days of the week, numbers, letters, months of the year, etc.)

Baum, A., and Baum, J. (1962). *One bright Monday morning.* New York: Random House.
Brown, M. (1957). *The three Billy Goats Gruff.* New York: Harcourt Brace Jovanovich, Inc.
Carle, E. (1969). *The very hungry caterpillar.* New York: Philomel.
Keats, E. J. (1971). *Over in the meadow.* New York: Scholastic.
Mack, S. (1974). *10 bears in my bed.* New York: Pantheon.
Roy, R. (1980). *The three ducks went wandering.* New York: Scholastic.
Schulevitz, U. (1967). *One Monday morning.* New York: Scribner's.

d. Cumulative Patterns (as the story progresses, the previous line is repeated)

Aardema, V. (1975). *Why mosquitos buzz in people's ears.* New York: Dutton.
Brett, J. (1985). *Annie and the wild animals.* Boston: Houghton Mifflin.
Brooke, L. (1986). *Johnny Crow's garden.* New York: Frederick Warne.
Emberley, B. (1967). *Drummer Hoff.* Englewood Cliffs, NJ: Prentice Hall.
Guilfoile, E. (1962). *The house that Jack built.* New York: Holt, Rinehart & Winston.
Kent, J. (1971). *The fat cat.* New York: Scholastic.
Lobel, A. (1984). *The rose in my garden.* New York: Greenwillow.
Mayer, M. (1975). *What do you do with a kangaroo?* New York: Scholastic.
McGovern, A. (1967). *Too much noise.* Boston: Houghton Mifflin.
Prelutsky, J. (1970). *The terrible tiger.* New York: Macmillan.
Waber, B. (1966). *"You look ridiculous," said the rhinoceros to the hippopotamus.* Boston: Houghton Mifflin.
Westcott, N. B. (1980). *I know an old lady who swallowed a fly.* Boston: Little, Brown.

e. Familiar/Popular Stories

Arno, E. (1970). *The gingerbread man.* New York: Scholastic.
Brown, M. (1957). *The three Billy Goats Gruff.* New York: Harcourt Brace Jovanovich.
Galdone, P. (1972). *The three bears.* New York: Seabury Press.
Galdone, P. (1975). *The little red hen.* New York: Scholastic.

GRABOFF, A. (1970). *Old MacDonald had a farm.* New York: Scholastic.
PIPER, W. (1954). *The little engine that could.* New York: Platt & Munk.
SEUSS, DR. (1957). *The cat in the hat.* Boston: Houghton Mifflin.
SLOBODKINA, E. (1947). *Caps for sale.* Reading, MA: Addison-Wesley.

f. Stories with Conversation

BROWN, M. W. (1972). *The runaway bunny.* New York: Harper & Row, Publishers.
FLACK, M. (1971). *Ask Mr. Bear.* New York: Macmillan.
GALDONE, P. (1972). *The three bears.* New York: Seabury Press.
HOBAN, R. (1964). *Bread and jam for Frances.* New York: Harper & Row, Publishers.
KELLOGG, S. (1971). *Can I keep him?* New York: Dial Press.
McGOVERN, A. (1971). *Stone soup.* New York: Scholastic.
WABER, B. (1966). *"You look ridiculous," said the rhinoceros to the hippopotamus.* Boston: Houghton Mifflin.
ZOLOTOW, C. (1962). *Mr. Rabbit and the lovely present.* New York: Harper & Row, Publishers.

16. Books That Can Foster Critical Discussions

FREEMAN, D. (1964). *Dandelion.* New York: Viking.
GALDONE, P. (1962). *The hare and the tortoise.* New York: McGraw-Hill.
GALDONE, P. (1972). *The three bears.* New York: Seabury Press.
GALDONE, P. (1984). *The three little pigs.* New York: Clarion.
LINDQUIST, W. (1970). *Stone soup.* New York: Western Publishing Co., Inc.
LOWREY, J. (1942). *The poky little puppy.* New York: Golden Press.
LIONNI, L. (1973). *Swimmy.* New York: Random House.
PIPER, W. (1979). *The little engine that could.* New York: Scholastic.
SILVERSTEIN, S. (1964). *The giving tree.* New York: Harper & Row, Publishers.
VIORST, J. (1976). *Alexander and the terrible, horrible, no good, very bad day.* New York: Atheneum.
ZOLOTOW, C. (1972). *William's doll.* New York: Harper & Row, Publishers.

17. Books for Enhancing Listening and Discrimination of Sounds

BROWN, M. W. (1939). *The noisy book.* New York: Harper & Row, Publishers.
GARELICK, M. (1963). *Sounds of a summer night.* Reading, MA.: Addison-Wesley.
HEIDE, F. (1970). *Sound of sunshine, sound of rain.* New York: Parents' Magazine Press.

JOHNSTON, T. (1973). *Night noises and other mole and troll stories.* New York: Putnam's.

KAUFMAN, L. (1965). *What's that noise?* New York: Lothrop.

KUSKIN, K. (1962). *All sizes of noises.* New York: Harper & Row, Publishers.

McGOVERN, A. (1967). *Too much noise.* Boston: Houghton Mifflin.

PERKINS, A. (1968). *The ear book.* New York: Random House.

SEUSS, DR. (1970). *Mister Brown can moo: Can you?* New York: Random House.

SHOWERS, P. (1961). *The listening walk.* New York: Thomas Y. Crowell.

STEINER, C. (1959). *Listen to my seashell.* New York: Knopf.

TEAL, V. (1967). *The little woman wanted noise.* Chicago: Rand McNally.

18. Books for Building Sound–Symbol Relationships

a. Consonants

B

BERENSTAIN, S. and J. (1971). *The Berenstain B book.* New York: Random House.

BERENSTAIN, S. and J. (1986). *The Berenstain bears and too much birthday.* New York: Random House.

CALDER, L. (1985). *Blast off, barefoot bear!* New York: Tern Enterprises.

MONCURE, J. (1984). *My "B" sound.* Elgin, IL: Child's World Publishing.

PEET, B. (1977). *Big, bad Bruce.* Boston: Houghton Mifflin.

C (hard)

BERENSTAIN, S. and J. (1972). *C is for clown.* New York: Random House.

KRAUSS, R. (1945). *The carrot seed.* New York: Scholastic.

SLOBODKINA, E. (1968). *Caps for sale.* Reading, MA: Addison-Wesley.

C (soft)

McPHAIL, D. (1974). *Cereal box.* Boston: Little, Brown.

WILDSMITH, B. (1970). *Circus.* New York: Franklins Watts, Inc.

WOODMAN, J. (1986). *Bossy bear at the circus.* London: Brimax Books.

D

LEXAU, J. (1987). *The dog food caper.* New York: Dial Books.

MONCURE, J. (1984). *My "D" sound.* Elgin, IL: Child's World Publishing.

STEIG, W. (1982). *Doctor DeSoto.* New York: Farrar, Straus & Giroux.

ZEMACK, H. and M. (1973). *Duffy and the devil.* New York: Farrar, Strauss & Giroux.

F

LITTLEDALE, F. (1987). *The farmer in the soup.* New York: Scholastic.

LOBEL, A. (1970). *Frog and toad are friends.* New York: Harper & Row, Publishers.

McPHAIL, D. (1984). *Fix-it*. New York: Dutton.
MONCURE, J. (1984). *My "F" sound*. Elgin, IL: Child's World Publishing.

G (hard)

BURINGHAM, J. (1976). *Mr. Gumpy's motor car*. New York: Thomas Y. Crowell.
GALDONE, P. (1981). *The three Billy Goats Gruff*. Boston: Houghton Mifflin.
SHARMAT, M. (1984). *Gregory the terrible eater*. New York: Scholastic.

G (soft)

GALDONE, P. (1975). *The gingerbread boy*. New York: Clarion Books.
REY, H. A. (1973). *Curious George*. Boston: Houghton Mifflin. (Other titles in this series include *Curious George rides a bike, Curious George goes to the circus, and Curious George learns the alphabet*.)

H

JOHNSON, C. (1960). *A picture for Harold's room*. New York: Harper & Row, Publishers.
KUSKIN, K. (1979). *Herbert hated being small*. Boston: Houghton Mifflin.
MONCURE, J. (1984). *My "H" sound*. Elgin, IL: Child's World Publishing.
ZION, G. (1976). *Harry the dirty dog*. New York: Harper & Row, Publishers.

J

ETS, M. (1965). *Just me*. New York: Viking.
KUSKIN, K. (1959). *Just like everyone else*. New York: Harper & Row, Publishers.
MONCURE, J. (1984). *My "J" sound*. Elgin, IL: Child's World Publishing.
STOBBS, W. (1969). *Jack and the beanstalk*. New York: Delacorte.
WHITNEY, A. (1971). *Just awful*. Reading, MA: Addison-Wesley.

K

MAESTRO, B. and G. (1982). *The key to the kingdom*. New York: Harcourt Brace Jovanovich, Inc.
MONCURE, J. (1984). *My "K" sound*. Elgin, IL: Child's World Publishing.
SCHONGUT, E. (1983). *Look kitten*. New York: Little Simon.

L

COSGROVE, S. (1985). *Leo the lop*. Los Angeles: Price, Stern & Sloan Publishers.
DEREGNIERS, B. S. (1979). *Laura's story*. New York: Atheneum.
KRAUSS, R. (1971). *Leo the late bloomer*. New York: Windmill Books, Simon & Schuster.
MONCURE, J. (1984). *My "L" sound*. Elgin, IL: Child's World Publishing.

M

BEMELMANS, L. (1977). *Madeline*. New York: Puffin Books.
KELLOGG, S. (1976). *Much bigger than Martin*. New York: Dial Press.
MONCURE, J. (1984). *My "M" sound*. Elgin, IL: Child's World Publishing.
WOLCOTT, P. (1974). *Marvelous mud washing machine*. Reading, MA: Addison-Wesley.

N

BROWN, M. W. (1939). *The noisy book.* New York: Harper.
GUILFOILE, E. (1957). *Nobody listens to Andrew.* Chicago: Follett.
McGOVERN, A. (1967). *Too much noise.* Boston: Houghton Mifflin.
WEZEL, P. (1967). *The naughty bird.* Chicago: Follett.

P

BROWN, R. (1973). *Pig in the pond.* New York: D. McKay.
DePAOLA, T. (1978). *The popcorn book.* New York: Holiday House.
DUVOISIN, R. (1950). *Petunia.* New York: Knopf.
KEATS, E. J. (1972). *The pet show.* New York: Macmillan.
ROTH, S. (1966). *Pick a peck of puzzles.* New York: Arnold Norton.

Q

BEATTY, J. (1967). *The queen wizard.* New York: Macmillan.
BLUE, R. (1969). *A quiet place.* New York: Franklin Watts, Inc.
HURD, T. (1978). *The quiet evening.* New York: Greenwillow.
JOHNSTON, T., and DePAOLA, T. (1985). *The quilt story.* New York: Putnam's.
ZOLOTOW, C. (1963). *The quarreling book.* New York: Harper & Row, Publishers.

R

FISHER, A. (1983). *Rabbits, rabbits.* New York: Harper & Row, Publishers.
KENT, J. (1982). *Round robin.* Englewood Cliffs, NJ: Prentice Hall.
SENDAK, M. (1975). *Really Rosie.* New York: Harper & Row, Publishers.
SHULEVITZ, U. (1969). *Rain, rain, rivers.* New York: Farrar, Straus & Giroux.
WATTS, B. (1968), *Little Red Riding Hood.* New York: Scholastic.

S

BROWN, M. (1947). *Stone soup.* New York: Scribner's.
KEATS, E. J. (1976). *The snowy day.* New York: Puffin Books.
KESSLER, E. and L. (1973). *Slush, slush!* New York: Parents Magazine Press.
LIONNI, L. (1973). *Swimmy.* New York: Random House.
STADLER, J. (1985). *Snail saves the day.* New York: Thomas Y. Crowell.

T

COSGROVE, S. (1984). *Tee-tee.* Vero Beach, FL: Rourke Enterprises, Inc.
LEXAU, J. M. (1971). *T for Tommy.* New York: Garrard.
NESS, E. (1965). *Tom tit tot.* New York: Scribner's.
PRESTON, E. M. (1969). *The temper tantrum book.* New York: Viking.
SEULING, B. (1976). *Teeny-tiny woman.* New York: Viking.

V

CARLE, E. (1969). *The very hungry caterpillar.* New York: Philomel.
DeARMOND, F. U. (1963). *The very, very special day.* New York: Parents' Magazine Press.
DUVOISIN, R. (1961). *Veronica.* New York: Knopf.

W

KEATS, E. J. (1964). *Whistle for Willie*. New York: Viking.
NYBLOM, H. (1968). *The witch of the woods*. New York: Knopf.
SENDAK, M. (1963). *Where the wild things are*. New York: Harper & Row, Publishers.

X

MONCURE, J. (1979). *My "X, Y, Z" sound box*. Elgin, IL: Child's World Publishing.

Y

MARSHALL, J. (1973). *Yummers*. Boston: Houghton Mifflin.
SEUSS, DR. (1958). *Yertle the turtle and other stories*. New York: Random House.

Z

SEUSS, DR. (1950). *If I ran to the zoo*. New York: Random House.
SEUSS, DR. (1955). *On beyond Zebra*. New York: Random House.

b. Vowels (long and short)

A

BAYER, J. (1984). *A, my name is Alice*. New York: Dial Press.
BOYNTON, S. (1983). *A is for angry: An animal and adjective alphabet*. New York: Workman Publishers.
HIAWYN, O. (1982). *Angry Arthur*. New York: Harcourt Brace Jovanovich, Inc.
MONCURE, J. (1984). *Short a and long a: Play a game*. Elgin IL: Child's World Publishing.

E

FRESCHET, B. (1977). *Elephant and friends*. New York: Scribner's.
KENT, J. (1975). *The egg book*. New York: Macmillan.
MILHOUS, K. (1951). *The egg tree*. New York: Scribner's.
MONCURE, J. (1984). *Short e and long e: Play a game*. Elgin, IL: Child's World Publishing.
ROCKWELL, A. and H. (1985). *The emergency room*. New York: Macmillan.

I

BONSHALL, C. (1974). *And I mean it, Stanley*. New York: Harper & Row, Publishers.
FISCHER, A. (1965). *In the woods, in the meadow, in the sky*. New York: Scribner's.
MONCURE, J. (1984). *Short i and long i: Play a game*. Elgin, IL: Child's World Publishing.
ORAM, H. (1985). *In the attic*. New York: Holt, Rinehart & Winston.
ZOLOTOW, C. (1966). *If it weren't for you*. New York: Harper & Row, Publishers.

O

ALLEN, L. J. (1979). *Ottie and the star.* New York: Harper & Row, Publishers.

KESSLER, L. (1976). *Ghosts and crows and things with O's.* New York: Scholastic.

MONCURE, J. (1984). *Short o and long o: Play a game.* Elgin, IL: Child's World Publishing.

THALER, M. (1982). *Owly.* New York: Harper & Row, Publishers.

U

MONCURE, J. (1984). *Short u and long u: Play a game.* Elgin, IL: Child's World Publishing.

PINKWATER, D. (1982). *Umbrellas and parasols.* New York: Dutton.

YASHIMA, T. (1969). *Umbrella.* New York: Viking.

c. Digraphs

CH

BROWN, M. W. (1982). *Little chicken.* New York: Harper & Row, Publishers.

HOFF, S. (1961). *Little chief.* New York: Harper & Row, Publishers.

KWITZ, M. (1983). *Little chick's breakfast.* New York: Harper & Row, Publishers.

SENDAK, M. (1962). *Chicken soup with rice.* New York: Harper & Row, Publishers.

PH

GOVAN, C. (1968). *Phinny's fine summer.* New York: World Publishing.

SH

ADAMS, A. (1981). *Shoemaker and the elves.* New York: Macmillan.

KLINE, S. W. (1984). *SHHH!* New York: Whitman Publishers.

ROGERS, P. (1986). *Sheepchase.* New York: Viking.

TH

LOEDHAS, S. (1962). *Thistle and thyme.* Toronto: Alger.

d. Word Families

BROWN, M. W. (1984). *Goodnight moon.* New York: Harper & Row, Publishers.

EICHENBERG, F. (1952). *Ape in a cape.* New York: Scholastic.

LIVERMORE, E. (1979). *The three little kittens lost their mittens.* Boston: Houghton Mifflin.

PATRICK, G. (1974). *A bug in a jug.* New York: Scholastic.

SEUSS, DR. (1957). *The cat in the hat.* New York: Random House.

19. Books for Following Directions

Asche, F. (1976). *Good lemonade.* New York: Franklin Watts, Inc.
Benjamin, C. (1982). *Cartooning for kids.* New York: Thomas Y. Crowell.
Bogle, K., and Cutler, K. (1974). *Crafts for Christmas.* New York: Lothrop.
dePaola, T. (1978). *Pancakes for breakfast.* New York: Harcourt Brace Jovanovich, Inc.
Hoban, T. (1971). *Look again.* New York: Macmillan.
Hutchins, P. (1968). *Rosie's walk.* New York: Macmillan.
Kunhardt, D. (1962). *Pat the bunny.* New York: Western Publishing Co., Inc.
McGovern, A. (1971). *Stone soup.* New York: Scholastic.

20. Series Books

Allard, H. (1977). *The stupids step out.* Boston: Houghton Mifflin.
   The stupids die.
   The stupids have a ball.
Bemelmans, L. (1977). *Madeline.* New York: Puffin Books.
   Madeline and the gypsies.
   Madeline in London.
   Madeline's rescue.
Freeman, D. (1968). *Corduroy.* New York: Viking.
   Corduroy's party.
   Corduroy's toys.
   A pocket for Corduroy.
Gramathy, H. (1978). *Little Toot.* New York: Putnam's.
   Little Toot on the Grand Canal.
   Little Toot on the Mississippi.
   Little Toot through the Golden Gate.
Hargreaves, R. (1980). *The Mr. Men books.* Los Angeles: Price, Stern & Sloan Publishers.
   Mr. Happy. Mr. Noisy. Mr. Impossible.
   Mr. Strong. Mr. Small. Mr. Fussy.
Hoban, R. (1976). *Bedtime for Frances.* New York: Harper & Row, Publishers.
   A baby sister for Frances.
   A birthday for Frances.
   Bread and jam for Frances.
Lindgren, B. (1982). *Sam's cookie.* New York: Morrow.
   Sam's bath.
   Sam's ball.
   Sam's teddy bear.
Lobel, A. (1979). *Frog and toad are friends.* New York: Harper & Row, Publishers.
   Days with frog and toad.
   Frog and toad all year.
   Frog and toad together.

Lowrey, J. S. (1942). *The poky little puppy*. New York: Golden Press.
   The poky little puppy and the patchwork blanket.
   The poky little puppy follows his nose home.
   The poky little puppy's first Christmas.
Minarik, E. H. (1978). *Little bear*. New York: Harper & Row, Publishers
   A kiss for little bear.
   Little bear's friend.
   Little bear's visit.
Parish, P. (1970). *Amelia Bedelia*. New York: Scholastic.
   Amelia Bedelia goes camping.
   Amelia Bedelia goes shopping.
   Amelia Bedelia helps out.
   Good work, Amelia Bedelia.
Rey, H. A. (1973). *Curious George*. Boston: Houghton Mifflin.
   Curious George flies a kite.
   Curious George goes to the circus.
   Curious George learns the alphabet.
   Curious George rides a bike.
Taylor, M. (1976). *Henry the explorer*. New York: Atheneum.
   Henry explores the jungle.
   Henry explores the mountains.
   Henry explores the castaway.
Waber, B. (1975). *The house on East 88th Street*. Boston: Houghton Mifflin.
   Lyle and the birthday party.
   Lyle finds his mother.
   Lyle, Lyle crocodile.
Wells, R. (1979). *Max's first words*. New York: Dial Press.
   Max's new suit.
   Max's ride.
   Max's toys.
Zion, C. (1976). *Harry the dirty dog*. New York: Harper & Row, Publishers.
   Harry and the lady next door.
   Harry by the sea.
   No roses for Harry.

21. Children's Books Related to Themes

a. All about Me Books

Blaine, M. (1975). *The terrible thing that happened at our house*. New York: Four Winds Press. (realistic literature)
Carlson, N. (1988). *I like me*. New York: Viking Press. (picture book)
Giff, P. (1988) *Ronald Morgan goes to bat*. New York: Viking Press. (picture book)
Joosse, B. (1989). *Dinah's mad, bad wishes*. New York: Harper & Row, Publishers. (picture book)

HOBAN, R. (1968). *A birthday for Frances*. New York: Scholastic. (picture book)

KALMAN, B. (1985). *Happy to be me*. New York: Crabtree Publishing Co. (realistic)

MAYER, M. (1988). *Just my friend and me*. Racine, WI: Western Publishing Co., Inc. (picture book)

PARISH, P. (1988) *Amelia Bedelia's family album*. New York: Greenwillow Books. (picture book)

SHARMAT, M. (1977). *I'm terrific*. New York: Holiday House. (realistic)

b. Animal Books

CARLE, E. (1969). *1,2,3 to the zoo*. New York: Philomel Books. (counting book)

CARLE, E. (1989). *Animals animals*. New York: Philomel Books. (poetry)

CROWTHER, R. (1982). *A jungle jumble*. Kansas City: Hallmark Children's Edition. (wordless moveable book)

DUVOISIN, R. (1950). *Petunia on the farm*. New York: Alfred A. Knopf. (serial picture book)

EMBERLY, R. (1986). *Jungle sounds*. Boston: Little, Brown & Co. (audiotape available)

GUARINO, D. (1989). *Is your mama a llama?* New York: Scholastic. (Big Book)

MAYER, M. (1989). *What do you do with a kangaroo?* New York: Scholastic. (Big Book)

NATIONAL WILDLIFE FEDERATION. *Your Big Backyard*. Washington, DC: National Wildlife Federation. (magazine)

PRELUTSKY, J. (1983). *Zoo doings*. New York: Greenwillow Books. (poetry)

TAFURI, N. (1988). *Junglewalk*. New York: Greenwillow Books. (wordless)

WALT DISNEY PRODUCTIONS. (1986). *The jungle book*. New York: Gallery Books. (traditional)

c. Dinosaurs

ALIKI. (1985). *Dinosaurs are different*. New York: Harper & Row, Publishers. (informational)

BARTON, B. (1989). *Dinosaurs, dinosaurs*. New York: Crowell. (informational)

DEPAOLA, T. (1990). *Little Grunt and the big egg*. New York: Holiday House. (fairytale)

HENNESSEY, B. G. (1988). *The dinosaur who lived in my backyard*. New York: Viking Press. (picture book)

HOFF, S. (1975). *Dinosaur dos and dont's*. New York: Windmill Books. (picture book)

KINGDON, J. (1982). *The ABC dinosaur book*. Chicago, IL: Children's Press. (picture book)

MOST, B. (1990). *Four & twenty dinosaurs*. New York: Harper & Row, Publishers. (adapted nursery rhymes)

PRELUTSKY, J. (1988). *Tyrannosaurus was a beast.* New York: Greenwillow Books. (poetry)
ROWE, E. (1989). *Giant dinosaurs.* New York: Scholastic. (Big Book)
WALTON, R. & A. (1989). *Fossil follies!: Jokes about dinosaurs.* New York: Lerner. (joke book)

d. Ecology

BLOOME, E. (1971). *The air we breath.* Garden City, NY: Doubleday. (informational)
CARLE, E. (1987). *The tiny seed.* Saxonville, MA: Picture Book Studio. (picture book)
GWYNNE, F. (1971). *The story of Ick.* New York: Windmill Books. (informational)
KUDLINSKI, K. (1988). *Rachel Carson, pioneer of ecology.* New York: Viking Kestrel. (biography)
LIONNI, L. (1968). *The alphabet tree.* New York: Pantheon Books. (alphabet book)
MARGOLIS, R. (1980). *Big bear spare that tree.* New York: Greenwillow Books. (picture book)
NATIONAL WILDLIFE FEDERATION. *Ranger Rick.* Vienna, VA: Author. (magazine)
SEUSS, DR. (1971). *The Lorax.* New York: Random House. (picture book)
TRESSALT, A. R. (1972). *The dead tree.* New York: Parents' Magazine Press. (picture book)
UDRY, J. M. (1956). *A tree is nice.* New York: Harper & Row, Publishers. (picture book)

e. Five Senses

ADOLPH, A. (1989). *Chocolate dreams.* New York: Lothrop, Lee & Shephard. (picture book)
ALIKI. (1989). *My five senses.* New York: Harper & Row, Publishers. (informational)
BAUM, A. & J. (1962). *One bright Monday morning.* New York: Random House. (picture book)
BOON, E. (1987). *1,2,3 how many animals do you see?* New York: Orchard Books. (counting book)
GARDNER, B. (1980). *The turn about, think about, look about book.* New York: Lothrop, Lee & Shepard. (picture book)
RYLANT, C. (1988). *All I see.* New York: Orchard Books. (picture book)
SHOWERS, P. (1990). *Ears are for hearing.* New York: Harper & Row, Publishers. (informational)

f. Insects and Reptiles

CARLE, E. (1984). *The mixed up chameleon.* New York: Crowell. (picture book)

CARLE, E. (1986). *The very hungry caterpillar.* New York: Philomel Books. (big book)
FARBER, N. (1979). *Never say ugh to a bug.* New York: Greenwillow Books. (poetry)
FISHER, A. (1986). *When it comes to bugs.* New York: Harper & Row, Publishers. (poetry)
HABERMAN, M. A. (1976). *Bugs: Poems.* New York: Viking Press. (poetry)
LIONNI, L. (1975). *A color of his own.* New York: Pantheon Books. (realistic)
NATIONAL CEOGRAPHIC WORLD. *National Geographic Society.* Washington, DC. (magazine)
PARKER, J. (1988). *I love spiders.* New York: Scholastic. (informational)
PETIE, H. (1975). *Billions of bugs.* Englewood Cliffs, NJ: Prentice Hall. (counting/rhymes)
ROOP, P. (1986). *Going buggy: Jokes about insects.* Minnneapolis: Lerner Publications Co. (joke book)

g. Ocean Life

ANDERSON, H. C. (1971). *The little mermaid.* New York: Harper & Row, Publishers. (traditional)
CARLE, E. (1987). *A house for a hermit crab.* Saxonville, MA: Picture Book Studio. (informational)
CARLE, E. (1989). *Animals animals.* New York: Philomel Books. (poetry)
GIBBONS, G. (1988). *Sunken treasures.* New York: Crowell. (realistic)
HAUSER, H. (1984). *Book of marine fishes.* Los Angeles: Petersen Publishing Co. (informational)
LESTER, H. (1988). *Tacky the penguin.* Boston: Houghton Mifflin. (picture book)
LIONNI, L. (1973). *Swimmy.* New York: Random House. (picture book)
RAFFI. (1987). *Down by the bay.* New York: Crown Publishers. (song book)
TOKUDA, W., and HALL, R. (1986). *Humphrey, the lost whale.* Union City, CA: Heian International. (realistic)
VASILIS, M. (1977). *A day at the beach.* New York: Random House. (informational)
WILDSMITH, B. (1968). *Fishes.* New York: Franklin Watts, Inc. (informational)

h. Seasons and Holidays

1. Books about the Seasons
BORDEN, L. (1988). *Caps, hats, socks, and mittens: A book about the four seasons.* New York: Scholastic. (Big Book)
HOPKINS, L. B. (1980). *Moments: Poems about the seasons.* San Diego, CA: Harcourt Brace Jovanovich. (poetry)
LARRICK, N. (selector). (1973). *More poetry for the holidays.* Champaign, IL: Garrard Publishing Co. (poetry)

2. Autumn

BRIDWELL, N. (1986). *Clifford's Halloween.* New York: Scholastic. (picture book)

BUSCAGLIA, L. (1982). *The fall of Freddie the leaf.* New York: Holt, Rinehart & Winston. (informational)

DUTTON, S. (1988). *The Cinnamon Hen's autumn day.* New York: Atheneum. (picture book)

KRAUS, R. (1973). *How spider saved Halloween.* New York: Scholastic. (picture book)

McGOVERN, A. (1973). *The Pilgrims' first Thanksgiving.* New York: Scholastic. (informational)

NIELSON-BARSUHN, R. (1985). *In fall.* Chicago: Children's Press. (poetry)

PRELUTSKY, J. (1977). *It's Halloween.* New York: Scholastic. (informational)

SANTREY, L. (1983). *Autumn.* Mahwah, NJ: Troll Associates. (informational/photography)

STEVENSON, J. (1986). *Fried feathers for Thanksgiving.* New York: Scholastic. (picture book)

3. Winter

BRETT, J. (1989). *The mitten.* New York: Putnam. (Ukranian folk tale)

BRIGGS, R. (1985). *The snowman.* Boston: Little, Brown. (wordless picture book)

FROST, R. (1978). *Stopping by the woods on a snowy evening.* New York: Dutton. (poetry)

KEATS, E. J. (1962). *The snowy day.* New York: Viking Press. (Big Book)

KROLL, S. (1987). *It's Groundhog Day!* New York: Scholastic. (picture book)

NEITZEL, S. (1989). *The jacket I wear in the snow.* New York: Greenwlllow Books. (repetitive story)

PRELUTSKY, J. (1984). *It's snowing! It's snowing!* New York: Greenwillow Books. (poetry)

PRELUTSKY, J. (1983). *It's Valentine's Day.* New York: Scholastic. (poetry)

4. Spring

ALLINGTON, R. (1981). *Spring.* Milwaukee: Raintree Children's Books. (informational)

DELTON, J. (1989). *Spring sprouts.* New York: Young Yearling; Dell. (read aloud)

HOBAN, L. (1973). *The sugar snow spring.* New York: Harper & Row, Publishers. (picture book)

HOLMELUND, E. (1989). *It's spring!* New York: Greenwillow Books. (picture book)

KALMAN, B. (1985). *We celebrate spring.* New York: Crabtree Publishing Co. (informational)

KRENSKY, S. (1990). *Lionel in the spring.* New York: Dial Books for Young Readers. (picture book)

LYON, G. E. (1990). *Come a tide.* New York: Orchard Books. (picture book)

WILHELM, H. (1985). *Bunny trouble.* New York: Scholastic. (picture book)

5. Summer

GARELICK, M. (1973). *Down to the beach.* New York: Four Winds Press. (informational)

KEATS, E. J. (1973). *Over in the meadow.* New York: Four Winds Press. (w/tape, rhyming story)

KROLL, S. (1990). *Gone fishing.* New York: Crown Publishers. (picture book)

McCLOSKEY, R. (1976). *Blueberries for Sal.* New York: Puffin Books. (picture book)

MONCURE, J. B. (1985). *In summer.* Chicago, IL: Children's Press. (poetry)

PRELUTSKY, J. (1984). *What I did last summer.* New York: Greenwillow Books. (poetry)

ZION, G. (1965). *Harry by the sea.* New York: Harper & Row, Publishers. (picture book)

i. Space

CARLE E. (1986). *Papa please get the moon for me.* New York: Scholastic. (picture storybook)

COLE, J. (1990). *The magic school bus lost in the solar system.* New York: Scholastic. (informational)

ETRA, J., and SPINNER, S. (1988). *Aliens for breakfast.* New York: Random House. (picture book)

FREEMAN, M. (1971) *You will go to the moon.* New York: Beginner Books. (informational)

JOHNSON, C. (1957). *Harold's trip to the sky.* New York: Harper & Row, Publishers. (picture book)

KEATS, E. J. (1981). *Regards to the man in the moon.* New York: Four Winds Press. (picture book)

LIVINGSTON, M. C. (1988). *Space songs.* New York: Holiday House. (poetry)

MUIRDEN, J. (1987). *Going to the moon.* New York: Random House. (informational)

NATIONAL AIR and SPACE MUSEUM. (1988). *Discovery: A tour of space flight vehicles for children grades pre-school through 3.* Washington, DC: Smithsonian Institution. (informational)

REY, H. A. (1951). *Curious George gets a medal.* Boston: Houghton Mifflin. (picture book)

SADLER, M. (1984). *A stair in outer space.* Englewood Cliffs, NJ: Prentice Hall. (picture book)

SCHOBERLE, C. (1986). *Beyond the Milky Way.* New York: Crown Publishers. (picture book)

UNGERER, T. (1984). *Moon man.* New York: Harper & Row, Publishers. (picture book w/film)

YOLEN, J. (1987). *Owl moon.* New York: Scholastic. (picture book)

j. Weather Books

BARRETT, J. (1978). *Cloudy with a chance of meatballs.* New York: Atheneum. (picture book)

BRANLEY, F. M., and CROWELL, T. Y. (1985). *Flash, crash, rumble, and roll.* New York: Crowell. (informational)

DePAOLA, T. (1975). *The cloud book.* New York: Scholastic. (informational)

KEATS, E. J. (1978). *The snowy day.* New York: Puffin. (picture book)

KNIGHT, D. C. (1967). *Let's find out about the weather.* New York: F. Watts. (informational)

PRELUTSKY, J. (1980). *Rainy rainy Saturday.* New York: Greenwillow Books. (poetry)

SHAW, C. G. (1947). *It looked like spilt milk.* New York: Harper & Row, Publishers. (picture book)

22. Children's Literature Related to Cultural Diversity

a. African–American Books

AARDEMA, V. (1975). *Why mosquitoes buzz in people's ears.* New York: Dutton. (Big Book/folktale)

AARDEMA, V. (1989). *Bringing the rain to Kapiti Plain.* New York: Scholastic. (rhyming Big Book)

LOTRIDGE, C. (1990). *The name of a tree.* New York: Margaret K. McElderry. (folktale)

MAYER, M. (1976). *Liza Lou and the Yellow Belly Swamp.* New York: Parents' Magazine Press. (folktale)

MENDEZ, P. (1989). *The black snowman.* New York: Scholastic. (picture book)

SAN SOUCI, R. (1989). *The boy and the ghost.* New York: Simon & Schuster. (folklore)

STEPTOE, J. (1987). *Mufaro's beautiful daughters.* New York: Lothrop, Lee & Shephard. (folktale)

b. Asian Books

BIRDSEYE, T. (1990). *A song of stars.* New York: Holiday House. (legend).

MAHY, M. (1990). *The seven Chinese brothers.* New York: Scholastic. (legend)

McDERMOTT, G. (1975). *The stone cutter.* New York: Viking Press. (myth)

PITTMAN, H. C. (1988). *The gift of the willows.* Minneapolis: Carolrhoda Books. (cultural story)

TORRE, B. (1990). *The luminous pearl.* New York: Orchard Books. (picture book)

YOUNG, E. (1989). *Lon Po Po: A Red Riding Hood story from China.* New York: Philomel. (folktale)

c. Hispanic Books

ETS, M. (1963). *Gilberto and the wind.* New York: Viking.

EVERETT, L. (1988). *Amigo means friend.* Mahwah, NJ: Troll Associates. (realistic)

O'Dell, S. (1983). *The amethyst ring*. Boston: Houghton Mifflin. (historical fiction)

Pena, S. (1981). *Kikiriki: Stories and poems in English and Spanish for children*. Houston, TX: Arte Publico. (stories and poems)

Roberts, M. (1986). *Henry Cisneros: Mexican American mayor*. Chicago: Children's Press. (biography)

d. Native American Books

Clark, A. N. (1975). *In my mother's house*. New York: Viking Press. (informational)

Goble, P. (1990). *Iktomi and the ducks*. New York: Orchard Books. (folktale)

Goble, P. (1990). *Dream wolf*. New York: Bradbury. (traditional tale)

Jones, H. (selector). (1971). *The trees stand shining: Poetry of the North American Indians*. New York: Dial. (Indian songs)

Longfellow, H. W. (1983). *Hiawatha*. New York: Dial. (epic poem)

McDermott, G. (1975). *Arrow to the sun*. New York: Viking Press. (myth)

23. Children's Literature about Children's Special Needs

a. Communication Problems (Speech and language differences)

Christopher, M. (1975). *Glue fingers*. Toronto: Little, Brown.

Fleischman, P. (1980). *The Half-a-Moon Inn*. New York: Harper & Row, Publishers.

Flournoy, V. (1985). *The patchwork quilt*. New York: Dial.

Greenfield, E. (1974). *She came bringing me that little baby girl*. Philadelphia: Lippincott.

Hamilton, V. (1985). *The people could fly*. New York: Alfred A. Knopf.

Mathis, S. B. (1975). *The hundred penny box*. New York: Puffin.

Mayer, M. (1976). *Liza Lou and the Yellow Belly Swamp*. New York: Four Winds Press.

White, E. B. (1970). *The trumpet of the swan*. New York: Harper & Row, Publishers.

b. Physical Disabilities (visual, hearing, physical)

Visual

Brighton, C. (1984). *My hands, my world*. New York: Macmillan.

Cohen, M. (1983). *See you tomorrow, Charles*. New York: Greenwillow Books.

MACLACHLAN, P. (1979). *Through Grandpa's eyes.* New York: Harper & Row, Publishers.

YALEN, J. (1977). *The seeing stick.* New York: Thomas Y. Crowell.

Hearing

CHARLIP, R. (1987). *Handtalk birthday: A number and storybook in sign language.* New York: Four Winds Press.

PETERSON, J. W. (1984). *I have a sister. My sister is deaf.* New York: Harper & Row, Publishers.

RISKIND, M. (1981). *Apple is my sign.* New York: Harcourt Brace Jovanovich.

Physical

FREVERT, P. D. (1983). *It's OK to look at Jamie.* Mankato, MN: Creative Education.

HENRIOD, L. (1982). *Grandma's wheelchair.* Niles, IL: Whitman.

HONEYMAN, A. (1980). *Sam and his cart.* St. Paul, MN: EMC.

RABE, B. (1981). *The balancing girls.* New York: Dutton.

c. Learning Disabilities

BALDWIN, A. (1978). *A little time.* New York: Viking Press.

HERMES, P. (1983). *Who will take care of me?* New York: Harcourt Brace Jovanovich.

HIRSCH, K. (1977). *My sister.* Minneapolis, MN: Carolrhoda Books.

OMINSKY, E. (1977). *Jon O, a special boy.* Englewood Cliffs, NJ: Prentice Hall.

SMITH, D. B. (1975). *Kelly's creek.* New York: Thomas Y. Crowell.

SOBOL, H. (1977). *My brother Stephen is retarded.* New York: Macmillan.

APPENDIX B

Additional Literature Resources

1. Book Clubs

The Book Plan, 921 Washington Avenue, Brooklyn, NY 11238.

Firefly Book Club, P.O. Box 485, Pleasantville, NY 10570.

Junior Deluxe Editions Club, Garden City, NY 11530.

My Weekly Reader Book Club, 1250 Fairwood Avenue, P.O. Box 2639, Columbus, OH 43216.

Parents' Magazine Read-Aloud Book Club for Little Listeners and Beginning Readers, Division of Parents' Magazine Enterprises, 52 Vanderbilt Avenue, New York, NY 10017.

Scholastic Book Services, See Saw Club (K–1), 904 Sylvan Avenue, Englewood Cliffs, NJ 07632.

Troll Book Club, 320 Route 17, Mahwah, NJ 07430

Trumpet Club, P.O. Box 604, Holmes, PA 19043

Young America Book Club, 1250 Fairwood Avenue, Columbus, OH 43216

2. Companies That Distribute Storybooks, Records, and Cassettes

Caedmon, 1995 Broadway, New York, NY 10023.

Doubleday, 277 Park Avenue, New York, NY 10017.

Kaplan School Supply Corporation, 1310 Lewisville–Clemmons Road, Lewisville, NC 27023.

Random House, Inc., 201 E. 50th Street, New York, NY 10022.

Scott Foresman, Talking Story Book Box, 1900 E. Lake Avenue, Glenview, IL 60025.

Troll Book Associates, 320 Route 17, Mahwah, NJ 07430.
Weston Woods, Weston, CT 06883.

3. Children's Book Awards

American Book Awards. Association of American Publishers, One Park Avenue, New York, NY 10016.

Annual awards for best books chosen by children. National Council of Teachers of English, 1111 Kenyon Road, Champaign-Urbana, IL 61801.

Caldecott Medal. American Library Association, 50 East Huron Street, Chicago, IL 60611.

Children's Book Showcase. Children's Book Council, 67 Irving Place, New York, NY 10003.

Newbery Award. American Library Association, 50 East Huron Street, Chicago, IL 60611.

APPENDIX C

Resources for Parents

1. Books

Barton, B. (1986). *Tell me another.* Exeter, NH: Heinemann Educational Books.

Butler, D. (1980). *Babies need books.* New York: Atheneum.

Butler, D., and Clay, M. (1982). *Reading begins at home.* Exeter, NH: Heinemann Educational Books.

Hearne, B. (1981). *Choosing books for children: A commonsense guide.* New York: Delacorte.

Kaye, P. (1984). *Games for reading: Playful ways to help your child read.* New York: Pantheon.

Kimmel, M. M., and Segel, E. (1983). *For reading out loud.* New York: Delacorte.

Lamme, L. (1985). *Highlights for children: Growing up reading.* Washington, DC: Acropolis Books, Ltd.

Larrick, N. (1985). *A parent's guide to children's reading* (5th ed.). New York: Bantam.

Rosi, M. J. M. (1982). *Read to me: Teach me.* Wauwatosa, WI: American Baby Books.

Taylor, D., and Strickland, D. S. (1986). *Family storybook reading.* Exeter, N.H.: Heinemann Educational Books.

Tiedt, I. M. (1979). *Exploring books with children.* Boston: Houghton Mifflin.

Trelease, J. (1982). *The read aloud handbook.* New York: Penguin.

White, D. (1986). *Books before five.* Exeter, NH: Heinemann Educational Books.

2. Pamphlets and Booklets

Choosing a children's book. New York: Children's Book Council.
  A four-page folder giving advice on nine booklets along with sources and prices. Free with stamped, self-addressed envelope sent to Children's Book Council, 67 Irving Place, New York, NY 10003.

Janes, D. *Reading in the home.* New York: Scholastic Magazines.
  A six-page folder for parents. Free from Scholastic Magazines, 50 West 44th Street, New York, NY 10036.

SCHICKEDANZ, J. (1983). *Helping children learn about reading.* Washington, DC: NAEYC.

Free with stamped, self-addressed envelope sent to National Association for the Education of Young Children, 1834 Connecticut Avenue NW, Washington, DC 20009. (800-424-2460)

IRA Micromonographs. Published by the International Reading Association, 800 Barksdale Road, P.O. Box 8139, Newark, DE 19714.

This valuable series of twelve-to-twenty-four-page pamphlets focuses on answering questions parents often ask about the reading education of their children.

What books and records should I get for my preschooler? Norma Rogers. (No. 872)

How can I prepare my young child for reading? Paula Grinnell. (No. 881)

Why read aloud to children? Julie M. T. Chan. (No. 877)

How can I help my child build positive attitudes toward reading? Susan Mandel Glazer. (No. 879)

What is reading readiness? Norma Rogers. (No. 870)

How can I help my child get ready to read? Norma Rogers. (No. 876)

IRA Parent Brochures. Published by the International Reading Association, 800 Barksdale Road, P.O. Box 8139, Newark, DE 19714.

These brochures focus on practical reading concerns of parents and on ways for parents to help their children develop reading skills and a lifetime reading habit.

Your home is your child's first school.

You can encourage your child to read.

Good books make reading fun for your child. Glenna Davis Sloan.

You can use television to stimulate your child's reading habits. Nicholas P. Criscuolo.

U. S. government publications. Available from U.S. Government Printing Office, North Capitol and H Streets NW, Washington, DC 20401.

Children and television (free).

Parents and beginning readers (free).

APPENDIX D

Quality Television Programs with Associated Children's Books

Educational Programs

Sesame Street

Hautzey, D. (1986). *It's not fair: A Sesame Street start to read book*. New York: Random House.

Stiles, N., and Wilcox, D. (1974). *Grover and the everything in the whole wide world museum*. New York: Random House.

Stone, J. (1971). *The monster at the end of this book*. Racine, WI: Western Publishing Co., Inc.

Mr. Rogers' Neighborhood

Rogers, F. (1983). Mister Rogers' *Planet Purple*. Dallas: Texas Instruments, Inc.

Rogers, F. (1986). *Going to the doctor*. New York: Putnam's.

Rogers, F. (1987). *Making friends*. New York: Putnam's.

Reading Rainbows

Cauley, B. (1979). *The ugly duckling*. New York: Harcourt Brace Jovanovich, Inc.

Keats, E. J. (1967). *Peter's chair*. New York: Harper & Row, Publishers.

Lobel, A. (1972). *Frog and toad together*. New York: Harper & Row, Publishers.

Sendak, M. (1963). *Where the wild things are*. New York: Harper & Row, Publishers.

Viorst, J. (1972). *Alexander and the terrible, horrible, no good, very bad day*. New York: Macmillan.

Muppets

Bruce, S. B. (1982). *Gonzo and the giant chicken.* New York: Random House.

Kates, L. (1986). *Make believe with the Muppet babies: A storybook.* New York: Random House.

Stevenson, J. (1986). *Bo saves the show.* New York: Random House.

Romper Room

Anastasio, D. (1985). *Romper Room book of ABC's.* New York: Doubleday.

Favata, R. (1984). *Romper Room song book of musical adventures: Alphabetcha!* New York: Caedmon.

Karnovsky, B. N. (1984). *Romper Room bedtime story book.* New York: Doubleday.

Nickelodeon (cable)

Rey, H. A. (1973). *Curious George.* Boston: Houghton Mifflin.

Rey, H. A. (1977). *Curious George flies a kite.* Boston: Houghton Mifflin.

Rey, H. A. (1985). *Curious George visits the zoo.* Boston: Houghton Mifflin.

Disney (cable)

Chase, A. (1964). *Mary Poppins.* Racine, WI: Western Publishing Co., Inc.

Disney, W. (1950). *Alice in Wonderland.* Racine, WI: Western Publishing Co., Inc.

Gag, W. (1938). *Snow White and the seven dwarfs.* New York: Putnam's.

Knights, H. (1978). *Cinderella.* New York: Random House.

Milne, A. A. (1957). *The world of Pooh.* New York: Dutton.

Popular Cartoon Shows

Berenstain Bears

Berenstain, S. and J. (1981). *The Berenstain bears' moving day.* New York: Random House.

Berenstain, S. and J. (1981). *The Berenstain bears go to the doctor.* New York: Random House.

Charlie Brown

Schulz, C. M. (1976). *Life is a circus.* New York: Scholastic.
Schulz, C. M. (1976). *It's the Easter beagle, Charlie Brown.* New York: Scholastic.
Schulz, C. M. (1976). *A Charlie Brown Thanksgiving.* New York: Scholastic.

Smurfs

Peyo. (1982). *A Smurf in the air.* New York: Random House.
Peyo. (1982). *Smurphony in C.* New York: Random House.
Peyo. (1982). *The wandering Smurf.* New York: Random House.

Dr. Seuss

Seuss, Dr. (1957). *How the Grinch stole Christmas.* New York: Random House.
Seuss, Dr. (1957). *The cat in the hat.* New York: Random House.
Seuss, Dr. (1961). *Sneetches and other stories.* New York: Random House.
Seuss, Dr. (1971). *The Lorax.* New York: Random House.

Other Books Featured as Television Specials

Baum, E. (1984). *Wizard of Oz.* New York: Random House.
Lofting, H. (1920). *The story of Doctor Doolittle.* New York: Lippincott.
Tolkien, J. R. (1984). *The hobbit.* Boston: Houghton Mifflin.
Wilder, L. I. (1935). *Little house on the prairie.* New York: Harper & Row, Publishers.

Computer Software for Early Literacy Development

1. *ADVENTURES OF KRISTEN AND FAMILY*   *Grade: PreK–2*

DESCRIPTION: Prereader develops computer literacy through sequencing and storytelling activities that value family and community.

HARDWARE: Apple II Family

AVAILABILITY: Rhiannon Software

2. *CHARLIE BROWN'S ABC'S*   *Grade: K–2*

DESCRIPTION: Uses animation to introduce children to letters and words. Includes off-screen activity cards.

HARDWARE: Apple II Family, Commodore 64.

AVAILABILITY: Random House School Division

3. *DELTA DRAWING*   *Grade: PreK–7*

DESCRIPTION: User creates colorful drawings on the computer screen with single-key commands that control the Delta Cursor.

HARDWARE: Apple II Family, Atari, Commodore 64, IBM

AVAILABILITY: Spinnaker Software Corporation

4. *EZ LOGO, REVISED EDITION*   *Grade: PreK–3*

DESCRIPTION: Children explore computer capabilities and experiment with turtle graphics using twenty-four open-ended activities.

HARDWARE: Apple 64K

AVAILABILITY: Minnesota Educational Computing Consortium

5. FIRST–LETTER FUN   Grade: PreK–3

DESCRIPTION:	Enjoyable animated stories that help children match letters with initial sounds of words.
HARDWARE:	Apple 48K, Commodore 64, IBM
AVAILABILITY:	Minnesota Educational Computing Consortium

6. THE FRIENDLY COMPUTER   Grade: PreK–3

DESCRIPTION:	Children learn the major parts of a computer system while playing games with Zebug, an animated character.
HARDWARE:	Apple 48K, Commodore 64, IBM
AVAILABILITY:	Minnesota Educational Computing Consortium

7. KIDWRITER   Grade: PreK–3

DESCRIPTION:	Children create a graphically illustrated story.
HARDWARE:	Apple II Family, Atari, Commodore, IBM
AVAILABILITY:	Spinnaker Software Corporation

8. LETTER MATCH   Grade: PreK–2

DESCRIPTION:	A game for learning upper- and lowercase letters.
HARDWARE:	Atari, Commodore 64, TRS-80.
AVAILABILITY:	Computer Applications Tomorrow

9. MAKE A MATCH   Grade: PreK–1

DESCRIPTION:	Electronic book of favorite nursery rhymes with music and color graphics, used to enhance children's cognition and recall.
HARDWARE:	IBM, Tandy
AVAILABILITY:	Sunstar Systems

10. PAINT WITH WORDS   Grade: PreK–2

DESCRIPTION:	Children exercise their creativity and develop their vocabulary as they choose words and turn them into colorful images.
HARDWARE:	Apple 64K
AVAILABILITY:	Minnesota Educational Computing Consortium

APPENDIX F

Resources for Teachers

1. School Supply Companies

Childcraft Education Corp., 20 Kilmer Road, Edison, NJ 08818-3018.

Didex Inc. Educational Resources, 5 Fourth Street, Peabody, MA 01960.

DLM Teaching Resources, P.O. Box 4000, One DLM Park, Allen, TX 75002.

Educational Teaching Aids, 159 West Kinzie Street, Chicago, IL 60610.

J. L. Hammett Co., Box 545, Braintree, MA 02184.

Kaplan School Supply Corp., 1310 Lewisville-Clemons Road, Lewisville, NC 27023.

Scholastic Inc., P.O. Box 7501, 2931 East McCarty Street, Jefferson City, MO 65102.

Totline Press/Warren Publishing House, Inc., P.O. Box 2255, Everett, WA 98203.

Toys 'n' Things Press/Resources for Child Caring, Inc., 906 North Dale Street, Box 23, St. Paul, MN 55103.

2. References for Teacher-Made Materials

Baratta, L. M. (1972) *Workjobs activity-centered learning for early childhood education.* Menlo Park, CA: Addison-Wesley.

Coudron, J. *Alphabet puppets.* (1983). Belmont, CA: Fearon Teacher Aids.

Flemming, B., and Hamilton, D. (1977). *Resources for creative teaching in early childhood education.* New York: Harcourt Brace Jovanovich, Inc.

Forgan, H. W. (1977). *The reading center: Ideas, games and activities for individualizing reading.* Santa Monica, CA: Goodyear.

Forte, P. T. (1973). *Center stuff for nooks, crannies and corners.* Nashville: Incentive Press Inc.

Greff, K., and Askov, E. (1977). *Learning centers: An idea book for reading and language arts.* Dubuque, IA: Kendall/Hunt.

Spice Series Teacher Handbooks. (1960). *Spice primary language arts.* Stevensville, MI: Educational Service, Inc.

3. Professional Associations and Related Journals Dealing with Early Literacy

- American Library Association, 50 E. Huron Street, Chicago, IL 60611.
- American Montessori Society, Inc. (AMS), 150 Fifth Avenue, New York, NY 10010.
- Association for Childhood Education International (ACEI), 11141 Georgia Avenue, Suite 200, Wheaton, MD 20902.
  Journal: *Childhood Education*
- Capital Publications, Inc., 2430 Pennsylvania Avenue NW, Washington, DC 20037.
  Journal: *Report on Preschool Education*
- Child Welfare League of America, Inc., 67 Irving Place, New York, NY 10010.
  Journal: *Child Welfare*
- Children's Bureau, Office of Child Development, U.S. Department of Health, Education and Welfare, Washington, DC 20201.
  Journal: *Children Today*
- College Reading Association (CRA), Department of Curriculum and Instruction, College of Education, Appalachian State University, Boone, NC 28608.
  Journal: *Reading Research & Instruction*
- Education Today Company, 530 University Avenue, Palo Alto, CA 94301.
  Journal: *Learning*
- Educational Resource Information Center/Early Childhood Education (ERIC/ECE), University of Illinois, 804 West Pennsylvania Avenue, Urbana, IL 61801.
- Gordon and Breach Science Publishers, Inc., One Park Avenue, New York, NY 10016.
  Journal: *Early Child Development and Care*
- Highlights for Children, Inc., P.O. Box 1266, Darien, CT 06820.
  Journal: *Early Years*

- The Instructor Publications, Inc., P.O. Box 6099, Duluth, MN 55806.
  Journal: *Instructor*
- International Reading Association (IRA), 800 Barksdale Road, P.O. Box 8139, Newark, DE 19711.
  Journals: *Reading Teacher; Reading Research Quarterly;*
  brochures, pamphlets, and monographs
- National Association for the Education Of Young Children (NAEYC), 1834 Connecticut Avenue NW, Washington, DC 20009.
  Journal: *Young Children*
  pamphlets and monographs
- National Council of Teachers of English (NCTE), 1111 Kenyon Road, Urbana, IL 61801.
  Journal: *Language Arts*
  pamphlets and monographs
- National Education Association (NEA), 1201 16th Street NW, Washington, DC 20036.
  Journal: *Today's Education*
- National Reading Conference (NRC), 1070 Sibley Tower, Rochester, NY 14604.
  Journal: *Journal of Reading Behavior*
- Society for Research in Child Development, 5750 Ellis Avenue, Chicago, IL 60637.
  Journal: *Child Development*

BIBLIOGRAPHY

ADAMS, M. J. (1990). *Beginning to read: Thinking and learning about print.* Urbana: University of Illinois Center for the Study of Reading.

ALLEN, R. V. (1976). *Language experience in communication.* Boston: Houghton Mifflin.

ALTWERGER, A., DIEHL-FAXON, J., and DOCKSTADER-ANDERSON, K. (1985). Reading aloud events as meaning construction. *Language Arts, 62,* 476–484.

ANDERSON, A., and STOKES, S. (1984). Social and institutional influences on the development and practice of literacy. In H. Goelman, A. Oberg, and F. Smith (eds.), *Awakening to literacy.* Exeter, NH: Heinemann Educational Books.

ANDERSON, R. C., HIEBERT, E. H., SCOTT, J. A., and WILKINSON, I. A. G., (1985). *Becoming a nation of readers.* Washington, DC: National Institute of Education.

ANDERSON, R. C., MASON, J., and SHIRLEY, L. (1984). The reading group: An experimental investigation of a labyrinth. *Reading Research Quarterly, 20,* 6–38.

ANDERSON, R. C., WILSON, P. T., and FIELDING, L. G. (1985, December). A new focus on free-reading. Symposium presentation at the National Reading Conference, San Diego.

APPLEBEE, A. N., and LANGER, J. A. (1983). Instructional scaffolding: Reading and writing as natural language activities. *Language Arts, 60,* 168–175.

ARBUTHNOT, M. H., and SUTHERLAND, Z. (1977). *Children and books* (5th ed.). Glenview, IL: Scott, Foresman.

ASHTON-WARNER, S. (1959). *Spinster.* New York: Simon & Schuster.

ASHTON-WARNER, S. (1963). *Teacher.* New York: Bantam.

ATHEY, I. (1971). Synthesis of papers on language development and reading. *Reading Research Quarterly, 7,* 9–16.

BADEN, M. J. P. (1981). A comparison of composition scores of third grade children with reading skills, pre-kindergarten verbal ability, self-concept, and sex. *Dissertation Abstract International, 42,* 1517A.

BAGHBAN, M. (1984). *Our daughter learns to read and write.* Newark, DE: International Reading Association.

BASE, G. (1986). *Animalia.* New York: Harry N. Abrams.

BAUMANN, J. F. (1984). The effectiveness of a direct instruction paradigm for teaching main idea comprehension. *Reading Research Quarterly, 20,* 93–115.

BECKMAN, D. (1972). Interior space: The things of education. *National Elementary Principal, 52,* 43–49.

BEMELMANS, L. (1939). *Madeline.* New York: Viking.

BEMELMANS, L. (1953). *Madeline's rescue.* New York: Viking.

BERENSTAIN, S. J. (1985). *The Berenstain bears and too much birthday.* New York: Random House.

BERGERON, B. (1990). What does the term whole language mean? A definition from the literature. *Journal of Reading Behavior, 23,* 301–329.

BIEHLER, R. F. (1976). *Child development: An introduction.* Boston: Houghton Mifflin.

BIPPUS, A. C. (1977). The relationship of the quality of students' written and reading comprehension in grades four and six. *Dissertation Abstracts International, 38,* 3993A.

BIRNBAUM, J. (1981). A study of reading and writing behaviors of selected fourth grade and seventh grade students. Doctoral dissertation, Rutgers University.

BIRNBAUM, J., and EMIG, J. (1983). Creating minds: Created texts. In R. Parker and F. Davis (eds.), *Developing literacy., Young children's use of language.* Newark, DE: International Reading Association.

BISSETT, D. (1969). The amount and effect of recreational reading in selected fifth grade classes. Doctoral dissertation, Syracuse University.

BISSETT, D. (1970). The usefulness of children's books in the reading program. In J. Catterson (ed.), *Children and literature.* Newark, DE: International Reading Association.

BISSEX, G. (1980). *GNYS at work: A child learns to write and read.* Cambridge, MA: Harvard University Press.

BLACHMAN, B. A., and JAMES, S. L. (1985) Metalinguistic abilities and reading achievement in first-grade children. In J. Niles and R. Lalik (eds.), *Issues in literacy: A research perspective,* pp. 280–286. Rochester, NY: National Reading Conference.

BLOOM, B. (1964). *Stability and change in human characteristics.* New York: John Wiley.

BLOOM, B. (1972). *Language development: Form and function in emerging grammars.* Cambridge, MA: MIT Press.

BOOK INDUSTRY STUDY GROUP. (1984). *The 1983 consumer research study on reading and book publishing.* New York.

BOORSTIN, D. (1984). Letter of transmittal. In *Books in our future: A report from the Librarian of Congress to the Congress.* Washington, DC: U.S. Congress, Joint Committee on the Library.

BRENNER, B. (1972). *The three little pigs.* New York: Random House.

BRIGGS, C., and ELKIND, D. (1973). Cognitive development in early readers. *Developmental Psychology, 9,* 279–280.

BRITTON, J. (1982a). *Retrospect and prospect.* Upper Montclair, NJ: Boynton/Cook.

BRITTON, J. (1982b). The spectator role and the beginnings of writing. In M. Nystrand (ed.), *What writers know: The language, process and structure of written discourse.* New York: Academic Press.

BRITTON, J. (1983). Writing and the story world. In B. Kroll and G. Wells (eds.), *Explorations in the development of writing: Theory, research and practice.* Chichester, England: John Wiley.

BROWN, A. (1975). Recognition, reconstruction and recall of narrative sequences of preoperational children. *Child Development, 46,* 155–166.

BROWN, M. (1939). *The noisy book.* New York: Harper.

Brown, M. (1957). *The three Billy Goats Gruff.* New York: Harcourt, Brace.

Brown, R. (1973). *A first language: The early stages.* Cambridge, MA: Harvard University, Press.

Brown, R., and Bellugi, U. (1964). Three processes in the child's acquisition of syntax. *Harvard Educational Review, 34,* 133–151.

Brown, R., Cazden, C., and Bellugi-Klima, U. (1968). The child's grammar from one to three. In J. P. Hill (ed.), *Minnesota symposium on child development.* Minneapolis: University of Minnesota Press.

Brunner, J. (1975). The ontogenesis of speech acts. *Journal of Child Language, 3,* 1–19.

Bumsted, L. A. (1981). Influencing the frequency of children's cooperative and learning task-related behavior through change in the design and management of the classroom. Master's thesis, Cornell University.

Burton, V. L. (1943). *Katy and the big snow.* Boston: Houghton Mifflin.

Bushner, D. E. (1979). The relationship between the reading comprehension ability of seventh grade subjects and the syntactic complexity of their written language. *Dissertation Abstracts International, 40,* 4978A.

Calkins, L. M. (1983). *Lessons from a child: On the teaching and learning of writing.* Exeter, NH: Heinemann Educational Books.

Calkins, L. M. (1986). *The art of teaching writing.* Exeter, NH: Heinemann Educational Books.

Cambourne, B. (1984). "Language, learning and literacy." In A. Butler and J. Turbill, *Towards a Reading-Writing Classroom.* Primary Teaching Association. Exeter, NH: Heinemann Educational Books.

Carey, M. (1972). *Peter Pan.* New York: Random House.

Carle, E. (1970). *The very hungry caterpillar.* New York: Philomel.

Carroll, Lewis, pseud. (Charles L. Dodgon) (1963). *Alice's adventures in wonderland.* New York: Macmillan. (original work published 1865)

Cazden, C. (1972). *Child language and education.* New York: Holt, Rinehart & Winston.

Chall, J. S., Conrad, S. S., and Harris-Sharples, S. H. (1983). *Textbooks and challenges: An inquiry into textbook difficulty, reading achievement, and knowledge acquisition.* Final Report to the Spencer Foundation. Chicago, IL.

Chomsky, C. (1965). *Aspects of a theory of syntax.* Cambridge, MA: MIT Press.

Chomsky, C. (1969). *The acquisition of syntax in children from five to ten.* Cambridge, MA: MIT Press.

Chomsky, C. (1972). Stages in language development and reading. *Harvard Educational Review, 42,* 1–33.

Chukovsky, K. (1963). *From two to five.* Berkeley: University of California Press.

Clark, M. M. (1976). *Young fluent readers.* London: Heinemann Educational Books.

Clark, M. M. (1984). Literacy at home and at school: Insights from a study of young fluent readers. In H. Goelman, A. Oberg, and F. Smith (eds.), *Awakening to literacy.* Exeter, NH: Heinemann Educational Books.

CLAY, M. M. (1966). *Emergent reading behavior.* Doctoral dissertation, University of Auckland.

CLAY, M. M. (1972). *Reading: The patterning of complex behavior.* Auckland, New Zealand: Heinemann Educational Books.

CLAY, M. M. (1975). *What did I write?* Auckland, New Zealand: Heinemann Educational Books.

CLAY, M. M. (1979a). *Reading: The patterning of complex behavior* (2nd ed.). Auckland, New Zealand: Heinemann Educational Books.

CLAY, M. M. (1979b). *The early detection of reading difficulties: A diagnostic survey with recovery procedures.* Auckland, New Zealand: Heinemann Educational Books.

CLAY, M. M. (1987). Implementing reading recovery: Systematic adaptations to an educational innovation. *New Zealand Journal of Educational Studies, 22,* 35–58.

COCHRAN-SMITH, M. (1984). *The making of a reader.* Norwood, NJ: Ablex Publishing Corp.

COHEN, D. (1968). The effects of literature on vocabulary and reading achievement. *Elementary English, 45,* 209–213, 217.

COODY, B. (1973). *Using literature with young children.* Dubuque, IA: Wm. C. Brown.

CULLINAN, B. E. (1977). Books in the life of a young child. In B. Cullinan and C. Carmichael (eds.), *Literature and young children.* Urbana, IL: National Council of Teachers of English.

CULLINAN, B. E. (ed.). (1987). *Children's literature in the reading program.* Newark, DE: International Reading Association.

CULLINAN, B. E. (1989). *Literature and the child* (2nd ed.). Orlando, FL: Harcourt Brace Jovanovich, Inc.

DANFORD, H. (1973). The effects of purposeful reading upon comprehension of and interest in social studies materials. Doctoral dissertation, Temple University.

DEAN, J. (1977). Peter, Peter, pumpkin eater. In Dean's *Mother Goose book of rhymes.* London: Dean & Son.

DEPAOLA, T. (1973). *Charlie needs a clock.* Englewood Cliffs, NJ: Prentice Hall.

DEWEY, J. (1966). *Democracy and education.* New York: Free Press. (original work published 1916)

DEWITZ, P., and STAMMER, J. (1980). The development of linguistic awareness in young children from label reading to word reading. Paper presented at the Annual Meeting of the National Reading Conference, San Diego.

DOWNING, J. (1970). The development of linguistic concepts in children's thinking. *Research in the Teaching of English, 4,* 5–19.

DURKIN, D. (1966). *Children who read early.* New York: Teachers College Press.

DUVOISIN, R. (1950). *Petunia.* New York: Knopf.

DYSON, A. H. (1983). The role of oral language in early writing processes. *Research in the Teaching of English, 17,* 1–30.

DYSON, A. H. (1985). Individual differences in emerging writing. In M. Farr (ed.), *Advances in writing research: Vol. 1: Children's early writing development.* Norwood, NJ: Ablex Publishing Corp.

Dyson, A. H. (1986). Children's early interpretations of writing: Expanding research perspectives. In D. Yoden and S. Templeton (eds.), *Metalinguistic awareness and beginning literacy*. Exeter, NH: Heinemann Educational Books.

Eastman, P. D. (1960). *Are you my mother?* New York: Random House.

Ehri, L. C. (1979). Linguistic insight: Threshold of reading acquisition. In T. G. Waller and G. E. MacKinnon (eds.), *Reading research: Advances in theory and practice* (Vol. 1). New York: Academic Press.

Emberley, B. (1967). *Drummer Hoff.* Englewood Cliffs, NJ: Prentice Hall.

Evanechko, P., Ollila, L., and Armstrong, R. (1974). An investigation of the relationships between children's performance in written language and their reading ability. *Research in the Teaching of English, 8,* 315–326.

Ferreiro, E. (1978). What is written in a written sentence? *Journal of Education, 160,* 24–39.

Ferreiro, E., and Teberosky, A. (1982). *Literacy before schooling.* Exeter, NH: Heinemann Educational Books.

Flack, M. (1932). *Ask Mr. Bear.* New York: Macmillan.

Flood, J. (1977). Parental styles in reading episodes with young children. *Reading Teacher, 30,* 864–867.

Foster, C. R. (1982). Diffusing the issues in bilingualism and bilingual education. *Phi Delta Kappan, 63,* 338–345.

Froebel, F. (1974). *The education of man.* Clifton, NJ: Augustus M. Kelly.

Fujikawa, A. (1980). *Jenny learn a lesson.* New York: Grosset & Dunlap.

Galdone, P. (1973). *The little red hen.* Boston: Houghton Mifflin.

Gambrell, L., Pfeiffer, W., and Wilson, R. (1985). The effect of retelling upon comprehension and recall of text information. *Journal of Educational Research, 78,* 216–220.

Genishi, C., and Dyson, A. (1984). *Language assessment in the early years.* Norwood, NJ: Ablex Publishing Corp.

Gesell, A. (1925). *The mental growth of the preschool child.* New York: Macmillan.

Gibson, E., and Levin, H. (1975). *The psychology of reading.* Cambridge, MA: MIT Press.

Gillian, S. (1936). The reading mother. In H. Fellerman (ed.), *Best loved poems of American people.* New York: Doubleday.

Glazer, S. M., and Searfoss, L. (1988). *Reading diagnosis and instruction: A C-A-L-M approach.* Englewood Cliffs, NJ: Prentice Hall.

Gonzales-Mena, J. (1976). English as a second language for preschool children. *Young Children, 32,* 14–20.

Goodman, K. S. (1967). Reading: A psycholinguistic guessing game. *Journal of the Reading Specialist, 4,* 126–135.

Goodman, Y. (1980). The roots of literacy. In M. Douglas (ed.), *Claremont Reading Conference forty-fourth yearbook.* Claremont, CA: Claremont Reading Conference.

Goodman, Y. (1984). The development of initial literacy. In H. Goelman, A. Oberg, and F. Smith (eds.), *Awakening to literacy.* Exeter, NH: Heinemann Educational Books.

Goodman, Y. (1986). Children coming to know literacy. In W. H. Teale and E. Sulzby (eds.), *Emergent literacy: Writing and reading.* Norwood, NJ: Ablex Publishing Corp.

GOODMAN, Y., and ALTWERGER, B. (1981). *Print awareness in preschool children: A study of the development of literacy in preschool children* (Occasional Paper 4). Tucson: University of Arizona, College of Education, Arizona Center for Research and Development, Program in Language and Literacy.

GRAVES, D., and HANSEN, J. (1983). The author's chair. *Language Arts, 60,* 176–183.

GRAVES, D. H. (1983). *Writing: Teachers and children at work.* Exeter NH: Heinemann Educational Books.

GREANEY, V. (1980). Factors related to amount and type of leisure reading. *Reading Research Quarterly, 15,* 337–357.

GREEN, J. (1985). Children's writing in an elementary school postal system. In M. Farr (ed.), *Advances in writing research: Vol. 1. Children's early writing development.* Norwood, NJ: Ablex Publishing Corp.

GRIEVE, R., and HOOGENRAAD, R. (1979). First words. In M. Garmen (ed.), *Language acquisition: Studies in first language development.* Cambridge, England: Cambridge University Press.

GRIMMER, F. L. (1970). The effects of an experimental program in written composition on the writing of second-grade children. *Dissertation Abstracts International, 31,* 5666A.

GUNDLACH, R., McLANE, J., SCOTT, F., and McNAMEE, G. (1985). The social foundations of early writing development. In M. Farr (ed.), *Advances in writing research: Vol. 1. Children's early writing development.* Norwood, N.J.: Ablex Publishing Corp.

HALL, M. A., (1976). *Teaching reading as a language experience.* Columbus, OH: Chas. E. Merrill.

HALLIDAY, M. A. K. (1975). *Learning how to mean: Exploration in the development of language.* London: Edward Arnold.

HANSEN, J. S. (1969). The impact of the home literacy environment on reading attitude. *Elementary English, 46,* 17–24.

HARDY, B. (1968). Toward a poetics of fiction: An approach through narrative. In *The novel: A forum on fiction.* Providence: Brown University Press.

HARRIS, L., and SMITH, L. (1980). *Reading instruction and diagnostic teaching in the classroom* (3rd ed.). New York: Holt, Rinehart & Winston.

HARSTE, J., WOODWARD, V., and BURKE, C. (1984). *Language stories and literacy lessons.* Exeter, NH: Heinemann Educational Books.

HEATH, S. B. (1980). The function and uses of literacy. *Journal of Communication, 30,* 123–133.

HEATH, S. B. (1982). What no bedtime story means. *Language in Society, 11,* 49–76.

HEATH, S. B. (1983). *Ways with words.* New York: Oxford University Press.

HENNESSY, B. G. (1991). *The missing tarts.* New York: Puffin Books.

HIEBERT, E. H. (1978). Preschool children's understanding of written language. *Child Development, 49,* 1231–1234.

HIEBERT, E. H. (1981). Developmental patterns and interrelationships of preschool children's print awareness. *Reading Research Quarterly, 16,* 236–260.

HIEBERT, E. (1986). Using environmental print in beginning reading instruction. In M. R. Sampson (ed.), *The pursuit of literacy: Early reading and writing.* Dubuque, IA: Kendall/Hunt.

Hipple, M. (1985). Journal writing in kindergarten. *Language Arts, 62,* 255–261.

Hittleman, D. (1983). *Developmental reading: A psycholinguistic perspective.* Chicago: Rand McNally.

Hoban, R. (1960). *Bedtime for Frances.* New York: Harper & Row Publishers.

Hoban, R (1964). *Bread and jam for Frances.* New York: Harper & Row Publishers.

Holdaway, D. (1979). *The foundations of literacy.* Sydney: Ashton Scholastic.

Holdaway, D. (1986). The structure of natural learning as a basis for literacy instruction. In M. Sampson (ed.), *The pursuit of literacy: Early reading and writing.* Dubuque, IA: Kendall/Hunt.

Holdsworth, W. (1968). *The Gingerbread Boy.* New York: Farrar, Straus & Giroux.

Huck, C. (1976). *Children's literature in the elementary school* (3rd ed.). New York: Holt, Rinehart & Winston.

Hunt, K. W. (1970). *Syntactic maturity in children and adults.* Monograph of the Society for Research in Child Development (Vol. 25). Chicago: University of Chicago Press.

IRA (International Reading Association). (1985). *Literacy development and pre–first grade.* Newark, DE.

Irving, A. (1980). *Promoting voluntary reading for children and young people.* Paris: UNESCO.

Izawa, T. (1968a). *Goldilocks and the three bears.* New York: Grosset & Dunlap.

Izawa, T. (1968b). *The little red hen.* New York: Grosset & Dunlap.

Jagger, A. (1985). Allowing for language differences, In G. S. Pinnell (ed.), *Discovering language with children.* Urbana, IL: National Council of Teachers of English.

Jewell, M., and Zintz, M. (1986). *Learning to read naturally.* Dubuque, IA: Kendall/Hunt.

Johnson, C. (1955). *Harold and the purple crayon.* New York: Harper & Row Publishers.

Johnson, P., and Pearson, P. D. (1982). *Prior knowledge connectivity and the assessment of reading comprehension* (Technical Report 245). Urbana, IL: University of Illinois.

Juel, C. (1989). The role of decoding in early literacy instruction and assessment. In L. Morrow and J. Smith (eds.), *Assessment for instruction in early literacy,* pp. 135–154. Englewood Cliffs, NJ: Prentice Hall.

Juel, C., Griffith, P. L., and Gough, P. B. (1986). Acquisition of literacy: A longitudinal study of children in first and second grade. *Journal of Educational Psychology, 78,* 243–255.

Karbon, J. C. (1984). An investigation of the relationship between prior knowledge and vocabulary development using semantic mapping with culturally diverse students. Unpublished doctoral dissertation, University of Wisconsin at Madison.

Kasza, K. (1988). *The pig's picnic.* New York: Putnam.

Keats, E. (1974). *Pet show.* New York: Aladdin Books.

Keats, E. (1962). *The snowy day.* New York: Viking.

KEATS, E. (1966). *Jenny's hat.* New York: Harper & Row, Publishers.

KEATS, E. (1967). *Peter's chair.* New York: Harper & Row, Publishers.

KEATS, E. (1971). *Over in the meadow.* New York: Scholastic Book Services.

KING, E. M., and FRIESEN, D. T. (1972). Children who read in kindergarten. *Alberta Journal of Educational Research, 18*, 147–161.

KOCH, A., and PEDEN, W. (eds.). (1974). *The life and selected writings of Thomas Jefferson.* New York: Random House.

KRESS, G. (1982). *Learning to write.* Sydney: Oxford University Press.

KRIPPNER, S. (1963). The boy who read at eighteen months. *Exceptional Child, 30*, 105–109.

LAMME, L. (1981). *Learning to love literature: Preschool through grade 3.* Urbana, IL: National Council of Teachers of English.

LEICHTER, H. P. (1984). Families as environments for literacy. In H. Goelman, A. Oberg, and F. Smith (eds.), *Awakening to literacy.* Exeter, NH: Heinemann Educational Books.

LENNENBERG, E. (1967). *Biological foundations of language.* New York: John Wiley.

LENNENBERG, E., and KAPLAN, E. (1970). Grammatical structures and reading. In H. Levin and J. Williams (eds.), *Basic studies in reading.* New York: Basic Books.

LENSKI, L. (1965). *The little farm.* New York: Henry Z. Walek.

LESIEG, T. (1961). *Ten apples up on top.* New York: Random House.

LEU, D. J., and KINZER, C. (1991). *Effective reading instruction. K–8* (2nd ed.). New York: Merrill.

LINDEN, M., and WITTROCK, M. C. (1981). The teaching of reading comprehension according to the model of generative learning. *Reading Research Quarterly, 17*, 44–57.

LIONNI, L. (1963). *Swimmy.* New York: Pantheon.

LOBAN, W. (1976). *Language development: Kindergarten through grade twelve.* Urbana, IL: National Council of Teachers of English.

McCLOSKEY, R. (1948). *Blueberries for Sal.* New York: Viking.

McCORMICK, C., and MASON, J. (1981). What happens to kindergarten children's knowledge about reading after summer vacation? *Reading Teacher, 35*, 164–172.

McCRACKEN, M., and McCRACKEN, J. (1972). *Reading is only the tiger's tail.* San Rafael, CA.: Leswing Press.

McGEE, L., and RICHGELS, D. (1990). *Literacy's beginnings: Supporting young readers and writers.* Boston: Allyn and Bacon.

McGOVERN, A. (1967). *Too much noise.* Boston: Houghton Mifflin.

McGRAW, B., and GROTELEUSCHEN, A. (1972). Direction of the effect of questions in prose materials. *Journal of Educational Psychology, 63*, 580–588.

McNEIL, D. (1970). *The acquisition of language: The study of developmental psycholinguistics.* New York: Harper & Row Publishers.

MANDLER, J., and JOHNSON, N. (1977). Remembrance of things parsed: Story structure and recall. *Cognitive Psychology, 9*, 111–151.

MARTINEZ, M., and TEALE, W. (1987). The ins and outs of a kindergarten writing program. *Reading Teacher, 40*, 444–451.

MARTINEZ, M., and TEALE, W. (1988). Reading in a kindergarten classroom library. *Reading Teacher, 41*, 6, 568–572.

Mason, J. (1977). *Reading readiness: A definition and skills hierarchy from preschoolers' developing conceptions of print* (Technical Report 59). Urbana: University of Illinois, Center for the Study of Reading.

Mason, J. (1980). When do children begin to read: An exploration of four year old children's letter and word reading competencies. *Reading Research Quarterly, 15*, 203–227.

Mason, J. (1982). Acquisition of knowledge about reading. Paper presented at the Annual Meeting of the American Educational Research Association, New York.

Mason, J. (1984). Early reading from a developmental perspective. In P. D. Pearson (ed.), *Handbook of reading research.* New York: Longman.

Mason, J. (1986). *Reading instruction for today.* Glenview, IL: Scott, Foresman.

Mason, J., and McCormick, C. (1981). *An investigation of pre-reading instruction: A developmental perspective* (Technical Report 224). Urbana: University of Illinois, Center for the Study of Reading.

Mason, J., Stewart, J., and Dunning, D. (1986). *Testing kindergarten children's knowledge about reading* (Technical Report 368). Urbana: University of Illinois, Center for the Study of Reading.

Menyuk, P. (1977). *Language and maturation.* Cambridge, MA: MIT Press.

Mitchell, J. N. (1984). Advantages and disadvantages of retelling for reading assessment. Presentation at the International Reading Association Conference, Atlanta.

Montessori, M. (1965). *Spontaneous activity in education.* New York: Schocken Books.

Morphett, M. V., and Washburne, C. (1931). When should children begin to read? *Elementary School Journal, 31*, 496–508.

Morrison, G. S. (1984). *Early childhood education today* (3rd ed.). Columbus, OH: Chas. E. Merrill.

Morrow, L. M. (1978). Analysis of syntax in the language of six-, seven-, and eight-year-olds. *Research in the Teaching of English, 12*, 143–148.

Morrow, L. M. (1980). The parent corner. *Home ideas for reading. New Jersey Reading Association Newsletter.* Volume 2, 3–4.

Morrow, L. M. (1981). *Supertips for storytelling.* New York: Harcourt Brace Jovanovich, Inc. Instructor Books.

Morrow, L. M. (1982). Relationships between literature programs, library corner designs and children's use of literature. *Journal of Educational Research, 75*, 339–344.

Morrow, L. M. (1983). Home and school correlates of early interest in literature. *Journal of Educational Research, 76*, 221–230.

Morrow, L. M. (1984). Reading stories to young children: Effects of story structure and traditional questioning strategies on comprehension. *Journal of Reading Behavior, 16*, 273–288.

Morrow, L. M. (1985a). *Promoting voluntary reading in school and home.* Bloomington, IN: Phi Delta Kappa Educational Foundation.

Morrow, L. M. (1985b). Retelling stories: A strategy for improving children's comprehension, concept of story structure and oral language complexity. *Elementary School Journal, 85*, 647–661.

Morrow, L. M. (1986a). Promoting responses to literature: Children's sense of story structure. Paper presented at the National Reading Conference, Austin, TX.

Morrow, L. M. (1986b). *Promoting voluntary reading: A curriculum guide for Reading Rainbow Program.* New York: WNET/13; Public Broadcasting Corporation.

Morrow, L. M. (1987a). The effects of one-to-one story readings on children's questions and comments. In S. Baldwin and J. Readance (eds.), *Thirty-sixth Yearbook of the National Reading Conference.* Rochester, NY.

Morrow, L. M. (1987b). Promoting voluntary reading: The effects of an inner city program in summer day care centers. *The Reading Teacher, 41,* 266–274.

Morrow, L. M. (1988a). Young children's responses to one-to-one story readings in school settings. *Reading Research Quarterly, 23,* 1, 89–107.

Morrow, L. M. (1988b). Retelling as a diagnostic tool. In S. M. Glazer, L. W. Searfoss, and L. Gentile. (eds.). *Re-examining reading diagnosis: New trends and procedures in classrooms and clinics.* Newark, DE: International Reading Association.

Morrow, L. M. (1990). Preparing the classroom environment to promote literacy during play. *Early Childhood Research Quarterly, 5,* 537–554.

Morrow, L. M. (1991) The impact of a literature based program on reading achievement, attitudes and use of literature of urban youth. Paper presented at the American Educational Research Association Conference, April 1991, Chicago.

Morrow, L. M., O'Connor, E., and Smith, J. K. (1990). Effects of a story reading program on the literacy development of at risk kindergarten children. *Journal of Reading Behavior, 22,* 225–275.

Morrow, L. M., and Smith, J. K. (1990). The effect of group setting on interactive storybook reading. *Reading Research Quarterly, 25,* 213–231.

Morrow, L. M., and Weinstein, C. S. (1982). Increasing children's use ot literature through program and physical design changes. *Elementary School Journal, 83,* 131–137.

Morrow, L. M., and Weinstein, C. S. (1986). Encouraging voluntary reading: The impact of a literature program on children's use of library centers. *Reading Research Quarterly, 21,* 330–346.

Neuman, S., and Roskos, K. (1990). The influence of literacy-enriched play settings on preschoolers' engagement with written language. In J. Zutell and S. McCormick (eds.), *Literacy theory and research: Analyses from multiple paradigms, pp. 179–187. Thirty-ninth yearbook of the National Reading Conference.* Chicago: National Reading Conference.

Newman, J. (1984). *The craft of children's writing.* Exeter, NH: Heinemann Educational Books.

Newman, J. (ed.). (1985). *Whole language: Theory in use.* Exeter, NH: Heinemann Educational Books.

Ninio, A. (1980). Picture book reading in mother–infant dyads belonging to two subgroups in Israel. *Child Development, 51,* 587–590.

NINIO, A., and BRUNNER, J. (1978). The achievement and antecedents of labeling. *Journal of Child Language, 5*, 1–15.

PALINCSAR, A. S., BROWN, A. L., and MARTIN, S. M. (1987). Peer interaction in reading, comprehension instruction. *Journal of Educational Psychology 23*, 231–253.

PARKER, R. (1983). Language development and learning to write. In R. Parker and F. Davis (eds.), *Developing literacy: Young children's use of language*. Newark, DE: International Reading Association.

PEARSON, P. D., HANSON, J., and GORDON, C. (1979). Effects of background knowledge on young children's comprehension of explicit and implicit information. *Journal of Reading Behavior, 11*, 201–209.

PEARSON, P. D., and JOHNSON, D. D. (1978). *Teaching reading comprehension*. New York: Holt, Rhinehart & Winston.

PELLEGRINI, A., and GALDA, L. (1982). The effects of thematic fantasy play training on the development of children's story comprehension. *American Educational Research Journal, 19*, 443–452.

PFLAUM, S. (1986). *The development of language and literacy in young children* (3rd ed.). Columbus, OH: Chas. E. Merrill.

PHYFE-PERKINS, E. (1979). Application of the behavior–person–environment paradigm to the analysis and evaluation of early childhood education programs. Doctoral dissertation, University of Massachusetts.

PIAGET, J., and INHELDER, B. (1969). *The psychology of the child*. New York: Basic Books.

PINNELL, G. S., FREID, M. D., and ESTICE, R. M. (1990). Reading recovery: Learning how to make a difference. *The Reading Teacher, 43*, 4, 282–295.

PINNELL, G. S., and MATLIN, M. L. (eds.). 1989. *Teachers and research: Language learning in the classroom*. Newark, DE: International Reading Association.

PIPER, W. (1954) *The little engine that could*. New York: Platt and Munk.

PITTELMAN, S. D., LEVIN, K. M., and JOHNSON, D. P. (1985). An investigation of two instructional settings in the use of semantic mapping with poor readers (Program Report 85-4). Madison: Wisconsin Center for Educational Research, University of Wisconsin.

PLESSAS, G. P., and OAKES, C. R. (1964). Prereading experiences of selected early readers. *Reading Teacher, 17*, 241–245.

POTTER, B. (1902). *The tale of Peter Rabbit*. New York: Scholastic Book Services.

PRESCOTT, O. (1965). *A father reads to his child: An anthology of prose and poetry*. New York: Dutton.

QUAKENBUSH, R. (1972). *Old MacDonald had a farm*. New York: Lippincott.

QUAKENBUSH, R. (1973). *Go tell Aunt Rhody*. New York: Lippincott.

READ, C. (1971). Pre-school children's knowledge of English phonology. *Harvard Educational Review, 41*, 1–34.

READ, C. (1975). Children's categorization of speech sounds in English (National Research Report 17). Urbana, IL: National Council of Teachers of English.

REY, H. A. (1941). *Curious George*. Boston: Houghton Mifflin.

RICHARDS, J. (1979). Adjunct post questions in text: A critical review of methods and processes. *Review of Educational Research, 49*, 181–196.

ROBINSON, V., STRICKLAND, D., and CULLINAN, B. (1977). The child: Ready or not? In L. Ollila (ed.), *The kindergarten child and reading*. Newark, DE: International Reading Association.

ROSEN, H., and ROSEN, C. (1973). *The language of primary school children*. London: Penguin Education.

ROSENTHAL, B. A. (1973). An ecological study of free play in the nursery school. Doctoral dissertation, Wayne State University.

ROSER, N., and MARTINEZ, M. (1985). Roles adults play in preschool responses to literature. *Language Arts, 62*, 485–490.

ROUSSEAU, J. (1962). *Emile*. (ed. and trans. William Boyd). New York: Columbia University Teachers College. (original work published 1762)

ROUTMAN, R. (1988). *Transitions*. Portsmouth, NH: Heinemann.

ROUTMAN, R. (1991). *Invitations*. Portsmouth, NH: Heinemann.

RUDDELL, R. (1971). *Oral language and development of other language skills: Listening and speaking*. London: Macmillan.

RUSK, R., and SCOTLAND, J. (1979). *Doctrines of the great educators*. New York: St. Martin's Press.

SCHICKEDANZ, J. A. (1978). Please read that story again: Exploring relationships between story reading and learning to read. *Young Children, 33*, 48–55.

SCHICKEDANZ, J. A. (1986). *More than ABC's: The early stages of reading and writing*. Washington, DC: National Association for the Education of Young Children.

Scholastic *Big Books*. (1986). Toronto: Scholastic–Tab Publications.

SCHULZ, J., CARPENTER, C. D., and TURNBULL, A. P. (1991). *Mainstreaming exceptional students: A guide for classroom teachers*. Boston: Allyn and Bacon.

SEEFELDT, C., and BARBOUR, N. (1986). *Early childhood education: An introduction*. Columbus, OH: Chas. E. Merrill.

SENDAK, M. (1962). *Chicken soup with rice*. New York: Harper & Row, Publishers.

SENDAK, M. (1963). *Where the wild things are*. New York: Harper & Row, Publishers.

SEUSS, DR. (1940). *Horton hatches the egg*. New York: Random House.

SEUSS, DR. (1957). *How the Grinch stole Christmas*. New York: Random House.

SEUSS, DR. (1960). *Green eggs and ham*. New York: Random House.

SEUSS, DR. (1970). *Mr. Brown can moo! can you?* New York: Random House.

SHARON, S. (1980). Cooperative learning in small groups: Recent methods and effects on achievement, attitudes, and ethnic relations. *Review of Educational Research, 50*, 241–271.

SHURE, M. B. (1963). Psychological ecology of a nursery school. *Child Development, 34*, 979–992.

SKINNER, B. F. (1957). *Verbal behavior*. Boston: Appleton-Century-Crofts.

SLAVIN, R. (1977). Student learning teams and scores adjusted for past achievement: A summary of field experience (Rep. No. 227). Baltimore, MD: Johns Hopkins University Center for Social Organization of Schools.

SLOBODKINA, E. (1947). *Caps for sale*. Reading, MA: Addison-Wesley.

SMITH, F. (1971). *Understanding reading.* New York: Holt, Rinehart & Winston.

SMITH, F. (1972). The learner and his language. In R. Hodges and E. H. Rudorf (eds.), *Language and learning to read.* Boston: Houghton Mifflin.

SMITH, F. (1973). *Psycholinguistics and reading.* New York: Holt, Rinehart & Winston.

SMITH, F. (1978). *Understanding reading* (2nd ed.). New York: Holt, Rinehart & Winston.

SMITH, F. (1983). A metaphor for literacy: Creating words or shunting information? In F. Smith, *Essays into literacy.* Exeter, NH: Heinemann Educational Books.

SMITH, J. A., and PARKER, M. (1977). *Words music and word magic: Children's literature methods.* Newton, MA: Allyn & Bacon.

SNOW, C., and PERLMANN, R. (1985). Assessing children's knowledge about bookreading. In L. Galda and A. Pellegrini (eds.), *Play, language, and stories.* Norwood, NJ: Ablex Publishing Corp.

SNOW, C. E. (1983). Literacy and language: Relationships during the preschool years. *Harvard Educational Review, 53,* 165–189.

SOUNDY, C. (1987). Effect of writing experiences in the expressive mode on children's reading comprehension and writing ability. Doctoral dissertation, Rutgers University.

SPIEGEL, D. L. (1981). *Reading for pleasure: Guidelines.* Newark, DE: International Reading Association.

SPIELBERG, S. (1987). Acceptance speech at the Academy Award Ceremonies. Los Angeles.

STAUFFER, R. G. (1970). A reading teacher's dream come true. *Wilson Library Bulletin, 45,* 282–292.

STAUFFER, R. G. (1980). *The language-experience approach to the teaching of reading* (2nd ed.). New York: Harper & Row, Publishers.

STEWART, J., BENJAMIN, L., and MASON, L. (1987). An early literacy program: Putting research into practice. Paper presented at the University of the Virgin Islands.

STEWIG, J. W., and SEBESTA, S. (eds.). (1978). *Using literature in the elementary classroom.* Urbana, IL: National Council of Teachers of English.

SULZBY, E. (1985). Children's emergent reading of favorite storybooks. *Reading Research Quarterly, 20,* 458–481.

SULZBY, E. (1986a). Children's elicitation and use of metalinguistic knowledge about "word" during literacy interactions. In P. Yaden and S. Templeton, *Metalinguistic awareness and beginning literacy.* Exeter, NH: Heinemann Educational Books.

SULZBY, E. (1986b). Kindergarteners as writers and readers. In M. Farr (ed.), *Advances in writing research: Vol. 1. Children's early writing.* Norwood, NJ.: Ablex Publishing Corp.

SULZBY, E. (1986c). Writing and reading: Signs of oral and written language organization in the young child. In W. Teale and E. Sulzby (eds.), *Emergent literacy: Writing and reading.* Norwood, NJ: Ablex Publishing Corp.

SULZBY, E. (1987). Simplified Version of Sulzby's (1985) Classification Scheme for "Children's Emergent Reading of Favorite Storybooks."

Paper presented at the International Reading Association Conference, Anaheim, CA.

SUTFIN, H. (1980). The effects on children's behavior of a change in the physical design of a kindergarten classroom. Doctoral dissertation, Boston University.

TAYLOR, B. M., FRYE, B. J., and MARUGAMA, M. (1990). Time spent reading and reading growth. *American Educational Research Journal, 27,* 351–362.

TAYLOR, D. (1983). *Family literacy.* Exeter, NH: Heinemann Educational Books.

TAYLOR, D., and STRICKLAND, D. (1986). *Family storybook reading.* Exeter, NH: Heinemann Educational Books.

TEALE, W. (1978). Positive environments for learning to read: What studies of early readers tell us. *Language Arts, 55,* 922–932.

TEALE, W. (1981). Parents reading to their children: What we know and need to know. *Language Arts, 58,* 902–911.

TEALE, W. (1982). Toward a theory of how children learn to read and write naturally. *Language Arts, 59,* 555–570.

TEALE, W. (1984). Reading to young children: Its significance for literacy development. In H. Goelman, A. Oberg, and F. Smith (eds.), *Awakening to literacy.* Exeter, NH: Heinemann Educational Books.

TEALE, W. (1986). The beginning of reading and writing: Written language development during the preschool and kindergarten years. In M. Sampson (ed.), *The pursuit of literacy: Early reading and writing.* Dubuque, IA: Kendal/Hunt.

TEALE, W. (1987). Emergent literacy: Reading and writing development in early childhood. In J. Readance and R. S. Baldwin (eds.), *Thirty-sixth Yearbook of the National Reading Conference.* Rochester, NY.

TEALE, W., HIEBERT, E., and CHITTENDEN, E. (1987). Assessing young children's literary development, *Reading Teacher, 40,* 772–778.

TEMPLETON, S. (1991). *Teaching the integrated language arts.* Boston: Houghton Mifflin.

THORNDYKE, R. (1977). Cognitive structures in comprehension and memory of narrative discourse. *Cognitive Psychology, 9,* 77–110.

TOBIN, A. W. (1981). A multiple discriminant cross-validation of the factors associated with the development of precocious reading achievement. Doctoral dissertation, University of Delaware.

TORREY, J. (1969). Learning to read without a teacher. *Elementary English, 46,* 556–559.

TORVEY, D. R., and KERBER, J. E. (eds.). (1986). *Roles in literacy learning: A new perspective.* Newark, DE: International Reading Association.

TUNMER, W. E., and NESDALE, A. R. (1985) Phonemic segmentation skill and beginning reading. *Journal of Educational Psychology, 77,* 417–427.

VEATCH, J., SAWICKI, F., ELLIOT, G., BARNETT, E., and BLACKEY, J. (1973). *Key words to reading. The language experience approach begins.* Columbus, OH: Chas. E. Merrill.

VIORST, J. (1972). *Alexander and the terrible, horrible, no good, very bad day.* New York: Atheneum.

VUKELICH, C., and GOLDEN, J. (1984). Early writing: Developmental teaching strategies. *Young Children, 38,* 3–5.

Vygotsky, L. S. (1978). *Mind in society: The development of psychological processes.* Cambridge, MA: Harvard University Press.

Vygotsky, L. S. (1981). The genesis of higher mental functions. In J. J. Wertsch (ed.), *The concept of activity.* White Plains, NY: M. E. Sharpe.

Ward, M., and McCormick, S. (1981). Reading instruction for blind and low vision children in the regular classroom. *The Reading Teacher, 34,* 434, 444.

Weinstein, C. S. (1977). Modifying student behavior in an open classroom through changes in the physical design. *American Educational Research Journal, 14,* 249–262.

Wells, G. (1986). *The meaning makers: Children learning language and using language to learn.* Exeter, NH: Heinemann Educational Books.

Westcott, N. B. (1980). *I know an old lady.* Boston: Little, Brown.

White, E. B., (1952). *Charlotte's web.* New York: Scholastic.

Whitehead, F., Capey, A. C., and Maddren, W. (1975). *Children's reading interests.* London: Evans & Methuen.

Williams, J. P. (1985). The case for explicit decoding instruction. In J. Osborn, P. T. Wilson, and R. C. Anderson (eds.), *Reading education: Foundations for a literate America.* Lexington, MA: Heath, Lexington Books.

Wiseman, D. E., and Robeck, C. P. (1983). The written language behavior of two socio-economic groups of preschool children. *Reading Psychology, 4,* 349–363.

Wittrock, M. C. (1974). Learning as a generative process. *Educational Psychologist, 11,* 87–95.

Wittrock, M. C. (1981). Reading comprehension. In F. J. Pirozzolo and M. C. Wittrock (eds.), *Neuropsychological and cognitive processes in readings.* New York: Academic Press.

Yaden, D. (1985). Preschoolers' spontaneous inquiries about print and books. Paper presented at the Annual Meeting of the National Reading Conference, San Diego.

Yager, S., Johnson, D. W., and Johnson, R. T. (1985). Oral discussion, group to individual transfer, and achievement in cooperative learning groups. *Journal of Educational Psychology, 77,* 60–66.

Ylisto, I. P. (1967). An empirical investigation of early reading responses of young children. Doctoral dissertation, University of Michigan.

Zolotow, C. (1962). *Mr. Rabbit and the lovely present.* New York: Harper & Row, Publishers.

Index